Too Busy To Cook?

Too Busy To Cook?

Time-Saving Recipes
and Easy Menus
from Bon Appétit®
magazine

The Knapp Press   Publishers   Los Angeles

The Viking Press   Distributors   New York

Published in the United States of America in 1981
The Knapp Press
5900 Wilshire Boulevard, Los Angeles, California 90036
Copyright © 1981 by Knapp Communications Corporation
Library of Congress Cataloging in Publication Data
Main entry under title:

Too busy to cook?

    Includes index.
    1. Cookery. I. Bon appétit.
TX652.T657   641.5'55   81-5959

ISBN 0-89535-049-1   AACR2

Printed and bound in the United States of America

Contents

or a quick guide to Do-Ahead
d Microwave sections of each chapter,
e page 1.

about the cover: Italian Stir-Fried Chicken
s a ready-in-minutes combination of
ucculent chicken, Italian green beans, red
eppers, tomatoes, green onions and lively
easonings. Recipe page 83.

FOREWORD

Sometimes the busier we are, the more we do! Because our time is so valuable, we budget it, plan ahead and above all "get organized." The Editors of **Bon Appétit** are delighted to present this newest cookbook, designed and planned especially for all of us who have ever had that feeling that we are too busy to cook.

The idea of doing a monthly feature in the magazine and calling it TOO BUSY TO COOK? was a natural for us. We had found in discussions among ourselves that everyone has tips, hints and ideas for surviving those busy times, for making them fun, and for creating recipes that are delicious and different. When we asked readers to share *their* special secrets with us, the response was tremendous.

So this book is a collection of favorites from our readers. It is a book by the subscribers of **Bon Appétit** magazine— and we think it is perfect for everyone.

All of the recipes presented in this book have been tested in the kitchens of **Bon Appétit.** And as they were being tested we kept several questions in mind: Is the recipe easy to prepare from ingredients on hand without making a trip to the market or specialty shop, *and* is this a recipe to be proud of. Only those recipes that rated an unqualified "Yes" were published in the magazine and gathered together in this distinctive volume.

You will find that the easy-to-read style—plus a generous sampling of glorious color photographs—make the recipes simple to master at a glance. And the book is organized around chapters on everything from hors d'oeuvres to desserts. Each chapter begins with hints, tips and ideas, and contains the exciting recipes you expect from **Bon Appétit.**

And what recipes! From the chapter on hors d'oeuvres there are ethnic specialties such as Chinese-style Spareribs, Mexican Meatballs and Scallops Veracruz. These are dishes that get any menu off to a good start.

In the chapter on beverages we have included tempting drinks with tempting names: South Seas Banana Punch, The Lemon Icecap and Skiers Brew are just a few of them.

And since the heart of any menu is always the main course, there is a bountiful selection of entrées for fish and shellfish such as flounder, salmon, shrimp and crab; for poultry, one of the most economical standbys of the busy cook; for meat—how about a really quick chili recipe or an easy, one-dish supper called Chinese One-Dish Lamb? And there are dozens of recipes for vegetable, egg and cheese entrées that are ready in minutes.

To round out the meal there are ideas for new ways with vegetables, pasta, rice and bread. And to top it off with a grand finale there are pages and pages of exciting desserts such as Dutch Butter Cake and Chocolate Fudgy Brownies, Instant Orange Mousse and Easy Zabaglione, Magic Pie Crust and 60-Second Lemon Chiffon Pie.

TOO BUSY TO COOK? contains much more—sections just for time-saving microwave recipes; a guide to freezing; a checklist for stocking your pantry; and very special selections of do-ahead recipes that make it easy to deal with impromptu entertaining.

The Editors of **Bon Appétit** have a particular affection for TOO BUSY TO COOK? because it solves a problem we all face, and it does it with ease, with ideas and with a sense of fun. We know that you will enjoy it, too.

Marilou Vaughan

Marilou Vaughan
Managing Editor
Bon Appétit magazine

HOW TO USE **TOO BUSY TO COOK?**

Each chapter opens with special tips and hints from *Bon Appétit.* We've then subdivided the chapters into quick recipes, do-ahead recipes and microwave recipes. For your convenience and handy reference, the page numbers for the do-ahead and microwave sections are listed to the right.

HORS D'OEUVRES

Rules for Presentation and Serving

■ First of all, be sure to offer a variety of hors d'oeuvres. Make them visually inviting—colorful and tempting. Present them in unusual dishes, trays, baskets. Be aware of balance and design when arranging them. Choose for texture, seasoning, color; offer crunchy things as well as smooth; bland as well as piquant; white ingredients—and dark—to play up the brightly colored ones.

■ Make a smorgasbord of appetizers: Offer a variety of herrings in wine and cream sauces with rye and pumpernickel breads. Spread steak tartare on cucumber rounds. Layer sliced roast beef with softened cream cheese and lumpfish caviar. Roll the slices like a Champagne biscuit and arrange fanlike on a platter. Add a selection of fine cheeses and assorted salamis.

■ Make a zesty wine and cheddar spread by blending 1 pound of sharp cheddar cheese with ⅓ cup dry, robust wine, such as zinfandel or mountain burgundy. Zing it up with 3 tablespoons finely minced chives and ½ teaspoon prepared mustard. To blend by hand, soften the cheese to room temperature, or grate before mixing with the other ingredients. A food processor will do the job in seconds. Pack the cheese into small lidded crocks and store in the refrigerator. Great with mini-loaves of cocktail rye and pumpernickel.

COLD

DIPS AND SPREADS

GALLEY DIP FOR VEGETABLES

MAKES 2 CUPS

- 1 pint plain yogurt
- 1 package dried Italian salad dressing mix

Mix together and chill.

MEXICAN DIPPING SAUCE

Excellent with cooked, chilled artichokes or other crudités.

MAKES ¾ CUP

- 5 tablespoons mayonnaise
- 1 tablespoon salsa tomatillo (green tomato sauce) or to taste
- 2 to 3 teaspoons mustard with seeds
- 1 teaspoon fresh lemon juice
  Dash of garlic powder

Combine all ingredients, blend well and refrigerate until ready to serve.

SALSA CRUDA DIP

MAKES ABOUT 2 CUPS

- 6 to 8 green tomatoes, peeled and quartered, or 1½ cups canned tomatillos, drained
- 1 medium onion, cut into pieces
- ½ cup diced canned green chilies
- 2 jalapeño peppers, seeded and minced, or to taste
- 1 teaspoon salt
  Tortilla chips

Puree tomatoes in processor or blender. Add all remaining ingredients except chips and mix well. Transfer to serving bowl, cover and refrigerate. Serve with tortilla chips.

SPINACH DIP

6 SERVINGS

- 1 8-ounce package cream cheese, room temperature
- 1 cup sour cream
- ½ cup mayonnaise
- 1 envelope onion soup mix
- ¼ teaspoon garlic powder
  Pinch of dried dill (optional)

Salt

- 1 10-ounce package frozen chopped spinach, thawed, drained and squeezed dry
  Crudités

Combine cream cheese and sour cream and blend well. Stir in mayonnaise and soup mix. Add seasonings. Gently stir in spinach. Serve with assorted crudités.

TANGY CHILI-BEAN DIP

MAKES ABOUT 4 CUPS

- 4 cups shredded sharp cheddar cheese
- 1 11½-ounce can bean with bacon soup
- ½ to ⅔ cup jalapeño relish
- ¼ cup chopped sweet red pepper
- 2 tablespoons chopped pimiento-stuffed olives
  Freshly chopped parsley (garnish)
  Tortilla chips

Combine first 3 ingredients in large bowl and beat well. Stir in pepper and olives. Pack into crock or serving bowl. Cover and refrigerate. Sprinkle with parsley. Serve with tortilla chips.

Quick Ideas for Hors d'Oeuvres

■ Serve crabmeat fingers (the tiny, sweet-meated claws)—fresh, frozen or canned—as a deliciously delicate and not-too-filling appetizer. Arrange the crab fingers around the perimeter of a blue and white platter. In the center place a little bowl of piquant dipping sauce.

■ Drain a can of artichoke bottoms. Cream together 1 cup fresh ricotta cheese, a few tablespoons of chopped lean prosciutto ham, ¼ cup finely chopped green onion, a dash or two of Worcestershire sauce and ¼ cup of finely minced cilantro (use Italian parsley if cilantro is not available). Mound the mixture in the artichoke bottoms. Lay a strip of bright red pimiento across the tops. Cut the stuffed artichokes into quarters.

■ Potted shrimp makes a great appetizer. Have ready eight demitasses or diminutive pôts de crème pots. You'll need two 7½-ounce cans of small shrimp, drained. Place 1 can of shrimp in food processor. Add ¼ pound softened sweet butter, a good dash of Worcestershire sauce, 2 teaspoons lemon juice, 1 teaspoon grated onion, salt and freshly ground pepper. Blend until smooth. Transfer to a bowl. Now add the second can of shrimp, left whole or cut in half, and mix with a wooden spoon until smooth. Pack the mixture into the cups, cover and chill overnight. Serve the cups on saucers, placing a sprig of parsley on top of each cup and a small wedge of lemon on the saucer. Serve with rounds of melba toast.

■ Pâté and good red wine are ready revivers. A suavely silken chicken liver pâté is quickly made in the food processor. Sauté one pound of chicken livers in a little sweet butter until the livers lose their pink color. Turn into your food processor, add half a small white onion, ½ stick of softened sweet butter, 3 tablespoons Cognac, 1 tablespoon lemon juice, salt and pepper and a miser's pinch of allspice, cloves and thyme. Blend until pureed and smooth. Pack into a lidded earthenware crock and store in the refrigerator. This will keep up to a week.

■ Pour amontillado sherry in all purpose wine glasses and surround with inviting nibbles: toasted almonds; pecans; green, black and stuffed olives; a platter of mild cheeses.

TAPENADE

4 TO 6 SERVINGS

- 1 8-ounce can pitted black olives, drained
- 1 7-ounce can albacore tuna packed in oil, drained
- ¼ cup capers, rinsed and drained
- ¼ cup fresh lemon juice
- 1 tablespoon dark rum or to taste
- 1 large garlic clove
- ½ cup olive oil
  Freshly ground pepper
  Crudités

Combine first 6 ingredients in processor or blender and mix until smooth. Slowly add olive oil, blending thoroughly. Season to taste with pepper. Serve with crudités.

VEGETARIAN HORS D'OEUVRE

6 SERVINGS

- 1 pound fresh green beans
- 2 tablespoons (¼ stick) butter
- 1 large onion, very thinly sliced
- 2 hard-cooked eggs, halved
- 2 slices white bread (crusts trimmed), toasted and broken into pieces
- 4 walnut halves, toasted
  Salt and freshly ground pepper
  Crudités or crackers

Cook beans in salted water to cover until tender. Drain well. Melt butter in medium skillet over medium heat. Add onion and sauté until well browned. Combine with beans, eggs, toast, walnuts, salt and pepper in processor or blender and mince finely. Transfer to bowl, cover and chill. Serve with crudités or crackers.

CURRY DIP

MAKES ABOUT 1¼ CUPS

- 1 cup mayonnaise
- ¼ cup chili sauce
- 1 teaspoon lemon juice
- 1 teaspoon minced onion
- 1 teaspoon curry powder or to taste
- ½ teaspoon Worcestershire sauce
- ½ teaspoon hot pepper sauce or to taste
  Salt and freshly ground pepper

Thoroughly combine all ingredients. Cover and chill until ready to serve.

CURRIED EGG SALAD SPREAD

MAKES ABOUT 2 CUPS

- 8 water chestnuts, chopped
- 6 hard-cooked eggs, chopped
- ¼ to ½ cup mayonnaise
- 2 green onions, chopped
- 1 teaspoon curry powder or to taste
- ½ teaspoon Worcestershire sauce
  Salt and freshly ground pepper

Combine all ingredients and blend well. Cover and chill in refrigerator until ready to serve.

SARDINE SPREAD

MAKES 1½ CUPS

- 1 can skinless and boneless sardines
- 1 8-ounce package cream cheese
- 1 tablespoon anchovy paste
- 1 teaspoon lemon juice
- 1 teaspoon Worcestershire sauce
  Crackers or crudités

Blend all ingredients together in mixer, blender or food processor. Serve with crackers or crudités.

SARDINE-EGG SPREAD

8 TO 10 SERVINGS

- 2 4⅜-ounce cans Portuguese sardines in oil, drained
- 1 hard-cooked egg
- 1 tablespoon mayonnaise
- 1 tablespoon tarragon vinegar
- 2 teaspoons Dijon mustard
- 1 teaspoon chives
- 1 teaspoon parsley
  Salt and freshly ground pepper
  Melba toast

Blend first 7 ingredients in food processor. Season to taste with salt and pepper. Serve with melba toast.

SEAFOOD SPREAD

8 TO 12 SERVINGS

- 1 8-ounce package cream cheese, room temperature
- 1 6½-ounce can crabmeat,* drained and patted dry with paper towels
- ½ teaspoon soy sauce
- ½ cup catsup
- 2 heaping teaspoons creamy horseradish
  Parsley or watercress sprigs (garnish)
  Crackers

Using hands, combine cream cheese, crab and soy sauce, forming mixture into ball. Cover and refrigerate. Just before serving, mix catsup and horseradish. Line plate with parsley and place ball in center. Pour sauce over and surround with assorted crackers.

*One 6½- or 7-ounce can of tuna or a 4½-ounce can of shrimp may be substituted.

CAMEMBERT SPREAD

6 SERVINGS

- 1 ripe Camembert
- 1 egg yolk
- 1 tablespoon finely minced onion
- ¼ teaspoon minced fresh garlic

Dash of paprika
Salt and freshly ground pepper
Onion rings, hard-cooked egg wedges and parsley (garnish)
Assorted crackers

Mash cheese with fork. Add yolk and blend well. Add onion, garlic, paprika, salt and pepper and mix thoroughly. Turn onto serving plate and shape into loaf. Garnish with onion rings, egg and parsley. Serve with crackers.

CHEDDAR-CREAM CHEESE SPREAD

8 TO 10 SERVINGS

- 1 8-ounce jar sharp cheddar cheese spread, room temperature
- 1 3-ounce package cream cheese, room temperature
- ¼ cup chopped pecans, toasted
- 1 garlic clove, minced

Thoroughly combine all ingredients. Pack into cheese crock and chill well. Bring to room temperature before serving for ease in spreading.

DUTCH CHEESE SPREAD

APPROXIMATELY 24 SERVINGS

- 1 1½- to 1¾-pound Gouda cheese
  Mayonnaise
- 1½ tablespoons chopped parsley
- 1 tablespoon dry white wine
- 1½ teaspoons dry mustard
- ¼ teaspoon Worcestershire sauce
- ¼ teaspoon cayenne pepper
  Dash of onion powder
  Wheat crackers

Cut a small lid from top of cheese. Scoop out cheese, leaving a thin but sturdy wall ¼- to ⅜-inch thick.

Grate cheese into pea-sized chunks in blender or food processor. Add enough mayonnaise to make a thick but spreadable consistency. Add remaining ingredients and mix well. Spoon mixture back into cheese shell, replace lid and chill. Serve with wheat crackers.

QUICK HERB CHEESE

6 TO 8 SERVINGS

- 1 8-ounce package cream cheese, room temperature
- 1 garlic clove, minced
- 1 teaspoon caraway seeds
- 1 teaspoon dried basil
- 1 teaspoon dill
- 1 teaspoon chives

Combine ingredients in bowl and blend well with electric mixer. Cover and chill. Roll into ball and serve.

THREE-CHEESE BALL

MAKES ABOUT 2½ CUPS

- 1 8-ounce package cream cheese, room temperature
- 5 ounces cheddar cheese spread, room temperature
- 10 ounces bleu cheese, room temperature
- 1 small onion, minced
- 1 garlic clove, minced
- 2 tablespoons brandy or medium dry sherry
  Chopped nuts (optional)
  Apples or crackers

Beat cheeses until well mixed and fluffy. Add onion, garlic and liquor and mix well. Chill. Shape into ball, coating with nuts, if desired. Chill again briefly before serving. Serve with slices of unpeeled apples and/or crackers.

Keeps several weeks in refrigerator.

COCKTAIL PARTY SPEEDY PATE

MAKES ABOUT 3 CUPS

- 1 pound liverwurst with bacon, casing removed
- ½ cup (2 sticks) butter or margarine, room temperature
- 4 ounces package cream cheese, room temperature
- ¼ cup minced parsley
- ¼ cup minced onion
- 3 tablespoons brandy
- 1 tablespoon curry powder
  Salt and freshly ground pepper
  Crudités and crackers

Using electric mixer or food processor fitted with steel knife, beat liverwurst until softened. Add butter and cream cheese and blend until light and fluffy. Add parsley, onion, brandy, curry powder, salt and pepper and mix well. Spoon into crock or other serving container. Swirl top, cover and chill. Serve with crudités and assorted crackers.

MUSHROOM AND NUT PATE

6 SERVINGS

- 2 tablespoons (¼ stick) butter
- 1 pound mushrooms, sliced
- 1 small onion, sliced
- 1 garlic clove, minced
- ¾ cup slivered almonds, toasted
- ¼ cup hazelnuts, toasted
- 2 tablespoons peanut oil
- ¼ teaspoon dried thyme
  Salt
  Dash of red pepper
  Toasted sesame seeds (garnish)
  Assorted crackers

Melt butter in large skillet over medium-high heat. Add mushrooms, onion and garlic and sauté until most of liquid has evaporated. Remove from heat.

Coarsely chop almonds and hazelnuts in blender or processor; remove 2 tablespoons and set aside. Continue chopping, slowly adding oil until mixture is well blended. Add seasoning and mushroom mixture and blend thoroughly. Stir in remaining nuts. Mold into loaf and sprinkle with sesame seeds. Serve with assorted crackers.

FISH

"BLACK TIE" APPETIZER

8 SERVINGS

- 1 8-ounce package cream cheese, room temperature

- 1 2-ounce jar black lumpfish caviar
- 2 hard-cooked eggs, chopped
- 3 green onions, chopped
  Lemon wedges
  Crackers, thin strips of toast, or cocktail rye or pumpernickel

Place block of cheese in center of serving plate. With small spreader, gently frost cheese with caviar. Cover with waxed paper and refrigerate until serving time. Surround with chopped egg, onion, lemon wedges and crackers or bread.

CAVIAR EGGS

Very pretty and very rich.

MAKES 24 HALVES

- 12 hard-cooked eggs
- 2 tablespoons mayonnaise
- 2 tablespoons sour cream
- 2 tablespoons minced onion
- ½ teaspoon lemon juice
- ¼ teaspoon dry mustard
- ¼ teaspoon salt
- 3 tablespoons red caviar
- 2 tablespoons black caviar

Halve eggs. Mix yolks with mayonnaise, sour cream, onion, lemon juice, mustard and salt. Divide evenly among halves. Cover each with red and black caviar.

HERRING TIDBITS

MAKES ABOUT 4 CUPS

- 2 cups (1 pint) sour cream
- 1 12-ounce jar herring tidbits in wine (undrained), chopped
- 2 apples, peeled, quartered, cored and chopped
- 1 medium Bermuda onion, quartered and chopped
- ½ cup seedless grapes
- 2 hard-cooked eggs, chopped
  Rye rounds

Combine first 5 ingredients in large bowl and mix thoroughly. Cover and refrigerate. Before serving, add eggs and toss lightly. Turn into dish. Serve with rye rounds.

QUICK GLASSBLOWER'S HERRING

6 SERVINGS

- 1 12-ounce jar marinated herring
- 1 medium carrot, sliced and cooked
- 1 large red onion, thinly sliced
- 1 teaspoon mustard seeds
- ½ teaspoon peppercorns

Pour marinated herring with liquid into a bowl. Add carrot, onion, mustard seeds and peppercorns. Refrigerate turning several times. Serve chilled. Remove peppercorns before serving if desired.

SMOKED SALMON ROLLS

6 SERVINGS

- 1 8-ounce package cream cheese, room temperature
- 3 tablespoons sour cream
- ½ pound thinly sliced smoked salmon
- 1 2-ounce jar red caviar

Blend cream cheese with sour cream. Gently fold in caviar and spread salmon slices with the mixture. Roll up and cut into 1½-inch lengths. Serve chilled.

CAROLINA PICKLED SHRIMP

6 TO 8 SERVINGS

- ½ cup vegetable oil
- ⅓ cup catsup
- ⅓ cup white vinegar
- 2 tablespoons Worcestershire sauce
- 2 teaspoons sugar
- 1 teaspoon salt
- ½ teaspoon dry mustard
  Dash of hot pepper sauce
- 1 pound shrimp, cooked and shelled
- 2 small red onions, thinly sliced
- 2 bay leaves, crushed

Combine first 8 ingredients and blend well. Layer shrimp, onion, bay leaves in bowl. Pour dressing over. Cover and chill before serving.

MARINATED SHRIMP AND CUCUMBER

6 SERVINGS

- 1 medium cucumber, peeled and diced
- ½ pound cooked small shrimp, chopped
- 6 tablespoons vinegar
- ¼ teaspoon coriander powder or ½ teaspoon dill
- 2 tablespoons vegetable oil
  Salt and pepper

Combine all ingredients and chill until ready to serve.

SHRIMP AND CAVIAR COCKTAIL

6 TO 8 SERVINGS

- 1 pound cooked medium shrimp, chilled
- 1 cup sour cream
- 1 2¼-ounce jar black caviar
  Juice of 1 lemon
  Lemon slices (garnish)

Arrange shrimp in chilled dishes. Combine next 3 ingredients and pour over shrimp. Garnish with lemon slices.

HORS D'OEUVRE SURPRISE

6 OR MORE SERVINGS

- 1 7-ounce can tuna with oil
- 2 to 3 tablespoons Cognac
- 2 3-ounce packages low-calorie cream cheese
- 2 hard-cooked eggs
  Freshly ground white pepper
  Salt to taste
- 3 tablespoons unsalted shelled pistachio nuts
- 1 10½-ounce can beef consommé, chilled until almost jelled
  Crackers or vegetable sticks

Place tuna, oil and Cognac in processor or blender and chop until tuna is well broken up. Add remaining ingredients except consommé, crackers or vegetable sticks, one at a time, chopping until all ingredients are well mixed.

When nuts are well ground, spoon mixture into 2-cup serving bowl. Smooth the surface. Spread with partially jelled consommé and refrigerate until firm. Serve with crackers or raw vegetable sticks.

MEAT AND VEGETABLE

KIWIFRUIT WITH PROSCIUTTO

6 SERVINGS

- 5 kiwifruit, cut into wedges
- ¼ pound prosciutto, sliced wafer thin
- 1 kiwifruit, cut into thin rounds

Wrap kiwifruit wedges in strips of prosciutto. Arrange on serving plate and garnish with kiwifruit rounds. Chill before serving.

STEAK TARTARE

6 SERVINGS

- ½ pound sirloin steak, well trimmed
- 1 egg yolk, beaten
- ½ teaspoon hot mustard
  Coarse salt
  Freshly ground pepper
  Dash of Worcestershire sauce
  Dash of hot pepper sauce
- 1 cup sour cream
  Caviar (optional)
- ½ cup finely chopped sweet onion (optional)
  Rye bread slices

Grind meat twice and mix with yolk. Blend mustard to a paste with water; add seasonings. Mix with meat; taste and adjust seasonings as desired. Shape meat into mound on chilled plate.

Cover with a layer of sour cream and top with caviar. Place chopped onion and rye bread on side of chilled plate and serve.

RAW ASPARAGUS WITH CREAM CHEESE DIPPING SAUCE

4 TO 6 SERVINGS

- 1 8-ounce package cream cheese, room temperature
- ⅓ to ½ cup sour cream
- 3 whole green onions, minced
- 2 tablespoons drained capers
- 2 tablespoons minced fresh parsley
- 1 tablespoon Dijon mustard
  Pinch each of tarragon, basil and marjoram
  Salt and freshly ground pepper
- 1½ to 2 pounds thin raw asparagus tips

Combine all ingredients except asparagus in medium mixing bowl and blend until smooth, using just enough sour cream to make soft consistency. Cover and chill until ready to serve.

Transfer to crock or serving dish and surround with asparagus tips.

Sauce will keep up to three days covered in refrigerator.

CELERIAC REMOULADE

6 SERVINGS

- 1 cup mayonnaise
- 2 tablespoons lemon juice
- 1½ tablespoons prepared mustard (preferably Dijon or Dusseldorf)
- 3 large celery roots, peeled and cut into matchstick slices
  Salt and freshly ground pepper
- 1 tablespoon minced chives (garnish)

Combine first 3 ingredients in large bowl and mix well. Stir in celery root. Season to taste with salt and pepper. Chill well. Sprinkle with chives just before serving.

HUMMUS SPREAD WITH YOGURT

MAKES ABOUT 2½ CUPS

- 2 15-ounce cans garbanzo beans (chick-peas), rinsed and drained
- 6 tablespoons plain yogurt
- ¼ cup olive oil
- 2 heaping tablespoons sesame seeds, toasted
- 2 green onions, chopped
- 2 large garlic cloves, chopped
  Juice of 1 lemon
  Salt and freshly ground pepper
  Pita bread

Puree all ingredients in processor or blender (if using blender, do in two batches). Refrigerate. Spread on pita bread. Add whatever stuffings you like. One of our favorites is a few slices of tomato, avocado slices and a sprinkling of bacon bits.

Keeps in refrigerator up to 1 week.

HARD-COOKED EGGS FLORENTINE

6 SERVINGS

- ½ pound fresh spinach, washed, stems removed
  Hot water
- 1½ cups mayonnaise (preferably homemade)*
- 3 tablespoons chopped parsley
- 6 hard-cooked eggs, shelled
  Watercress sprigs (garnish)

Wilt spinach by soaking in hot water 5 minutes. Drain well and mince. Combine with mayonnaise and parsley, mixing well. Halve eggs lengthwise and place cut side down on individual serving plates. Cover with mayonnaise mixture and chill before serving. Garnish with watercress sprigs.

*If mayonnaise is not homemade, add 1 teaspoon Dijon mustard and fresh lemon juice to taste.

MARINATED MUSHROOMS

8 TO 10 SERVINGS

- ⅔ cup olive oil
- ½ cup water
  Juice of 2 lemons
- ½ teaspoon salt
- 6 peppercorns
- 2 garlic cloves
- 1 bay leaf
- 1 pound large mushrooms, cleaned

Combine all ingredients except mushrooms in large saucepan, cover and bring to boil over medium heat. Reduce heat and simmer 15 minutes. Strain and return to saucepan. Add mushrooms and simmer 5 minutes, turning occasionally. Transfer to bowl, cover and chill.

TOASTED PUMPKIN SEEDS

These are good when served as snacks or with cocktails.

MAKES ABOUT 1 CUP

- 2 cups pumpkin seeds, shells left on, fibers rubbed off (not washed)
- 1 tablespoon peanut oil
- 1 tablespoon butter
- 1½ teaspoons kosher or other coarse salt

Preheat oven to 250°F. Combine all ingredients in small bowl and mix well. Spread on baking sheet or in shallow pan and toast, stirring frequently until seeds are evenly browned and crisp, about 30 to 40 minutes. Cool, then store in tightly covered containers. Remove shells before eating seeds.

MARINATED TOMATOES AND ONIONS

6 SERVINGS

- ½ cup red wine vinegar
- ⅓ cup olive oil
- 4½ teaspoons dried basil
- 1½ teaspoons dried tarragon
- ¼ teaspoon dried oregano
- 6 large tomatoes, peeled and thinly sliced

- 2 medium red onions, thinly sliced
- 4½ teaspoons sugar
  Salt and freshly ground pepper

Combine first 5 ingredients in small bowl and whisk until well blended. Layer half of tomatoes in large serving bowl and cover with half of onions. Sprinkle with half of sugar, and salt and pepper to taste. Drizzle with some of marinade. Repeat with remaining ingredients. Cover and chill before serving.

HOT

DIPS AND CHEESE

CHILI CON QUESO

6 TO 8 SERVINGS

- 1 15-ounce can chili con carne (without beans)
- 1 8-ounce package cream cheese, softened
  Corn or tortilla chips

Combine chili and cheese in small saucepan and heat. Serve hot as a dip with corn or tortilla chips.

QUESADILLAS

4 TO 6 SERVINGS

- 6 flour tortillas
- ¾ cup (about) thinly sliced or shredded Monterey Jack and/or cheddar cheese
- 6 tablespoons canned diced chilies
- 6 tablespoons diced pimiento

Preheat oven to 350°F. Lay tortilla on baking sheet or large baking dish. Sprinkle layer of cheese over half, dot with 1 tablespoon each chilies and pimiento, and fold. Repeat with remaining tortillas. Bake until cheese is melted, about 10 to 15 minutes. Cut into wedges and serve.

HOT CLAM DIP

Great for large gatherings.

MAKES 1½ QUARTS

- ½ cup (1 stick) butter
- 4 large onions, diced
- 2 6½-ounce cans minced clams, drained
- 2 cans white clam sauce
- 1 can whole baby clams, drained
- 8 ounces crackers, mashed
- ½ teaspoon garlic powder
  Assorted crudités

Preheat oven to 350°F. Melt butter in large saucepan over medium heat. Add onion and sauté until transparent. Reduce heat to low and add all remaining ingredients except crudités. Cook until heated through, about 8 minutes, stirring frequently. Transfer to baking dish, cover and bake 15 minutes. Remove cover and bake an additional 15 minutes. Serve hot with an assortment of crudités.

CHEESE SHOESTRINGS

ABOUT 4 SERVINGS

- 1 4-ounce can shoestring potatoes
- ⅓ cup grated Parmesan cheese

Preheat oven to 450°F. Spread potatoes evenly on cookie sheet or large baking dish and sprinkle with Parmesan. Heat about 4 minutes. Serve immediately.

EASY CHEESE CANAPES

MAKES 18 TO 24

- 6 slices sandwich bread
- 1 cup mayonnaise
- ½ cup Parmesan cheese
  Boiling onions, thinly sliced
  Cilantro

Toast bread. Mix mayonnaise and cheese. Cut out 4 rounds from each toast slice. Top with onion slice, sprinkle with cilantro and cover with a dollop of mayonnaise mixture. Broil briefly until tops are puffed and golden, 1 to 2 minutes.

MEXICAN HOT BITES

MAKES 30

- 6 tablespoons (¾ stick) butter
- 6 large flour tortillas
- 6 ounces Monterey Jack cheese, grated
- 1 7-ounce can green chili salsa

Preheat oven to 200°F. Melt 1 tablespoon butter in large skillet over medium-high heat. Add 1 tortilla and fry on each side until lightly browned, about 1 minute. Place about 1 ounce of cheese in center of tortilla and top with 2 tablespoons salsa. Fold sides of tortilla towards center, overlapping slightly. Continue frying until tortilla is golden brown and cheese is melted, about 2 to 3 minutes. Transfer to platter and keep warm in oven. Repeat with remaining ingredients. Cut each tortilla into 5 pieces and serve hot.

Mexican Hot Bites can be prepared ahead. Reheat in 375°F oven about 5 minutes.

SWEET BRIE

24 SERVINGS

- 1 8-inch round of Brie (24 ounces), not fully ripened, top rind removed
- 1 cup chopped pecans
- 2 cups firmly packed brown sugar
  Crackers

Preheat broiler. Place Brie in 10-inch quiche dish or pie plate and sprinkle with nuts. Cover top and sides with sugar, patting gently with fingertips (do not be concerned if sides are not fully covered). Broil on lowest rack until sugar bubbles and melts, about 3 minutes (cheese should retain its shape). Serve immediately with assorted crackers.

CHICKEN AND FISH

CHICKEN-CHEESE PUFFS

MAKES 24

- 2 cups finely diced cooked chicken

- 1 cup mayonnaise
- 2 large shallots, minced
- ¼ teaspoon dried basil, crumbled
- ¼ teaspoon dried thyme, crumbled
  Salt and freshly ground pepper
- ½ to ¾ cup grated Fontina, Gruyère or Swiss cheese
- ½ cup grated Parmesan cheese
  Very thin slices of rye bread

Preheat oven to 350°F. Combine first 3 ingredients in medium bowl. Blend in herbs and seasonings. Add Fontina, Gruyère or Swiss cheese and 2 tablespoons Parmesan, blending well. Slice bread in half. Spread mixture evenly over tops. Arrange on baking sheet. Sprinkle with remaining Parmesan and bake until lightly browned, about 10 minutes.

CHICKEN TRIANGLES

This is a quick and delicious variation of the classic Chinese shrimp toast.

MAKES 64

- 2 pounds chicken breasts, skinned, boned and cut into 1-inch pieces
- 1 cup chopped green onion
- 1 8½-ounce can bamboo shoots, drained and coarsely chopped
- 2 eggs, well beaten
- ¼ cup cornstarch
- 2 teaspoons salt
- 16 slices firm white bread, crusts trimmed
  Oil

Combine chicken, onion and bamboo shoots in blender or processor and mix to consistency of paste. Blend in eggs, cornstarch and salt. Cut each bread slice into 4 triangles. Spread with mixture. Refrigerate until ready to fry.

Heat ¾ inch of oil in large skillet over medium-high heat. Add triangles face down and fry until golden brown, about 1 to 2 minutes. Serve hot. (Or, fry up to one hour before serving and keep warm in preheated 250°F oven.)

Triangles can be frozen before cooking. Fry without thawing, allowing extra time to brown and heat thoroughly.

HONEY CHICKEN WINGS APPETIZER

APPROXIMATELY 10 SERVINGS

This recipe can be cooked all day in a slow cooker or oven-baked one hour before serving.

3 pounds chicken wings
  Salt and pepper
1 cup honey
½ cup soy sauce
2 tablespoons vegetable oil
2 tablespoons catsup
½ garlic clove, chopped

Cut off and discard chicken wing tips. Cut each wing into two parts and sprinkle with salt and pepper. Combine remaining ingredients and mix well. Place wings in slow cooker and pour sauce over. Cook all day on low setting. Or, preheat oven to 375°F. Place wings in shallow casserole, pour sauce over and bake until chicken is well done and sauce is caramelized, about 1 hour.

CHICKEN LIVERS IN SAGE CREAM

4 SERVINGS

1 to 1½ pounds chicken livers, cleaned and patted dry
  Coarse salt and freshly ground pepper
2½ tablespoons butter
1 teaspoon oil
2 tablespoons finely minced shallots
⅓ cup Marsala wine
½ cup brown chicken stock
½ cup whipping cream
1 tablespoon softened butter mixed into a paste with 1 tablespoon flour
2 tablespoons finely slivered fresh sage leaves

Season livers with salt and pepper. Heat 2 tablespoons butter with oil in large heavy skillet over medium-high heat. Add livers and sauté until nicely browned on both sides, about 2 to 3 minutes. Remove with slotted spoon and set aside in bowl.

Melt remaining butter in skillet, add shallots and sauté until just softened and lightly browned, about 1 minute, scraping up any browned bits clinging to pan. Stir in Marsala. Bring to boil and cook until reduced to a glaze. Add stock, return to boil and cook until reduced by half. Blend in cream and bring to boil. Whisk in butter-flour mixture and beat until sauce coats spoon. Taste and adjust seasoning.

Stir sage into sauce. Return chicken livers with any accumulated juices to skillet and turn in sauce until heated through. Serve immediately.

HOT SALMON SANDWICHES

MAKES 3 TO 4 DOZEN

1 15½-ounce can salmon, drained and boned
1 pound cheddar cheese, grated
¾ cup plain yogurt or mayonnaise
1 teaspoon onion salt
½ teaspoon paprika
  Dash of white pepper
2 loaves sliced miniature cocktail rye, French or sourdough bread
  Paprika

Mix together salmon, cheese (reserve 1 cup), yogurt, salt, paprika and pepper. Spread mixture on each bread slice. Top with remaining cheese and sprinkle with paprika.

Place sandwiches on greased cookie sheet and broil until cheese is completely melted and lightly browned, about 3 minutes. Serve immediately.

SCALLOPS VERACRUZ

Spoon from a large chafing dish into individual scallop shells for artful presentation. The sauce can be cooked one day ahead and refrigerated. Add scallops and reheat in a low oven just before serving.

25 SERVINGS

1 cup olive oil
4 cups chopped onion
2 cups chopped green pepper
5 large garlic cloves, finely minced
2 bay leaves
2 teaspoons paprika
2 teaspoons dried oregano leaves, crumbled
½ teaspoon dried thyme, crumbled
½ teaspoon ground red pepper or to taste
4 28-ounce cans diced tomatoes, drained
1 16-ounce can tomato sauce
7 pounds small scallops, rinsed, drained and patted dry (slice in half if large)
1 cup sliced green olives
¼ cup chopped cilantro
  Salt

Heat olive oil in stockpot or large Dutch oven over low heat. Add onion, green pepper and garlic and sauté until soft but not brown. Blend in bay leaves, paprika, oregano, thyme and red pepper. Add tomatoes and tomato sauce. Increase heat to medium and bring to boil. Reduce heat and simmer 10 minutes. (Can be prepared 1 day ahead to this point and refrigerated.)

Add scallops and continue cooking over low heat (or in low oven if reheating later) until scallops are just done. Stir in remaining ingredients. Adjust seasoning and transfer to chafing dish.

SHRIMP IN BACON

4 TO 6 SERVINGS

8 to 12 bacon slices, halved
  Hot spicy mustard
16 to 24 medium to large raw shrimp, shelled and deveined

Preheat broiler. Place bacon on waxed paper and brush generously with mustard. Wrap around shrimp, mustard side in, and secure with toothpick. Broil until bacon is crisp, turning once. Serve hot.

CLAM-STUFFED MUSHROOMS

12 SERVINGS

- 2 pounds medium mushrooms
- ½ cup (1 stick) butter
- 3 garlic cloves, minced
- 1 6½- or 8-ounce can minced clams, drained (juice reserved)
- ½ cup breadcrumbs
- ⅓ cup chopped fresh parsley
- ¾ teaspoon salt
- ¼ teaspoon freshly ground pepper

Remove mushroom stems; mince finely in blender or processor.

Combine butter and garlic in small saucepan and heat slowly until butter is melted, stirring occasionally. Coat mushroom caps with mixture and set on baking sheet.

Preheat broiler. Combine clam juice and minced mushroom stems in small saucepan over medium heat and cook until tender. Add clams, breadcrumbs, parsley, salt and pepper and heat through. Divide evenly among caps. Broil 6 inches from heat until lightly golden and heated through, about 5 to 8 minutes.

MEAT AND VEGETABLE

COCKTAIL PARTY MEATBALLS

MAKES 100 SMALL MEATBALLS

- 2 pounds lean ground beef
- ¼ cup peeled grated potato
- 1 egg
- 1 small onion, grated
  Salt and freshly ground pepper
- 1 13-ounce bottle chili sauce
- 5 ounces grape jelly
  Dash of Worcestershire sauce

Combine first 4 ingredients in large bowl and mix well. Season with salt and pepper. Form into small meatballs and set aside.

Blend remaining ingredients in large skillet over medium heat. Add meatballs. Cover and simmer about 30 minutes, stirring occasionally. Transfer meatballs to chafing dish or fondue pot. Skim excess fat from sauce. Pour sauce over meatballs. Serve warm from chafing dish.

PARTY MEATBALLS

MAKES 35 TO 40 SMALL MEATBALLS

- 32 Ritz crackers, crushed
- 1 egg
- 1 small onion, finely chopped
- ½ cup milk
- 2 ounces bleu cheese
- ⅛ teaspoon dried sage
  Salt and freshly ground pepper
- 1 pound ground beef

Combine all ingredients except meat and let stand until soft. Mix in meat. Shape into small balls and arrange on baking sheet. Preheat broiler. Broil meatballs until well browned, about 5 to 8 minutes.

Meatballs can be flash-frozen on baking sheet, then stored in plastic bags in freezer until ready to use.

PARTY MEATBALLS IN SWEET-SOUR SAUCE

6 TO 8 SERVINGS

- 1 10-ounce bottle sweet-sour sauce
- ½ cup catsup
- ¼ cup cider vinegar
- ¼ cup firmly packed brown sugar
- 1½ teaspoons cornstarch
- ½ teaspoon salt
- ½ teaspoon ground ginger
- 1 recipe Party Meatballs (see preceding recipe)
- 1 20-ounce can pineapple chunks, well drained

Combine all ingredients except meatballs and pineapple in medium saucepan. Cook over medium-high heat until sauce is thickened, stirring frequently. Add meatballs and heat through. Blend in pineapple. Serve from chafing dish.

MOCK EMPANADAS EMILIA

MAKES ABOUT 4 DOZEN

- 1 pound lean ground beef
- 1 envelope onion soup mix
  Pinch of ground red pepper
- 1 cup (4 ounces) grated cheddar cheese
- 3 8-ounce packages refrigerated crescent rolls

Combine first 3 ingredients in 10-inch skillet and cook over medium-high heat until browned. Drain off any excess fat. Add cheese and stir until melted, about 2 minutes. Remove from heat.

Preheat oven to 375°F. Separate dough into triangles; cut each in half. Spoon about 1 tablespoon meat mixture onto each triangle. Fold edges into center and seal well. Bake on ungreased baking sheet until golden, about 15 minutes.

QUICK PIROSHKI

6 SERVINGS

- 1 package or 2 sticks pie crust mix
- 2 large onions, minced
- 2 tablespoons (¼ stick) butter or margarine
- ¾ pound lean, twice-ground beef
- 1 teaspoon dried dill
- ¾ teaspoon salt
- ⅛ teaspoon pepper
- 2 hard-cooked eggs, chopped

Preheat oven to 400°F. Prepare pie crust according to package directions, roll out and cut into 2-inch circles using cutter or top of a glass.

Prepare filling by sautéing onions in butter until golden, add meat and cook, stirring until light brown. Cool mixture and add all remaining ingredients, blending thoroughly. Place a teaspoon of mixture in the center of one-half of each pastry circle, fold over to cover meat, crimp and seal edges with a fork dipped into cold water. Place piroshki on greased cookie sheets and bake until golden. Serve hot.

PRUNE AND BACON HORS D'OEUVRES

MAKES ABOUT 24

- ½ pound bacon, sliced into thirds
- 1 12-ounce package pitted prunes

Preheat oven to 375°F. Wrap piece of bacon around each prune, secure with toothpick and place on rack over broiler pan. Bake until bacon is cooked, about 15 to 20 minutes. Serve immediately.

HOT SALAMI

4 TO 6 SERVINGS

- 1 1-pound all beef salami, casing discarded
  Mustard
  Rye rounds and assorted mustards

Preheat oven to 400°F. Cut salami into slices ⅛ inch thick, but do not cut through. Transfer to baking sheet. Bake 45 minutes. Discard fat from pan. Generously brush salami slices with mustard. Continue baking until crusty, about 15 to 20 minutes. Serve immediately with rye rounds and assorted mustards.

HOT SAUSAGE AND CHEESE PUFFS

MAKES ABOUT 2 DOZEN

- ¼ pound Italian sausage, casings removed
- ¼ pound cheddar cheese, grated
- ¾ cup buttermilk baking mix
- 3 to 4 tablespoons water

Preheat oven to 375°F. Sauté sausage in medium skillet over medium-high heat, breaking up with fork until browned and finely crumbled, about 7 to 10 minutes. Drain off excess fat. Transfer sausage to medium bowl and let cool slightly. Add remaining ingredients and mix well. Form into 1-inch balls. Arrange on baking sheet. Bake until cheese is melted and puffs are lightly golden, about 10 to 12 minutes. Serve immediately.

Puffs can be baked ahead and frozen. Thaw and then reheat in 375°F oven until warmed through, about 5 to 7 minutes.

SAUSAGE APPETIZERS

MAKES 48

- 1 8-ounce package refrigerated butterflake rolls
- ½ pound hot sausage, crumbled
- 2 eggs, lightly beaten
- 1 cup cottage cheese
- 1 tablespoon snipped chives
  Dash of freshly ground pepper
- ¼ cup grated Parmesan cheese

Preheat oven to 375°F. Generously grease miniature muffin tins. Separate rolls into eight sections. Press each piece between ⅛ and ¼ inch thick and fit into muffin cups. Brown sausage in small skillet; drain well. Spoon equally over dough. Mix eggs, cottage cheese, chives and pepper. Stir in Parmesan. Spoon over sausage and bake until filling is lightly browned, about 20 minutes.

Sausage Appetizers can be made ahead and frozen before or after baking. Reheat before serving.

CREAM CHEESE-STUFFED MUSHROOMS

6 TO 8 SERVINGS

- Small amount of lemon juice diluted with water
- 1 pound fresh mushroom caps, stems removed
- 1 8-ounce package cream cheese, softened
- 1 small onion, grated
- 1 egg
  Salt and pepper

Preheat broiler. Dip cloth into lemon water and wring well; wipe mushroom caps with acidulated cloth. Mix together cheese, onion, egg, salt and pepper. Fill caps with mixture. Place on baking sheet and broil until bubbly and caps are cooked.

WALNUT AND CHEESE STUFFED MUSHROOMS

6 TO 8 SERVINGS

- 24 medium mushroom caps
  Juice of 1 large lemon
- 1 teaspoon olive oil
- 1 teaspoon butter
- 1 medium onion, minced
- 3 tablespoons coarsely chopped walnuts
- 2 green onions, minced
- 1 small garlic clove, minced
- 7 ounces fresh spinach, cooked, chopped and squeezed dry
- 1½ ounces feta cheese, crumbled
- 1 ounce Gruyère cheese, shredded
- 2 tablespoons minced fresh dill or 2 teaspoons dried dill, crumbled
  Salt and freshly ground pepper
- 1 tablespoon oil

Toss mushrooms with lemon juice; let stand while making stuffing.

Heat olive oil with butter in heavy medium nonaluminum skillet over medium-low heat. Add onion and cook until soft and transparent. Increase heat to medium high. Stir in walnuts and cook about 30 seconds. Add green onion and garlic and cook another 30 seconds, stirring constantly. Add spinach and cook briefly until excess moisture has evaporated. Let cool. Stir in cheeses, dill, salt and pepper.

If barbecuing prepare fire. When coals are very hot, spread sheet of foil over grill and brush with oil. Punch 12 holes into foil.

Meanwhile, stuff mushrooms. Arrange on foil and grill or bake on a cookie sheet in 375° oven until filling is hot, 8 to 10 minutes. Serve immediately while hot.

DO AHEAD

COLD

DIPPING SAUCE FOR SMOKED FISH

SERVES 4, MAKES ABOUT ⅓ CUP

- ¼ cup sour cream
- 2 tablespoons prepared horseradish
- ½ teaspoon Worcestershire sauce
- ½ teaspoon dry mustard
- 4 drops Tabasco
- ½ teaspoon salt

Combine ingredients and chill overnight for flavors to blend.

ORIENTAL DIP

MAKES ABOUT 2 CUPS

- ½ pint (1 cup) sour cream
- 1 6½-ounce can minced clams, drained
- 1 green onion, minced
- 1 medium garlic clove, minced
- 1 tablespoon chili sauce
- 1 teaspoon hoisin sauce
  Shrimp chips
  Assorted fresh vegetables (snow peas, asparagus, broccoli and celery)

Combine first 6 ingredients and mix thoroughly. Chill at least 2 hours. Serve with chips and vegetables.

RED CAVIAR-CHEESE DIP

MAKES ABOUT 1½ CUPS

- 12 ounces cream cheese, room temperature
- 2 tablespoons minced green onion, white part only
- ¼ teaspoon dried basil, crumbled
  Freshly ground pepper
- 1 2-ounce jar red caviar
  Crackers and crudités

Combine first 3 ingredients in blender or processor and mix until

smooth. Season with pepper. Add ⅓ of caviar and blend until light pink. Transfer to serving bowl. Add remaining caviar, stirring gently with wooden spoon. Cover and refrigerate overnight. Let stand at room temperature for about 30 minutes before serving. Serve with crackers and crudités.

THISTLE DIP

6 TO 8 SERVINGS

- 1 6-ounce jar marinated artichoke hearts, undrained
- 1 cup sour cream
- 1 small garlic clove, minced
- ¼ teaspoon onion salt
  Dash of ground red pepper
  Paprika
  Assorted crackers

Puree undrained artichoke hearts in blender or processor until very smooth. Transfer to bowl and blend in sour cream, garlic, onion salt and red pepper. Cover and refrigerate at least 1 hour. Sprinkle with paprika and serve with crackers.

ALMOND PATE

MAKES ABOUT 2½ CUPS

- 1 8-ounce package ripe Brie, rind discarded, then brought to room temperature
- ¾ cup (1½ sticks) butter, room temperature
- ½ cup slivered almonds, toasted
- 2 tablespoons dry sherry
- ¼ teaspoon dried thyme
  Crackers or crudités

Whip all ingredients except crackers or crudités together. Spoon into cheese crock; cover and chill at least 2 hours or overnight. Let stand at room temperature for about 1 hour before serving. Serve with crackers or crudités.

CURRIED CHICKEN BALLS

4 TO 6 SERVINGS

- 4 ounces cream cheese, room temperature
- 2 tablespoons mayonnaise

- 1 cup cooked chopped chicken
- 1 cup sliced blanched almonds
- 1 tablespoon curry powder or to taste
- 1 tablespoon finely chopped chutney
- ½ teaspoon salt
- ½ cup flaked coconut, toasted

Blend cream cheese and mayonnaise in mixing bowl. Add chicken, almonds, curry, chutney and salt and mix well. Chill. Shape into small balls and roll in coconut. Serve chilled.

ORIENTAL CHICKEN APPETIZER

4 TO 6 SERVINGS

- 1 whole skinned and boned chicken breast
- 1½ cups chicken broth
  Lettuce
  Oriental Sauce*

Poach chicken breast in broth 20 minutes. Let cool in the liquid. Remove and chill overnight. Slice into 1- by 2-inch strips. Place on a bed of lettuce. Pour Oriental Sauce over chicken and serve.

*Oriental Sauce

- 2 tablespoons soy sauce
- 1 tablespoon sesame oil
- 1 tablespoon honey
- 1 tablespoon dry sherry
- 1 teaspoon freshly grated ginger root or ¼ teaspoon dried
- 2 green onion tops, finely chopped
- 1 tablespoon toasted sesame seeds (optional)

Mix all ingredients together and pour over chicken.

BROOK TROUT MOUSSE

6 SERVINGS

- 1 small skinned and fileted smoked trout
- 1 3-ounce package cream cheese
  Juice and grated pulp of 1 small onion

2 tablespoons fresh lemon juice
Dash of hot pepper sauce
Dash of Worcestershire sauce
Rye or other crackers
Minced parsley (garnish)

Place first 6 ingredients into mixer or food processor and mix until smooth. Mound into serving dish. Round the top and refrigerate 2 hours or overnight.

Arrange crackers around mousse, garnish with parsley and serve.

ALL-IN-THE-BLENDER SALMON MOUSSE

8 SERVINGS

    1 envelope unflavored gelatin
    2 tablespoons lemon juice
    1 small onion, sliced
    ½ cup boiling water
    ½ cup mayonnaise
    ½ teaspoon paprika
    1 teaspoon dried dill
    1 1-pound can pink salmon, drained
    1 cup heavy cream
      Parsley (garnish)

Place first 4 ingredients in blender and blend at high speed until onion is pureed. Add next 4 ingredients and blend again. Add cream, ⅓ at a time, and blend until very smooth. Pour into 1-quart mold and chill overnight. To unmold, dip bottom and sides of mold into warm water and invert onto a serving plate. Decorate mousse with parsley.

SCALLOP-MUSHROOM APPETIZER

10 TO 12 SERVINGS

    1 pound bay scallops
    2 teaspoons minced onion
    1 bay leaf
    ¼ teaspoon salt
      Freshly ground pepper
    1 pound mushrooms, sliced
    1 cup minced fresh parsley or ½ cup dried parsley flakes

    1 envelope Italian or French salad dressing mix
    ⅔ cup olive oil
    ½ cup fresh lemon juice
    2 tablespoons water
      Butter lettuce leaves (optional)
      Minced parsley, paprika (garnish)

Combine scallops, onion, bay leaf, salt and pepper in medium saucepan; add water to cover. Place over high heat and bring to boil; immediately turn off heat, cover pan and let stand until scallops have lost translucent look and are firm, about 5 minutes. Drain. Transfer to medium bowl and add mushrooms and parsley.

Make dressing according to package directions, substituting olive oil for salad oil and lemon juice for vinegar. Pour over scallop-mushroom mixture, tossing gently. Cover and refrigerate overnight. Serve on lettuce leaves or with toothpicks, garnished with parsley and paprika.

SHRIMP AND DIP

8 TO 12 SERVINGS

    2 to 3 pounds cleaned, raw medium shrimp
    1 pint mayonnaise
    2 tablespoons chili sauce
      Juice of ½ lemon
    ¼ cup oil
    1 teaspoon celery seeds
      Salt and pepper
    1½ stalks celery, diced
    1 medium onion, minced

One day before serving, cook shrimp in boiling water for 5 minutes or until they turn pink. Chill. Combine remaining ingredients and chill thoroughly. Place dip in serving bowl and surround with shrimp.

DILLED MUSHROOMS

6 SERVINGS

    ½ pound sliced fresh mushrooms
    1 teaspoon butter or margarine

      Salt and pepper
    ¼ cup vinegar and oil dressing
    ½ bunch fresh chopped dill

Lightly sauté mushrooms in butter. Do not brown. Season with salt and pepper to taste and drain.

Mix with remaining ingredients and marinate overnight or longer in refrigerator. Serve cold.

HOT

SCALLOP KEBABS

See photograph page 32

8 SERVINGS

    12 strips thinly sliced bacon, partially cooked until light brown and cut into pieces same size as scallops
    16 sea scallops, halved horizontally
    16 small water chestnuts, halved horizontally
    32 5- to 6-inch bamboo skewers
    ⅓ cup soy sauce
    2 tablespoons rice wine vinegar
    1½ tablespoons sugar
    1 tablespoon Chinese rice wine or dry sherry
    1 garlic clove, minced
    1 teaspoon minced fresh ginger

Alternate bacon between scallop and water chestnut slices on skewers. Arrange in shallow dish. Combine remaining ingredients in processor or blender and mix well. Pour over kebabs, cover and marinate in refrigerator for 2 to 3 hours.

Prepare fire on barbecue, allowing coals to burn down to moderate temperature. Set grill about 4 inches above coals.

Spread coals in single layer. Drain off marinade and pat kebabs dry with paper towels. Grill until scallops are barely firm, about 6 minutes per side. Serve immediately.

VIETNAMESE PORK STICKS WITH LETTUCE CUPS

See photograph page 32

Tempting finger food with a delicous sauce. Just add Cucumber Stick Salad (page 57) and fresh fruit to complete the meal.

4 SERVINGS

Meat Mixture

- 1 pound finely ground lean pork butt
- 6 water chestnuts, minced
- 1 large garlic clove, minced
- 1 small green onion, minced
- 1 tablespoon Japanese soy sauce
- 2 teaspoons oil
- 1¼ teaspoons fresh lemon juice
- ½ teaspoon minced fresh ginger
- ¼ teaspoon sugar
- ¼ teaspoon Chinese hot chili oil
- ⅛ teaspoon salt
- 12 5- to 6-inch bamboo skewers

Garnishes

- 12 Boston or Bibb lettuce leaves
- ½ cup chopped fresh cilantro (also known as Chinese parsley or coriander)
- ½ cup chopped fresh mint leaves
- ½ cup chopped green onion

Dipping Sauce

- ½ cup Japanese soy sauce
- 5 tablespoons fresh lemon juice
- 3 tablespoons water
- 2 garlic cloves, minced
- 2 teaspoons sugar
- 1 teaspoon oyster sauce
- 1 teaspoon minced fresh ginger
- ⅛ to ¼ teaspoon ground red pepper

For meat: Combine all ingredients in large bowl and use hands to mix gently but thoroughly. Shape into 12 cylinders approximately 3 inches long and no more than 1 inch thick. Insert bamboo skewer through each cylinder and set aside.

Arrange garnishes in individual bowls; refrigerate.

For sauce: Combine all ingredients in small pan and bring to boil. Reduce heat and simmer 5 minutes. Let cool. Divide among 4 small bowls and set aside.

Heat coals on barbecue until gray ash forms. Spread into overlapping layer, knocking off ash so coals are hot and glowing. Place grill 2 to 3 inches above coals or, preheat oven to broil.

Arrange pork sticks on grill or broiling pan so they do not touch. Cook until meat is crisped, browned and firm, turning often with tongs, about 10 to 15 minutes.

Have each diner sprinkle lettuce leaf with other garnishes. Slip pork off skewer onto lettuce. Wrap around pork and use sauce for dipping.

Meat Mixture can be prepared and skewered up to 24 hours before barbecuing. Sauce will keep 2 weeks in refrigerator.

CHEDDAR RAMEKIN

10 TO 12 SERVINGS

- 12 ounces grated sharp cheddar cheese
- 1 baked deep 10-inch pie crust
- ½ cup canned diced green chilies
- 4 eggs
- 2 egg yolks
- 2 tablespoons freshly grated Parmesan cheese
- 1½ tablespoons flour
- ½ teaspoon salt
- 1½ cups whipping cream

Preheat oven to 350°F. Sprinkle half of cheddar cheese over bottom of pie crust. Top with diced chilies, then cover with remaining cheddar cheese. Beat together eggs, yolks, Parmesan, flour and salt. Add cream, stirring until just blended. Gently pour over cheese and chilies, blending with fingertip (so as not to pierce crust) until cheese is moistened. Bake

until filling is set in center, 50 to 60 minutes. Serve warm.

Can be baked ahead and frozen. Bring to room temperature before reheating gently in a low oven.

CLAM PUFFS

4 TO 8 SERVINGS

- 3 6½-ounce cans drained clams (reserve ¼ cup liquor)
- 2 eggs, separated
- 1 cup all purpose flour
- 2 teaspoons baking powder
- ¼ cup (½ stick) butter, melted
- ½ teaspoon salt
  Pepper
  Oil for deep frying

Combine clams, liquor and egg yolks in medium bowl. Add flour, baking powder, melted butter, salt and pepper. Mix well. Beat egg whites to stiff peaks. Fold into clam mixture. Chill overnight.

Heat oil in deep fryer or large frying pan to 375°F. Drop mixture by teaspoonfuls; don't crowd. Fry until brown and crisp, turning once. Drain on paper towel. Sprinkle lightly with salt and serve hot.

CHINESE-STYLE SPARERIBS

6 TO 8 SERVINGS

- ¼ cup chicken stock
- ¼ cup dark soy sauce
- ¼ cup sugar
- 3 tablespoons hoisin sauce
- 1 tablespoon sherry
- 4 garlic cloves, mashed
- 12 to 16 spareribs, cut into 2-inch pieces

Combine all ingredients except ribs in shallow baking dish just large enough to accommodate ribs in single layer. Add ribs, turning to coat evenly. Cover and marinate overnight in refrigerator.

Preheat oven to 375°F. Bake ribs in sauce 15 minutes. Reduce oven to 300°F, turn ribs and bake an additional 15 minutes. Transfer ribs to rack set over baking sheet and return to oven to crisp (or run under broiler 2 minutes to brown). Serve hot.

SESAME BEEF STRIPS

24 SERVINGS

- 3 cups sesame oil
- 1½ cups light soy sauce
- 1½ cups sherry
- 1½ cups firmly packed brown sugar
- 4 garlic cloves, finely minced
- ¾ teaspoon ground ginger
- 3 pounds sirloin tip or boneless eye of round, flash frozen and cut across grain into paper-thin strips
  Bamboo skewers soaked in water

Combine first 6 ingredients in large shallow dish and blend well. Add beef strips, turning to coat. Cover and marinate in refrigerator overnight turning occasionally.

Preheat broiler. Thread beef onto skewers. Dip into marinade, coating heavily. Place on rack and broil 6 inches from heat source for 1½ minutes. Remove, dip in marinade again and broil on second side to desired doneness. Serve hot or at room temperature.

MICROWAVE

COLD

FRESH VEGETABLE DIP

Best made one day before serving.

MAKES ABOUT 3 CUPS

- 1 10-ounce package frozen chopped spinach
- 1 cup sour cream
- ½ cup minced fresh parsley
- ½ cup chopped green onion
- ½ cup mayonnaise
- 1 tablespoon fresh lemon juice or to taste
- 1 teaspoon fines herbes
- 1 teaspoon minced fresh dill or ½ teaspoon dried dill

Salt and freshly ground pepper
Paprika

Place unopened package of spinach on plate. Cook on High 5 minutes. Let stand 5 minutes until completely defrosted. Remove spinach from package and drain thoroughly; squeeze dry.

Transfer spinach to processor or mixing bowl. Add all remaining ingredients except paprika and blend well. Dust with paprika. Cover and refrigerate.

LIVER PATE

MAKES ABOUT 3 CUPS

- 2 large onions, diced
- ¼ cup chicken fat or ¼ cup (½ stick) unsalted butter
- 1 pound chicken livers, rinsed and drained
- 1 teaspoon salt
- ¼ teaspoon freshly ground white pepper
  Pinch of garlic powder
- 1 hard-cooked egg, grated

Combine onions and chicken fat or butter in mixing bowl and cook on High until onion is softened, about 10 minutes. Set aside. Arrange chicken livers in single layer in shallow dish or pie plate. Cover loosely with paper towel and cook on Medium (50 percent power) until livers just lose pink color, about 5 minutes; do not overcook or livers with be tough. Drain off any accumulated liquid. Transfer livers to processor. Add onion, salt, pepper and garlic powder and mix until smooth. Spoon into bowl or container and chill. Sprinkle with grated egg before serving.

SEAFARER HORS D'OEUVRE

MAKES ABOUT 40

- 4 ounces cream cheese
- 1 6-ounce package frozen crabmeat or shrimp, thawed and drained
- 2 tablespoons fresh lemon juice

- 1 tablespoon ranch-style dry salad dressing mix
- 1 tablespoon mayonnaise
- 2 medium zucchini, thinly sliced
  Paprika (garnish)

Heat cheese in 1-quart bowl on High 30 seconds to 1 minute to soften. Add crab, lemon juice, dressing mix and mayonnaise and mix until well blended.

Arrange zucchini slices in serving dish(es). Top each slice with a teaspoonful of crab mixture. Sprinkle with paprika. Cook on High until zucchini is crisp-tender, about 1 to 2 minutes. Let cool slightly. Chill before serving.

HOT

CRAB PUFFS

MAKES 24 PUFFS

- 1 6½-ounce can crab (or 8 ounces fresh crab)
- ¼ cup chopped ripe black olives
- 2 tablespoons minced onion
- 2 tablespoons minced green pepper
- 2 tablespoons minced celery
- 3 drops hot pepper sauce
- ½ to ¾ cup mayonnaise
- 24 baked miniature cream puff shells, halved

Combine crab, olives, onion, green pepper, celery and pepper sauce in 1-quart mixing bowl. Blend in enough mayonnaise to moisten. Pile into bottom of puff shells, top with "lids" and arrange in a circular pattern on glass serving plate. Heat, uncovered, allowing 1½ to 2 minutes on High for 12 shells, rotating dish ¼ turn halfway through cooking time. Serve immediately.

May be made ahead and frozen. To serve, defrost in microwave for several minutes (exact time will depend on quantity) and heat as needed.

Tiny canned shrimp or tuna may be substituted for the crab.

SOMBRERO DIP
8 SERVINGS

- 1 pound lean ground beef
- 1 large yellow onion, chopped
- ½ cup catsup
- 1 tablespoon chili powder
- 1 teaspoon garlic salt
- 1 teaspoon ground cumin
- 1 teaspoon dried oregano leaves, crushed
  Hot pepper sauce to taste
- 1 24-ounce can kidney beans, undrained
- 1 2-ounce jar pimiento-stuffed green olives, sliced, at room temperature
- ½ pound cheddar cheese, grated, at room temperature
- 4 green onions, chopped (garnish)

Combine beef and yellow onion in 2-quart casserole and cook on High 5 minutes, stirring once to crumble beef. Add catsup, chili powder, garlic salt, cumin, oregano and hot pepper sauce and blend well. Puree beans in processor or blender and stir into beef mixture. Cover and cook on High 10 minutes, stirring once halfway through cooking time. Stir through several times. Blend in about ¾ of olive slices. (Can be prepared ahead to this point and reheated just before serving.) Sprinkle cheese over top and garnish with green onion and remaining olives. Serve immediately.

CHEESE MELTS
4 SERVINGS

- 2 English muffins, split and toasted
- 2 tablespoons (¼ stick) butter, room temperature
- 4 ½-inch tomato slices
- 8 slices bacon, cooked crisp
- 8 3x1-inch slices Swiss cheese

Arrange muffin halves in baking dish or on paper plate. Spread evenly with butter. Top each with tomato slice. Crisscross 2 bacon slices over each tomato, then overlap with 2 slices of cheese. Cook on High until cheese melts, about 1 minute.

NACHOS
8 SERVINGS

- 2 cups grated sharp cheddar cheese
- ½ cup taco sauce (mild or hot)
- ½ cup minced onion (optional)
- 1 2¼-ounce can sliced ripe olives, drained
- 1 10-ounce package tortilla or corn chips

Sprinkle cheese evenly over large glass plate with rim, leaving 1-inch border. Top with taco sauce, onion and olives. Microwave on High 3 minutes, rotating dish ¼ turn halfway through cooking time. Insert edges of tortilla chips into cheese, covering entire surface, and serve immediately.

CHICKEN WINGS PARMESAN

Here is a winning appetizer using halved chicken wings with the tips discarded.

6 TO 8 SERVINGS

- 15 chicken wings
- ¼ cup (½ stick) butter or margarine
- 18 Ritz crackers
- ½ cup grated Parmesan cheese
- 2 teaspoons minced dried parsley
- ¾ teaspoon garlic powder
- ½ teaspoon paprika
- ⅛ teaspoon freshly ground pepper

Cut off wing tips and discard. Separate wings at joint. Pat dry with paper towels. Melt butter in flat round dish (a 9-inch pie plate works well). Combine all remaining ingredients in processor or blender and mix well. Dip chicken in butter and then in seasoned coating. Return wings to pie plate and arrange meaty side up in spoke pattern with thicker portion of chicken toward outside. Cover loosely with paper towel and cook on High 15 minutes.

RUMAKI
MAKES 16

- 8 slices bacon, cut in half
- 8 water chestnuts, drained and cut in half
- ¼ pound chicken livers, trimmed and cut into 16 pieces
  Chinese mustard or plum sauce

Arrange bacon in single layer on paper towel-lined paper plate. Cook on High 4 to 5 minutes to soften. Place water chestnut and liver on bacon slice and roll up, securing with plain wooden toothpick. (Rumaki can be prepared ahead to this point and refrigerated.)

Arrange rumaki in circle on 7- to 9-inch round dish or plate. Cook on High until bacon is crisp, 3 to 4 minutes. Serve with mustard or plum sauce on the side.

ALBONDIGAS (MEXICAN MEATBALLS)
MAKES ABOUT 35

Meatballs

- 1 pound lean ground beef
- 1 slice bread, rinsed with water and squeezed dry
- 1 egg
- ¼ cup chopped fresh parsley
- ¼ cup minced onion
- 1 garlic clove, minced
- 1 teaspoon salt
- ⅛ teaspoon freshly ground pepper
- 1 4-ounce can diced green chilies

Sauce

- 1 cup tomato puree
- ¼ cup minced onion
- ¼ teaspoon chili powder
  Chopped fresh parsley (garnish)

For meatballs: Combine first 8 ingredients with half of chilies in medium bowl. Gently shape into meatballs. Arrange in circle on round microwave-safe rack set in shallow baking dish. Cook on High 7 minutes. Drain off fat. Transfer meatballs to shallow serving dish.

For sauce: Combine remaining chilies with tomato puree, onion and chili powder in large measuring cup. Cover and cook on High 5 minutes. Spoon over meatballs. Sprinkle with chopped parsley and serve immediately.

ARTICHOKE APPETIZERS

8 SERVINGS

- 2 14-ounce cans water-packed artichoke hearts, drained
- ¾ cup mayonnaise
- ½ cup grated Parmesan cheese
  Dash of tarragon vinegar

Place artichokes between paper towels and squeeze to remove excess moisture. Cut into quarters. Combine mayonnaise, cheese and vinegar in mixing bowl. Add artichokes and stir gently just to coat. Turn into glass pie plate and microwave on High 2 minutes, turning dish if necessary to cook evenly. Serve hot with toothpicks.

GREEK STUFFED MUSHROOMS

8 SERVINGS

- 1 10-ounce package frozen spinach
- ½ cup grated Parmesan cheese
- 4 ounces feta cheese, rinsed and crumbled
- ½ cup finely chopped green onion
- ½ cup finely chopped parsley
  Salt
- 24 fresh mushrooms, cleaned and stemmed

Cook frozen spinach on High setting until barely defrosted, about 3 minutes. Drain well in colander, gently pressing out moisture with wooden spoon. In mixing bowl, combine drained spinach, cheeses, onion, parsley and salt. Mix well.

Fill mushroom caps with spinach mixture, mounding high in center. Arrange on plate used for serving and cook on High setting until steaming hot, approximately 3 to 4 minutes. Serve immediately.

PARMESAN POTATOES

A quick appetizer easily adaptable to any number of servings. Keep a batch of the coating on hand in the refrigerator so you can whip up hors d'oeuvres at a moment's notice.

4 SERVINGS

- ¼ cup (½ stick) butter
- 1 pound russet potatoes, peeled and cut into 1-inch cubes
- ¼ cup freshly grated Parmesan cheese
- 8 crackers
- 1 teaspoon garlic powder
- ½ teaspoon salt or to taste
- ½ teaspoon freshly ground pepper
- ½ teaspoon paprika
- 3 tablespoons minced fresh parsley
- 1 tablespoon freshly grated Parmesan cheese

Melt butter in pie plate or au gratin dish just large enough to accommodate potatoes in single layer. Add potatoes, stirring to coat evenly. Remove with slotted spoon and set aside. Pour off any remaining butter and reserve.

Combine ¼ cup Parmesan, crackers, garlic powder, salt, pepper and paprika in food processor or blender and process to fine crumbs. Transfer to plastic bag. Add potatoes in batches, shaking to coat evenly. Return potatoes to dish in single layer. Cover with plastic wrap and cook on High 5 minutes. Add reserved butter and stir potatoes well. Cook uncovered on High until potatoes are fork tender, about 2 to 3 minutes. Combine parsley and remaining cheese and sprinkle over top. Spear potatoes with toothpicks and serve immediately.

Add a sprinkle of dill, oregano, tarragon or other favorite herb at begin-

ning of cooking time for a spicy variation if desired.

MONTEREY JACK RATATOUILLE

4 TO 6 SERVINGS

- 1 eggplant (about 1½ pounds)
- ¼ cup olive oil
- 2 large garlic cloves, minced
- 1 large onion, thinly sliced into rings
- ½ pound zucchini, thinly sliced into rings
- 1 green pepper, thinly sliced into rings
- 1 celery stalk, thinly sliced
- 3 firm large tomatoes, cut into wedges, or 1 14½-ounce can plum tomatoes, coarsely chopped
- 1 6-ounce can tomato paste
- 3 tablespoons flour
- 1½ teaspoons salt
- 1 teaspoon fines herbes
- ½ teaspoon freshly ground pepper
- ¼ teaspoon oregano
  Pinch of dried thyme, crumbled
- 2 cups shredded Monterey Jack cheese
  Chopped fresh parsley (garnish)

Set eggplant on microwave-safe rack and pierce well with fork. Cook on High 7 minutes. Set aside to cool.

Combine oil, garlic and onion in 3- to 4-quart casserole. Cover and cook on High 5 minutes. Stir in zucchini, green pepper and celery. Peel eggplant and cut into 1½-inch cubes. Add to vegetables, mixing well. Cover and cook 5 minutes. Combine all remaining ingredients except cheese and parsley and blend well. Spoon half over vegetables and sprinkle with half of cheese. Cover with remaining tomato mixture and cheese. Cook on High until mixture is hot and bubbly, about 2 minutes. Sprinkle with chopped parsley just before serving.

BEVERAGES

The Punch Bowl

■ Classic wine and food combinations carry over into the punch bowl—and with sufficient leeway for improvisation. Champagne and strawberries are compatible and cheerful, as are red wine and spices, brandy and pears. Pink champagne, cold duck and ever-reliable vin rosé make eye-catching additions. Most champagnes, even those labeled dry, are slightly sweet and the inexpensive wines may contain sugar as well. That's why some recipes instruct that punches be "sweetened to taste." For extra aromatics, add an ounce or two of liqueur.

Special tips

■ Adding fresh lemon—its juice, zest, or both— is wonderfully effective in making a drink really refreshing and appealing. In drinks, as in cooking, the zesty flavor of the lemon blends beautifully with other ingredients and, in fact, magically brings out and enhances the best in their intrinsic flavors.

■ Guests tend to congregate around the bowl. Help the conversation along by floating something attractive in it. You can make your own block of ice, using any handy mold, even an empty half-gallon milk carton. Add chunks or slices of fruit and water, and freeze. Float oranges sliced into cartwheels; use sliced lemons or limes or both. Orange segments and slices of pear can be frozen and dropped into glasses to serve as additional "ice."

COLD

SIBERIAN SOUSE

Savor this delectable mélange slowly for its sensuous combination of lemon juice, liqueurs and essence of fresh apricot. The spiked apricot serves as an added bonus.

FOR EACH SERVING

- 1 whole fresh apricot, blanched and peeled, or 1 whole canned apricot, well drained
- 1 ounce (2 tablespoons) fresh lemon juice
- 1 ounce (2 tablespoons) vodka liqueur
- 1 ounce (2 tablespoons) apricot brandy
- Crushed ice
- Sparkling mineral water or club soda

Pierce apricot on all sides with fork. Place in bottom of large chilled wine glass (preferably with 20-ounce capacity). Pour lemon juice, liqueur and brandy over apricot and stir gently. Fill glass slightly more than halfway with crushed ice. Add a splash or two of water and serve with small straw.

BANANA-COFFEE SHAKE

2 SERVINGS

- 1 pint French vanilla ice cream, softened
- 1 cup cold double-strength coffee
- 1 small banana
- Sugar to taste (optional)
- Shaved chocolate (garnish)

Mix first 3 ingredients until smooth in blender or processor. Add sugar if desired. Pour into wine glasses or goblets. Garnish each serving with shaved chocolate.

BANANA DAIQUIRI

ABOUT 6 SERVINGS

- 2 cups ½-inch ice cubes (or use crushed or shaved)
- 6 ounces (¾ cup) light rum
- 4 ounces (½ cup) sweet and sour mix
- 4 ounces (½ cup) half and half
- 2 ounces (¼ cup) Triple Sec or curaçao
- 2 very ripe medium or large bananas

Orange slices (optional garnish)

Put ice into blender. Add remaining ingredients except orange slices and blend on high or frappé speed about 1½ minutes. Serve in stemmed glasses, garnished if desired.

SOUTH SEAS BANANA PUNCH

MAKES ABOUT 2 GALLONS

- 7 cups water
- 5 cups sugar
- 5 ripe bananas, pureed
- 2½ cups orange juice
- 1½ cups fresh lemon juice
- 6 to 8 32-ounce bottles ginger ale, well chilled
- Sliced bananas (garnish)

Combine first 5 ingredients in large bowl and blend thoroughly. Pour into shallow pans and freeze (mixture will still be slushy). Fill glasses ⅓ full. Top with ginger ale and stir. Garnish with banana.

TIPSY CRANBERRY COCKTAIL

25 SERVINGS

- 2 48-ounce jars cranberry juice cocktail, chilled

■ Make your own personal recipe changes only with the greatest of care, remembering that the tastiest blends are a medley of flavors.

■ Measure all ingredients carefully. Don't imitate free-pouring bartenders who trust a flick of the wrist. The subtle blend of flavors that makes a mixed drink memorable results from a precise combination of ingredients. Many cocktail recipes look deceptively simple, but to throw the ingredients together casually can be disastrous. Use standard measures, whether teaspoons, jiggers, ounces, cups or liters. When you multiply quantities for party drinking, be mathematically accurate.

■ You don't have to use premium wines or liquors—in fact, you'll be wasting money if you do, because blending overpowers the subtleties that give premium brands their characteristic qualities. But you should like the basic taste of these ingredients because that will remain in the finished blend.

■ If you have trouble igniting brandy, here's a trick: after heating the brandy, take a tablespoon of it and place a sugar cube in the spoon. When the cube has soaked up some liquid, light it, then empty the rest of the tablespoon into the vessel containing the remaining brandy. The sugar will act as a wick, keeping the flame alive.

■ Unless a recipe advises to the contrary, don't cut fruit until just before serving. Earlier cutting permits the flavor-carrying juices to flow away; oxidation extracts a toll on taste.

■ Serve the drink in a suitable glass or cup and be sure that it's sparkling clean. Eye appeal being part of the pleasure of drinking, the wrong serving vessel can destroy the effect you seek. (Imagine serving eggnog in a mug that conceals the liquid's froth or an aromatic wine punch in an eyedropper-size glass that leaves no room for the aroma to develop.) A cold serving vessel will chill hot drinks prematurely, and one containing residues of detergent may affect taste.

■ Heat ingredients very carefully. Slow heating gives the flavors time to marry, but boiling drives flavor away and leaves an unpleasant "burned" flavor. Boiling also causes the alcohol to evaporate; the result is a punchless punch. Unless a recipe advises to the contrary, heat only until you see wisps of steam arise.

2 6-ounce cans frozen lemonade concentrate, thawed
2 cups gin
Grated peel of 2 large lemons
1 lemon, thinly sliced

Blend all ingredients in punch bowl.

LEMON FROTH

FOR EACH SERVING

2 ounces (¼ cup) fresh lemon juice
1 ounce (2 tablespoons) vodka or gin
1 egg white
1 teaspoon sugar (optional)
Ice cubes
Thin curl of lemon zest (garnish)

Combine all ingredients except zest in cocktail shaker or jar with tight-fitting lid and shake vigorously until well blended. Pour into chilled martini glass and garnish froth with lemon curl.

THE LEMON ICECAP

FOR EACH SERVING

1 ounce (2 tablespoons) fresh lemon juice

1 ounce (2 tablespoons) vodka liqueur
1 ounce (2 tablespoons) vodka
Ice cubes
Sparkling mineral water or club soda
Thin curl of lemon zest (garnish)

Combine first 3 ingredients with ice cubes in tall chilled glass and stir to blend. Fill with water or soda and mix well. Garnish with lemon curl.

PERFECT LEMONADE

This recipe makes a fairly tart beverage, so adjust the syrup and lemon juice if you prefer a sweeter version.

MAKES ABOUT 2½ QUARTS

1 cup superfine sugar
1 cup water
1⅓ cups fresh lemon juice
Finely grated zest of 4 lemons
2 quarts (8 cups) cold water
Ice cubes or crushed ice
Lemon slices and fresh mint leaves (garnish)

Combine sugar and 1 cup water in small saucepan over medium heat and bring to boil. Reduce heat and simmer 5 to 6 minutes, stirring occasionally. Remove from heat and cool completely.

Combine syrup, lemon juice and zest in large pitcher or jar with tight-fitting lid. Add cold water and stir vigorously. When ready to serve, fill tall glasses with ice and pour lemonade over. Garnish with lemon slices and mint.

WHISKEY SOUR

6 SERVINGS

1 6-ounce can frozen lemonade concentrate, thawed
1 lemonade can filled with beer
6 to 8 ounces (¾ to 1 cup) whiskey
3 large ice cubes
Crushed ice
Maraschino cherries and orange slices (garnish)

Combine first 4 ingredients in blender or processor and mix thoroughly. Pour over crushed ice in individual cocktail glasses. Garnish with a cherry and orange slice.

LIME COOLER

ABOUT 6 SERVINGS

- 2 cups cracked ice
- 1 6-ounce can frozen limeade concentrate, partially thawed
- ¼ cup lemon juice
- 1¼ cups vodka
- 1 10-ounce bottle club soda, chilled
  Fresh strawberries, pineapple cubes and mint sprigs (garnish)

Combine ice, limeade concentrate and lemon juice in blender and mix at medium speed 1 minute. Add vodka and blend well. Pour in soda and mix briefly on low speed. Serve in stemmed cocktail or wine glasses and garnish with strawberries, pineapple and mint.

ORANGE APPEAL

ABOUT 6 SERVINGS

- 2 cups finely cracked ice
- 8 ounces (1 cup) orange juice
- 6 ounces (¾ cup) light rum
- 2 ounces (¼ cup) lemon juice
- 2 ounces (¼ cup) brandy
- 2 ounces (¼ cup) orgeat syrup
  Ice cubes

Put ice into blender. Add remaining ingredients and blend on high or frappé speed until well mixed. Pour into tall glasses partially filled with ice and serve immediately.

WASHINGTON INDISCRETION

FOR EACH SERVING

- 6 parts fresh orange juice
- 5 parts tequila
- 1 part coffee liqueur
  Crushed ice
  Orange slice and fresh mint sprig (garnish)

Combine orange juice, tequila and liqueur in tall glass filled with crushed ice and stir well. Garnish with orange slice and sprig of mint.

SPECIAL RUM PUNCH

Roy Haughton, one of Jamaica's most popular barmen, serves his own rum punch at Moxon's in Ocho Rios, Jamaica.

6 TO 8 SERVINGS

- 3 ounces (6 tablespoons) orange juice
- 2½ ounces (5 tablespoons) lime or lemon juice
- 2 ounces (¼ cup) pineapple juice
- 2 ounces (¼ cup) dark rum
- 2 ounces (¼ cup) 151-proof rum
- 2 ounces (¼ cup) light rum
- 2 ounces (¼ cup) grenadine
  Dash of angostura bitters
  Dash of ground ginger
  Dash of nutmeg (optional)

Blend all ingredients. Pour into tall glasses partially filled with crushed ice and serve immediately.

PEAR COCONUT COOLER

The rum may be left out entirely for a refreshing nonalcoholic drink.

ABOUT 6 SERVINGS

- 3 cups pear nectar
- 1 15-ounce can coconut cream
- 1 cup light rum
- 1 cup club soda
- ½ cup lime juice

Combine all ingredients in large pitcher with ice; stir until chilled.

STRAWBERRY DAIQUIRI

ABOUT 6 SERVINGS

- 2 cups ½-inch ice cubes (or use crushed or shaved)
- 8 ounces (1 cup) light rum
- 5 ounces (½ cup plus 2 tablespoons) sweet and sour mix
- 1 10-ounce package frozen strawberries in syrup, unthawed

Put ice into blender. Add remaining ingredients and blend on high or frappé speed about 1½ to 2 minutes. Serve in stemmed wine or cocktail glasses.

POUR AND SERVE ROSE PUNCH

A "quick as a wink" punch you can make just as guests arrive.

25 SERVINGS

- 1 fifth rosé
- 1 23-ounce bottle sparkling mineral water
- 1 cup fresh lemon juice
- 1 cup orange liqueur
  Block of ice
- 2 fifths dry champagne
  Frozen orange slices (garnish)

Combine first 4 ingredients and pour over block of ice in punch bowl. Add champagne as guests arrive. Serve in champagne glasses, floating orange slice in each.

RANGOON RACQUET CLUB PUNCH

ABOUT 6 SERVINGS

- ¼ cup pineapple juice
- ¼ cup lemon juice
- ¼ cup orange juice
- ½ cup sugar
- 1½ ounces (3 tablespoons) dark rum
- 1½ ounces (3 tablespoons) curaçao
- 1½ cups dry red wine
- 1 half-bottle (375 ml) brut champagne, well chilled
- 1 cup club soda, well chilled
  Crushed ice

Combine pineapple juice, lemon juice, orange juice and sugar and stir until sugar is dissolved. Stir in rum, curaçao and red wine. Chill thoroughly. Just before serving pour over ice in pitcher. Add champagne and soda and stir gently to blend. Pour into tall glasses partially filled with crushed ice.

BATH HOUSE GOLDEN FIZZ

6 SERVINGS

- 1 cup ½-inch ice cubes (or use crushed or shaved)
- 1½ cups sweet and sour mix

5 eggs
5 ounces (½ cup plus 2 tablespoons) curaçao
3 ounces (6 tablespoons) Galliano
¾ cup gin
¾ cup half and half
1½ ounces (3 tablespoons) sugar syrup
½ ounce (1 tablespoon) orange flower water
Nutmeg (garnish)

Blend all ingredients except nutmeg in large blender about 20 seconds. Strain into stemmed 11-ounce glasses and lightly dust with nutmeg for garnish.

HOT

CAFE A LA RUSSE

4 SERVINGS

¾ cup boiling water
1 ounce semisweet chocolate
1½ tablespoons sugar
1¾ cups hot coffee
½ cup whipping cream, scalded
½ cup milk, scalded
2 ounces (¼ cup) Cognac
2 ounces (¼ cup) crème de cacao
Cinnamon
Nutmeg

Combine water, chocolate and sugar in top of double boiler. Place over hot, not boiling, water and simmer, stirring, until chocolate is melted and sugar dissolved, about 2 or 3 minutes. Stir in coffee, cream, milk, Cognac and crème de cacao. Pour into 4 large preheated mugs and sprinkle with cinnamon and nutmeg to taste.

CAFE BRULOT DIABOLIQUE

8 SERVINGS

1 cinnamon stick
8 whole cloves

Zest of 1 lemon, cut into thin strips
3 sugar cubes
3 jiggers (½ cup plus 1 tablespoon) brandy
3 cups strong black coffee

Combine spices, zest and sugar in hot chafing dish. Pour brandy into ladle and warm briefly. Ignite and pour into dish, ladling mixture until sugar dissolves. Add coffee and serve in demitasses.

CAFE CAFE

On the theory that if you're a coffee lover, you can't have too much of a good thing.

FOR EACH SERVING

6 ounces hot strong coffee
1 ounce (2 tablespoons) cream
2 teaspoons sugar
2 ounces (¼ cup) coffee-flavored liqueur
Sweetened whipped cream flavored with instant coffee

Combine coffee, cream, sugar and liqueur together in a heated cup. Top with a glob of whipped cream.

CAFE IBERICO

4 SERVINGS

24 ounces hot coffee
3 tablespoons fresh lemon juice
2 jiggers (¼ cup plus 2 tablespoons) anisette
4 thin lemon slices

Combine coffee and lemon juice in hot chafing dish. Heat anisette gently in separate small pan or pot, ignite and immediately pour into chafing dish, stirring constantly until flame dies. Serve immediately in heated cups with lemon slice floating on top.

CAFE LOUVOIS

This drink is Belgian in origin, and is almost as good without adding the Cognac.

FOR EACH SERVING

2 jiggers (¼ cup plus 2 tablespoons) hot black coffee

2 jiggers (¼ cup plus 2 tablespoons) hot chocolate
1 ounce (2 tablespoons) Cognac
Whipped cream, sweetened slightly

Mix coffee and chocolate in 8-ounce mug. Stir in Cognac and top with whipped cream.

CAFE MUCK

This one is from Holland. Well, they had to name it something.

FOR EACH SERVING

Espresso
1 small piece semisweet chocolate
Dash of cherry liqueur
Whipped cream

Fill a demitasse almost to the top with espresso. Drop in the piece of chocolate and stir until melted. Add liqueur and top with dollop of whipped cream.

CAFE ORANGE

FOR EACH SERVING

1 teaspoon grated fresh lemon zest
Coffee
1 jigger (3 tablespoons) orange liqueur

Place grated lemon zest in coffee cup, add coffee until it is about two-thirds full and stir in liqueur.

CAFE ROYALE

FOR EACH SERVING

Coffee
1 sugar cube
Brandy

Fill a demitasse half full with coffee. Add sugar and stir until dissolved. Slowly fill cup with brandy, pouring over back of spoon so brandy will float on top. Ignite brandy, and when you get bored watching the fire, quench it with spooned coffee.

CAPPUCCINO

18 SERVINGS

- 1 quart (4 cups) half and half
- 2 cups extra strong coffee or espresso
- ¼ cup honey
- 1 tablespoon unsweetened cocoa
- 1 tablespoon vanilla
- 6 ounces (¾ cup) Cognac or brandy
- 5 ounces (½ cup plus 2 tablespoons) coffee liqueur
- 4 ounces (½ cup) rum
- ½ ounce (1 tablespoon) Galliano
  Whipped cream and shaved chocolate (garnish)

Combine first 5 ingredients in large saucepan. Place over medium-high heat and stir until almost scalded. Remove from heat and add next 4 ingredients. Pour into heated cups or mugs and garnish with whipped cream and chocolate.

DUTCH TREAT

FOR EACH SERVING

- 5 ounces (½ cup plus 2 tablespoons) hot black coffee
- 1 teaspoon sugar
- 1 ounce (2 tablespoons) brandy
- 1 ounce (2 tablespoons) chocolate mint liqueur
- 1 strip of lemon zest

Pour coffee into preheated 8-ounce mug and stir in sugar. Add brandy and liqueur, stir again, twist lemon zest over the top and drop it in.

GNOME OF ZURICH

The Swiss and Dutch can never agree on who makes the best cocoa. Here's the Swiss version.

2 SERVINGS

- 1 tablespoon unsweetened cocoa

- 1 tablespoon sugar
- 1 tablespoon water
  Dash of salt
- 1 cup hot milk
- 1 cup hot coffee
- 3 ounces (¼ cup plus 2 tablespoons) crème de noyaux or almond liqueur

Combine cocoa, sugar, water and salt in small saucepan and heat just to boiling. Stir in hot milk, coffee and liqueur. Serve in heated mugs.

MEDITERRANEAN COFFEE

12 SERVINGS

- 2 quarts freshly brewed strong coffee
- ⅓ cup sugar
- ¼ cup chocolate syrup
- 4 cinnamon sticks
- 1½ teaspoons whole cloves
- ½ teaspoon aniseed, tied in cheesecloth
  Orange and lemon peel and whipped cream (garnish)

Combine first 6 ingredients in saucepan. Bring to boiling point over medium-high heat. Reduce heat and let simmer until ready to serve. Strain into warmed coffee mugs and top with orange and lemon twists and whipped cream.

MOCHA COFFEE

6 SERVINGS

- 6 ounces coffee liqueur
- 2 ounces crème de cacao
- 24 ounces hot strong coffee
- ¼ cup whipping cream, whipped
- 1 teaspoon cocoa

Combine coffee liqueur with crème de cacao and divide among 6 mugs or heated wine glasses. Add coffee. Top with cream and sprinkle with dash of cocoa.

Amaretto, Grand Marnier or any other dessert liqueur may be substituted for the coffee liqueur and crème de cacao.

GLOGG

See photograph pages 28-29

Glögg originated in Sweden. While any color of table wine may be used, the most popular version of the drink is made with red wine.

8 SERVINGS

- ¾ cup raisins
- 1 tablespoon whole cardamom
- 2 teaspoons whole cloves
- 1 cinnamon stick
- 1½ cups water
- 1 fifth red, white or rosé table wine
- ½ cup sugar
- ¼ cup blanched almonds

Rinse and drain raisins; peel and crush cardamom. Combine ½ cup raisins, spices and water in medium saucepan and simmer 30 minutes. Strain. Combine with wine, add sugar and heat thoroughly, stirring until sugar is dissolved. Serve in preheated mugs with almonds and remaining raisins in each cup.

GLUHWEIN

Legend has it that early Bavarians devised this drink as an after-ski warmer-upper. They skied in those days not for recreation but for transportation—barrel staves were the most efficient way of navigating the snowy trails of their mountainous communities. Once home, they would pour wine into a crock and add some sweetening ingredients, then thrust a red-hot poker into the mixture. The poker, in addition to heating the wine, made it luminous. Thus, the name Glühwein, or literally "glowing wine."

Which wine to use? Most people today favor a full-bodied red, but in old Bavaria almost all the available wine was white. Most people probably will also prefer a dry wine, which will be sweetened adequately by the other ingredients. But if your taste runs to the sweeter side, by all means use a medium-dry or sweetish wine.

6 SERVINGS

- 1 fifth red, white or rosé wine
- ½ cup sugar
- ¼ teaspoon cinnamon
- ¼ teaspoon allspice
- ¼ teaspoon cloves
- ⅛ teaspoon nutmeg

Combine all ingredients in medium saucepan. Bring to serving temperature over medium heat, stirring until sugar dissolves. Serve in preheated mugs while still warm.

MULLED WINE

6 SERVINGS

- 6 tablespoons sugar
- ¼ cup water
- 10 whole cloves
- 6 orange slices
- 6 lemon slices
- 4 cinnamon sticks
- 6 cups dry red wine

Combine all ingredients except wine in 2-quart saucepan. Heat slowly, stirring occasionally, until sugar is dissolved. Stir in wine and continue heating until mixture is just below boiling point. Strain into 6 heated mugs.

OLYMPIC WINE TORCH

This recipe is supposed to date from American Revolutionary times.

20 SERVINGS

- 3 cups apple juice
  Zest of 1 lemon, cut into thin strips
- 20 whole cloves
- 4 cinnamon sticks
  Juice of 1 lemon
- ½ gallon dry red table wine
- ½ gallon port
- ½ cup brandy

Combine apple juice, lemon zest, cloves and cinnamon sticks in 6- to 8-quart kettle or Dutch oven and simmer 15 minutes. Strain. Add lemon juice and wines and bring to simmer. Heat brandy briefly, ignite and ladle slowly into hot wine. Serve in preheated mugs.

MULLED RASPBERRIES AND PORT

6 SERVINGS

- 1 10-ounce package frozen sweetened raspberries
- 1 fifth port

Simmer raspberries in medium saucepan until thawed and soft, about 5 minutes. Force through fine strainer to remove seeds. Return to saucepan, add wine and heat gently. Serve in preheated mugs or large, stemmed glasses.

THE NEGUS

Here's another member of the family of hot punches known generically as "mulled wine" or "mulls." The name Negus has been attributed to the seventeenth-century English colonel, Francis Negus, who reportedly brought this recipe back to the United Kingdom after a campaign on the Continent.

Actually there were two colonels named Negus, the second serving in the American Revolutionary Army under George Washington. The punch may have been named after either or both.

Which port wine to use? Certainly not your most prized vintage port. Just about any port, imported or local, will do. The sweeter, redder version known as ruby port probably will appeal to more quaffers than tawny port.

8 SERVINGS

- 1 fifth port
- 2 teaspoons sugar
  Juice and grated peel of 1 lemon
- 1 cup boiling water
  Nutmeg

Combine port with sugar, lemon juice and peel. Heat until steam begins to rise, then stir in boiling water. Strain into preheated mugs and top with dusting of nutmeg.

SKIERS BREW

MAKES 3½ QUARTS

- 2 quarts ruby port
- 1 quart cranberry juice cocktail
- 2 cups lemon juice
- 1 small lemon, studded with cloves
- 2 cinnamon sticks

Combine all ingredients in 4-quart container and let stand. Heat thoroughly before serving.

TOM AND JERRY

A bit of care is required to make this all-time classic properly, but anyone who has tasted a perfect one will warm to the task.

2 SERVINGS

- ¾ cup milk
- 2 tablespoons (¼ stick) butter
- 2 eggs, separated
- 2 teaspoons sugar
- ⅛ teaspoon vanilla
- 3 ounces brandy
- 3 ounces dark or light rum
  Nutmeg

Combine milk and butter in medium saucepan and place over low heat until butter is melted. Meanwhile, in separate bowls beat yolks until slightly thickened and beat whites until frothy. Fold whites into yolks and stir in sugar and vanilla.

Remove milk from heat and slowly add egg mixture, whisking constantly. Return pan to heat and add brandy and rum. Continue whisking until mixture is thoroughly blended and warmed, then pour into preheated mugs or large, stemmed glasses and sprinkle top generously with nutmeg.

SPICED CIDER WITH CALVADOS

See photograph page 159

6 SERVINGS

    2 cinnamon sticks, broken
    1 tablespoon whole allspice
    1 quart (4 cups) apple cider
    6 ounces (¾ cup) Calvados
    6 cinnamon sticks

Tie broken cinnamon sticks and allspice in cheesecloth bag. Place in 1½- to 2-quart saucepan and add cider. Heat slowly until steaming but do not boil. Pour 1 ounce of Calvados into each heated mug. Add cider and stir gently with cinnamon stick. Serve immediately.

HOT BUTTERED RUM

This cold weather friend dates to Colonial times and reportedly was a favorite of Thomas Jefferson. The classic recipe calls for dark rum, but if you prefer light rum use it.

FOR EACH SERVING

    1 cup milk or water
    1½ teaspoons sugar
    1 cinnamon stick
    3 ounces rum
    1 tablespoon butter
       Nutmeg

Heat milk or water in small pan over low heat; do not let milk boil. Combine sugar, cinnamon stick and rum in preheated mug and stir until sugar is dissolved. Add milk or water, top with butter and dash of nutmeg. Serve immediately.

BULLSHOT

This one-time favorite of New York's Madison Avenue is normally served cold but also may be presented hot. Its preparation is simplicity itself.

FOR EACH SERVING

    ½ cup beef bouillon
    1½ ounces vodka
       Dash of salt
       Dash of freshly ground
       pepper

Heat bouillon. Pour into preheated mug or stemmed glass, add vodka

and salt and pepper to taste and stir well. Serve immediately.

DO AHEAD

COLD

"AQUAVIT"

12 TO 18 SERVINGS

    2 ounces caraway seeds
    1 fifth vodka

Add seeds to vodka. Place in freezer two days. Strain before serving.

BRANDY SMASH

MAKES ABOUT 3½ QUARTS

    9 cups water
    2 cups brandy
    1 12-ounce can frozen
       lemonade, thawed
    1 12-ounce can frozen orange
       juice, thawed
       Fresh mint sprigs (garnish)

Combine first 4 ingredients in 4-quart container. Cover and freeze overnight (mixture will remain slushy). Spoon into individual glasses and garnish with mint.

FISH HOUSE PUNCH

See photograph pages 30-31

This brew was invented by members of the Fish House Club founded in Philadelphia in 1732. The 30 original members made succeeding generations keep the recipe a guarded secret for almost 200 years!

20 TO 25 SERVINGS

    2 quarts (8 cups) water
    2 fifths dark rum
    1 fifth Cognac or brandy
    3 cups fresh lemon juice
    1 cup superfine sugar
    ½ cup peach brandy

Combine all ingredients in large bowl. Let stand several hours or overnight to "brew." Pour over ice in individual glasses.

STRAWBERRY COOLERS

6 TO 8 SERVINGS

    1 cup fresh strawberries or 1
       10-ounce package frozen
       strawberries, partially thawed
    3 cups water
    2 6-ounce cans frozen pink
       lemonade concentrate,
       thawed
    1 6-ounce can frozen limeade
       concentrate, thawed
    1 to 1½ cups light rum
    6 to 8 fresh pineapple chunks
       (garnish)
       Coconut snow

Puree strawberries in blender or processor until almost smooth. Mix with remaining liquids in plastic container. Cover and freeze overnight. Defrost to desired degree of slushiness and pour (or scoop) into serving glasses. Skewer pineapple on fancy picks and roll in coconut snow for garnish. Serve with straws.

Opposite
Chinese Hot and Sour Soup is brightened with ham, mushrooms, sliced bean curd and thin slivers of green onion.

Page 26
Shellfish Gazpacho requires no cooking. Create your own variations with condiments. Spiedini accompanies the soup, and chewy Raisin-Granola Cookies are for a tasty and nourishing dessert.

Page 27
Borscht is a hearty warm-up for frosty winter evenings.

Page 28
Glogg is an easy-to-blend medley of wine, almonds, raisins and spices.

Page 30–31
Fish House Punch is a potent mixture of rum, Cognac and peach brandy.

Page 32
Scallop Kebabs with bacon and water chestnuts, Vietnamese Pork Sticks with Lettuce Cups and Cucumber Stick Salad provide a crunchy menu combination.

Chinese Hot and Sour Soup
Recipe page 39

Shellfish Gazpacho
Recipe page 46
Spiedini
Recipe page 166
Raisin-Granola Cookies
Recipe page 173

Borscht
Recipe page 47

Glogg
Recipe page 22

Fish House Punch
Recipe page 24

32

Scallop Kebabs
Recipe page 13
Vietnamese Pork Sticks:
Recipe page 14
Cucumber Stick Salad
Recipe page 57

LEMON SANGRIA

MAKES ABOUT 1½ QUARTS

- 3½ cups dry white wine, chilled
- 3 unpeeled lemons, sliced
- 1 unpeeled orange, sliced (optional)
- 1 green apple, peeled, cored and cut into wedges
  Small bunches green grapes
- ½ cup Cognac
- ¼ cup sugar
- 1 10-ounce bottle club soda, chilled
  Ice cubes

Combine all ingredients except soda and ice cubes in large pitcher and chill overnight. Just before serving, add soda and ice cubes and stir lightly. Pour into glasses, adding additional fruit as desired.

HOT

HOT SANGRIA

A marvelous warming punch that somehow seems to retain all the freshness of the cold version.

16 SERVINGS

- 2 grapefruit, unpeeled
- ½ gallon dry white or red wine
- 6 cups apple juice
- 1½ cups frozen orange juice concentrate, thawed
- ¾ cup fresh lemon juice
- 1 lemon, thinly sliced
- 1 orange, thinly sliced
- 4 teaspoons brown sugar

Cut each grapefruit into 8 wedges. Combine with wine and juices in large saucepan, cover and let stand in cool room overnight. (Shorter standing time will produce a palatable drink but one lacking some of the tartness the liquid absorbs from the grapefruit skins.) Add lemon and orange slices and let stand 1 hour.

Preheat oven to 400°F. Remove grapefruit wedges, orange and lemon wheels; set aside. Heat liquid over low heat until steam rises. While liquid is heating, peel grapefruit wedges, press with brown sugar and bake until sugar forms hard coating, about 5 minutes. Place each wedge in preheated mug or large stemmed glass, ladle in hot liquid and add orange and lemon slices. Serve immediately.

SPICED APPLE BOWL

12 SERVINGS

- ¼ cup sugar
- ¼ teaspoon cinnamon
- 12 small apples
- 3 tablespoons light corn syrup
- 3 cups dry white wine
- 1½ cups apple cider
- ¼ teaspoon nutmeg
- 1 twist lemon peel

Preheat oven to 400°F. Combine sugar and cinnamon. Coat apples by rolling first in corn syrup, then in cinnamon/sugar mixture. Place in baking dish and bake 15 minutes.

Meanwhile, combine remaining ingredients in medium saucepan and heat slowly until apples finish baking. Place each apple in preheated mug. Serve punch from preheated bowl, ladling over apples in mugs. Or, if you prefer, keep things simpler by filling preheated mugs at the stove before serving.

MICROWAVE

HOT BUTTERED RUM

FOR EACH SERVING

- 2 ounces (¼ cup) dark rum
- 1 teaspoon unpacked light brown sugar
- ⅔ cup apple cider, room temperature
  Slice of sweet butter
  Mace to taste

Combine rum and sugar in a hot toddy glass or mug; blend well. Pour in cider until glass is ⅔ full; blend well. Cook on High uncovered 2 minutes. Top with butter and sprinkle lightly with mace. Give each guest a spoon for stirring the butter and mace into the drink.

HOT CHOCOLATE

MAKES ABOUT 2 CUPS SYRUP

- 1 cup water
- 4 1-ounce squares unsweetened chocolate, broken up
- 1 cup sugar
- ¼ teaspoon salt
- ½ teaspoon vanilla
  Milk
  Marshmallows

Place water and chocolate in 4-cup glass measuring cup. Cook on High, stirring several times, until chocolate is totally melted (no graininess will show on spoon or spatula), about 4 minutes. Stir to blend, then mix in sugar and salt. Cook 30 seconds; stir again. Repeat. Add vanilla.

For each serving of hot chocolate place 2 or 3 tablespoons of syrup into a cup and fill with milk until ⅔ full. Stir. Cook on High, until thoroughly heated, 1 minute 45 seconds. Add marshmallow and cook until melted, about 15 seconds.

SPICED CIDER

4 TO 5 SERVINGS

- 1 quart apple cider*
- 2 whole allspice
- 2 whole cloves
- 1 to 2 cinnamon sticks
- 5 tablespoons brown sugar
- ½ orange, unpeeled, thinly sliced

In 1½- to 2-quart pitcher or other glass container, combine cider, allspice, cloves, cinnamon sticks and brown sugar; float orange slices on top. Cover with waxed paper and cook on High 8 to 10 minutes, stirring halfway through cooking time. Serve steaming hot.

If using temperature probe, heat to 190°F before serving.

*Tea may be substituted for cider.

Quick Soups

■ You don't have to work hard to make different, company-pleasing soup. Simply combine 2 cups clam-tomato drink with an equal amount of beef broth, 1 cup dry white wine and ½ cup sherry in a medium-size saucepan over medium heat. Bring to a boil, reduce the heat and add 1 finely chopped green onion and 1 small clove of garlic, halved. Let this boil one minute, then remove the garlic. Serve piping hot and garnish with fresh minced parsley.

■ Make a quick Chinesey soup: Add a rounded tablespoon of shredded crab per serving to hot chicken consommé. Pep up the soup with a bit of light soy sauce, a dash of dry sherry. Garnish with green onion.

Mock Minestrone

■ A hearty soup is wonderfully satisfying, especially in blustery weather. It doubles as a luncheon entrée or late-night company comforter. A quick one to do is a mock minestrone: Combine 1 quart of rich beef stock with 1 cup each chopped onion, celery, carrots, green beans and a handful of precooked split peas. Bring to a boil, reduce heat, cover and simmer for 1 hour. Season with salt, freshly ground pepper, a bit of thyme, ¼ cup brandy and ½ cup dry red wine. Simmer another 10 minutes. (Tastes even better on reheating.)

Cold Soups Can Be Made Ahead

■ Prepare soup in the cool evening the day before. And because they add a festive note to any meal, they combine well with simple main courses—grilled chicken or fish, quickly sautéed veal scallops or shrimp, broiled steak. With an elegant soup as a highlight, summer entertaining is more appealing to cooks as well as their families and guests.

■ For a perfect cold soup to start a summer brunch, combine 3 cups chopped cantaloupe and 3 cups chopped honeydew. Puree half of mixture and finely chop the other half. Blend 2 cups fresh orange juice and about 3 tablespoons honey into the pureed melon, then add 2 cups brut Champagne and the remaining finely chopped melon. Serve the soup well chilled. For added elegance, serve it in crystal or glass stemware.

SOUPS

COLD

CHILLED CREAM OF ASPARAGUS SOUP

4 TO 6 SERVINGS

- 1 10¾-ounce can cream of asparagus soup
- 1 cup sour cream or yogurt
- 1 cup milk
- 1 cup crushed ice
- ½ teaspoon salt
  Hot pepper sauce to taste
  Chopped chives (garnish)

Combine all ingredients except chives in food processor or blender and mix until smooth. Chill thoroughly. Sprinkle with chives just before serving.

CHILLED CUCUMBER-YOGURT SOUP

4 SERVINGS

- 1 large cucumber, chopped
- 1 small yellow onion, chopped
- 2 bouillon cubes (chicken or beef)
- 1½ cups plain yogurt
- 1 tablespoon snipped chives or minced green onion
- ½ teaspoon dill (garnish)

Combine cucumber and onion in medium saucepan; add water just to cover. Stir in bouillon cubes and simmer until vegetables are tender. Let cool, then cover and chill.

When ready to serve, blend in yogurt and chives or green onion. Transfer to serving bowl and sprinkle lightly with dill.

COLD YOGURT SOUP

8 SERVINGS

- 3 cups plain yogurt
- ½ cup half and half
- 1 chopped hard-cooked egg
- ½ cup water
- 1 cucumber, chopped
- ½ cup chopped green onions
- ¼ to ½ cup raisins (optional)
- 2 teaspoons salt or to taste
- ½ teaspoon white pepper or to taste
- 1 tablespoon chopped parsley (garnish)
- 1 tablespoon chopped dill (garnish)

Place yogurt in a large bowl. Add half and half, egg, water, cucumber, green onions, raisins, salt and pepper. Mix well and refrigerate.

Top with chopped parsley and dill.

For more flavor dissolve 1 teaspoon curry powder in a little water and add to soup.

LEFTOVER SALAD SOUP

4 SERVINGS

- 2 to 3 cups leftover dressed salad, tossed
- 1 cup (about) fresh or canned chicken broth, not dehydrated
  Salt and pepper
  Sour cream (garnish)
  Chopped chives or other fresh herbs (garnish)

SAUCES

■ A number of soups are robust and nutritious enough to become the mainstay of a warming meal. Add a crusty loaf of bread, a crisp salad, some perfectly ripe pears, cheese and a bottle of wine and your meal is complete. And you can fill a vacuum bottle or two with your favorites, add sandwiches, fruit and wine for an extra-special picnic. Or invite friends over for a cozy Sunday lunch.

■ A tablespoon or two of juice adds special zip to a wide range of soups—chicken, vegetable, black bean, sorrel vichyssoise, fruit—even hot or cold consommés.

Hints For Sauces

■ A simple sauce of melted butter, lemon juice and a dash of hot pepper sauce can be put together in seconds. Great over broiled fish, cauliflower and superb as a sauce for asparagus.

■ Store olive oil in a cool, dark spot, not in the refrigerator. Many experts claim that it will keep indefinitely but actually once opened, oil can go rancid in hot weather. Buy only in sizes you can use up within about two months. Unopened oil will keep no more than a year.

■ Since many sauces are based on a sauté of onion, there are several tricks here too. If onions are sautéed slowly, they become mild and sweet, complementing tomato sauces perfectly. A quick sauté over high heat produces a more robust onion flavor, ideal for many meat and vegetable dishes.

Place leftover greens in blender or food processor with ½ cup stock. Blend briefly, then add enough remaining broth to achieve desired consistency. Add salt and pepper to taste. Chill thoroughly. Top with sour cream and chives or other fresh herbs.

CURRIED CREAM OF PEA SOUP

6 SERVINGS

- 1 cup shelled fresh or frozen peas
- 1 medium onion, sliced
- 1 carrot, sliced
- 1 celery stalk (with leaves), sliced
- 1 medium potato, peeled and sliced
- 1 garlic clove
- 1 teaspoon curry powder or to taste
  Salt and freshly ground pepper
- 2 cups chicken stock
- 1 cup half and half

Combine vegetables and seasonings with 1 cup stock in saucepan. Bring

---

to boil; reduce heat, cover and simmer 15 minutes. Puree in batches in processor or blender. Pour into bowl and whisk in remaining stock and half and half. Serve chilled or at room temperature.

PEA AND YELLOW SQUASH SOUP

Good before grilled fish or meat.

6 SERVINGS

- 5 cups chicken stock
- 5 large crookneck squash, coarsely chopped (about 3 cups)
- 1 cup shelled fresh or frozen peas
- 1 garlic clove
- ½ teaspoon dried chervil
  Salt and freshly ground white pepper
- 1 cup sour cream or plain yogurt

Combine first 5 ingredients with salt and pepper in large saucepan. Bring to boil; reduce heat, cover and simmer until vegetables are very soft, about 30 minutes. Puree in batches in processor or blender. Transfer to bowl and let cool to room tempera-

---

ture. Stir in sour cream or yogurt, blending thoroughly. Cover and chill well before serving.

GAZPACHO

4 SERVINGS

- 1 16-ounce can whole tomatoes, undrained
- 1 cucumber, peeled and cut into chunks
- 1 small onion, quartered
- 1 small garlic clove, halved
- 1 whole pimiento
- ½ green pepper, cut into chunks
- ¼ cup fresh lemon juice
  Salt and freshly ground pepper
  Sour cream (garnish)
  Black caviar (optional garnish)

Combine first 7 ingredients with salt and pepper to taste in blender or processor and mix until thick. Cover tightly and chill thoroughly to blend flavors. Serve in chilled bowls, garnishing each with dollop of sour cream topped with caviar.

TOMATO-YOGURT SOUP
6 SERVINGS

2½ pounds ripe tomatoes, peeled, seeded and chopped
2 cups plain yogurt
1 garlic clove, pressed
¼ teaspoon celery salt
¼ teaspoon curry powder or to taste
   Juice of 1 lemon
   Salt and freshly ground pepper
   Plain yogurt and minced fresh parsley (garnish)

Puree tomatoes in processor or blender. Add remaining ingredients except garnish and mix until smooth. Taste and adjust seasoning. Pour into bowl, cover and chill well. Garnish each serving with yogurt and minced parsley.

HOT

ARTICHOKE SOUP ANNETTE
6 TO 8 SERVINGS

¼ cup (½ stick) butter or margarine
1 medium onion, chopped
2 pounds fresh Jerusalem artichokes (sunchokes), cooked, peeled and coarsely chopped
5 cups chicken stock or 4 10¾-ounce cans chicken broth
   Salt and freshly ground white pepper
½ cup whipping cream
   Chopped fresh parsley (garnish)

Melt butter in medium skillet over medium heat. Add onion and sauté until translucent, about 10 minutes. Puree onion and artichokes in batches with some of stock in blender or processor. Pour into 3-quart saucepan. Blend in remaining stock. Simmer until heated through, about 15 minutes. Season with salt and white pepper. Ladle into bowls. Stir about 1 tablespoon

cream into center of each serving, combining just enough to show swirl of cream. Garnish with parsley.

This soup can also be served cold.

ASPARAGUS SOUP
4 TO 6 SERVINGS

1 to 2 tablespoons butter
4 to 5 escarole leaves, shredded
1 pound thin raw asparagus, trimmed and cut diagonally into ¼-inch pieces
6 cups canned chicken stock, boiling
   Salt and freshly ground pepper
2 whole green onions, minced
   Freshly grated Parmesan cheese

Heat butter in skillet over medium-high heat. Add escarole and asparagus and sauté 2 minutes. Add to stock, increase heat to high and boil just until asparagus is crisp-tender. Season to taste with salt and pepper. Sprinkle each serving with green onion and pass freshly grated Parmesan cheese.

For a richer soup, combine 3 egg yolks with ½ cup whipping cream. After soup has cooked, remove from heat and slowly beat 1 cup broth into yolk mixture. Return to saucepan and stir constantly over low heat several minutes until slightly thickened. Do not let soup boil or yolks will curdle. Pour into heated bowls and serve immediately.

CREAM OF BROCCOLI SOUP
6 SERVINGS

2 tablespoons (¼ stick) butter
1 medium onion, chopped
3 tablespoons flour
½ teaspoon salt
½ teaspoon freshly ground pepper
1 14½-ounce can chicken broth
1 10-ounce package frozen chopped broccoli, thawed and well drained

2 cups milk
   Grated Parmesan cheese (garnish)

Melt butter in large saucepan over medium heat. Add onion and sauté until light golden, about 10 minutes. Blend in flour, salt and pepper and stir constantly about 2 minutes. Gradually add broth, then broccoli and bring to boil, stirring frequently. Cover and simmer until broccoli is tender. Puree in batches in blender or processor. Return to saucepan, add milk and bring to simmer, stirring occasionally. Ladle into bowls and sprinkle with Parmesan. Run under preheated broiler until cheese is browned. Serve immediately.

CORN CHOWDER
4 SERVINGS

1 medium potato, peeled and diced
1 onion, chopped
1 cup water
1 16-ounce can cream-style corn
2 cups milk
2 tablespoons (¼ stick) butter
   Salt and freshly ground pepper
1 egg, lightly beaten
   Chopped fresh chives (garnish)

Combine first 3 ingredients in medium saucepan over medium-low heat and simmer until potatoes are tender, about 10 to 15 minutes. Add corn, milk and butter and blend well. Season with salt and pepper. Bring to boil. Remove from heat. Stir some of chowder into egg. Add mixture to saucepan and blend well. Simmer until heated through, about 1 minute. Ladle into bowls, garnish with chives and serve.

SOPA DE MAIZ (MEXICAN CORN SOUP)
6 SERVINGS

3½ cups fresh or thawed frozen corn
1 cup chicken stock
¼ cup (½ stick) butter

2 cups milk
1 garlic clove, pressed
1 teaspoon dried oregano
  Salt and freshly ground pepper
2 to 3 tablespoons rinsed, seeded and finely chopped green chilies
1 cup peeled, diced tomatoes
1 cup cubed Monterey Jack cheese
  Chopped fresh parsley or cilantro (garnish)

Combine corn and stock in blender or processor and mix to fine puree. Melt butter in large saucepan over medium heat. Add corn and simmer 5 minutes, stirring frequently. Blend in milk, garlic, oregano, salt and pepper and bring to boil. Reduce heat, add chilies and simmer another 5 minutes.

Divide tomato among serving bowls. Remove soup from heat and stir in cheese until completely melted. Pour over tomatoes and garnish with parsley or cilantro. Serve immediately.

EGGPLANT SOUP AU GRATIN

8 SERVINGS

2 tablespoons olive oil
1 Spanish onion, sliced
2 garlic cloves, minced
2 medium or large eggplants, peeled and cubed
1 teaspoon oregano
½ teaspoon thyme
4 cups chicken broth
½ cup sherry
  Salt and freshly ground pepper
2 tomatoes, sliced
1½ cups grated Swiss cheese
  Freshly grated Parmesan cheese

Heat oil in large kettle or Dutch oven over medium-high heat. Add onion and garlic and sauté until onion is transparent. Add eggplant, oregano and thyme and sauté 2 minutes. Blend in broth, reduce heat, cover and simmer 20 minutes. Add sherry

and continue simmering 3 minutes more. Add salt and pepper to taste. At this point, soup may be refrigerated.

Preheat broiler. Pour soup into oven-proof bowls. Top soup with tomato slices and cheeses. Brown under broiler until cheese is melted and lightly browned, about 2 minutes. Serve immediately.

LETTUCE SOUP

6 SERVINGS

2 tablespoons minced onion
1 tablespoon butter
1 tablespoon flour
½ teaspoon salt
¼ teaspoon nutmeg
  Dash of pepper
4 chicken bouillon cubes
3½ cups boiling water
1 medium head iceberg lettuce, shredded
1 slightly beaten egg yolk
½ cup heavy cream

Sauté onion in butter until lightly golden. Stir in flour, salt, nutmeg and pepper. Dissolve bouillon cubes in boiling water; add to onion mixture slowly. Cook over medium heat. Stir till thickened. Add lettuce. Cover and let cook 3 minutes.

Mix together egg yolk and cream. Stir ¼ cup soup into yolk-cream mixture. Pour mixture into soup, stirring constantly. Cook over low heat, stirring, until soup comes to a boil. Remove from heat. Serve at once.

CHRYSANTHEMUM SOUP

4 TO 6 SERVINGS

2 large dried Japanese mushrooms
3 cups homemade chicken broth or 2 13½-ounce cans chicken broth, warmed
¼ cup sherry
1 teaspoon light soy sauce or to taste
  Petals of 1 large chrysanthemum, well washed and drained (garnish)

Soak mushrooms in warm broth several hours. Strain, reserving broth. Cut mushrooms into small strips, discarding hard stems. Combine reserved broth with mushrooms and all remaining ingredients except chrysanthemum petals in medium saucepan and simmer about 10 minutes. Stir in chrysanthemum petals, ladle into individual bowls and serve immediately.

ONION SOUP GRATINEE

This hearty soup can be prepared in advance and served for supper with a tossed green salad and crusty French bread.

FOR EACH SERVING

2 tablespoons (¼ stick) butter
1 cup frozen diced onion, thawed and patted dry
1 teaspoon flour
  Freshly ground pepper
2 cups chicken broth
½ ounce (1 tablespoon) red wine or Cognac (optional)
  Butter
1 slice French bread, cut 1 inch thick
  Garlic salt
  Grated Gruyère or Swiss cheese
  Grated Parmesan cheese

Melt butter in heavy saucepan over medium-high heat. Add onion and sauté until golden. Stir in flour. Add pepper to taste. Reduce heat, add chicken broth and wine and simmer 30 minutes. Soup may be refrigerated at this point until serving time.

To make crouton, generously butter bread and sprinkle lightly with garlic salt. Place under broiler and toast until crisp and golden. Let cool.

At serving time bring soup to boiling point. Transfer to heatproof serving crock. Cover with grated Gruyère or Swiss, top with crouton and sprinkle with Parmesan. Run under broiler until cheese is bubbly and slightly crusty. Serve immediately.

FROTHY VEGETABLE SOUP

6 SERVINGS

- 1 14-ounce can chicken broth
- 1 sliced zucchini
- 2 sliced carrots
- 1 sliced celery stick
  Dash of nutmeg
  Salt and pepper

Combine all ingredients in medium saucepan. Bring to boil and simmer until vegetables are tender, about 15 to 20 minutes. Place in blender or food processor and blend about 30 seconds. Serve in mugs.

Other combinations of vegetables may be used for variety. Beef bouillon may be substituted for chicken broth and is especially good with cabbage or beets.

GREENS SOUP

Reprinted with permission from Irena Chalmers Cookbooks, Inc., AMERICAN WINE/CALIFORNIA FOOD by Barbara Kafka, © 1981.

6 SERVINGS

- 1 tablespoon unsalted butter
- 1 cup (about ¼ pound) shredded tender young mustard greens or kale
- 2 cups hot chicken stock
- 1 cup shredded fresh sorrel leaves or ¼ cup canned
- 4 egg yolks
- ½ cup whipping cream
- 1 cup zucchini cut into fine julienne
- ¼ cup shredded fresh basil leaves
- 3 tablespoons Pesto*
- ½ teaspoon coarse salt
  Freshly ground pepper

Melt butter in medium saucepan over medium heat. Stir in greens, tossing to coat, and cook about 1 minute. Add stock and bring to boil. Reduce heat and simmer until greens are tender, about 15 minutes longer. Blend in sorrel and simmer 5 more minutes.

Beat egg yolks with cream in small bowl. Stir in small amount of hot soup. Stir back into soup, mixing constantly. Add zucchini, basil, pesto, salt and pepper. Continue stirring over medium heat until slightly thickened and soup coats back of wooden spoon. Serve hot.

*Pesto

MAKES ABOUT ¾ CUP

- 2 cups packed fresh basil leaves
- 2 garlic cloves
- ¼ cup olive oil
- 3 tablespoons freshly grated Parmesan cheese
- 2 tablespoons pine nuts, toasted

Combine basil leaves and garlic in processor and mix until finely chopped. Gradually add olive oil through feed tube. Add Parmesan and nuts and process until smooth.

MULLIGATAWNY SOUP

6 SERVINGS

- ¼ cup (½ stick) butter
- 1 medium onion, sliced
- 1 medium carrot, diced
- 1 green pepper, diced
- 1 celery stalk, trimmed and diced
- 1 medium-size tart apple, peeled, cored and sliced
- 1 cup chopped cooked chicken
- ¼ cup all purpose flour
- 2 whole cloves
- 1 teaspoon curry powder or to taste
- 1 parsley sprig, minced
  Pinch of nutmeg
- 2 10½-ounce cans chicken broth
- 1 16-ounce can whole tomatoes, chopped (reserve liquid)
  Salt and freshly ground pepper

Melt butter in 3-quart saucepan over medium-high heat. Add onion and sauté until softened, about 2 to 3 minutes. Blend in carrot, green pepper, celery, apple and chicken and sauté until vegetables are tender, about 10 minutes. Stir in flour. Add cloves, curry powder, parsley and nutmeg. Blend in broth with tomatoes and reserved liquid. Season with salt and pepper. Reduce heat, cover and simmer until heated through, about 30 minutes. Ladle into bowls. Serve immediately.

QUICK POTAGE SAINT-GERMAIN

See photograph page 109

The foundation of this recipe is an enriched canned chicken broth that comes in handy for a number of other recipes. This same technique can be used with beef broth.

MAKES ABOUT 5 CUPS/6 SERVINGS

- 2 13½-ounce cans chicken broth
- 1 onion, chopped
- 1 celery stalk with leaves
- 1 small carrot, chopped
- 2 10-ounce packages frozen tiny peas, thawed
- 2 small green onions, chopped
- ¼ teaspoon minced fresh garlic
- 1 cup whipping cream
  Salt and freshly ground white pepper

Combine broth, onion, celery and carrot in saucepan. Cover and simmer for 30 to 45 minutes.

Add peas, green onion and garlic. Cover and simmer 5 minutes. Transfer to blender in batches and puree until smooth. Turn into saucepan, blend in cream and heat through. Season with salt and pepper. Serve hot or chilled.

Soup can be made up to 2 days ahead and refrigerated.

CHEESE SOUP

6 SERVINGS

- 1 small onion, coarsely chopped
- 1 small green pepper, coarsely chopped
- 2 celery stalks, cut into small pieces
- 2 carrots, cut into small pieces

¼ cup (½ stick) butter
¼ cup all purpose flour
3½ cups canned chicken broth
3 cups grated cheddar cheese
1½ cups milk
2 tablespoons sherry or favorite liqueur (optional)
Salt and freshly ground pepper
Minced parsley (garnish)
Beer (room temperature)

Combine first 4 ingredients in blender and finely chop. Melt butter in 3-quart saucepan over medium heat. Add vegetables and cook 8 to 10 minutes, stirring occasionally. Add flour and stir until well blended. Pour in chicken broth and bring to boil, stirring constantly until soup is slightly thickened. Remove from heat. Add cheese and allow to melt. Add milk, liqueur, salt and pepper to taste and mix thoroughly. Ladle into warmed mugs and sprinkle with parsley. Top with small amount of beer before serving.

CHINESE HOT AND SOUR SOUP

See photograph page 25

4 SERVINGS

4 dried black oriental mushrooms
¼ pound ham, slivered
½ cup slivered bamboo shoots
1 tablespoon soy sauce
4 cups chicken stock
Salt and freshly ground white pepper (optional)
1 cup finely sliced bean curd
3 tablespoons red wine vinegar
2 tablespoons cornstarch mixed with 3 tablespoons cold water
1 egg, lightly beaten
1 tablespoon sesame oil
1 green onion, finely chopped (garnish)

Soak mushrooms in warm water until softened. Drain; remove stems and slice caps. Combine mushrooms, ham, bamboo shoots, soy

sauce and chicken stock in large saucepan and bring to boil over high heat. Reduce heat and simmer 3 minutes. Taste and add salt and pepper if necessary. Add bean curd and vinegar and bring to boil again. Stir in dissolved cornstarch and cook, stirring constantly, until soup is slightly thickened.

Slowly add egg, stirring gently. Remove from heat and stir in oil. Ladle into bowls and garnish with finely chopped green onion.

If preferred, green onion can be cooked. Add along with bean curd.

GREEN SOUP

8 SERVINGS

2 10-ounce packages frozen peas
2 10-ounce packages frozen chopped spinach
1 onion, chopped
Bouquet garni (1 bay leaf, 2 parsley sprigs, ½ teaspoon each chervil and tarragon tied in cheesecloth bag)
4 cups chicken stock or broth
2 cups milk, half and half or whipping cream
2 to 4 tablespoons soy sauce (optional)
½ to 1 teaspoon curry powder or to taste
Salt and white pepper

Combine peas, spinach, onion and bouquet garni with chicken stock in 4-quart saucepan and simmer 25 to 30 minutes. Remove bouquet garni and puree soup in batches in blender or food processor. Return to pan, add milk and seasonings and bring to serving temperature, but do not allow to boil.

Good hot or chilled.

HOT MOCK TURTLE SOUP AND SHERRY

FOR EACH SERVING

4 ounces mock turtle soup
2 ounces dry sherry
Dash of salt
Dash of freshly ground pepper

Heat soup. Pour into preheated mug or stemmed glass, add sherry, salt and pepper to taste and stir well.

ITALIAN CHEESE CHOWDER

6 TO 8 SERVINGS

1 16-ounce can stewed tomatoes, undrained
1 15½-ounce can garbanzo beans, drained
½ pound zucchini, sliced
2 onions, chopped
1½ cups dry white wine
¼ cup (½ stick) butter
2 teaspoons salt
2 teaspoons instant minced garlic
1 teaspoon dried basil, crumbled
¼ teaspoon freshly ground pepper
1 bay leaf
1 cup grated Monterey Jack cheese
1 cup grated Romano cheese
1 cup whipping cream

Preheat oven to 400°F. Combine first 11 ingredients in 4-quart baking dish. Cover tightly and bake 1 hour, stirring once or twice. Blend in remaining ingredients. Cover and bake until cheese melts, about 10 minutes. Serve immediately.

INDIAN SOUP

4 SERVINGS

1 11-ounce can bisque of tomato soup
11 ounces milk (use soup can as measure)
1 tablespoon curry powder
½ teaspoon cumin
Plain yogurt or sour cream (garnish)

Combine all ingredients except garnish in medium saucepan and bring to boil, stirring several times to blend. Reduce heat, simmer 2 minutes and serve in heated bowls or mugs topped with dollop of yogurt or sour cream.

BRANDIED PUMPKIN SOUP

MAKES ABOUT 2 QUARTS

- 2½ cups canned pumpkin
- ¼ cup (½ stick) butter
- ½ cup finely chopped onion
- ¼ teaspoon ginger
- ¼ teaspoon nutmeg
- 3½ cups chicken broth
- 1 cup half and half
- 2 tablespoons brandy
  Salt and white pepper
  Croutons or sour cream
  (garnish)

Melt butter in a large deep saucepan. Add onion and cook, stirring occasionally, until transparent. Blend in spices and chicken broth. Bring to boil. Blend in pumpkin and half and half. Reduce heat and cook until soup is thoroughly heated, stirring occasionally. Blend in brandy. Season to taste with salt and pepper.

Serve hot with croutons, or chilled, with a dollop of sour cream.

COMPANY TUNA CHOWDER

4 SERVINGS

- 2 7-ounce cans chunk tuna, drained
- 3 tablespoons (⅜ stick) butter
- 1 large onion, sliced
- 1 12-ounce can whole kernel corn, undrained
- 2 tablespoons tomato paste
- 2 10½-ounce cans cream of celery soup
- 2 cups milk or more
- 3 to 4 large potatoes, peeled and cubed
- 1 teaspoon dry mustard
- 1 teaspoon dill
- ¼ teaspoon basil
- ¼ teaspoon fennel
  Salt and pepper to taste
  Parsley (garnish)

Break tuna into pieces. In a deep heavy pot heat butter and sauté onion until transparent. Add tuna, corn, tomato paste, soup, 2 cups milk, potatoes, mustard, herbs, salt and pepper. Bring to a simmer, stirring several times. Cover and cook until potatoes are tender, about 30

minutes. Thin with milk if necessary. Garnish with parsley.

Serve with tossed salad and rolls.

BEGGAR'S BOUILLABAISSE

6 TO 8 SERVINGS

- 2 16-ounce cans stewed tomatoes
- 2 8-ounce cans tomato sauce
- 2 medium potatoes, peeled and cut into 1-inch cubes
- 2 onions, coarsely chopped
- 2 green peppers, seeded and diced
- 2 garlic cloves, minced
- 1 bay leaf
- ⅓ cup minced fresh parsley
- 1 teaspoon Italian herb seasoning
- 1 teaspoon salt
- ½ teaspoon freshly ground white pepper
- 2½ pounds red snapper fillets or any firm-fleshed fish, cut into large pieces
- ½ pound cooked small to medium shrimp
- 1 6½-ounce can chopped clams, undrained

Combine first 11 ingredients in 3-quart saucepan and bring to boil over medium-high heat. Reduce heat, cover and simmer until vegetables are almost tender, about 30 minutes. Add snapper, shrimp and clams and continue simmering until fish flakes easily with fork, about 10 minutes. Taste and adjust seasoning before serving.

CRAB AND HAM SOUP

4 TO 6 SERVINGS

- 1½ cups chicken broth
- 1 11-ounce can whole kernel corn
- 1 6½-ounce can crabmeat, drained
- 3 ounces diced ham
- 1 tablespoon sherry
- 1 tablespoon cornstarch dissolved in 2 tablespoons water
- 2 eggs, lightly beaten

Salt
- 1 ounce julienned ham

Combine broth and corn in large saucepan and bring to boil. Add crabmeat, diced ham and sherry and return to boil. Add cornstarch mixture and stir until soup thickens. Slowly add eggs, whisking constantly. Season with salt. Ladle into bowls and garnish each serving with julienned ham.

HERBED TUNA CHOWDER

4 SERVINGS

- ¼ cup (½ stick) butter
- ½ cup chopped celery
- 1 medium onion, chopped
- 1 medium potato, peeled and chopped
- 3 tablespoons flour
- 3 cups milk
- 2 6-ounce cans drained and flaked tuna
- 1 cup grated Jack cheese
- ½ teaspoon thyme
- ½ teaspoon dill
- 1 teaspoon salt
- ½ teaspoon pepper
- ¼ cup chopped fresh parsley (garnish)

Melt butter in a large skillet and sauté vegetables about 3 to 5 minutes. Stir in flour until well blended. Gradually add milk. Cook over low heat until thick, stirring frequently. Add tuna, cheese, thyme, dill, salt and pepper. Heat thoroughly, about 5 minutes. Garnish with parsley.

OYSTER SOUP

4 SERVINGS

- 6 tablespoons olive oil
- 4 slices French bread
- 1 large garlic clove, mashed
- 2 8-ounce jars oysters, undrained
- 1 8-ounce bottle clam juice
- ¾ cup red wine
- 1 tablespoon catsup
- ½ teaspoon oregano
- ½ teaspoon garlic salt
- ¼ teaspoon freshly ground pepper

2 tablespoons chopped fresh parsley (garnish)

Heat 3 tablespoons olive oil in large saucepan over medium heat. Add bread and brown on both sides. Remove and set aside. Add remaining oil and garlic and cook 2 to 3 minutes to season oil and pan. Remove and discard garlic.

Add all remaining ingredients except parsley and bring to boil. Reduce heat and simmer 10 minutes. Place a slice of bread in each bowl and ladle soup over. Garnish with chopped parsley.

SOPA DE CUARTO DE HORA (QUARTER HOUR SOUP)

6 SERVINGS

2 tablespoons olive oil
1 onion, finely chopped
¼ pound ham, finely chopped
¼ pound uncooked shrimp, shelled and cleaned
¼ cup blanched almonds, finely ground
3 tomatoes, peeled and chopped
6 cups chicken stock
1 6½-ounce cans minced clams, undrained
1 cup cooked rice
½ cup peas, fresh or frozen
2 hard-cooked eggs, minced (garnish)

Heat oil in large saucepan over medium heat. Add onion and sauté until tender but not browned. Add ham, shrimp and almonds and cook until shrimp turn pink. Remove shrimp; chop and set aside. Add tomatoes to pan and blend well. Stir in stock and undrained clams and bring to boil. Add rice and peas and simmer 5 minutes. Add shrimp and cook 1 minute longer. Garnish with minced egg.

QUICK CRAB CHOWDER

4 TO 6 SERVINGS

3 tablespoons (⅜ stick) butter
½ cup chopped onion
½ cup chopped celery

3 cups milk
1 10¾-ounce can cream of potato soup
1 8-ounce can creamed corn
1 6½-ounce can crabmeat, drained
1 bay leaf
¼ teaspoon dried thyme
¼ teaspoon salt
¼ cup dry sherry
¼ cup chopped fresh parsley or 2 tablespoons dried parsley flakes (garnish)

Melt butter in large saucepan over medium heat. Add onion and celery and sauté until softened, about 15 minutes. Add all remaining ingredients except sherry and parsley and continue cooking until heated through, stirring frequently, about 15 minutes. Stir in sherry and heat an additional 2 minutes. Discard bay leaf. Garnish with parsley.

QUICK MANHATTAN-STYLE CHOWDER

6 TO 8 SERVINGS

¼ pound bacon, diced
1 large garlic clove, minced
1 onion, chopped
1 green pepper, seeded and chopped
2 cups chicken stock or broth
1 28-ounce can stewed tomatoes
2 8-ounce cans minced clams, undrained
1 10-ounce can baby clams, undrained
½ cup barley
Tomato juice (optional)
Salt and freshly ground pepper
Hot pepper sauce
Rye toast

Brown bacon with garlic in heavy-bottomed large saucepan or Dutch oven over medium-high heat. When bacon is almost crisp, add onion and green pepper and sauté until tender.

Stir in stock and tomatoes. Add clams and barley and blend well. Bring mixture to boil, reduce heat and simmer to desired thickness, about 20 to 30 minutes. Add tomato juice to thin, if desired. Season to taste with salt, pepper and hot pepper sauce.

Serve with crisp buttered rye toast.

CONDIMENTS

APFELKREN (RELISH)

This spicy Austrian relish is good with pork or goose.

MAKES ABOUT 1½ CUPS

3 eating apples, peeled, cored and grated
¼ cup sugar, or to taste
1 tablespoon prepared horseradish, drained
2 teaspoons paprika
2 tablespoons dry white wine or more

Combine all ingredients in medium bowl and blend well, adding wine to give desired consistency.

FIVE-DAY PICKLES

MAKES ABOUT 2 QUARTS

2 to 3 large cucumbers (unpeeled), thinly sliced
2 large onions, thinly sliced
2 cups sugar
2 cups white wine vinegar
¾ teaspoon celery seeds
¾ teaspoon lemon pepper
¾ teaspoon turmeric
¾ teaspoon mustard seeds
¼ teaspoon salt

Layer cucumber and onion in sterilized jars, packing tightly. Combine remaining ingredients in medium saucepan over low heat and stir constantly until sugar is dissolved, about 10 minutes. Pour evenly into jars and seal. Let cool slightly. (Refrigerate at least 5 days before serving.)

CHUNKY APRICOT PRESERVES

This easy preserve makes delightful and delicious gifts.

MAKES ABOUT 3½ CUPS

- 1 6-ounce package dried apricots
- 1 cup water
- 4 cups sugar
- 1 8¼-ounce can crushed pineapple packed in its own juice, undrained
- 1 10-ounce package frozen yellow squash, thawed and drained (optional)

Combine apricots and water in medium saucepan and let stand about 1 hour to plump. Place over medium heat and cook until apricots are tender, about 10 minutes. Mash into course chunks. Add sugar, pineapple and squash, blending well. Continue cooking over low heat until thickened, stirring occasionally, about 15 minutes. Pour into sterilized jars and seal. Let cool. Store in refrigerator.

MUSTARD

MAKES ABOUT 1½ CUPS

- 2 eggs
- ½ cup firmly packed brown sugar
- ½ cup canned consommé
- ½ cup white wine vinegar
- ¼ cup dry mustard
- 1½ teaspoons flour
  Dash of hot pepper sauce

Beat eggs in medium bowl. Add remaining ingredients and mix well. Pour into saucepan and cook over low heat until thickened, stirring constantly, about 10 minutes. Pour into sterilized jar and seal. Let cool. Store in refrigerator.

SWEET AND HOT SWEDISH MUSTARD

MAKES 2 CUPS

- 2 eggs
- ½ cup sugar
- 5 tablespoons dry mustard
- 2 teaspoons salt
  Dash of freshly ground pepper
- 1 cup whipping cream
- ¼ cup white vinegar

Place eggs in top of double boiler over gently simmering water and whisk until light. Add sugar, mustard, salt and pepper and blend well. Gradually add cream, stirring constantly with wooden spoon until it drops in thin ribbon, about 8 to 10 minutes. Do not boil or mixture will curdle. Remove from heat and slowly add vinegar, beating constantly to blend. Mixture will thicken as it cools. Store in refrigerator.

SPINACH MAYONNAISE

MAKES ABOUT 3 CUPS

- 2 10-ounce packages frozen spinach, thawed, drained and squeezed
- 2 cups mayonnaise
- 1 medium onion, chopped
- 1 cup parsley
- 1 tablespoon vinegar
- 1 tablespoon fresh dill or 1 teaspoon dried
  Salt and pepper to taste

Place all ingredients in blender or food processor and mix until smooth.

SAUCES

COLD

ALL PURPOSE MEAT SAUCE

MAKES ABOUT 5 CUPS

- 1 14-ounce bottle catsup
- 1 12-ounce bottle chili sauce
- 1 6-ounce bottle sauce Robert
- ½ 5-ounce bottle steak sauce
- 5 shakes Worcestershire sauce
  Hot pepper sauce to taste

Combine all ingredients in bowl or jar with lid and mix well. Cover and refrigerate for use as needed.

AMARETTO-APRICOT SAUCE

MAKES ABOUT 3 CUPS

- ½ cup (1 stick) unsalted butter
- ⅓ cup (about) thinly sliced shallot
- ¾ cup fresh orange juice, strained (2 or 3 oranges)
- ¼ cup (scant) fresh lemon juice (2 small lemons)
- 2 tablespoons prepared mustard (preferably Dijon)
- 2 cups washed, pitted and halved fresh apricots*
  Salt and freshly ground pepper
- 1 cup Amaretto liqueur
- ½ cup slivered almonds, toasted

Melt butter in saucepan. Add shallot, orange juice, lemon juice, mustard, apricots and salt and pepper and cook briefly to soften shallot and combine ingredients. Add Amaretto and simmer, stirring occasionally, until sauce coats spoon, about 35 minutes. Stir in slivered almonds just before serving.

*If fresh apricots are not available, use canned apricot halves. Rebalance "bite" of the sauce by adding 2 tablespoons Cognac and juice of another lemon.

LEMON CREAM

A refreshing dip for artichokes.

MAKES 4 CUPS

- 2 cups mayonnaise
- 2 cups sour cream
- ¼ cup fresh lemon juice
- 2½ teaspoons finely grated lemon peel
- 2 teaspoons white horseradish
- 2 teaspoons Dijon mustard
- 1 teaspoon salt

Combine all ingredients in large bowl and blend. Cover and refrigerate. Adjust seasoning before serving.

HORSERADISH SAUCE

MAKES ABOUT 1 CUP

- ½ cup whipping cream
- 2 tablespoons creamy horseradish
- 1 teaspoon lemon juice
  Pinch of sugar (optional)

Whip cream in small bowl. Add remaining ingredients and mix well. Refrigerate until chilled.

HORSERADISH MOUSSELINE SAUCE

MAKES 2 CUPS

- 1 cup Hollandaise Sauce*
- 1 cup whipped cream
- 1 teaspoon freshly grated horseradish or 1½ teaspoons drained prepared white horseradish, or to taste

Combine all ingredients. Serve at room temperature.

May be prepared 2 days ahead and stored in the refrigerator. Whisk to fluff just before ready to serve.

*Hollandaise Sauce

MAKES 1 CUP

- 4 egg yolks
- 2 tablespoons fresh lemon juice
- 1 teaspoon white vinegar
- ¼ teaspoon salt
- ⅛ teaspoon cayenne pepper
- ¾ cup (1½ sticks) butter

Place yolks, lemon juice, vinegar, salt and cayenne in blender or food processor. Blend 5 seconds. Heat butter until it sizzles. Pour in a steady stream into running blender. Turn off motor as soon as mixture is creamy.

PUNGENT FRUIT SAUCE

MAKES 1¼ CUPS

- 1 cup orange marmalade
- 2 tablespoons orange juice
- 2 tablespoons lemon juice

- 1½ teaspoons horseradish
- 1 small piece fresh ginger, pressed
- 1 teaspoon dry mustard

Mix marmalade, orange and lemon juices in blender or food processor until combined. Mix in remaining ingredients.

May be stored in refrigerator for several weeks.

Good with wontons, egg rolls, spareribs, ham and roast pork.

SALSA DELLE API

Excellent over boiled meat or ham.

MAKES ABOUT ¾ CUP

- ¾ cup honey
- 5 to 6 whole walnuts, blanched, peeled and chopped
- 1 tablespoon beef or chicken broth
- 1 tablespoon Dijon mustard

Blend all ingredients in small bowl.

SAUCE SUEDOISE

Try this with cold pork or roast goose or duck.

MAKES ABOUT 2 CUPS

- 1 cup mayonnaise
- 1 cup thick applesauce
- 1 tablespoon freshly grated horseradish

Combine all ingredients in small bowl and mix well. Chill in refrigerator before serving.

YOGURT SAUCE
See photograph page 129

The tangy zing of yogurt is perfect as an accompaniment with lamb.

MAKES ABOUT 1½ CUPS

- 1 cup plain yogurt
- ½ cup chopped onion
- 1 teaspoon prepared mustard

Combine all ingredients and mix well. Cover and chill before serving.

COCKTAIL SAUCE

Can be made three days ahead.

MAKES ABOUT 7½ CUPS

- 1½ quarts (6 cups) chili sauce
- 1 14-ounce bottle catsup
- ¼ cup prepared red horseradish
- 2 teaspoons Worcestershire sauce
- 1 teaspoon hot pepper sauce or to taste
  Juice of ½ lemon

Blend all ingredients. Cover and refrigerate. Adjust seasoning to taste before serving.

MAISON SAUCE

Can be made three days ahead.

MAKES ABOUT 4½ CUPS

- 1 quart (4 cups) mayonnaise
- 3 tablespoons dry white wine
- 3 tablespoons prepared mustard
- ½ teaspoon Worcestershire sauce
- ½ teaspoon hot pepper sauce or to taste
  Juice of ½ lemon

Blend all ingredients. Cover and refrigerate. Adjust seasoning to taste before serving.

QUICK SAUCE FOR SHRIMP

MAKES ABOUT 1½ CUPS

- ¾ cup oil
- ⅓ cup red wine vinegar
- 1 egg yolk
- 2 tablespoons snipped fresh chives
- 2 tablespoons minced shallot
- 2 tablespoons chopped fresh parsley
- 2 tablespoons Dijon mustard

Combine all ingredients and blend thoroughly until smooth. Serve over chilled shrimp.

TANGY FISH SAUCE

MAKES 1¼ CUPS

- 1 cup mayonnaise, preferably homemade
- ¼ cup fresh lemon juice
- 1 teaspoon Dijon mustard

Combine all ingredients in small bowl and blend until smooth. Cover and chill before serving.

HOT

QUICK BROWN SAUCE

MAKES ABOUT 1½ CUPS

- ¼ cup dry white wine
- 2 shallots, minced
- ½ cup beef gravy
- ¾ cup whipping cream
- 1 teaspoon sauce Robert
  Pinch of thyme
  Pinch of tarragon
  Salt and freshly ground pepper
- 1 teaspoon Dijon mustard

Simmer wine and shallots in small saucepan until most of wine has evaporated, about 10 minutes. Stir in gravy, cream, sauce, herbs and salt and pepper and let simmer 10 minutes. Remove from heat and blend in mustard. Serve with steaks, roasts, short ribs or hamburger patties.

INSTANT BURGUNDY SAUCE

MAKES 1½ CUPS

- 1 10¾-ounce can cream of mushroom soup
- 4 fresh mushrooms, diced
- 2 tablespoons dry red wine
  Dash Kitchen Bouquet

Stir all ingredients together over low heat until hot.

Add 1½ to 2 cups diced leftover roast beef to sauce to make Beef Burgundy. To make Beef Stroganoff, add the beef to sauce, plus ½ green pepper, sliced and sautéed, and 2 tablespoons or more sour cream.

BUTTER SAUCE FOR COOKED ARTICHOKES

4 SERVINGS

- 1 cup (2 sticks) melted butter
- ¼ cup lemon juice
- ¼ cup chopped parsley
- 1 teaspoon salt
- ½ teaspoon dry mustard

Combine all ingredients and simmer 5 minutes. Serve warm as dipping sauce with hot artichokes.

CONEY ISLAND CHILI SAUCE

4 SERVINGS

- ½ pound lean ground beef
- ¼ cup finely chopped onion
- 1 garlic clove, minced
- 1 8-ounce can tomato sauce
- ¼ cup water
- ½ to ¾ teaspoon chili powder or to taste

Combine beef, onion and garlic in large skillet over medium-high heat and stir until mixture is finely crumbled. Pour off any excess fat. Add remaining ingredients and simmer about 10 minutes, stirring occasionally. Serve immediately.

MARINADES

BARBECUE SAUCE AND MARINADE

MAKES ABOUT 1½ CUPS

- 1 tablespoon butter
- ½ onion, chopped
- ½ cup water
- ½ cup catsup
- 2 tablespoons brown sugar
- 1½ tablespoons Worcestershire sauce
- 1 tablespoon vinegar
- 1 teaspoon dry mustard

Melt butter in medium skillet over medium-high heat. Add onion and sauté until tender, about 5 minutes. Blend in remaining ingredients. Cook until heated through, about 10 minutes. Let cool slightly. Transfer to jar or other container. Cover tightly. Store in refrigerator.

MULTI-PURPOSE MARINADE

Good for spareribs, butterflied leg of lamb and chicken. Serve excess sauce on the side or over noodles, rice or potatoes. Leftover fresh marinade can be refrigerated and kept handy for another time.

MAKES APPROXIMATELY 3 CUPS

- 1 cup soy sauce
- 1 cup catsup
- ½ cup sugar
- 2 tablespoons hoisin sauce
- 1 tablespoon sherry
- 1 tablespoon wine vinegar
- 4 garlic cloves, chopped
- 1 1-inch piece fresh ginger, chopped
  Freshly ground pepper

Mix all ingredients well and pour over meat. Marinate in refrigerator at least 2 hours before cooking.

SALSA SAPORITA

An excellent sauce for marinating meats, poultry or fish. The recipe makes enough for marinating three pounds.

MAKES 1 CUP

- 1 cup dry sherry or Marsala wine
- 2 tablespoons honey
- 1 teaspoon Dijon mustard
- ¼ teaspoon ground ginger
- 2 bay leaves
- 2 garlic cloves or 1 onion, quartered

Combine all ingredients in blender or processor until liquified.

SHANGHAI MARINADE

MAKES ¾ CUP

- ¼ cup soy sauce
- ¼ cup oil
- ¼ cup white wine
- 1 teaspoon sugar
- 1 garlic clove, minced
- 2 dashes hot pepper sauce
- 1 2-inch strip fresh orange, lemon or tangerine peel

Combine all ingredients in small bowl. Pour over meat and let marinate from 1 hour to overnight, depending on thickness of meat and amount of flavor desired. Pan- or oven-broil or barbecue.

SPANISH SHERRY MARINADE

MAKES ¾ CUP

- ½ cup dry Spanish sherry
- ¼ cup olive oil (preferably Spanish)
- 1 small onion, minced
- 1 bay leaf
- ¼ teaspoon thyme
- ⅛ teaspoon freshly ground pepper
  Additional dash of thyme

Combine all ingredients except additional thyme in small bowl and pour over meat. Marinate from 1 hour to overnight. During last 5 minutes of cooking sprinkle additional thyme over coals.

WHITE BARBECUE SAUCE

Good baste for chicken.

MAKES ABOUT 1 CUP

- 6 tablespoons mayonnaise
- 2 tablespoons sugar
- 1 teaspoon salt
- 1 teaspoon freshly ground pepper
- 3 tablespoons lemon juice
- 3 tablespoons vinegar

Combine first 4 ingredients in small bowl. Gradually whisk in lemon juice and vinegar and blend thoroughly until smooth.

BUTTERS

ANCHOVY BUTTER

MAKES ABOUT ½ CUP

- ½ cup (1 stick) unsalted butter, room temperature
- 4 anchovy fillets, rinsed, drained and chopped
- 1 teaspoon fresh lemon juice
  Dash of hot pepper sauce

Combine all ingredients in small bowl and mix well. Dollop on cooked steaks or pass separately.

BASIL BUTTER

MAKES ABOUT ½ CUP

- ½ cup (1 stick) unsalted butter, room temperature
- 1 tablespoon basil
- 1 teaspoon tomato paste
- ½ teaspoon minced garlic
  Salt and freshly ground pepper

Combine all ingredients in small bowl and mix well. Dollop on cooked steaks or pass separately.

GARLIC BUTTER

MAKES ABOUT ½ CUP

- ½ cup (1 stick) unsalted butter, room temperature
- 1 tablespoon minced parsley
- 1 tablespoon minced shallot
- 1 teaspoon minced garlic or more to taste
- 1 teaspoon dry white wine
- ½ teaspoon lemon juice

Combine all ingredients in small bowl and mix well. Dollop on cooked steaks or pass separately.

HOMEMADE BUTTER

MAKES ABOUT 1 CUP

- 2 cups whipping cream
- ¼ cup ice-cold water

Mix cream in processor or blender until thick. Add water and continue mixing until separated. Turn into strainer and hold under cold running water, kneading to remove as much milky liquid as possible. Pat dry with paper towels and mold into desired shape. Chill about 30 minutes (or longer) before serving.

SHALLOT-TARRAGON BUTTER

MAKES ABOUT ½ CUP

- ½ cup (1 stick) unsalted butter, room temperature
- 3 shallots, minced
- 1 to 2 teaspoons dried, finely crumbled tarragon
  Salt and freshly ground pepper

Combine all ingredients in small bowl and mix well. Dollop on cooked steaks or pass separately.

DO AHEAD SOUPS

COLD

BLENDER BORSCHT

4 SERVINGS

- 2 16-ounce cans whole beets, drained (reserve ½ cup liquid)
- ¾ cup chicken broth
- 2 tablespoons coarsely chopped onion
- 4 teaspoons fresh lemon juice
- ½ teaspoon salt
- ⅛ teaspoon sugar
  Dash of freshly ground pepper
  Whipped sour cream (garnish)
  Minced chives (garnish)

Combine beets and reserved liquid with next 6 ingredients in blender or processor and puree until smooth. Taste and adjust seasoning. Transfer to medium bowl. Cover and refrigerate overnight. Serve in chilled bowls. Garnish with dollop of sour cream and sprinkle with chives.

COLD MINT-CUCUMBER SOUP

A delicate and unusual combination that is refreshing on a hot day.

4 TO 6 SERVINGS

- 3 tablespoons (⅜ stick) butter
- 1 medium onion, finely chopped
- 1 small garlic clove, minced
- 3 medium cucumbers, peeled and thinly sliced
- 3 tablespoons flour (preferably rice flour)
- 2 cups chicken stock
- 2 tablespoons finely chopped fresh mint
- 1 cup half and half
- 1 cup plain yogurt
  Salt and freshly ground white pepper
  Sliced cucumber (garnish)

Melt butter in large skillet over medium heat. Add onion and garlic and sauté until limp but not brown. Add sliced cucumber and cook slowly until soft. Remove from heat. Stir in flour, then stock, blending well. Place over medium-high heat and bring to boil. Reduce heat and simmer 5 minutes. Transfer to processor or blender in batches and puree. Pour into bowl and blend in mint. Cover and chill well. Just before serving, stir in half and half and yogurt and mix well. Taste and season with salt and pepper. Garnish each serving with sliced cucumber.

ONE-OF-EACH SOUP

6 SERVINGS

- 1 tablespoon butter or margarine
- 1 onion, chopped
- 1 medium apple, peeled and diced

- 1 potato, peeled and diced
- 1 banana, peeled and diced
- 1 celery stalk, chopped
- 2 cups chicken broth
- 1 teaspoon curry powder or to taste
- ½ teaspoon salt
- 1 cup half and half
  Lemon slices or melon balls (garnish)

Melt butter or margarine in large saucepan over medium-high heat. Add next 5 ingredients. Stir in broth, curry powder and salt. Reduce heat, cover and simmer 20 to 30 minutes, stirring occasionally. Puree in blender. Chill thoroughly.

At serving time blend in half and half. Turn into chilled soup tureen and garnish with lemon slices or melon balls.

FRENCH TARRAGON SOUP

Ladle into lettuce-lined bowls for a refreshingly cool presentation.

4 SERVINGS

- 5 cups chicken stock
- 4 teaspoons chopped fresh tarragon or 2 teaspoons dried, crumbled
- 1 envelope unflavored gelatin
- ¼ cup cold water
- ¼ pound cooked shrimp, coarsely chopped
  Chopped fresh parsley
  Fresh lemon juice
  Lemon slices

Bring chicken stock to boil in saucepan. Reduce heat and simmer 5 minutes. Add tarragon. Dissolve gelatin in water and add to hot stock, mixing well. Remove from heat and let cool. Cover and chill.

Stir soup gently and ladle into individual bowls. Sprinkle each serving with shrimp, parsley and lemon juice and top with a lemon slice.

SHELLFISH GAZPACHO
See photograph page 26

6 SERVINGS

- 4 cups fresh French or Italian breadcrumbs
- 4 tomatoes, peeled, seeded and chopped
- 2 cucumbers, peeled and coarsely chopped
- 1 onion, chopped
- 1 green pepper, seeded and chopped
- 2 teaspoons minced fresh garlic
- 4 cups water
- ¼ cup wine vinegar
- 1 tablespoon salt
  Freshly ground pepper
- ¼ cup olive oil
- 1 tablespoon tomato paste
- 1½ pounds cooked, cleaned shellfish (shrimp, lobster, crab, scallops or combination), chopped or shredded

Garnishes

- 1 cup croutons
- ½ cup minced onion
- ½ cup peeled, chopped cucumber
- ½ cup minced green pepper
- ½ cup minced fresh parsley
- ¼ cup snipped fresh chives

Combine first 6 ingredients in large bowl and blend well. Add water, vinegar, salt and pepper and stir thoroughly. Puree about 2 cups at a time in blender, food processor or food mill. Pour into another large bowl or Dutch oven and slowly whisk in oil and tomato paste. Cover and chill overnight. Just before serving, add shellfish. Pass garnishes in separate bowls.

BORSCHT

See photograph page 27

- 1 raw beet, peeled and shredded
- ⅓ cup water
- 1 pound lean beef, cubed
- 3 cups beef stock
- 2 cups water
- 1½ teaspoons salt
- ½ cup coarsely grated carrot
- ½ cup coarsely grated turnip
- 1 small onion, chopped
- 2 tablespoons vinegar or to taste
- 1 tablespoon tomato paste
- 1 tablespoon butter
- ½ teaspoon sugar
- 1 16-ounce can sliced or shredded beets, drained (juice reserved)
- 1 cup shredded cabbage
- 1 bay leaf
  Freshly ground pepper
  Sour cream and dill sprigs (garnish)

Combine raw beet and water and let stand for several hours.

Combine beef, stock, water and salt in large saucepan and simmer, skimming surface frequently, until meat is tender, about 1½ to 2 hours.

While meat is cooking, combine carrot, turnip, onion, vinegar, tomato paste, butter and sugar in small saucepan. Cover and simmer about 15 minutes, checking occasionally to be sure mixture isn't too dry. Add canned beet juice and cabbage and cook 10 minutes.

When meat is tender, add vegetable mixture, canned beets, bay leaf and a few grindings of pepper and cook until heated through. Add undrained raw beet. Taste and adjust salt and vinegar as necessary. Ladle soup into bowls and garnish with sour cream and dill.

TURKISH LENTIL SOUP

6 TO 8 SERVINGS

- 1 cup dried lentils
- 3 cups beef stock
- 2 tablespoons chopped fresh parsley
- 3 tablespoons (⅜ stick) butter
- 1 large onion, finely chopped
- 3 cups tomato juice
  Dash of ground red pepper
  Additional stock or tomato juice (optional)
  Salt and freshly ground pepper (optional)

Combine lentils, stock and parsley in medium saucepan. Cover and cook until lentils are tender, about 30 minutes. Stir occasionally.

Melt butter in large saucepan over medium heat. Add onion and sauté until golden. Stir in lentils and stock, tomato juice and red pepper. Cover and simmer 30 minutes. If too thick, stir in additional stock or tomato juice. Taste and adjust seasoning with salt, pepper and additional red pepper if necessary.

CREAM OF VEGETABLE SOUP NORMANDY

6 SERVINGS

- ¼ cup (½ stick) butter
- 6 medium carrots, thinly sliced
- 3 large leeks (with 1-inch green stem), cleaned and thinly sliced
- 2 large onions, thinly sliced
- 2 large turnips, peeled and thinly sliced
- 6 potatoes, peeled and sliced
- 8 cups chicken stock
  Salt and freshly ground pepper
- 1 cup Crème Fraîche*

Melt butter in Dutch oven or large saucepan over medium heat. Add carrots, leeks, onions, and turnips and sauté until golden. Add potatoes, stock and salt (if necessary) and pepper to taste Increase heat and bring to boil. Reduce heat and simmer until vegetables are tender. Transfer to processor or blender in batches and puree. Return to saucepan and stir in Crème Fraîche. Cook over low heat until just warmed through. Do not boil.

*Crème Fraîche

MAKES 1 CUP

- 1 cup whipping cream
- 1 tablespoon buttermilk

Combine cream and buttermilk in jar with tight-fitting lid and shake briskly 1 minute. Let stand at room temperature overnight until thickened. Shake again. Refrigerate until ready to use.

VICHYSSOISE

2 SERVINGS

- ⅓ cup dry leek soup mix
- 1 cup water
- 1 cup whipping cream
  Freshly ground pepper
  Chopped chives (garnish)

In 4-cup glass measuring cup, thoroughly combine soup mix and water. Cover with plastic wrap and cook 3 minutes on High, stirring once. Stir well, add cream and mix. Cover and cook about 3 more minutes on High, stirring once, until soup comes to a full boil (cream will not curdle). Cool slightly, cover and refrigerate. Serve well chilled, seasoned with pepper and garnished with chives.

SALADS AND DRESSINGS

Salads make simple first courses

■ Mix a little imagination with a full measure of assistance from your well-stocked pantry shelf and vegetable bin. Easy-to-store provisions like marinated artichoke hearts, marinated mushrooms, pickled vegetables, anchovies and pimientos add interest to salads when combined with lettuce, spinach, sprouts, tomatoes, mayonnaise and bottled dressings from the refrigerator. Other good salad standbys include: vinegar and fresh garlic, olive and safflower oil, mustard, dry and prepared, and onions, both white and bermuda.

Quick Salads

■ Individual Salades Niçoise are delightful. In a large bowl place several cans of solid-pack tuna broken into large chunks, drained cooked green beans, cooked cubed potatoes, and a tablespoon or two of drained capers. Toss the ingredients in a light vinaigrette seasoned with salt, pepper and a hint of garlic. Place a tablespoon or so on individual Bibb lettuce leaves. Garnish with flat, drained anchovies, cherry tomatoes, quartered hard-cooked eggs and black olives. Serve with warm French loaves and sweet butter.

■ Quick crab salad: Bind lump crabmeat with a light, mustard-spiked mayonnaise, season with salt, pepper and grated onion. Mound the salad on chilled salad plates. Shower with lots of finely minced chives and garnish plates with slices of lime and whole-kernel corn (canned or frozen) dressed with oil and vinegar and brightened with fragments of chopped red pimiento and green pepper.

SALADS

ANTIPASTO CENTERPIECE SALAD

See photograph page 156

6 TO 8 SERVINGS

Here's when having the pantry stocked with an assortment of canned and bottled goodies really pays off. It saves the tedious job of slicing and chopping usually associated with combination salads. The concept is simple: a basket filled with artfully arranged whole vegetables and salad greens for everyone to slice and break according to taste, along with bowls of marinated mushrooms, artichokes, pickled peppers, garbanzo beans, thinly sliced salami and whatever else strikes your fancy.

Salad

   1 small head escarole
   1 small head romaine
   1 basket cherry tomatoes
   1 bunch small green onions, trimmed
   1 small head cauliflower, core removed

   2 branches of broccoli, stems peeled
   1 or 2 green peppers, seeded and cut into strips
   1 bunch radishes (including tops if possible)
      Handful of sugar snap peas or snow peas
      Handful of tender green beans

Dressing

   ⅓ cup red or white wine vinegar
   ⅔ cup light olive oil
      Salt and freshly ground pepper

Antipasto accompaniments

   1 cup marinated artichoke hearts
   1 cup marinated mushrooms
   1 cup sweet or hot pickled peppers
   1 cup oil-cured olives
   1 cup pickled or stuffed eggplant
   1 15-ounce can garbanzo beans (chick-peas), rinsed and drained

For salad: Rinse all vegetables with cold water. Line 10- to 12-inch shallow basket with plastic wrap, then with colorful napkin. Make a bed of salad greens. Arrange remaining vegetables attractively atop greens. Cover with plastic wrap and cool.

For dressing: Combine ingredients and pour into serving bowl.

For antipasto accompaniments: Place each item in a separate bowl. Serve at room temperature.

TOSSED ANTIPASTO SALAD

6 TO 8 SERVINGS

   1 cup bottled Italian dressing
   1 tablespoon fresh lemon juice
      Salt and freshly ground pepper
   1 large zucchini, thinly sliced
   ½ medium cauliflower, broken into small florets
   ¼ cup sliced green onion
   8 cups crisp salad greens
   6 slices Italian salami, cut into strips
   4 large mushrooms, sliced
   2 firm tomatoes, cut into wedges
   ¼ pound provolone cheese, cut into strips
   1 2-ounce can black olives, drained (optional)

Dressing Ideas

■ To dress a salad of seasonal greens, try a vinaigrette made with fragrantly fruity, ruby-red raspberry vinegar combined with a light French olive oil. The raspberry taste, with its delicate flavor and hint of sweetness, offers an unusual foil for the greens.

■ With crinkly forest-green spinach leaves and sliced raw mushrooms, combine a full-bodied red wine vinegar, with salad oil and a miser's touch of Dijon mustard.

■ Serve an attractive mélange of briefly cooked snow pea pods, raw turnips or black winter radishes and mushrooms dressed with a light vinaigrette. Cook fresh or frozen Chinese pea pods in boiling water 2

minutes; drain and cut into julienne strips. Peel white turnips (or tart, firm winter radishes), slice thinly, then stack the slices and cut into julienne strips. Wipe fresh white mushrooms with damp towel, cut off stems and slice caps as thinly as possible. Sprinkle the mushrooms with a little lemon juice to keep them white. Combine vegetables in a large bowl and toss very gently with light oil, vinegar, garlic powder, salt and fresh pepper.

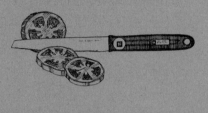

■ With tart, crunchy sliced endive bejeweled with bright green shards of scallion use a dressing of champagne vinegar and light French olive oil, a flick of tarragon leaves and pepper.

■ For an unusual salad and crunch, color and zest, slice red radishes into paper-thin rounds, sprinkle with rounds of sliced green onion and drizzle with lemon juice. Serve on chilled plates with a lemon wedge.

■ For barely cooked florets of broccoli or cauliflower use a dressing of sherry wine vinegar blended with a light oil and a sprinkling of chervil.

■ Dress a salad of cubed fresh apples, pineapple and pears with a vinaigrette made of raspberry vinegar, salad oil and garnish with slivered almonds.

---

    1 cup seasoned croutons
    ¼ cup freshly grated Parmesan
       cheese

Combine Italian dressing, lemon juice, salt and pepper in medium bowl and mix well. Add zucchini, cauliflower and onion and toss lightly to coat. Cover and marinate in refrigerator.

Combine next 6 ingredients in large salad bowl. Add vegetables with marinade and toss well. Add croutons, sprinkle with Parmesan cheese and toss again.

BEEF SALAD WITH ASPARAGUS AND BROCCOLI
See photograph page 68

4 SERVINGS

    1 small flank steak
       Salt
    4 cups fresh asparagus
       diagonally sliced into 2-inch
       pieces
    1 bunch broccoli, cut into
       bite-size florets

Ginger Dressing

    ⅓ cup light soy sauce
    ¼ cup white vinegar

    3 tablespoons sesame oil
    1 1½-inch piece fresh ginger,
       peeled and grated
    1 teaspoon sugar
       Freshly ground white pepper

Broil or pan-fry flank steak according to basic recipe to desired doneness. Cool and slice.

Bring large pot of salted water to rapid boil. Add asparagus and blanch 30 seconds. Remove with slotted spoon or strainer and set aside to cool. Add broccoli to same water and blanch 30 seconds. Drain well and let cool.

For dressing: Combine all ingredients in small bowl.

When ready to serve, toss beef slices with dressing. Add vegetables and toss. Serve at room temperature.

BEET SALAD

6 SERVINGS

    1 8¼-ounce jar diced pickled
       beets

    1 medium onion, finely
       chopped
    ½ cup finely chopped pickled
       herring
    2 hard-cooked eggs, diced
    1 hard-cooked egg yolk, sieved
       (garnish)

Drain beets and reserve juice. Mix beets with onion, herring and hard-cooked eggs. Pour in and gently mix 3 tablespoons of the reserved beet liquid.

BIBB AND WALNUT SALAD
See photograph page 159

6 SERVINGS

    2 heads Bibb lettuce, washed,
       dried and torn into bite-size
       pieces
    ⅔ cup coarsely chopped
       walnuts, toasted
    ½ cup walnut oil or to taste
    3 to 6 tablespoons wine
       vinegar
       Salt and freshly ground
       pepper

Arrange lettuce in salad bowl. Sprinkle with walnuts and toss with walnut oil and vinegar. Season to taste with salt and freshly ground pepper and serve immediately.

CARAWAY COLE SLAW

8 SERVINGS

- 1 large head cabbage
- 1 medium onion, finely minced
- 2 tablespoons lemon juice
  Salt and pepper
- ¾ cup mayonnaise
- 1 tablespoon caraway seeds

Shred cabbage with food processor, blender or hand grater. Add onion, lemon juice, salt and pepper. Stir in mayonnaise and caraway seeds. Chill before serving.

SPICY CUCUMBER SALAD

8 SERVINGS

- 2 medium cucumbers, peeled, halved crosswise, seeded
- 1 tablespoon vinegar
- 1 tablespoon sugar
- 1 teaspoon soy sauce
- 1 teaspoon sesame oil
- ½ teaspoon salt
- 5 to 6 dashes hot pepper sauce

Slice cucumbers ⅛ inch thick. Combine remaining ingredients in small bowl and mix well. Add cucumbers and toss to coat. Chill.

WALNUT AVOCADO SALAD

4 TO 6 SERVINGS

- ½ head iceburg lettuce, shredded
- ½ head romaine lettuce, shredded
- 1 cup chopped walnuts
- 1 avocado, diced and sprinkled with lemon juice
- ⅓ cup wine vinegar
- ⅔ cup oil
- 2 garlic cloves, minced
- 1 teaspoon salt
- ¼ teaspoon pepper

Combine lettuce, nuts and avocado in a bowl; chill thoroughly.

Combine remaining ingredients in jar; refrigerate. Toss with chilled vegetables just before serving.

GARDEN SALAD

See photograph page 72

4 SERVINGS

- 3 cups cauliflower cut into bite-size florets
- 1 pound green beans, trimmed
- ¼ cup oil
- 1 tablespoon minced fresh garlic
- 3 tablespoons light soy sauce
- 3 tablespoons white vinegar
- 2 tablespoons dry sherry
- 1 tablespoon sugar or to taste
  Dash of salt
- 2 cups fresh or canned lotus root,* fresh radish or zucchini, thinly sliced
- ¼ cup sesame seeds, toasted

Bring large pot of salted water to rapid boil. Add cauliflower and blanch briefly. Remove with slotted spoon or strainer and set aside to cool. Add beans to same water and blanch 2 minutes. Drain and cool.

Heat oil in small saucepan over medium-high heat. Add garlic and let sizzle briefly; do not burn. Remove from heat and stir in soy sauce, vinegar, sherry, sugar and salt.

Arrange cauliflower and lotus root, radish or zucchini in center of large platter. Place beans along both sides. Drizzle with sauce and sprinkle with sesame seeds. Let cool and serve at room temperature.

*Available in oriental markets.

CABBAGE SALAD

6 SERVINGS

- ½ head cabbage, shredded
- ½ cup tiny frozen peas, thawed
- 2 tablespoons chopped shallot or white part of green onion
- 2 tablespoons chopped fresh parsley
- ⅓ cup mayonnaise flavored with ½ teaspoon curry powder
  Spanish peanuts (garnish)
  Fresh sliced fruit (optional garnish)

Combine first 4 ingredients in bowl and toss with mayonnaise. Garnish with peanuts and fresh sliced fruit. Serve immediately.

LEBANESE SALAD

4 TO 6 SERVINGS

- 1 head of lettuce, torn into pieces
- 3 to 4 green onions, finely chopped
- 3 tomatoes, cut into wedges
- 2 small cucumbers, peeled and thinly sliced
- ½ small green pepper, sliced into thin strips
- 5 parsley sprigs, coarsely chopped
- 4 mint sprigs, coarsely chopped
  Dressing*

Combine all ingredients except dressing in large bowl and toss lightly. Just before serving, pour dressing over and toss.

*Dressing

- ¼ cup oil
- ¼ cup lemon juice
- 1 teaspoon salt
- 1 garlic clove, minced
  Salt and freshly ground pepper

Combine all ingredients in jar with tight-fitting lid and shake well. Refrigerate. Shake before serving.

POTATO, HAM AND SWISS CHEESE SALAD WITH SHALLOT DRESSING

See photograph page 71

A pleasant rustic salad, perfect for a picnic or light supper.

4 SERVINGS

- 1½ pounds new potatoes (preferably red-skinned variety)
- 3 tablespoons white wine
- 2 tablespoons white wine vinegar
- 2 tablespoons minced shallot
- 1½ tablespoons Dijon mustard
- ¾ teaspoon salt

¼ teaspoon freshly ground pepper

½ cup olive oil

¼ cup minced fresh parsley

¾ pound cooked ham, julienned and chilled (about 2 cups)

½ pound imported Swiss cheese, coarsely shredded or julienned and chilled (about 2½ cups)

Finely shredded red cabbage or coarsely shredded chicory

½ cup walnut halves, toasted

Boil potatoes in lightly salted water until barely tender. Drain in colander. When cool enough to handle, cut in 1½-inch pieces into large bowl, peeling only if skin is coarse.

Combine next 6 ingredients in jar with tight-fitting lid and shake well. Add oil and parsley and mix well. Pour ⅔ of dressing over potatoes and toss lightly. Cover and cool at room temperature.

Add ham, cheese and half of remaining dressing and blend well. Toss cabbage or chicory with remaining dressing and arrange on platter. Mound salad in center and sprinkle with toasted nuts.

QUICK MIXED SALAD

Adaptable to any number of servings. Be sure to use first 4 ingredients in equal amounts.

Young uncooked string beans, halved or quartered

Onions, coarsely chopped

Pepperoni, sliced

Feta cheese, rinsed, patted dry and crumbled

Generous dash of oregano leaves

Cheese-garlic salad dressing mix to taste (use dry)

Combine all ingredients and toss lightly. Arrange attractively on serving platter.

SAUERKRAUT SALAD

8 SERVINGS

⅓ cup salad oil

⅓ cup vinegar

1 2-pound jar sauerkraut, drained

1 cup chopped onion

1 cup shredded carrots

1 cup diced green pepper

⅔ to ¾ cup sugar to taste

Boil oil and vinegar in small saucepan 3 minutes. Let cool. Combine remaining ingredients and pour dressing over. Cover and chill. Drain and toss well before serving.

SPINACH, BACON AND APPLE SALAD

6 SERVINGS

¼ cup olive oil

3 tablespoons wine vinegar

1 teaspoon sugar

½ teaspoon prepared mustard

Salt and freshly ground pepper

5 slices bacon

⅓ cup sliced almonds

1 pound fresh spinach (stems discarded), torn into bite-size pieces

1 unpeeled red apple, cored and coarsely chopped

3 green onions, thinly sliced

Combine first 4 ingredients with salt and pepper in jar with tight-fitting lid and shake well. Refrigerate until ready to use.

Cook bacon in large skillet over medium-high heat until browned and crisp. Drain well on paper towels. Crumble and set aside. Discard all but 1 tablespoon fat from skillet. Add almonds to skillet and shake pan over medium-high heat until nuts are lightly toasted. Remove from heat. Combine spinach with bacon, apple, onion and almonds and toss lightly. Shake dressing, pour over salad and toss again.

FISH AND SHELLFISH

AVOCADO AND SHRIMP SALAD

See photograph page 65

4 SERVINGS

3 tablespoons olive oil

2 tablespoons white wine vinegar (preferably French)

1 teaspoon Dijon mustard

1 pound fresh shrimp, cooked, shelled, deveined and cubed

1 cup mayonnaise

2 tablespoons chili sauce

1 large garlic clove, crushed

Hot pepper sauce

Salt and freshly ground pepper

1 ripe large avocado

Juice of ½ lemon

2 tablespoons finely minced fresh dill

2 tablespoons finely minced fresh chives

Dill sprigs, lemon wedges and avocado slices (garnish)

Whisk together first 3 ingredients until well blended. Add to shrimp, toss thoroughly, cover and marinate.

Meanwhile, whisk mayonnaise, chili sauce, garlic, hot pepper sauce, salt and pepper until smooth. Set aside.

Peel, pit and cube avocado. Sprinkle with lemon juice.

Drain shrimp. Add cubed avocado, dill and chives and toss lightly. Fold in enough mayonnaise mixture to coat lightly. Taste and adjust seasoning. Cover and chill until ready to serve.

Divide salad among chilled plates and garnish with dill sprigs, lemon wedges and avocado slices.

ORIENTAL SURPRISE SALAD

6 SERVINGS

- 1 20- to 24-ounce package frozen tiny peas, thawed and drained
- 1 8-ounce can shrimp, lobster or crab
- 1 cup finely chopped celery
- ¾ cup mayonnaise
- 1 tablespoon fresh lemon juice
- ½ teaspoon curry powder
  Garlic salt
- ½ cup unsalted cashews
- 1 5½-ounce can chow mein noodles
  Lettuce leaves (garnish)

Combine first 7 ingredients in large bowl and toss well. Cover and refrigerate at least 30 minutes. Add cashews and noodles and toss again. Serve on lettuce.

SHRIMP AND CARNATION SALAD

4 SERVINGS

- 1 pound cooked shrimp, chilled
- 1 11-ounce can mandarin orange sections, drained
- ¼ cup thinly sliced red onion or ¼ cup chopped green onion
- ¼ cup almonds, lightly toasted
- 3 tablespoons fresh lemon juice
- 2 tablespoons honey
- 1 teaspoon sesame seeds, lightly toasted
- 1 teaspoon salt
- ½ teaspoon ginger
  Endive and watercress
- 4 carnations, washed (stalks removed and discarded)

Combine all ingredients except carnations in large salad bowl and toss gently but thoroughly to mix. Divide among plates and garnish each with carnation.

SHRIMP AND SCALLOP SALAD WITH SNOW PEAS

See photograph pages 66-67

4 SERVINGS

- 2 dozen large shrimp, shelled and deveined

- 1½ pounds scallops
- ½ pound snow peas
- 2 cucumbers, peeled, seeded and sliced

Mustard Dressing

- ⅓ cup water
- ⅓ cup white vinegar
- ¼ cup vegetable oil
- 3 tablespoons light soy sauce
- 2 to 3 tablespoons dry mustard or to taste
- 2 tablespoons sesame oil
- 2 tablespoons dry sherry
- 1 tablespoon sugar
  Salt
- 4 celery stalks, thinly sliced

Cook shrimp in boiling water until just pink. Drain well and transfer to bowl. Cook scallops in boiling water until translucent; drain well. Add to shrimp and set aside to cool.

Place snow peas in colander and pour boiling water over; drain well. Transfer to another bowl, add cucumber and toss lightly. Let cool.

For dressing: Combine all ingredients in small bowl. Set aside.

Add celery to seafood mixture and blend well. Add half of dressing and toss to coat. Add remaining dressing to snow pea-cucumber mixture and toss well. Mound seafood on serving platter and surround with snow pea mixture. Chill slightly before serving.

SQUID SALAD WITH GREEN GINGER SAUCE

See photograph page 72

2 SERVINGS

- 1¼ pounds squid
  Boiling water

Green Ginger Sauce

- ¼ cup vegetable oil
- 3 to 4 tablespoons green onion, finely chopped
- 2 tablespoons dry sherry
- 1 1-inch piece fresh ginger, peeled and cut into several pieces

- Juice of 1 lemon
  Salt
- 2 green peppers, seeded and finely shredded
- 1 cup finely shredded bamboo shoots
- 1 small leek (white part only), finely shredded
- 1 medium carrot, finely shredded

Open and clean squid. Score diamond pattern on underside and cut into 1-inch pieces. Cook in boiling water until white and curled, about 1 minute; do not overcook. Drain well and let cool.

For sauce: Combine all ingredients in food processor and mix until onion and ginger are finely minced.

Combine remaining ingredients in bowl and toss lightly. Arrange on platter. Toss squid in sauce and arrange over vegetables. Spoon any remaining sauce over top. Serve at room temperature.

MARINATED BEAN, TUNA AND TOMATO SALAD

6 TO 8 SERVINGS

- 2 20-ounce cans cannellini beans
- ¼ cup olive oil
- 1 tablespoon fresh lemon juice
- ½ teaspoon oregano
  Salt and freshly ground pepper
- 1 12½- or 13-ounce can tuna, drained and separated into chunks
- 2 medium tomatoes, chopped
- 1 small onion or 2 green onions, minced
- 2 tablespoons chopped fresh parsley

Place beans in colander and rinse thoroughly with cold water. Dry on paper towels and transfer to large serving bowl. Combine oil, lemon juice, oregano, salt and pepper in small bowl or jar with lid and stir or shake well. Pour over beans. Add tuna, tomatoes, onion and parsley, and toss gently to combine. Chill well before serving.

MOCK CRAB SALAD

A great way to serve leftover rice.

6 TO 8 SERVINGS

- 2 cups cold cooked rice
- 1 13-ounce can tuna, drained and flaked
- 1 4-ounce jar pimientos, diced (optional)
- 4 green onions, finely sliced or 1 to 2 tablespoons instant minced onion, rehydrated
  Mayonnaise
  Onion and garlic powders
  Salt and freshly ground pepper
  Lettuce leaves
  Parsley sprigs

Combine rice, tuna, pimientos and green onions with mayonnaise to moisten in medium bowl. Add seasonings to taste and mix well. Serve on lettuce-lined salad plates and garnish with sprigs of parsley.

SALADE PROVENCALE

4 TO 6 SERVINGS

- 3 cups cooked rice
- 1½ to 2 cups canned white beans, rinsed and drained
- 2 7½-ounce cans tuna, drained
- ½ cup chopped green pepper
- ½ cup chopped red onion
- ½ cup chopped green olives
- ¼ cup fresh lemon juice
- 3 tablespoons olive oil
- 1 tablespoon wine vinegar
- 1 teaspoon salt
  Freshly ground pepper
  Lettuce leaves
  Tomato wedges and quartered hard-cooked eggs (garnish)

Combine all ingredients except lettuce and garnish in large mixing bowl and toss thoroughly. Cover and chill overnight. Line salad bowl or platter with lettuce and mound salad in center. Garnish with tomato wedges and hard-cooked eggs.

Salade Provençale may also be served in well-drained, hollowed-out tomatoes.

TERRIFIC TUNA SALAD

4 TO 6 SERVINGS

- 2 7½-ounce cans white tuna, well drained and flaked
- 2 medium-size ripe tomatoes, cut into wedges
- ¼ head lettuce, broken into small pieces
- ¼ pound fresh mushrooms, sliced
- ½ pound Muenster, Jack or mild cheddar cheese (or a combination) cut into 1-inch cubes
- 1 tablespoon capers
- 1 ripe avocado, peeled, pitted and chopped
  Vinaigrette Dressing*

Assemble all ingredients except avocado and dressing in large salad bowl. Chill. Add avocado and Vinaigrette Dressing just before serving.

*Vinaigrette Dressing

- ½ cup olive oil
- 3 tablespoons wine vinegar
- 1 teaspoon sugar
- 1 garlic clove, peeled
  Dash of seasoned salt
  Pinch of oregano
- 1 teaspoon red wine

Place all ingredients in jar and let stand for several hours or overnight in the refrigerator. Discard garlic clove before serving.

TUNA, PASTA, BROCCOLI AND RED PEPPER SALAD
See photograph page 69

4 SERVINGS

Dressing

- ½ cup olive oil
- 2 tablespoons red wine vinegar
- 2 tablespoons drained capers
- 1 teaspoon crumbled oregano leaves
- ¾ teaspoon salt
- ½ teaspoon finely minced garlic
- ¼ teaspoon freshly ground pepper

Salad

- 1 bunch broccoli
- ½ pound freshly cooked farfalle noodles or shell macaroni
- 3 to 4 red peppers, cut into 1-inch pieces
- 2 7- to 7½-ounce cans solid white tuna, drained and coarsely chunked

For dressing: Combine all ingredients in jar with tight-fitting lid, shake well and refrigerate.

For salad: Peel broccoli stems and cut diagonally ½ inch thick. Divide florets into 1-inch pieces. Steam stems and florets separately in batches until crisp-tender. Transfer to colander and run under cold water until cooled completely. Pat dry with paper towels. Transfer florets to bowl and toss with about ¼ of dressing.

Combine pasta, peppers and broccoli stems in large serving bowl and toss lightly with remaining dressing. Add tuna and toss gently. Make border of florets around salad. Cover and chill before serving.

PASTA AND RICE

CHILLED RICE SALAD

6 SERVINGS

- 1 9-ounce package rice pilaf, cooked according to package directions and cooled slightly
- 1 pound mushrooms, sliced
- 1 bunch green onions, minced
- ¼ cup olive oil
- 3 tablespoons red wine vinegar
- ½ teaspoon Dijon mustard
- ½ teaspoon salt
- ¼ teaspoon freshly ground pepper

Toss rice, mushrooms and onions together in large bowl. Combine remaining ingredients in small bowl or jar with tight-fitting lid and blend well. Pour over rice mixture and toss gently but thoroughly. Cover and let stand overnight before serving. Serve at room temperature.

SWEET AND TART RICE SALAD

4 TO 6 SERVINGS

- 2 cups cooked long-grain rice, chilled
- ½ cup chopped carrots
- ½ cup chopped green onion
- ½ cup chopped cucumber
- ¼ cup white wine vinegar
- 2 tablespoons sugar
- ½ teaspoon salt
- 3 dashes ground red pepper
  Lettuce leaves
  Toasted sesame seeds (garnish)
  Cooked chilled shrimp (garnish)

Combine first 4 ingredients. Mix vinegar, sugar, salt and red pepper. Gently stir into rice mixture. Cover and chill well. Line serving dish with lettuce and mound rice in center. Sprinkle with sesame seeds and garnish with shrimp.

GREEN PASTA SALAD

4 SERVINGS

- 1 pound green noodles
- ¼ to ½ cup chopped green onion (including tops)
- ¼ cup Italian dressing
- 1 2-ounce jar or can chopped pimientos, drained
- ½ to ¾ cup mayonnaise
- ½ to ¾ cup sour cream
  Salt and freshly ground pepper
- ½ cup sunflower seeds, toasted (optional)

Cook noodles in rapidly boiling water until al dente. Cool quickly under cold running water; drain thoroughly. Transfer to large bowl and toss gently with green onion, dressing and pimientos. Combine equal parts mayonnaise and sour cream and add to pasta with salt and pepper. Toss again, adding sunflower seeds just before serving.

This salad will keep several days stored covered in refrigerator.

SPAGHETTI SALAD

24 SERVINGS

- 2 pounds spaghetti
- 2 tablespoons olive oil
- 3 pounds mozzarella cheese, shredded
- 12 tomatoes, chopped
- 6 bunches watercress, finely chopped
- 4 garlic cloves, finely minced
- 3 pounds fresh pea pods
- 3 10-ounce packages frozen green peas, thawed
  Salt and freshly ground pepper
  Freshly grated Parmesan cheese

Cook spaghetti in large pot of boiling water with olive oil until al dente. Drain well. Return to pot, add mozzarella and toss until cheese melts (cheese will be gummy and seemingly inseparable but will break up as other ingredients are added). Cook over low heat 15 minutes. Remove from heat, add remaining ingredients except Parmesan and toss gently but thoroughly (using hands if necessary). Serve at room temperature. Pass bowl of Parmesan cheese.

FRUIT

COOL FRUIT SALAD

4 SERVINGS

- 1 cup plain yogurt
- 1 tablespoon honey
- 1 teaspoon vanilla or almond extract
- ½ teaspoon cinnamon
  Pinch of nutmeg
  Assorted fresh fruit (apples, bananas, pineapple, peaches, strawberries, grapes)
  Shredded coconut (garnish)

Combine first 5 ingredients in small bowl and mix well. Arrange fruit in individual serving dishes. Spoon some of sauce over top. Garnish with coconut.

CRANBERRY SALAD

10 TO 12 SERVINGS

- 2 3-ounce packages cream cheese, room temperature
- 2 tablespoons mayonnaise
- 2 tablespoons sugar
- 1 16-ounce can whole cranberry sauce
- 1 11-ounce can mandarin oranges, drained
- ½ cup chopped walnuts, lightly toasted
- 1 cup whipping cream, whipped

Grease 1½-quart plain ring mold. Line with plastic wrap or foil, overlapping edges by at least 1 inch.

Beat cream cheese with mayonnaise and sugar until smooth. Gently blend in cranberry sauce, oranges and walnuts using wooden spoon. Fold in whipped cream. Pour into mold. Freeze. Unmold onto platter and serve immediately.

CRANBERRY-CITRUS SALAD

8 SERVINGS

- Escarole, Boston and romaine lettuce, washed and chilled
- 2 8-ounce cans chilled cranberry sauce, whole berry style
- 1 8-ounce can grapefruit sections, chilled and drained
- 1 8-ounce can orange sections, chilled and drained
  Pomegranate seeds (optional)
  Sweet-Sour Dressing*

Line a large platter with lettuce leaves. Slice contents of chilled cans of cranberry sauce into four rounds each. Put cranberry slices, grapefruit and orange sections on lettuce. Sprinkle with pomegranate seeds if desired. Serve with Sweet-Sour Dressing on the side.

*Sweet-Sour Dressing

MAKES ½ CUP

- ½ cup mayonnaise
- 1 tablespoon honey
- 2 teaspoons vinegar

½ teaspoon celery seeds

Combine all ingredients and refrigerate until ready to use. (This is best if made ahead.)

TOSSED FRUIT SALAD

8 SERVINGS

Dressing

- 1 cup safflower oil
- ⅓ cup white vinegar
- ¼ cup sugar or to taste
- 1 tablespoon poppy seeds (optional)
- 1 teaspoon dry mustard
- 1 teaspoon salt

Salad

- 2 heads lettuce, washed, dried and torn into bite-size pieces
- 1 pint fresh strawberries (if available), hulled and halved
- 2 oranges, peeled and diced
- 2 avocados, peeled and diced

For dressing: Combine ingredients in blender and mix until thickened. Chill thoroughly.

For salad: Combine ingredients except avocado in salad bowl. Cover and chill. Add avocado just before ready to serve.

Pour dressing over and toss to coat.

VERMONT FRUIT SALAD

8 TO 10 SERVINGS

- 2 cups plain yogurt
- 3 tablespoons maple syrup
- ½ teaspoon cinnamon
- 1 pound trail mix
- 3 large navel oranges, peeled and separated into sections
- 3 large bananas, peeled and sliced into ¼-inch rounds
- 3 large firm pears, quartered, cored and sliced
- 2 pink grapefruits, peeled and separated into sections.

Mix first 3 ingredients in small bowl. Combine remaining ingredients in large serving bowl. Pour sauce over and toss lightly. Cover and chill thoroughly. Toss before serving.

WINTER FRUIT SALAD

4 SERVINGS

- 2 firm medium apples, cored and cubed
- 2 bananas, halved lengthwise, then cut into 1-inch pieces
- 8 dried apricots or 4 dried peach or nectarine halves, coarsely chopped
- 4 dried pitted prunes, coarsely chopped
- ½ cup raisins
- 3 to 5 heaping tablespoons plain yogurt
- ½ tablespoon honey
  Dash of nutmeg
- 1 to 2 tablespoons orange or apple juice or Grand Marnier
- 2 tablespoons coarsely chopped toasted almonds

Combine first 8 ingredients in medium bowl and mix well. Stir in juice or liqueur to taste. Cover and chill. When ready to serve, gently mix in almonds.

SALAD DRESSINGS

BLEU BUTTERMILK DRESSING

MAKES ABOUT 2 CUPS

- 1 cup mayonnaise
- ¾ cup crumbled bleu cheese
- ½ cup buttermilk or plain yogurt
- 2 garlic cloves, minced
- 1 teaspoon Worcestershire sauce
- ½ teaspoon dry mustard
- 3 dashes hot pepper sauce
  Freshly ground pepper

Combine all ingredients in jar. Cover tightly and shake well. Refrigerate until ready to use. Shake again before serving.

CAPER VINAIGRETTE

MAKES ABOUT 4½ CUPS

- 2½ cups oil
- 1 cup white wine vinegar
- ½ cup fresh lemon juice
- ½ cup capers, rinsed and drained

- 1 tablespoon sugar
- 1 teaspoon salt
- ½ teaspoon freshly ground white pepper

Combine all ingredients in mixing bowl and blend well. Cover and refrigerate. Stir and adjust seasoning before serving.

CREAMY VINAIGRETTE SALAD DRESSING

MAKES ABOUT 1½ CUPS

- ½ cup oil
- ½ cup half and half
- 1 egg, lightly beaten
- 1 garlic clove, minced
- 5 tablespoons tarragon vinegar
- 2 tablespoons olive oil
- 2 teaspoons salt
- 1 teaspoon freshly ground white pepper
- ½ teaspoon freshly ground pepper
- ½ teaspoon dry mustard
- ¼ teaspoon sugar
  Juice of ½ lemon

Combine all ingredients in jar with tight-fitting lid and shake well. Refrigerate. Shake again before using.

HERBED BUTTERMILK DRESSING

MAKES ABOUT 2 CUPS

- 1 cup buttermilk
- 1 cup mayonnaise
- 1½ teaspoons fresh lemon juice
- 1½ teaspoons parsley flakes
- 1 teaspoon salt
- ½ teaspoon dried chives
- ¼ teaspoon dried oregano, crumbled
- ¼ teaspoon dried basil, crumbled
- ¼ teaspoon dried tarragon, crumbled
- ¼ teaspoon garlic powder
  Freshly ground pepper

Whisk all ingredients in small bowl until well blended. Pour into jar. Cover and refrigerate thoroughly.

Crumbled bleu cheese can be added.

ORIENTAL SALAD DRESSING

MAKES ABOUT 1½ CUPS

- ⅓ cup vinegar
- ¼ cup soy sauce
- 2 tablespoons water
- 1 tablespoon sesame oil
- ½ teaspoon sesame seeds
- ⅔ cup oil

Combine first 5 ingredients in jar with tight-fitting lid and shake well. Add oil and shake again. Chill until ready to serve.

SWEET AND SOUR DRESSING

4 TO 6 SERVINGS

- 3 hard-cooked eggs, separated
- ⅓ cup oil
- ¼ cup sugar
- ½ teaspoon salt
- ½ teaspoon celery seeds
- ⅓ cup vinegar
  Freshly ground pepper

Mash egg yolks in small bowl; chop whites separately and refrigerate. Blend oil, sugar, salt and celery seeds with yolks. Cover and chill. Just before serving, add vinegar and pepper and mix thoroughly. Pour over salad greens and toss lightly. Sprinkle with egg whites.

SOY-SESAME VINAIGRETTE FOR BIBB LETTUCE

Reprinted with permission of Barbara Kafka from the as yet untitled book to be published by Harper & Row in 1981.

Colonel Bibb was a genuine Kentucky colonel who bred an outstanding lettuce. It deserves to have dressing as special as it is.

MAKES ABOUT ½ CUP

- ¼ cup olive oil
- 2½ tablespoons tarragon vinegar
- 2½ tablespoons Japanese soy sauce
- ¼ teaspoon tightly packed chopped fresh tarragon leaves (if available) or pinch of dried

- ⅛ teaspoon coarse salt
- ⅛ teaspoon dry mustard
- ⅛ teaspoon (scant) oriental sesame oil
  Freshly ground pepper

Mix all ingredients in small bowl.

VINAIGRETTE DRESSING

MAKES ABOUT ½ CUP

- 6 tablespoons olive oil
- 2 tablespoons lemon juice
- 1 teaspoon Dijon mustard
- ½ teaspoon sugar
- 1 garlic clove, halved
- 1 teaspoon salt
  Freshly ground pepper

Combine all ingredients and blend thoroughly. Remove garlic clove before serving.

DO AHEAD

AVOCADO FROSTED CAULIFLOWER SALAD

6 TO 8 APPETIZER SERVINGS OR 4 MAIN COURSE SERVINGS

- 1 head cauliflower

Marinade

- 6 tablespoons salad oil
- 3 tablespoons white vinegar
  Salt and freshly ground pepper

Sauce

- 3 medium avocados
- 1 small onion, minced
- 3 tablespoons marinade
  Dash of nutmeg
  Salt
  Toasted sliced almonds
  Lettuce leaves
  Cherry tomatoes (garnish)

Steam cauliflower until tender but still firm. Place in bowl.

For marinade: Combine ingredients and pour over cauliflower while still warm. Chill overnight.

For sauce: Mash avocados with fork in medium bowl. Add onion, mari-

nade, nutmeg and salt and mix well. Frost cauliflower completely. Cover with toasted almonds. Serve on bed of lettuce and garnish with cherry tomatoes.

GRATED BEET AND CAVIAR SALAD

8 TO 10 SERVINGS

- 1½ pounds raw beets, well chilled*
- 1 small white onion, finely chopped
- 2 tablespoons Italian olive oil
- 2 tablespoons mild wine vinegar
- ¼ teaspoon salt
- ¼ teaspoon freshly ground pepper
- 1 cup sour cream
- 1 to 2 tablespoons grated white horseradish
- 8 ounces salmon caviar

Peel beets and cut julienne. Mix with onion, olive oil, vinegar, salt and freshly ground pepper.

Combine sour cream and horseradish and mix thoroughly.

When ready to serve, drain beets. Mound in rectangular shape on small platter. Carefully spread sour cream down center. Cover with salmon caviar.

*If fresh beets are not available, 3 8-ounce cans julienne beets can be substituted. Chill well, then drain and pat dry with paper towels.

CALYPSO SALAD

4 SERVINGS

- 1 cup mayonnaise
- 1 tablespoon curry powder or to taste
- 1 tablespoon minced onion
- 1 tablespoon soy sauce
- 1 tablespoon catsup
- 1 tablespoon lemon juice
- ½ teaspoon ground ginger
- 1 pound lump crabmeat, chicken, turkey or tuna
- 1 cup chopped green pepper

1 cup seedless green grapes

1 8-ounce can water chestnuts, drained and sliced

1 8-ounce can pineapple chunks, drained

1 2-ounce jar chopped pimientos, drained
Lettuce leaves

1 cup slivered almonds, toasted
Thinly sliced cantaloupe (optional garnish)
Sliced avocado (optional garnish)

Combine first 7 ingredients in large bowl. Add next 6 ingredients and mix well. Cover and chill overnight.

When ready to serve, shape lettuce into cups on individual plates. Add half of almonds to salad and toss lightly. Divide among lettuce cups. Sprinkle with remaining almonds and garnish with cantaloupe and avocado slices if desired.

CHERRY TOMATO SALAD

8 SERVINGS

1 cup olive oil

½ cup red wine vinegar

2 tablespoons chopped fresh parsley

1½ tablespoons Dijon mustard

1 tablespoon fresh lemon juice

1 tablespoon fresh dill

3 green onions, chopped

1 garlic clove
Coarse salt and freshly ground pepper

2 pints cherry tomatoes, stemmed and halved

1 hard-cooked egg, grated (garnish)
Dill (garnish)

Combine first 8 ingredients with salt and pepper to taste in food processor or blender and mix well. Pour over tomatoes in serving bowl and toss lightly. Cover and chill 1 to 2 hours. Sprinkle with grated egg and additional dill just before serving.

CUCUMBER STICK SALAD

See photograph page 32

4 SERVINGS

2 cucumbers, peeled, halved horizontally, seeded and cut into thin sticks

1 tablespoon cider vinegar or rice wine vinegar or to taste

2 teaspoons soy sauce

1 teaspoon sugar or to taste
Few dashes Chinese sesame seed oil

Place cucumbers in mixing bowl. Cover and refrigerate overnight. Drain off accumulated liquid. Add remaining ingredients and toss well. Serve chilled.

LIMA BEAN, CARROT AND ZUCCHINI SALAD WITH FETA CHEESE

4 TO 5 SERVINGS

4 small, firm zucchini, trimmed

4 to 5 carrots, peeled if desired

1 10-ounce package frozen baby lima beans

1 cup plain yogurt

2 tablespoons corn oil

1 tablespoon fresh lemon juice
Salt and freshly ground pepper

6 ounces feta cheese, rinsed, cut into small cubes
Chopped parsley or watercress sprigs (garnish)

Cut zucchini in half lengthwise. Cut each half lengthwise again and then into strips. Repeat with carrots. Steam carrots 5 to 7 minutes. Add zucchini and steam an additional 5 to 7 minutes. Add lima beans and continue steaming until all vegetables are crisp-tender, transferring to colander as they are cooked and holding under cold running water until cool to touch. Transfer to salad bowl, cover and chill.

Combine yogurt, oil, lemon juice, salt and pepper in small bowl and blend well. Cover and chill thoroughly.

When ready to serve, add cheese to vegetables and toss lightly. Spoon

yogurt mixture over and garnish with parsley or sprigs of watercress.

MAJESTIC LAYERED SALAD

8 SERVINGS

1 cup mayonnaise

½ teaspoon sugar

½ teaspoon curry powder or to taste

4 cups (1 quart) shredded lettuce

2 cups sliced mushrooms

1½ cups thinly sliced red onion

2 10-ounce packages frozen peas, cooked and drained

2 strips bacon, cooked crisp and crumbled

Combine first 3 ingredients in small bowl. Layer half (each) of lettuce, mushrooms, onion and peas in 2½-quart glass bowl. Repeat. Spread sauce evenly over top. Cover tightly and refrigerate overnight. Sprinkle with bacon and serve.

MARINATED SALAD

6 SERVINGS

1 17½-ounce can garbanzo beans, drained

1 16-ounce can pitted black olives, drained

1 8½-ounce can artichoke hearts packed in water, drained

1 8-ounce can green beans, drained

1 4-ounce jar diced pimientos, drained

1 cucumber, thinly sliced

1 16-ounce bottle Italian dressing

1 teaspoon dried dill

1 teaspoon dried oregano, crumbled
Freshly ground pepper

Combine first 6 ingredients in large bowl with enough Italian dressing to moisten. Toss lightly. Add seasonings and toss again. Refrigerate overnight and toss before serving.

PEAS AND BACON SALAD

6 SERVINGS

- 1 cup sour cream
- 1 teaspoon seasoned salt
- ¼ teaspoon lemon pepper
- ¼ teaspoon garlic powder
- 1 20-ounce bag frozen, thawed peas (not cooked)
- ½ pound bacon, cooked, drained and crumbled
- 1 small tomato, diced
- ¼ cup minced red onion

Combine sour cream and seasonings in a medium bowl. Add remaining ingredients, mix thoroughly and chill overnight.

SESAME BEAN SPROUT SALAD

4 SERVINGS

- ½ pound fresh bean sprouts
- 1 4-ounce jar or can sliced pimientos, drained
- ¼ cup chopped green onions
- 2 tablespoons sesame oil
- 2 tablespoons rice or wine vinegar
- 2 tablespoons soy sauce
- 2 tablespoons sesame seeds, toasted
- ½ teaspoon garlic salt
- ½ teaspoon minced fresh ginger
- ½ teaspoon sugar
- ½ teaspoon freshly ground pepper

Rinse sprouts in cool water, drain and place in large bowl. Thoroughly mix remaining ingredients, pour over sprouts and toss. Cover and refrigerate overnight.

SHRIMP, CORN AND TOMATO SALAD

See photograph page 70

A brightly colored salad of fresh shrimp and sweet summer vegetables, enlivened with the bite of hot peppers and cumin.

4 SERVINGS

- 5 large ears corn (about 3 cups kernels)
- ½ small red onion, minced
- ⅓ cup minced fresh cilantro
- 3 tablespoons red wine vinegar
- 1 tablespoon olive oil
- 2 teaspoons minced seeded fresh hot peppers
- 1 teaspoon ground cumin
- 2 teaspoons salt
- 6 cups water
- 1 teaspoon whole peppercorns
- 1½ to 1¾ pounds unshelled small raw shrimp
- 1 small tomato, peeled, seeded and diced
- 1 egg yolk
- ¾ cup olive oil
- 3 medium tomatoes, thinly sliced
- ½ small red onion, thinly sliced and separated into rings
- 1 2-ounce jar small stuffed green olives, drained and sliced (garnish)

Add corn to large pot of boiling salted water. Return to rolling boil. Drain well and cool until easy to handle. Cut off kernels and transfer to large bowl. Add minced onion, 2 tablespoons cilantro, 2 tablespoons vinegar, oil, 1 teaspoon hot peppers, cumin and ½ teaspoon salt. Toss lightly, cover and set aside.

Combine water, peppercorns and 1 teaspoon salt in large saucepan and bring to boil. Add shrimp and immediately remove from heat. Let stand 20 minutes. Drain shrimp, peel and devein. Transfer to bowl, cover and chill thoroughly.

Combine small tomato and yolk with remaining vinegar, hot peppers and salt in blender or food processor and mix until light and fluffy. With machine running, gradually add oil, blending well until sauce is consistency of mayonnaise. Add 2 tablespoons cilantro and mix well.

Cover and chill until serving time. If refrigerated well ahead, let stand at room temperature before using, as sauce should be softly spoonable.

Arrange sliced tomatoes and onion rings around edge of large serving platter. Spoon corn into center, leaving well in middle. Toss shrimp with about ¼ of sauce and mound in well. Garnish salad with sliced green olives and remaining cilantro. Pass sauce separately.

DAY-AHEAD SPINACH SALAD

6 SERVINGS

- ½ to ¾ pound fresh spinach, stems discarded, well dried and torn into bite-size pieces
- ½ medium cucumber, thinly sliced
- ½ cup thinly sliced radishes
- ¼ cup thinly sliced green onion
- 2 hard-cooked eggs, sliced
- ¾ to 1 cup thick commercial bleu cheese dressing
- 5 slices bacon, crisply fried and crumbled
- ½ cup salted Spanish peanuts

Arrange spinach evenly in shallow salad bowl. Layer with all of cucumber slices, then radishes, onion and egg. Spread dressing evenly over top. Cover and chill overnight. Just before serving, sprinkle with bacon and peanuts. To serve, lift out portions with salad spoon and fork, being careful to pick up all layers.

TABBOULEH

See photograph page 129

A zesty salad of bulgur wheat tossed with herbs and an oil and lemon dressing is splendid with lamb cooked in any fashion.

6 SERVINGS

- 1¾ cups bulgur wheat
- 7 cups boiling water
- ¾ cup minced fresh parsley
- ⅓ cup minced fresh mint
- ½ cup minced green onion

1 cup peeled, seeded and chopped tomato
⅓ cup fresh lemon juice
⅓ cup olive oil
  Salt and freshly ground pepper
  Romaine leaves

Measure bulgur into large bowl or saucepan and add boiling water. Cover and let stand until wheat has expanded and is light and fluffy, about 2 to 3 hours. Drain off excess water. Transfer bulgur to sieve and shake until very dry. Return to bowl. Add remaining ingredients except romaine and mix thoroughly. Cover and chill.

To serve, mound tabbouleh in center of large platter and surround with greens. Use romaine leaves as "scoops" for each serving.

ZUCCHINI SALAD WITH SAFFRON

6 SERVINGS

5 tablespoons olive oil
1½ pounds small zucchini, thinly sliced
3 shallots or 1 onion, finely chopped
  Pinch of saffron infused in 2 tablespoons boiling water
1 teaspoon dill seeds or 2 teaspoons chopped fresh dill
1 teaspoon sugar
  Salt and freshly ground pepper
4 to 5 tablespoons white wine vinegar
  Fresh dill or parsley (garnish)

Heat oil in large skillet over low heat. Add zucchini and shallot or onion and cook 5 minutes, stirring occasionally (do not allow mixture to brown). Add dissolved saffron, dill, sugar, and salt, pepper and vinegar to taste. Continue cooking until zucchini is just tender, about 5 minutes. Transfer to salad bowl and let cool slightly. Cover and chill. To serve,

bring to room temperature and sprinkle with dill or parsley.

MICROWAVE

EASY POTATO SALAD

FOR EACH SERVING

1 medium potato (about 7 ounces), rinsed and patted dry (do not pierce)
2 to 3 tablespoons mayonnaise
1 hard-cooked egg, grated
1 small stalk celery, finely chopped
1 small green onion, finely chopped
¼ teaspoon salt
⅛ teaspoon freshly ground pepper
1 large Bibb or Boston lettuce leaf
  Minced fresh parsley (garnish)

Cook potato on High on microwave-safe rack until just done, but still firm, about 6 minutes. Let cool 5 minutes. Peel and cut potato into ½-inch dice.

Transfer potato to bowl. Add mayonnaise, egg, celery, onion, salt and pepper and blend well. Spoon onto lettuce leaf and sprinkle with parsley. Chill thoroughly before serving.

GREEN SALAD WITH DILL DRESSING

5 TO 6 SERVINGS

1 16-ounce can French-style green beans, well drained
1 head butter lettuce, washed, dried and torn into bite-size pieces
1 cup seasoned croutons
  Dill Dressing*
½ cup grated cheddar cheese (garnish)
4 radishes, thinly sliced (garnish)

Combine beans, lettuce and croutons in salad bowl and toss

gently. Cover and chill.

When ready to serve, pour desired amount of dressing over and toss again. Garnish with cheese and sliced radishes.

*Dill Dressing

MAKES ABOUT 1 CUP

⅔ cup oil
¼ cup red wine vinegar
1 tablespoon sugar
1 teaspoon salt
½ teaspoon dill
⅛ teaspoon curry powder
⅛ teaspoon freshly ground pepper

Combine all ingredients in 2-cup glass measure and microwave on High 2 minutes, stirring once. Cover and chill before pouring over salad.

SPINACH SALAD

4 SERVINGS

6 slices bacon, diced
¼ cup vinegar
2 tablespoons water
½ teaspoon salt
¼ teaspoon freshly ground pepper
¼ teaspoon dry mustard
12 ounces fresh spinach, stems removed
4 green onions, thinly sliced
1 cup sliced mushrooms
1 hard-cooked egg, grated

Place bacon in 4-cup measure and cover with paper towel. Cook on High until bacon is crisp. Remove with slotted spoon and drain on paper towel. Add next 5 ingredients to drippings and blend well. Cook on High until mixture boils, about 1 to 2 minutes.

Combine spinach, onion and mushrooms in large salad bowl. Pour hot dressing over top and toss lightly. Sprinkle with grated egg and reserved bacon. Serve immediately.

ENTREES: Fish and Shellfish

Special Hints

■ Baking: With bony fish allow 1 pound per person; for plump fish without head allow 10 to 12 ounces per person. Fish can be any size, but all must be the same size for even cooking. Allow the following cooking times at 350°: For fish weighing 2 to 3 pounds—12 minutes per pound; for fish 3 to 6 pounds—10 minutes per pound; for fish 6 to 12 pounds—9 minutes per pound.

■ Poaching: To oven-poach your fish, place the fillets or steaks in a shallow buttered baking pan and pour over the liquid suggested for the particular recipe. Cover with foil or buttered waxed paper and place in a preheated oven. Count on cooking the fish slightly less than 10 minutes per inch of thickness (measured at the thickest point) from the time the liquid reaches a boil.

■ Watching your weight? For a variation on plain broiled fish, try dipping the fillets in low fat milk and seasoning them with tarragon, dill and onion powder as well as salt and pepper. Broil the fish about 3 inches from the heat source for about 3 to 4 minutes, then baste it with the drippings, turn, baste and season again. Continue broiling the fillets until done, an additional 3 to 4 minutes.

■ Add a crunch to sautéed flounder or fillet of sole: Dip fillets first in lemon juice, then into finely chopped walnuts. Sauté in butter until golden on each side and serve with a puree of broccoli seasoned with salt, freshly ground pepper and finely minced shallots and chopped parsley.

■ Stash a two-pound piece of Nova Scotia or Scotch salmon in the coldest part of the refrigerator, tightly wrapped in plastic or foil. Slice as needed, as thin as onion skin, using your thinnest, sharpest knife. Serve with little dishes of finely chopped onion, drained capers and wedges of lemon. Have a pepper mill handy.

■ To rid clams or mussels of their sand and to plump them, scrub thoroughly and place in deep bowl. Cover with cold water and sprinkle with 2 tablespoons cornmeal. Cover and refrigerate overnight. Rinse and drain well just before cooking.

■ Lemon juice combined with yogurt and dill makes a simple, refreshing sauce for cold poached fish.

FISH

BAKED FISH MOZZARELLA

6 SERVINGS

- 2 pounds thick flounder or sole fillets
- 1 cup shredded mozzarella cheese
- 1 large tomato, thinly sliced
- ½ teaspoon dried oregano
  Granulated garlic
  Salt and freshly ground pepper

Preheat oven to 375°F. Butter large baking dish. Rinse fillets in salted or acidulated water and pat dry. Arrange in single layer in dish. Sprinkle with cheese and layer with tomato. Dust with oregano, garlic, salt and pepper to taste. Bake until fish is opaque, about 10 minutes. Transfer to heated platter and serve.

PESCADO COREY

4 TO 6 SERVINGS

- 6 tablespoons (¾ stick) butter or margarine
- 1½ pounds flounder, sole or haddock fillets
- ½ teaspoon paprika
  Salt and freshly ground pepper
- 6 medium carrots, diced
- 4 to 5 medium potatoes, peeled and thinly sliced
- 2 medium onions, quartered
- 1 16- or 17-ounce can (2 cups) stewed tomatoes
- ¼ cup dry white wine

Preheat oven to 350°F. Spread 2 tablespoons butter or margarine on bottom of 9×13-inch glass baking dish. Season fish with paprika, salt and pepper and place in single layer in dish. Arrange carrots, potatoes and onions around outer edge. Combine tomatoes and wine and pour over. Dot with remaining butter or margarine. Cover with foil and bake until potatoes are tender, about 20 to 30 minutes.

STUFFED FLOUNDER

4 SERVINGS

- 4 tablespoons (½ stick) butter, melted
- 1 2- to 3-pound flounder, boned, or 8 small sole fillets
  Salt and freshly ground pepper

Stuffing

- ¼ cup (½ stick) butter
- ½ cup chopped white onion
- ½ cup chopped celery
- ½ cup chopped shallot
- ¼ cup chopped green pepper
- 1 garlic clove, pressed
- 1 tablespoon flour
- ½ cup dry white wine
- ½ cup milk
- ½ pound boiled shrimp, chopped
- ½ pound lump crabmeat, shredded
- ½ cup breadcrumbs
- 2 tablespoons chopped fresh parsley
- 1 egg, lightly beaten
  Salt and freshly ground pepper
  Cayenne pepper

Preheat oven to 375°F. Grease shallow baking pan with 3 tablespoons melted butter. Brush fish with remaining melted butter and season with salt and pepper.

For stuffing: Melt butter in medium skillet over medium-high heat. Add

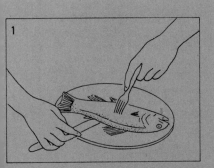

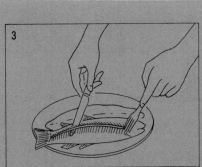

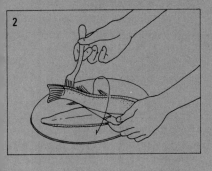

Boning Trout

■ There's no mystery to boning fish at the table. It really is as easy as the maître d' makes it look. Practice this simple procedure.

1. Steady the trout on the plate with a fork in the left hand, the fish head facing left (reverse if left-handed). Insert a fish knife or butter knife about a half-inch deep, just behind the head, and slip it along the entire length of the backbone. Separate the head from the bottom fillet with the knife. 2. Gently lift away the top fillet (including head, bones and tail) and flip it over, skin side down, on the plate. 3. Lift away the head, tail and spine with bones in one piece. 4. *Voilà*, you have a boneless trout feast for your guests.

onion, celery, shallot, green pepper and garlic and sauté just until tender. Blend in flour. Add wine and milk and stir until thickened. Remove from heat. Add next 5 ingredients and mix well. Season to taste with salt, pepper and cayenne.

To assemble: Stuff flounder and press edges together to close. If using fillets, divide stuffing over 4, top with remaining fillets and press edges together to seal. Place fish in baking dish, cover and bake 25 minutes. Remove cover and bake 5 minutes longer to brown lightly.

CREAMED SALMON WITH MUSHROOMS

4 SERVINGS

- 1 tablespoon butter
- 1 tablespoon minced onion
- 1½ teaspoons finely chopped shallot (optional)
- ¼ pound fresh mushrooms, thinly sliced
- 1 tablespoon flour
- ¼ cup dry white wine

- ¼ cup liquid from canned salmon or ¼ cup bottled clam juice
- ¼ cup whipping cream
- 1 tablespoon chopped parsley
  Salt and freshly ground pepper
- 1 1-pound can salmon, drained and broken into bite-size pieces
  Toast triangles or baked patty shells

Heat butter in deep skillet. Add onion and shallot, stirring until onion wilts. Mix in mushrooms. Sprinkle evenly with flour. Add wine and salmon liquid, stirring rapidly with wire whisk until thickened and smooth. Simmer 5 minutes. Add cream, parsley and salt and pepper to taste. Fold in salmon and heat through. Serve over toast triangles or in patty shells.

OVEN-POACHED SALMON

4 SERVINGS

- 4 salmon steaks
- 1 cup white wine
- 1 lemon, thinly sliced

- 1 onion, thinly sliced
- 6 whole peppercorns
  Several parsley sprigs
  Cucumber Sauce*

Preheat oven to 350°F. Place salmon steaks in an ovenproof pan. Pour wine over steaks. Add remaining ingredients except Cucumber Sauce. Cover with buttered waxed paper, greased side down. Poach in oven for 15 minutes.

Serve with Cucumber Sauce.

*Cucumber Sauce

MAKES 1 CUP

- 1 cucumber, peeled and seeded
- 2 tablespoons mayonnaise
- ½ cup sour cream
- 1 tablespoon lemon juice
  Salt and white pepper

Grate cucumber in food processor. Mix thoroughly with remaining ingredients. Serve at room temperature over hot salmon. Or serve chilled over cold salmon.

SALMON ZUCCHINI QUICHE

4 TO 6 SERVINGS

- 1 unbaked 9-inch deep-dish pie shell
- 1 egg white, lightly beaten
- 1 tablespoon butter
- 1½ cups thinly sliced zucchini
- ½ cup chopped onion
- 1 7¾-ounce can salmon, skin and bones discarded, flaked (reserve liquid)
- ⅔ cup grated Swiss cheese
- 3 eggs
- 1½ cups half and half
- ½ teaspoon salt
- 1 teaspoon minced fresh dill or ¼ teaspoon dried dill
  Freshly ground pepper

Preheat oven to 375°F. Brush pie shell with egg white. Melt butter in medium skillet over medium-high heat. Add zucchini and onion and sauté until crisp-tender, about 2 minutes. Let cool slightly. Layer salmon, zucchini mixture and cheese on bottom of pie shell. Beat eggs in medium bowl. Gradually beat in half and half, reserved salmon liquid and seasonings. Pour into shell. Bake until set, about 40 minutes. Cool slightly before serving.

SALMON WITH APPLES, PEARS AND LIMES

See photograph page 132

6 SERVINGS

- 6 salmon steaks, 1¼ inches thick
- 2 tablespoons (¼ stick) butter
  Freshly ground pepper
- 2 limes, thinly sliced (including ends)
- 1 unpeeled apple, halved, cored and thinly sliced
- 1 unpeeled pear, quartered, cored and thinly sliced

Preheat broiler. Place salmon on broiler pan. Melt butter in large skillet over low to medium heat. Sprinkle with pepper. Add lime slices and turn to coat with butter. Add

apple and pear and sauté until butter is absorbed by fruit, about 5 minutes; fruit should be tender but not browned. Remove lime ends from skillet and rub over salmon, simultaneously squeezing juice. Broil about 5 inches from heat source until browned on both sides, about 7 minutes per side. Serve immediately with sautéed fruit.

SMOKED SALMON TART

See photograph page 112

6 TO 8 SERVINGS

- 1 unbaked 9-inch pastry shell
- 1 egg white, lightly beaten
- ½ pound smoked salmon,* chopped
- 1 cup grated Swiss cheese
- 4 eggs
- 1¼ cups half and half
- 1 tablespoon finely snipped fresh dill or 1 teaspoon dried dill
- ½ teaspoon salt
- ¼ teaspoon freshly ground pepper
  Red caviar (optional garnish)

Preheat oven to 400°F. Brush pastry shell lightly with egg white and bake for 5 minutes. Let cool slightly.

Preheat oven to 450°F. Distribute salmon over bottom of pastry and sprinkle with cheese. Beat all remaining ingredients together except garnish and pour over cheese. Bake 15 minutes. Reduce oven temperature to 350°F and continue baking until top is golden, about 15 minutes. Garnish with caviar.

*Use ends and trimmings of smoked salmon if available, as they are less costly and produce the same results.

WHOLE SALMON BAKE

6 SERVINGS

- 1 whole salmon (about 6 pounds), cleaned and scaled
- 3 lemons, sliced
- ½ cup white wine

Preheat oven to 350°F. Place salmon on large sheet of heavy foil. Layer

lemon slices over fish. Pour wine over and seal with foil. Bake until fish flakes when tested with a fork, about 45 to 60 minutes.

FILLET OF SOLE IN TARRAGON BUTTER

3 TO 4 SERVINGS

- 4 tablespoons (½ stick) butter
- ¼ pound mushrooms, sliced
- 1 small onion, chopped
- 1 pound sole fillets
- ¼ cup dry vermouth
- 1½ teaspoons dried tarragon
  Salt and freshly ground pepper

Preheat oven to 350°F. Line 9×13-inch baking dish with foil. Melt butter in medium skillet over medium-high heat. Add mushrooms and onion and sauté until softened, about 5 minutes. Arrange fillets in dish. Pour vermouth over fish. Dot each piece generously with butter and sprinkle with tarragon, salt and pepper to taste. Spoon mushroom mixture evenly over top. Cover with foil and bake until fish loses its translucency, about 30 minutes.

FISH FILLETS FLORENTINE

4 SERVINGS

- 4 6- to 8-ounce sole fillets (or other thin fish fillets)
- ½ cup dry white wine
- 2 10-ounce packages frozen chopped spinach, thawed and well drained
  Salt and freshly ground pepper
- 1 10¾-ounce can cream of shrimp soup, undiluted
- 4 tablespoons (½ stick) butter
  Freshly grated Parmesan cheese
  Paprika

Preheat oven to 350°F. Butter an 8-inch square baking dish. Poach fish in wine 4 to 5 minutes; drain. Spread spinach evenly in dish and season with salt and pepper to taste. Arrange fish over spinach and top with soup. Dot with butter and sprinkle with cheese and paprika. Bake 20 minutes. Serve immediately.

FILLET OF SOLE WITH WHITE GRAPES

2 SERVINGS

½ pound sole fillets
1 tablespoon butter
3 large mushrooms, sliced
24 seedless grapes
¼ cup sour cream
¼ cup mayonnaise
Juice of ¼ lemon

Preheat oven to 350°F. Generously butter au gratin or similar shallow dish. Arrange fish fillets in dish. Melt butter in small saucepan over low heat. Add mushrooms and sauté until softened. Add grapes, stirring gently. Add remaining ingredients and blend well. Spoon over fish. Tent with foil and bake until fish is flaky and sauce is heated through, about 20 minutes.

PARMESAN FISH FILLETS

6 SERVINGS

2 pounds firm fish fillets, ½ inch thick (sole, halibut, sea bass, haddock or scrod)
1 cup mayonnaise
¼ cup snipped chives
1 egg white, stiffly beaten
2 to 3 tablespoons grated Parmesan cheese
1 tablespoon minced fresh parsley
Lemon slices (garnish)

Preheat oven to 425°F. Rinse fillets in salted or acidulated water and pat dry. Arrange dark side down in single layer in large greased baking dish. Combine mayonnaise with chives. Fold ½ to ¾ of egg white into mixture to lighten mayonnaise; do not add too much or mixture will be too loose. Spread evenly over fish.

Sprinkle with Parmesan and parsley. Bake until topping is puffed, about 5 minutes, then broil until top is golden, about 2 minutes. Garnish with lemon slices.

KEDGEREE

4 TO 6 SERVINGS

1½ cups cooked flaked fish
1 cup cooked rice
¼ cup whipping cream
2 hard-cooked eggs chopped
2 tablespoons minced fresh parsley
1 tablespoon butter
1 teaspoon curry powder or to taste
Salt and freshly ground pepper

Combine all ingredients in top of double boiler and blend well. Set over hot water and heat through, stirring frequently.

SHELLFISH

RAMEKINS FRUITS DE MER

6 SERVINGS

4 tablespoons (½ stick) butter
1 shallot, chopped
½ cup sliced mushrooms
½ teaspoon tarragon vinegar
¼ cup sour cream, room temperature
¼ teaspoon dry mustard
Salt
1 cup coarsely shredded lump crabmeat
½ cup coarsely chopped cooked shrimp
1 egg, beaten
Grated Parmesan cheese

Italian seasoned breadcrumbs
Paprika

Melt 2½ tablespoons butter in 10-inch skillet over medium-high heat. Add shallot and sauté lightly. Stir in mushrooms and vinegar and cook 1 to 2 minutes. Remove from heat and stir in sour cream, mustard, and salt to taste. Fold in crabmeat, shrimp and egg. Spoon into individual ramekins and sprinkle with Parmesan, breadcrumbs and paprika. Dot with remaining butter. Run under broiler just until golden.

SAVORY CREAMED CRABMEAT

A simple but satisfying meal. Serve over rice or noodles, accompanied by leaf spinach cooked in butter and seasoned with a dusting of nutmeg.

4 SERVINGS

3 tablespoons (⅜ stick) butter
⅓ cup finely diced onion
⅓ cup finely diced green pepper
⅓ cup finely diced celery
3 tablespoons flour
1¼ cups warm milk
⅓ cup finely diced pimiento
Juice of ½ lemon
Dash of Worcestershire sauce
Salt and freshly ground white pepper
1½ cups flaked crabmeat
Chopped fresh parsley (garnish)

Melt butter in large skillet over medium heat. Add onion and sauté until transparent. Add pepper and celery and sauté until limp. Sprinkle with flour and cook, stirring constantly, until well blended. Gradually add milk, stirring until sauce is smooth and thickened. Blend in pimiento, lemon juice, Worcestershire sauce, salt and white pepper. Add crabmeat and cook 10 minutes, stirring gently. Taste and adjust seasoning as necessary. Sprinkle with parsley just before serving.

CARIBBEAN BAKED CRAB

6 SERVINGS

- 3 6½-ounce cans crabmeat, rinsed and drained, or ¾ to 1 pound fresh crab, drained
- 6 slices bacon, cooked crisp and crumbled
- 1½ cups mayonnaise
- ½ cup dry white wine
- 1 teaspoon vinegar
- 1 teaspoon dry mustard
- ½ teaspoon paprika
- ¼ teaspoon celery salt
- 3 to 5 drops hot pepper sauce
- 6 tablespoons breadcrumbs

Preheat oven to 350°F. Break crab into chunks and divide evenly among 6 individual baking dishes or ramekins. Sprinkle with bacon. Place dishes in large shallow baking pan and warm 4 to 5 minutes.

Meanwhile, combine next 7 ingredients in small bowl and mix thoroughly. Remove crab from oven and preheat broiler. Spoon sauce over crab, top with breadcrumbs.

Place baking dishes 5 inches from broiler and broil just long enough to heat topping through. Serve.

SCALLOPS IN KIRSCH

4 SERVINGS

- 1 pound fresh scallops
- 1 cup chicken stock
- ¼ cup and 1 tablespoon kirsch
- 3 tablespoons (⅜ stick) butter
- 3 tablespoons flour
- ½ cup whipping cream
- 1 teaspoon tarragon
   Grated nutmeg
   Salt and freshly ground pepper
   Cooked brown rice (optional)

Combine scallops, stock and ¼ cup kirsch in medium saucepan and bring to simmer; poach until scallops begin losing translucency. Drain, reserving liquid.

Melt butter in 2- to 3-quart saucepan over medium heat. Add flour and stir constantly to form a roux. Pour in reserved liquid and stir until mixture becomes smooth. Add cream and additional kirsch and cook until thickened, stirring constantly. Stir in tarragon, nutmeg, salt and pepper to taste. Add scallops and simmer about 1 minute. Serve over brown rice.

If desired, divide among scallop shells and place under preheated broiler until sauce is lightly browned and bubbly, about 1 to 2 minutes.

SEA SCALLOP CURRY

3 TO 4 SERVINGS

- 2 tablespoons (¼ stick) butter
- 2 tablespoons oil
- 1 pound sea scallops
- 2 teaspoons curry powder or to taste
- ¼ cup white vermouth
- 1 tablespoon lemon juice
- 1 tablespoon chopped parsley
   Cooked rice

Heat butter and oil in medium skillet. Add scallops and cook a few minutes, stirring constantly. Sprinkle with curry powder and mix well. Cook a few more minutes. Remove scallops and keep warm. To same skillet, add vermouth, lemon juice and parsley. Stir, scraping brown bits from bottom of pan. Pour sauce over scallops and serve immediately over cooked rice.

BAKED SHRIMP

6 TO 8 SERVINGS

- 1 cup (2 sticks) butter, melted
- ¼ cup dry white wine
- ¼ cup minced parsley
- 2 tablespoons fresh lemon juice
- 3 large garlic cloves, minced
- 2 teaspoons basil
- 1 teaspoon Worcestershire sauce
- ¾ to 1 teaspoon hot pepper sauce
- ½ teaspoon salt
- 2 pounds large shrimp (about 32), shelled and deveined, tails left intact
- ½ cup dry unseasoned breadcrumbs

Preheat oven to 450°F. Combine first 9 ingredients in shallow 2-quart baking dish and mix well. Remove ¼ cup of this mixture and set aside.

Add shrimp to baking dish and mix thoroughly. Combine breadcrumbs with reserved butter sauce and sprinkle over shrimp. Bake 10 to 15 minutes. Serve immediately.

Opposite
Avocado and Shrimp Salad gives luster to the flavors of shrimp and avocado.

Page 66
Shrimp and Scallop Salad with Snow Peas balances the subtle flavor of seafood with the crunch of fresh vegetables.

Page 68
Beef Salad with Asparagus and Broccoli is a refreshing treat for any occasion.

Page 69
Tuna, Pasta, Broccoli and Red Pepper Salad is as delightful as an afternoon on the Italian Riviera.

Page 70
Shrimp, Corn and Tomato Salad lends a Latin accent to healthy dining.

Page 71
Potato, Ham and Swiss Cheese Salad is enlivened with toasted walnuts for an inspired garnish.

Page 72
Garden Salad (above) is a dazzling meatless entrée. Squid Salad (below) provides an intriguing change of pace.

Avocado and Shrimp Salad
Recipe page 51

Shrimp and Scallop Salad with Snow Peas
Recipe page 52

Beef Salad with Asparagus and Broccoli
Recipe page 49

una, Pasta, Broccoli and
led Pepper Salad
Recipe page 53

70

Shrimp, Corn and Tomato Salad
Recipe page 58

Potato, Ham and Swiss Cheese Salad
recipe page 50

Above: Garden Salad
Recipe page 50
Below: Squid Salad
Recipe page 52

CHUTNEY SHRIMP ON SHELLS OF PASTRY

6 SERVINGS

- 1 recipe single 10-inch pie crust
- 6 4- to 5-inch extra deep scallop shells
- ½ cup chopped onion
- ¼ cup (½ stick) butter
- 2½ teaspoons curry powder or to taste
- ½ cup chopped chutney (mango preferred)
- 3 cups shelled, deveined small shrimp, cooked
- 1 hard-cooked egg, finely chopped
- 3 tablespoons minced parsley

Pastry shells: Preheat oven to 375°F. Prepare a favorite pie crust recipe.

Roll pastry ⅛ inch thick on lightly floured surface. Oil each scallop shell and line with pastry, trimming edges with dull knife. Gently press pastry against shell so all indentations will be imprinted in the pastry. Place parchment or heavy duty waxed paper atop pastry and weigh down with baker's aluminum pellets,* dried lima beans or rice. Bake on middle rack until pastry shells are golden, about 10 minutes. Allow to cool before removing pastry from shell.

*Aluminum pellets may be purchased at some store houseware sections and in gourmet shops.

Note: Baked shells may be frozen for 2 weeks. Be very careful when wrapping. Bring to room temperature and freshen in 200°F oven 10 minutes before filling.

Pastry shells may also be baked in individual tart or cupcake pans.

For Chutney Shrimp: Sauté onion in butter until golden. Stir in curry powder and chutney; mix well. Add shrimp, tossing until well coated with sauce and heated through. Do not allow to boil. Spoon evenly onto pastry shells. Sprinkle with egg and minced parsley.

Chutney Shrimp is also delicious on rice or toast rounds.

CURRIED SHRIMP IN SOUR CREAM

4 SERVINGS

- 3 tablespoons (⅜ stick) butter
- 1 green pepper, chopped
- ½ cup chopped onion
- 1 garlic clove, crushed
- 1 teaspoon curry powder or to taste
- ¼ teaspoon salt or to taste
  White pepper
  Pinch of turmeric
- 1 pint (2 cups) sour cream, room temperature
- 1¼ pounds cooked shelled shrimp, deveined
  Freshly cooked rice

Melt butter in large skillet over medium-high heat. Add green pepper, onion and garlic and sauté until golden. Blend in curry, salt, pepper and turmeric. Just before serving, add sour cream and shrimp and stir over low heat until warmed through; do not boil. Serve over rice.

EASY SCAMPI

4 SERVINGS

- ¾ cup (1½ sticks) unsalted butter
- ¼ cup finely chopped onion
- 3 to 4 garlic cloves, crushed
- 4 parsley sprigs, chopped
- 1 pound uncooked medium shrimp, deveined
- ¼ cup dry white wine
- 2 tablespoons fresh lemon juice
  Salt and freshly ground pepper

Melt butter in medium skillet over low heat. Add onion, garlic and parsley and sauté until golden; about 10 minutes. Add shrimp and stir just until pink. Remove shrimp and place in ovenproof dish. Cover lightly and keep warm. Add wine and lemon juice to skillet and simmer about 2 to 3 minutes. Season to taste with salt and pepper and pour over shrimp.

PEAS A LA VENITIENNE

See photograph page 130

This is a lovely spring dish. The peas are not presented in their usual role as accompaniment to a main course but are introduced as an appetizer or a simple supper. For supper you may serve a good homemade pâté as an appetizer and for dessert a tray of cheese with a seasonal fruit.

4 TO 6 SERVINGS

- 3 pounds fresh peas, shelled
  Salt
- 1 to 2 teaspoons sugar (optional)
- 1 pound uncooked small shrimp
- ¼ cup (½ stick) sweet butter
- 2 tablespoons minced shallots
- 1 cup cubed prosciutto (use ¼-inch-thick slices)
  Freshly ground white pepper
  Chopped parsley (garnish)
  Grated Parmesan cheese (garnish)

Add peas to 4 cups boiling salted water in a 4-quart saucepan. Simmer uncovered until barely tender, about 5 to 7 minutes. (If using large peas, add sugar to the water.) Drain peas and plunge them into cold water to stop cooking. Drain.

In a 2-quart saucepan, bring 1 cup salted water to a boil. Add shrimp, return to a boil, cook until shrimp just turn pink, about 3 to 5 minutes. Drain and plunge into cold water. Peel and devein.

Melt butter in a 10- or 12-inch skillet and add shallots. Cook until tender but not browned, about 2 to 3 minutes. Add shrimp and shake pan to coat shrimp evenly with butter. Add peas and prosciutto and heat through. Add white pepper to taste. Sprinkle with parsley and serve immediately with bowl of Parmesan cheese on the side.

SEAFOOD SUCCOTASH

See photograph page 106

Reprinted with permission from Irena Chalmers Cookbooks, Inc., AMERICAN WINE/CALIFORNIA FOOD by Barbara Kafka, © 1981.

6 SERVINGS

Succotash

- 1 tablespoon unsalted butter
- ½ teaspoon minced fresh garlic
- 2 10-ounce packages frozen baby lima beans, defrosted (4 cups)
- 2 10-ounce packages frozen corn, defrosted, or 4 cups fresh kernels
- 1 cup whipping cream
- 2 tablespoons snipped fresh chives
- 1½ tablespoons fresh lemon juice
- ¾ teaspoon coarse salt
  Freshly ground pepper

Seafood

- 1 tablespoon unsalted butter
- 1 tablespoon olive oil
- ½ teaspoon minced fresh garlic
- 1 1½-pound live lobster cut into 16 pieces
- 12 large shrimp, peeled and deveined (tails left on)
- 2 tablespoons bourbon
- 4 cups peeled, seeded and coarsely chopped tomatoes
- ½ cup chopped fresh parsley
- 1½ to 2 teaspoons coarse salt
  Generous amount of freshly ground pepper
  Pinch of ground red pepper
- 18 fresh mussels or clams, well scrubbed (mussels debearded)

For succotash: Melt butter in large skillet over medium heat. Add garlic and cook about 30 seconds. Reduce heat, add beans, corn and cream and simmer about 10 minutes. Stir in chives, lemon juice, salt and pepper. If mixture is too thick, add a little more cream.

For seafood: Heat butter with oil in large skillet over medium-high heat. When hot, add garlic, then lobster and shrimp, and cook, stirring or shaking frequently, about 1 minute. Add bourbon and ignite, shaking skillet until flame dies. Transfer shellfish to plate.

Return skillet to heat and add tomatoes, parsley, salt and peppers. Cover and cook over high heat until tomatoes begin to give off juice, about 3 minutes.

Add mussels or clams, lobster and shrimp (along with any juices on plate). Cover and cook, shaking pan occasionally, until mussels have opened, about 2 minutes. Taste and adjust seasoning.

Spoon succotash in a ring on each plate and mound seafood in center.

SHRIMP CONGELIA

4 TO 6 SERVINGS

- ½ cup (1 stick) butter
- 2 tablespoons lemon juice
- 1 pound shelled medium shrimp, deveined
- ¼ cup chili sauce or catsup
- 1 tablespoon Worcestershire sauce
  Dash of hot pepper sauce
- 1 cup sour cream
  Grated Parmesan cheese
  Toast triangles
  Lemon wedges (garnish)

Melt butter with 1 tablespoon lemon juice in large skillet over medium heat. Add shrimp and stir-fry until barely cooked, 1 to 2 minutes. Remove shrimp with slotted spoon and keep warm. Stir next 3 ingredients and remaining lemon juice into skillet. Remove from heat, return shrimp to pan and add sour cream. Transfer to individual shells or heatproof dishes. Sprinkle generously with Parmesan and run under broiler until lightly browned. Serve with toast triangles and garnish of lemon wedges.

SHRIMP CURRY

6 TO 8 SERVINGS

- 2 10½-ounce cans white sauce
- 2 tablespoons sherry
- 1 tablespoon Worcestershire sauce
- 1 tablespoon curry powder or to taste
  Pinch of cayenne pepper
- 2 pounds uncooked medium shrimp, shelled and deveined
- 2 4-ounce cans whole button mushrooms, drained
- 1 to 2 6-ounce jars marinated artichoke hearts, drained
- 1½ to 2 5-ounce cans water chestnuts, drained
  Freshly grated Parmesan cheese
  Seasoned salt or paprika
- 3 cups cooked rice (hot)
- 2 6-ounce packages frozen snow peas, thawed, or 1½ to 2 cups fresh
  Salt and freshly ground pepper
  Pine nuts, raisins, chutney, coconut chips or flakes (condiments)

Preheat oven to 425°F. Combine first 5 ingredients and blend thoroughly. Pour into 9×13-inch baking dish.

Alternate shrimp, mushrooms, artichoke hearts and water chestnuts in rows over sauce, standing them up as well as possible. Sprinkle top with cheese and seasoned salt or paprika. Bake until bubbly and top is slightly browned, about 20 or 30 minutes. (It may be necessary to cover with foil if cheese begins browning too fast.)

Just before serving, combine hot cooked rice, snow peas, salt and pepper and toss gently to mix. Place in steamer or strainer, set over 2 inches rapidly boiling water, cover and steam 1 to 2 minutes or until peas are crisp-tender. Serve curry over rice; pass condiments separately.

SHRIMP ETOUFFEE

4 SERVINGS

- ½ cup (1 stick) butter
- ½ cup chili sauce
- ¼ cup chopped onion

¼ cup chopped celery

2 pounds shrimp, shelled, deveined, and seasoned with salt, pepper and cayenne

¼ cup dry white wine

¼ cup chopped parsley

2 tablespoons minced shallot
Freshly cooked rice

Melt butter in large skillet over medium-high heat. Add chili sauce, onion and celery and sauté until vegetables are tender. Add shrimp and wine and sauté until shrimp loses its transparency, about 5 minutes. Stir in parsley and shallot. Serve immediately over rice.

SHRIMP FLAMBE

6 SERVINGS

¼ cup all purpose flour

1 garlic clove, minced

¾ teaspoon salt

¼ teaspoon freshly ground pepper

1 pound medium shrimp, shelled and deveined

¼ cup oil

¼ cup canned diced green chilies

¼ cup dry sherry
Freshly cooked rice

Combine first 4 ingredients in large plastic bag. Add shrimp in batches and coat well, shaking off excess. Heat oil in medium skillet over medium-high heat. Add shrimp and sauté until golden, about 5 to 8 minutes. Blend in chilies. Warm sherry in small saucepan, ignite and pour over shrimp. Spoon over rice.

SCALLOPED OYSTERS

4 SERVINGS

1 cup cracker crumbs

½ cup (1 stick) melted butter

1 teaspoon salt

1 teaspoon Worcestershire sauce

1 cup whipping cream

2 8-ounce cans oysters, drained

Preheat oven to 350°F. Combine cracker crumbs, melted butter, salt and Worcestershire sauce. Place half of the crumb mixture in a 1-quart baking dish or in 4 ovenproof seafood shells. Gently pat.

Combine cream and oysters and place evenly over crumbs. Top with remaining crumbs. Bake until heated thoroughly, 15 to 20 minutes.

DO AHEAD

FISH

COLD BASS IN SORREL SAUCE
See photograph pages 130-131

Accompany with crusty bread and sweet butter and chilled asparagus with lemon dressing.

4 TO 6 SERVINGS

6 cups water

1 carrot, peeled and finely sliced

1 celery stalk, diced

1 large onion, chopped

1 bay leaf

1 large parsley sprig

¼ cup white wine vinegar

8 peppercorns
Salt to taste

1 2½- to 3-pound whole bass (see Note)
Salt and freshly ground white pepper
Sorrel Sauce*
Chopped chives, parsley sprigs, lemon slices (garnish)

Preheat oven to 325°F. In 2-quart pot, combine water, vegetables, bay leaf, parsley, vinegar and peppercorns. Add salt and bring to boil over high heat. Reduce heat and simmer 20 minutes.

Clean and dry fish. Season with salt and white pepper. Place in baking dish large enough to hold entire fish. Pour in boiled stock with vegetables and spices. Butter a large piece of waxed paper and place over fish. Perforate paper in several places with tip of sharp knife. Bake until fish feels firm but flakes easily when tested with tip of sharp knife at thinnest part, about 30 to 40 minutes. Remove from oven and let cool in poaching liquid. Make sauce.

Lift fish from poaching liquid and remove skin. Place on serving platter. Cover fish with sauce, sprinkle with chopped chives and surround with parsley sprigs. Garnish with lemon slices. Refrigerate until serving time.

Note: In addition to bass—striped bass is particularly good if it's available in your area—ocean perch, flounder, pike, red snapper, ling cod or trout can be used with great success in this recipe.

*Sorrel Sauce

1 cup well-washed fresh spinach leaves

2 cups well-washed sorrel leaves

1 cup boiling salted water

2 whole eggs

2 teaspoons Dijon mustard

2 teaspoons white wine vinegar

1 cup peanut oil

3 tablespoons finely minced green onions
Salt and freshly ground white pepper

Add spinach and sorrel leaves to water and cook 2 to 3 minutes. Drain thoroughly, pressing out all moisture. Mince finely and reserve.

In blender or food processor combine eggs, mustard and vinegar; blend until smooth. With machine on high speed, start adding oil by drops, blending until mixture is thick and smooth.

Add spinach and sorrel mixture with onions and blend until smooth. Season with salt and pepper to taste. Chill thoroughly.

The sauce can be prepared one or two days ahead of time and chilled.

SPINACH SOLE WITH PESTO SAUCE

The sunny Italian flavor of the pesto-touched sauce combines well with ratatouille, crusty French or Italian bread and a crisp green salad.

6 SERVINGS

- 6 6- to 7-ounce sole fillets
  Salt and freshly ground pepper
- 1 cup dry white vermouth
- 1 tablespoon fresh lemon juice
- 2 tablespoons (¼ stick) butter
- ¼ cup chopped onion
- 1 garlic clove, minced
- 1 10-ounce package frozen chopped spinach, thawed and very well drained
- ¾ cup freshly grated Parmesan cheese
- ½ teaspoon oregano
  Salt and freshly ground pepper
- 1 cup sour cream
- ¼ cup pesto sauce (available dried or frozen)
  Salt and freshly ground pepper

Preheat oven to 400°F. Pat fish dry with paper towels. Place in single layer in two 9×13-inch baking dishes. Sprinkle with salt and pepper and cover with vermouth and lemon juice. Bake, covered, until fish loses its translucency, about 10 to 15 minutes. Pour off liquid and reserve. Remove fish and set aside to cool. Pour liquid into saucepan and reduce over medium-high heat to ½ cup.

Meanwhile, melt butter in medium skillet over moderate heat. Add onion and garlic and sauté until just golden. Turn into bowl. Add spinach, ¼ cup Parmesan, oregano, salt and pepper and mix well (it will be quite thick). Return fillets to baking dishes. Divide spinach mixture over each, spreading evenly.

Add sour cream and pesto sauce to reduced liquid. Season to taste with salt and pepper. Spoon over fillets and sprinkle with remaining Parmesan. Dish may be covered and refrigerated at this point. Remove from refrigerator 2 hours before reheating.

Just before serving, preheat oven to 350°F. Bake, uncovered, until heated through, about 5 to 10 minutes, then run under broiler several minutes until cheese is melted and bubbly.

SWEET AND SOUR FISH

6 TO 8 SERVINGS

- 1½ cups water
- 1 cup white vinegar
- ¾ cup sugar
- ½ teaspoon salt
- 2 carrots, cut into ¼-inch rounds
- 2 pounds mackerel or cod steaks, fileted and cut into 1-inch cubes
- 1 medium onion, sliced into rounds
- 2 celery stalks, cut into 2-inch pieces

Combine water, vinegar, sugar and salt in large saucepan and bring to boil. Reduce heat, add carrots, cover and simmer until crisp-tender. Add fish and simmer uncovered until opaque. Remove from heat and immediately add onion and celery. Let cool. Marinate overnight in refrigerator, stirring occasionally. When ready to serve, arrange fish and vegetables on platter and pass marinade separately.

DANISH BAKED FILLETS

With these delicately herbed fillets, consider serving steamed new potatoes with butter and parsley, and slender fresh asparagus.

6 SERVINGS

- 6 6- to 7-ounce fish fillets
- ½ cup chicken broth or more
  Juice of ½ lemon
  Salt
- 3 tablespoons (⅜ stick) butter
- 2 tablespoons flour
- ⅓ cup sour cream, room temperature
- 1½ teaspoons dried dill or 2 tablespoons fresh
  Salt and freshly ground pepper
  Minced fresh parsley (garnish)

Preheat oven to 400°F. Pat fish dry with paper towels. Place in single layer in two 9×13-inch baking dishes. Cover with ½ cup broth and lemon juice and sprinkle lightly with salt. Bake, covered, until fish loses its translucency, about 10 to 15 minutes. Transfer fillets to platter. Measure liquid. If there is less than 1 cup, add chicken broth.

Melt butter in medium skillet over medium heat. Stir in flour and cook several minutes but do not brown. Remove from heat and gradually add reserved liquid. Return to heat, stirring constantly until thick and smooth. Over low heat, blend in sour cream and dill. Do not boil, or sour cream will curdle. If sauce is too thick, add more chicken broth. Season with salt and pepper to taste. Cool thoroughly.

Spoon sauce evenly over fish, covering completely. Dish may be covered and refrigerated at this point. Remove from refrigerator 2 hours before serving.

Just before serving, preheat oven to 400°F. Bake uncovered until sauce is bubbly around edges and fish is heated through, about 10 to 12 minutes. Sprinkle with parsley and serve.

SHERRY-POACHED FISH WITH ORANGES

Serve with rice pilaf, fresh spinach salad with crumbled bacon, chopped red onion and cucumber slices, hot biscuits and a soft, rounded wine like a Johannisberg Riesling or a Chenin Blanc.

6 SERVINGS

- 6 6- to 7-ounce fish fillets
  Salt
- ½ cup dry sherry
- 3 tablespoons (⅜ stick) butter
- 2 green onions, minced
- ½ cup whipping cream

2 tablespoons orange juice
  Slivered zest of 1 orange

Preheat oven to 400°F. Pat fish dry with paper towels. Place in single layer in two 9×13-inch baking dishes. Sprinkle with salt and cover with sherry. Bake, covered, until fish loses its translucency, about 10 to 15 minutes. Transfer fillets to platter. Pour liquid into saucepan and reduce over medium-high heat to ⅔ cup.

Melt butter in small saucepan over medium heat. Add onion and sauté until limp. Remove from heat and stir in reserved poaching liquid, cream, orange juice and zest. Return to burner, bring to simmer over low heat and cook 5 minutes, stirring frequently. Cool. Return fillets to baking dish and cover with sauce. Dish may be covered and refrigerated at this point. Remove from refrigerator 2 hours before reheating.

Just before serving, preheat oven to 400°F. Bake, covered, until sauce is bubbly, about 8 to 10 minutes.

If thicker sauce is preferred, dissolve 1 to 2 tablespoons flour in small amount of whipping cream in small saucepan or heatproof dish over low heat. Stir into sauce, return to burner and bring to simmer, stirring occasionally, until sauce has thickened.

SPICED FISH

6 SERVINGS

3 cups cooked fish, cut into chunks
  Onion slices
⅔ to ¾ cup white wine vinegar
¼ to ⅓ cup oil
¼ cup water
1 to 2 tablespoons sugar
1 tablespoon pickling spices
1 teaspoon salt

Alternate layers of fish with onion in plastic container with tight-fitting lid. Combine remaining ingredients in small saucepan, bring to boil and boil 3 minutes. Let cool. Pour over fish and onion. Cover and refrigerate overnight, tipping container 2 or more times to mix. Before serving adjust

seasoning to taste (dressing should have sweet-sour flavor).

SHELLFISH

SHERRIED SCALLOPS WITH SNOW PEAS AND BELGIAN ENDIVE

See photograph pages 110-111

The imported Spanish Sherry wine vinegar, available in gourmet shops and specialty food stores, is vital to this dish as it maintains the sweet-tart contrast.

4 TO 6 SERVINGS

1 quart water
1 pound sea scallops, trimmed of tough muscle and halved
3 tablespoons light olive oil
3 to 4 tablespoons imported Spanish Sherry wine vinegar
4 heads Belgian endive, separated
½ pound fresh snow peas, trimmed (do not substitute frozen pea pods), or ½ pound green beans cooked until crisp-tender
  Salt and freshly ground pepper
2 tablespoons minced green onion tops or chives (garnish)

Bring water to boil in saucepan. Add scallops and simmer (do not let water boil) until barely firm, about 1 to 2 minutes. Remove immediately, drain in colander and rinse with cold water to stop cooking process. Transfer scallops to bowl and toss with oil and vinegar. Cover and marinate overnight in refrigerator.

Shortly before serving, arrange endive on platter in sunburst pattern. Top with snow peas. Toss scallops with salt and pepper to taste and mound in center of platter. Sprinkle with onion tops or chives and serve.

COLD BAY SCALLOPS

2 TO 4 SERVINGS

1 cup water
1 cup dry white wine

1 bay leaf
1 large slice fresh lemon
6 peppercorns
1 pound bay or sea scallops
1 cup sour cream
1 cup mayonnaise
2 tablespoons fresh dill
1 tablespoon fresh lemon juice
1 teaspoon salt
¼ teaspoon crushed garlic
¼ teaspoon freshly ground pepper
  Lettuce leaves

Combine first 5 ingredients in medium saucepan and bring to boil. Reduce heat and simmer 5 minutes. Add scallops and continue cooking until scallops are opaque, about 2 to 3 minutes. Drain in colander and rinse under cold running water. Cool slightly, cover and chill.

Combine all remaining ingredients except lettuce and blend well. Cover and chill until ready to use. To serve, arrange scallops on lettuce-lined platter and spoon several dollops of sauce over top. Pass remaining sauce in separate dish.

GRILLED SHRIMP

2 SERVINGS

½ cup dry breadcrumbs
⅓ cup olive oil
1 garlic clove, minced
1 tablespoon minced fresh parsley
1½ teaspoons finely chopped fresh basil
  Salt and freshly ground pepper
1 pound large shrimp (15 or less), peeled and deveined

Combine first 5 ingredients with salt and pepper to taste. Pat generous amount onto each shrimp. Cover and refrigerate overnight.

Position rack in upper third of oven and preheat to 425°F. Place shrimp on baking sheet and bake, turning once, until shrimp lose translucency and coating is golden brown, about 3 to 4 minutes per side (exact time will depend on size of shrimp).

SAUTE OF SHRIMP L'ANTIBOISE

See photograph pages 134-135

4 SERVINGS

- 8 to 10 Italian plum tomatoes, peeled, quartered and seeded
  Salt
- 5 tablespoons full-bodied olive oil
- 1 medium zucchini, finely cubed
  Salt and freshly ground pepper
- 1 red bell pepper, roasted, peeled, cored and finely sliced
- 1 small dried hot chili pepper, crumbled
- 1 pound fresh uncooked shrimp, peeled and deveined
- 2 large garlic cloves, finely sliced
- 1 large sprig fresh thyme
- 3 tablespoons finely minced fresh parsley
- 2 garlic cloves, finely minced
- 2 tablespoons finely minced fresh thyme
  Lemon wedges (garnish)
  French bread

Place tomatoes in colander, sprinkle with salt and let drain in sink 30 to 60 minutes.

Heat 2 tablespoons oil in heavy medium skillet over medium-high heat. Add zucchini, season with salt and pepper to taste and sauté until zucchini is nicely browned. Add red pepper and continue cooking, stirring gently, for 1 minute. Remove from heat and set aside.

Heat remaining oil with chili pepper in heavy large skillet over high heat. When pepper has darkened, remove and discard. Add shrimp, sliced garlic and thyme sprig and sauté, shaking pan constantly, until shrimp turn bright pink. Season with salt and pepper. Discard garlic if it has burned. Add tomatoes and cook until excess liquid has evaporated, 2 to 3 minutes. Add zucchini mixture, parsley, minced garlic and thyme.

Taste and adjust seasoning. Remove from heat and garnish with lemon wedges. Serve directly from skillet, accompanied by French bread.

MICROWAVE

FISH

FILLET OF FLOUNDER AMANDINE

4 SERVINGS

- 4 6- to 8-ounce flounder fillets
- 2 tablespoons dry white vermouth
- 2 tablespoons fresh lemon juice
- 1½ teaspoons salt
- 2 tablespoons (¼ stick) butter, room temperature
- ⅓ cup slivered almonds, toasted

Place fish fillets in 7×11 or 9×13-inch baking dish. Sprinkle each with vermouth, lemon juice and salt, then dot with butter. Cover with waxed paper and cook 3 minutes on High. Sprinkle with almonds, rotate ½ turn and cook until fish barely flakes when tested with a fork, about 3 minutes. Let stand several minutes before serving.

FLOUNDER FILLETS WITH LEMON-YOGURT

4 SERVINGS

- 4 flounder fillets (about 1½ pounds total weight)
- ⅓ cup plain yogurt
- 2 tablespoons fresh lemon juice
- 1 tablespoon Dijon mustard
- 1 tablespoon prepared horseradish

Place fillets side by side in shallow glass baking dish. Blend yogurt, lemon juice, mustard and horseradish in a small bowl. Spread mixture over fish. Cover with waxed paper and cook 2 minutes on High. Rotate dish ½ turn. Cook 2 minutes more. Let set, covered with foil, 3 minutes. Fish is properly cooked when it flakes easily with a fork.

BAKED SALMON STEAKS

4 SERVINGS

- 4 salmon steaks, 1 inch thick (defrosted if frozen)
- 2 tablespoons (¼ stick) butter
- 2 tablespoons fresh lemon juice
  Salt and freshly ground pepper
- 1 small onion, thinly sliced
  Paprika
- 8 lettuce leaves, rinsed, undrained
  Lemon slices or wedges

Arrange salmon in 4 corners of 10-inch glass casserole, placing narrow ends of fish toward center. Melt butter 30 seconds on High in glass measuring cup. Add lemon juice, stir and pour evenly over salmon. Sprinkle with salt and pepper to taste. Top with onion slices and a dash of paprika. Cover each steak with damp lettuce leaf. Cook 5 to 7 minutes on High, rotating dish ¼ turn halfway through cooking time. Let stand 5 minutes. Serve with lemon slices or wedges.

MARINATED SALMON STEAKS

4 SERVINGS

- 2 tablespoons olive oil
- 4 tablespoons (½ stick) melted butter
- 3 tablespoons fresh lime juice
- ½ teaspoon salt
- ½ teaspoon pepper
- 1 heaping teaspoon dill
- 4 fresh salmon steaks, ¾ inch thick

In a large measuring cup, or bowl, mix all ingredients except salmon.

Place salmon in a deep dish, pour marinade over fish, and marinate for 1 hour at room temperature.

Preheat browning skillet according to directions. Remove salmon from marinade and cook 2½ minutes on High; carefully turn (using a wide spatula), and cook 3 minutes more. Let set, covered, 2 minutes.

SHELLFISH

LOBSTER TAILS WITH CAPER BUTTER

4 SERVINGS

- 4 6-ounce lobster tails
- 2 tablespoons (¼ stick) melted sweet butter
- 1 tablespoon drained and rinsed capers
- 3 tablespoons (⅜ stick) butter
- ½ teaspoon pepper
- 2 tablespoons lemon juice

Cut the lobster tails lengthwise through shell, then open flat. In a glass dish, place the tails meat side up and liberally brush with melted butter. Cook 2 minutes on High; rotate dish ½ turn, cook 2 minutes more.

In a glass cup, place the capers, butter and pepper and cook on High until butter is melted and mixture begins to simmer, about ½ minute.

Add lemon juice and cook 5 seconds. Pour over the lobster tails.

SCAMPI

2 SERVINGS

- 2 large garlic cloves, minced
- 2 tablespoons corn oil
- 2 tablespoons dry white wine
- 2 tablespoons minced fresh parsley
- ⅛ teaspoon paprika
- ⅛ teaspoon onion powder
- ¾ pound large uncooked shrimp, cleaned, shelled (leave tails intact) and deveined, butterflied if desired
  Juice of ½ lemon
  Salt and freshly ground pepper
  Minced fresh parsley (garnish)

Combine garlic and oil in au gratin-type dish just large enough to accommodate shrimp. Cook on High 2 minutes. Add wine, parsley, paprika and onion powder and continue cooking on High 3 minutes. Add

shrimp, lemon juice, salt and pepper and stir to coat shrimp. Arrange shrimp with thickest part toward outside of dish. Cover with paper towel and cook on High, stirring once, until shrimp are just pink, about 3½ minutes; do not overcook or shrimp will be tough. Garnish with parsley.

Sauce can be reduced if desired. Remove shrimp with slotted spoon and cook liquid uncovered on High until desired flavor and thickness, about 1 to 2 minutes.

SHRIMP VERACRUZ

This recipe is a microwave adaptation of a dish originally developed to honor the president of Mexico and the wonderful shellfish the country provides. Cooking time for the onion and green pepper will leave them rather crisp, so if you prefer them less crunchy, cook a bit longer before adding shrimp.

4 SERVINGS

- 1 large onion, cut into chunks
- 1 large green pepper, seeded and cut into chunks
- 2 tablespoons oil
- 2 garlic cloves, crushed
- 1 8-ounce can tomato sauce
- ¼ cup dry white wine
- ½ teaspoon dried oregano
- ½ teaspoon salt
- ¼ teaspoon ground cumin
  Dash of hot pepper sauce
- 1 pound uncooked jumbo shrimp, shelled and deveined
- 2 tablespoons chopped fresh parsley (garnish)
  Freshly cooked rice or noodles

Combine onion, pepper, oil and garlic in shallow baking dish. Cook on High 3 minutes. Stir in tomato sauce, wine, oregano, salt, cumin and pepper sauce. Cover with waxed paper and cook on High 5 minutes. Add shrimp and toss lightly to coat with sauce. Cook on High until shrimp just turn pink, about 5 to 7 minutes. If you notice several shrimp are done before the others, move

them to center of dish, leaving uncooked shrimp on outside. Serve immediately, garnished with parsley and accompanied by hot rice or freshly cooked noodles.

SEAFOOD COMBO

5 TO 6 SERVINGS

- ½ cup minced celery (optional)
- ¼ cup minced onion
- 1 garlic clove, minced
- 2 tablespoons (¼ stick) butter
- ¾ pound scallops, cut into ½-inch pieces
- ¾ pound perch fillets (or other fillets as available), cut into ½-inch pieces
- ¼ cup seasoned breadcrumbs
- 1 tablespoon minced parsley
- 1 tablespoon butter
- 1 tablespoon flour
- ¼ teaspoon paprika
- ½ cup milk
- 2 tablespoons dry or medium sherry
  Salt and freshly ground pepper
  Paprika
  Buttered seasoned breadcrumbs

Combine celery, onion, garlic and 2 tablespoons butter in 1-quart glass casserole and microwave on High 2 to 3 minutes, stirring halfway through cooking time. Add scallops, fish, breadcrumbs and parsley and stir to blend well.

Microwave 1 tablespoon butter in 1-cup glass measure on High 30 seconds to melt. Stir in flour and paprika and blend. Add milk and sherry and microwave on High, stirring every 30 seconds, until sauce comes to boil and is thick, about 2 to 2½ minutes.

Pour sauce over fish mixture and stir to blend well. Microwave on High 5 to 6 minutes, stirring halfway through cooking time. Season with salt and pepper and sprinkle with additional paprika and crumbs before serving.

Boning a chicken breast

■ If you can't coerce a cooperative butcher into boning a chicken breast for you, learn how to do it yourself.

1. First put the whole breast (select large ones, about one pound each) skin side up on a flat surface. If the recipe calls for skinless breasts, run your thumbs between the flesh and skin to loosen the skin. Hold the breast firmly in one hand and pull off the skin with the other. Beginners may use a knife to remove any meat that clings to the skin.

Slip the knife point under the long first rib on the left and loosen it to make a little handle. Hold the handle in your left hand and lift. 2. Using your knife to ease the meat away from the bone, pull the rib cage bones away from the meat. Repeat this process on the right side and all you have left is the wishbone. 3. Cut that out with the point of your knife and you're ready to go. (Don't forget to put the bones in a pot with some water, carrots, onion, celery and a bay leaf to brew your own broth.) With a supply of boned breasts on hand, you are just minutes away from dozens of glamorous dishes that can be made quickly.

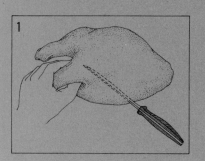

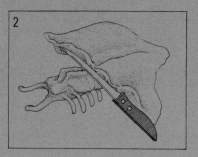

CHICKEN

BASIC ROAST CHICKEN

Boiled new potatoes tossed with butter and chives and the season's first asparagus would be fine accompaniments. A Pinot Chardonnay will round out the menu perfectly.

2 TO 4 SERVINGS

- 1 2½- to 3-pound fryer*
- 1 garlic clove, split
- ½ teaspoon salt
- ⅛ teaspoon freshly ground pepper

Preheat oven to 350°F. Remove fat from rear cavity of chicken. Rinse chicken under cold running water and pat dry with paper towels inside and out. Rub bird inside and out with split garlic and then place garlic in cavity. Sprinkle chicken with salt and pepper. Place breast side down in shallow roasting pan.

Roast until leg moves easily in its socket, about 25 minutes to the pound, basting several times with pan juices. Turn chicken breast up during last 20 minutes of cooking to ensure even browning. Cut into quarters and serve.

*Roasting chicken or capon may be substituted in any of these recipes. Roast smaller birds (3 to 5 pounds) about 25 minutes to the pound, and larger ones (5 to 8 pounds) 18 to 20 minutes to the pound.

BAKED CHICKEN PARMESAN

4 SERVINGS

- 2 cups breadcrumbs
- ½ cup grated Parmesan cheese
- ⅓ cup chopped fresh parsley
- 1 3-ounce can french-fried onions, crushed
- ½ cup (1 stick) unsalted butter
- 2 garlic cloves, crushed
- 1 teaspoon Worcestershire sauce
- 1 teaspoon dry mustard
- 4 whole chicken breasts, halved, boned and skinned

Preheat oven to 350°F. Line 9×13-inch baking dish with foil. Combine first 4 ingredients in shallow dish and mix thoroughly. Melt butter in saucepan over medium-high heat. Add garlic and sauté about 1 minute. Remove from heat. Stir in Worcestershire sauce and mustard. Dip chicken in butter mixture and then in breadcrumbs, coating well. Arrange in prepared dish. Pour remaining butter mixture over top. Bake until chicken tests done, about 50 to 60 minutes. Serve hot.

BASIL CHICKEN

Garlic mashed potatoes, deep-fried zucchini and Chenin Blanc ably complement the chicken's bouquet.

2 TO 4 SERVINGS

- 1 2½- to 3-pound fryer
- 1 small onion, minced
- 1 large bunch fresh basil

Follow directions for Basic Roast Chicken, adding onion and all but 12 large leaves of basil to cavity. Arrange remaining basil leaves over chicken and roast as directed in basic recipe. Remove basil from cavity and cut chicken into pieces.

BOX SUPPER CHICKEN

2 SERVINGS

Salt
Pepper

Cooking Tips

■ Don't roast your chicken on a rack, because you want the breast to rest in pan juices. But do use a shallow pan rather than a deep one. While your objective is a moist breast, you do not want the rest of the chicken to steam in its own juices. A bird cooked in a shallow pan is surrounded by dry heat, which produces crisp, brown skin and moist tender meat.

■ Keeping the chicken breast side down during the first two-thirds of the cooking time is the secret of moist white meat. Not only will the breast be juicy but the fat from the back will filter down through the bird. Then, for even browning, turn over during the last 20 minutes or so. This rule of thumb also applies when roasting a turkey. And, by the way, the reverse is true of duck

and goose, which have a good deal of fat in the breast area; always roast these breast up.

■ The secret of basting is to wait until the chicken has cooked 20 minutes, pour liquid over the bird and then baste every 20 minutes or so with the pan juices. Pan juices, cider, stock, wine, fruit juices or fruit-flavored liqueurs present myriad seasoning possibilities and ideas.

■ The noble bird may also be seasoned with herbs (thyme, tarragon, coriander, mustard, chervil, marjoram, oregano, basil, bay, dill, cumin, cinnamon, allspice, ginger or savory). Other delicious additions might be soy sauce, honey, onion, garlic, chutneys, tamarind, vinegar or your favorite barbecue sauce. Any one or more of these could be rubbed into the skin or basted over the chicken.

■ Always remember in microwave cooking, test for chicken tenderness after the setting or carryover cooking time. If not quite tender enough, it is a simple matter to microwave for another couple of minutes.

■ Stuff chicken breasts with shredded crabmeat and bake, basting with butter and white wine. Serve with linguine and a tossed green salad.

■ Sauté lots of chicken breasts in butter and oil until golden. Freeze in individual packets. To serve, heat breasts in a basil or oregano tomato sauce. Accompany the moist, succulent chicken with a mixture of either plain, long-grain or wild rice.

■ Marinate raw chicken breasts in lemon, oil, chopped fresh tarragon and salt and pepper before broiling.

1 whole frying chicken, cut in half
Paprika
1 medium tomato
1 medium green pepper
2 tablespoons minced onion
2 cups cooked rice

Preheat oven to 350°F. Thoroughly salt and pepper chicken halves. Sprinkle with paprika. Set aside.

Cut two slices from tomato and set aside. Chop the rest. Cut two slices from green pepper and set aside. Chop the rest.

Combine chopped tomato, chopped green pepper, onion and rice. Pack mixture firmly in chicken cavities. Place on two large sheets of aluminum foil, stuffing side down. Garnish chicken with tomato and green pepper slices. Fold up foil, envelope style. Bake 30 minutes. Unwrap top of foil and cook 15 to 20 minutes.

BREAST OF CHICKEN SHIRLEY

8 TO 10 SERVINGS

4 to 5 whole chicken breasts, skinned, boned and split
Salt and freshly ground pepper

Paprika
¼ to ⅓ cup (½ to ⅔ stick) butter
2 10¾-ounce cans cream of chicken soup
½ teaspoon curry powder or to taste
2 cups sour cream
1 cup sliced mushrooms, sautéed
3½ ounces (1 cup) slivered almonds

Preheat oven to 350°F. Season chicken generously with salt, pepper and paprika. Melt butter in large skillet over medium-high heat. Add chicken and brown quickly on both sides. Transfer to shallow baking dish large enough to accommodate pieces in 1 layer. Combine soup and curry. Pour over chicken, cover and bake 1 hour.

Remove chicken. Stir sour cream, mushrooms and almonds into sauce. Return chicken to dish. Spoon sauce over pieces. Bake uncovered until browned.

CHICKEN-ARTICHOKE-MUSHROOM SAUTE

4 SERVINGS

2 large chicken breasts, boned, skinned and halved
Flour
4 tablespoons (½ stick) butter
8 to 10 mushrooms, sliced
1 15-ounce can artichoke hearts, rinsed and well drained
½ cup chicken stock or broth
¼ cup white wine
Juice of ½ lemon or to taste
Salt and freshly ground pepper

Dredge chicken with flour; shake off excess. Heat butter in medium skillet, add chicken and sauté until golden brown and cooked. Transfer to heated platter. Add mushrooms to skillet and sauté 1 to 2 minutes. Stir in artichoke hearts, stock, wine, lemon juice, salt and pepper to taste and let cook until sauce is reduced slightly, stirring occasionally. Return chicken to skillet and warm through. Serve immediately.

Veal scallops may be used in place of chicken breasts.

CHICKEN WITH ASPARAGUS MOUSSE

This attractive main course goes well with buttered potato balls, tossed green salad and a chilled Chardonnay or Chablis.

6 TO 8 SERVINGS

Mousse

- 1 pound fresh or 1 9-ounce package thawed frozen asparagus
- 3 shallots or green onions, minced
- ⅔ cup hollandaise sauce (homemade or prepared)
- 4 large whole chicken breasts, skinned, boned and halved
  Flour seasoned with salt and pepper
- ¼ cup (½ stick) clarified butter
- ¼ cup dry white wine
- ⅓ cup grated Parmesan cheese

For mousse: Wash and trim fresh asparagus. Cut fresh or thawed asparagus into 1-inch pieces. Place in saucepan with shallots or onions and enough salted water to cover and cook until tender, about 12 to 15 minutes. Drain thoroughly, pressing out all water. Puree in blender or finely chop. Combine asparagus and hollandaise in mixing bowl and keep warm. (May be done ahead.)

Preheat broiler. Place chicken breasts between 2 sheets of waxed paper and pound them until thin (about ¼ inch). Dip chicken in seasoned flour, shaking off excess. Heat butter in 10- to 12-inch skillet over high heat and sauté chicken breasts quickly until golden brown, about 2 minutes on each side. Remove to large shallow casserole. Add white wine to skillet, scraping up any browned bits from bottom. Pour wine over chicken.

Evenly spoon mousse on each chicken breast. Sprinkle with Parmesan and place under broiler until top begins to brown lightly and cheese is bubbling. Serve immediately.

GINGER CREAM CHICKEN

Serve with chutney, curried rice and a salad of crisp cucumbers and watercress in a tart vinaigrette. Any good cold lager or Pilsner beer would go well with this spicy meal.

4 TO 8 SERVINGS

- 4 large whole chicken breasts, skinned, boned and halved
- ½ cup flour
- 1 teaspoon ginger
- 1 teaspoon salt
- ¼ teaspoon pepper
- 6 tablespoons (¾ stick) clarified butter
- 2 green onions, minced
- 3 tablespoons flour
- ¾ cup chicken broth
- ½ cup Madeira
- ¾ cup light cream
- 4 tablespoons minced crystallized ginger

Place chicken breasts between two sheets of waxed paper and pound them until thin (about ¼ inch). Combine flour, ginger, salt and pepper in a bag. Add breasts and coat well, shaking off any excess.

Heat clarified butter in a skillet and sauté chicken breasts until golden, about 2 to 3 minutes on each side, adding onions when chicken is turned. Remove to plate, set aside and keep warm.

Add flour to skillet and stir over low heat about 3 minutes. Blend in chicken broth, Madeira and cream and stir until thickened. Mix in 2 tablespoons ginger. Pour sauce over chicken breasts and garnish with remaining ginger.

HERBED CHICKEN WITH VEGETABLES

4 SERVINGS

- 1 pound new potatoes, cut into 1 × 1½-inch sticks
- ½ pound carrots, cut diagonally into 1-inch chunks
- ½ pound rutabaga, peeled and cut into 1 × 1½-inch sticks
- ½ pound pearl onions
- 1 2½- to 3-pound fryer

- 4 shallots, minced
- 1 teaspoon tarragon
- ¼ teaspoon summer savory
- ⅛ teaspoon marjoram
- ⅓ cup dry white wine
  Watercress (garnish)

Combine all vegetables in steamer basket or colander and steam over boiling water 5 minutes. Refresh under cold running water, let drain and set aside.

Follow directions for Basic Roast Chicken, sprinkling bird with shallots, tarragon, summer savory and marjoram. Roast 20 minutes. Arrange steamed vegetables around chicken and pour wine over top. Continue roasting, basting every 20 minutes with pan juices and turning vegetables to prevent sticking. Vegetables should be lightly browned and tender when chicken is done. If not, transfer chicken to heated platter and keep warm. Increase oven temperature to 400°F and cook vegetables, turning often, until tender and lightly browned. To serve, cut chicken into pieces and arrange on heated platter. Surround with separate mounds of vegetables and garnish with watercress.

For 6 to 8 servings, use 2 fryers side by side. Increase vegetables by one-half for 6 servings; double the amount for 8 portions.

ROAST CHICKEN WITH ROSEMARY BUTTER
See photograph page 109

A vertical roaster cuts cooking time by at least 25 percent and requires little attention.

2 SERVINGS (PLUS ENCORE)

- 1 small garlic clove, minced
- 3 tablespoons (⅜ stick) unsalted butter, room temperature
  Juice of 1 lemon
- 2 tablespoons fresh rosemary or 2 teaspoons dried leaves, crumbled
- ¼ teaspoon salt

⅛ teaspoon freshly ground
pepper
1 2½- to 3-pound frying
chicken, rinsed and patted
dry
½ lemon
Paprika (Hungarian preferred)
½ cup water

If using vertical roaster, place rack in lowest position and preheat oven to 450°F. Combine garlic, butter, lemon juice, rosemary, salt and pepper in processor or blender and mix well (lemon may not blend in completely). Stuff mixture under skin of chicken in breast and thigh areas. Rub skin with cut lemon and sprinkle with paprika.

Set on vertical roaster (or on rack) in shallow roasting pan. Add water to pan and roast chicken 15 minutes. Reduce oven to 375°F and continue roasting until chicken is done (allow about 15 minutes to the pound if using vertical roaster, or about 20 minutes to the pound if using regular rack). To serve, cut into quarters.

SAUTEED CHICKEN BREASTS PRINTANIER

Serve with parslied new potatoes and a well-seasoned salad.

6 TO 8 SERVINGS

1 cup fresh shelled peas
Large pinch of sugar
Salt
2 cups scraped and chopped asparagus spears (¾-inch pieces)
4 whole chicken breasts, skinned, boned and halved
Freshly ground white pepper
Flour
3 tablespoons (⅜ stick) butter
1 tablespoon oil
1 large onion, halved
1 cup chicken stock or bouillon
1 cup whipping cream
Salt and pepper
2 tablespoons beurre manié (1 tablespoon butter and 1 tablespoon flour, mashed into fine paste)
Finely minced parsley (garnish)

Add peas and sugar to 1 cup boiling salted water in 1-quart saucepan and cook over medium heat until just tender, about 5 minutes. Drain and set aside. In same pan bring another cup of salted water to boil, add asparagus and cook until barely tender, about 3 to 4 minutes. Drain and set aside. Separate asparagus tips from stalks.

Season chicken with salt and pepper. Dredge lightly in flour. Heat butter and oil in large heavy skillet over medium-high heat. Add chicken and onion and sauté until golden brown, about 3 to 5 minutes on each side. Remove and set aside. Add chicken stock and bring to boil over high heat; reduce to about 1 cup, 5 to 8 minutes.

Remove from heat and stir in cream. Season to taste with salt and pepper. Bring to boil over medium heat, stirring constantly. Return chicken to skillet, cover and simmer 10 to 12 minutes. Discard onion. Add peas and asparagus except tips, and heat briefly. With whisk stir in beurre manié a little at a time, using just enough so sauce is thick and heavily coats spoon. Taste and correct seasoning. Transfer chicken breasts to serving platter, spoon sauce over and garnish with reserved asparagus tips and parsley.

ITALIAN STIR-FRIED CHICKEN

See cover photograph

4 SERVINGS

3 tablespoons olive oil
1 garlic clove, minced
2 whole large chicken breasts, skinned, boned and cut into 1-inch squares
1 cup fresh or frozen thawed Italian green beans
½ cup chopped red bell pepper
¼ cup chopped green onion (white part only)
½ teaspoon salt
4 medium tomatoes, quartered
4 anchovies, mashed to a paste

2 tablespoons diced pimiento
1 tablespoon capers, rinsed and drained
1 to 2 tablespoons fresh lemon juice
1 teaspoon ground red pepper or to taste

Place wok or large skillet over high heat until very hot, about 30 seconds. Add oil and garlic and stir-fry 10 seconds. Add chicken, beans, chopped red bell pepper, onion and salt and continue stirring until chicken is cooked through, about 3 minutes. Add tomatoes, anchovies, pimiento and capers and stir-fry 1 minute. Sprinkle with lemon juice and toss through. Turn onto heated platter, sprinkle with ground red pepper and serve.

CURRIED CHICKEN AND BROCCOLI

4 TO 6 SERVINGS

4 chicken breast halves
1 10¾-ounce can cream of chicken soup
½ cup mayonnaise
½ teaspoon fresh lemon juice
½ teaspoon curry powder or to taste
¼ cup soft breadcrumbs
1 tablespoon butter
1 10-ounce package frozen broccoli spears, cooked and drained
½ cup shredded cheddar cheese
Freshly cooked rice

Place chicken in medium skillet and add water just to cover. Simmer until tender, about 20 to 30 minutes. Drain well. Let cool slightly. Remove meat from bones.

Preheat oven to 350°F. Combine next 4 ingredients in small bowl and blend well. Mix breadcrumbs and butter in another small bowl. Arrange broccoli in single layer in bottom of 1½-quart baking dish. Cover with chicken. Pour soup mixture over. Sprinkle with breadcrumbs and cheese. Bake until heated through, about 25 minutes. Serve over rice.

WRAPPED HERB CHICKEN

This easily prepared chicken—delicious served hot—may also be refrigerated and presented cold for lunches, picnics or a late supper.

3 TO 6 SERVINGS

- 3 whole chicken breasts, skinned, boned and halved
- 6 tablespoons chopped chives, tarragon or chervil (or any fresh herb)
- ¾ cup fresh lemon juice
- 6 teaspoons onion powder, or to taste
- 6 tablespoons (¾ stick) butter
- 6 tablespoons chopped fresh parsley

Preheat oven to 375°F. Place each chicken piece on large sheet of foil. Top each with 1 tablespoon chopped herbs, 2 tablespoons lemon juice, 1 teaspoon onion powder, 1 tablespoon butter and 1 tablespoon parsley. Fold foil tightly around chicken with double folds on each edge. Bake 30 minutes.

CHICKEN LIVERS WITH GINGER AND SHERRY

4 SERVINGS

- ¼ cup soy sauce
- 2 tablespoons dry sherry
- 1 teaspoon brown sugar
- 1 teaspoon grated fresh ginger or ½ teaspoon ground ginger
- 3 tablespoons (⅜ stick) butter
- 1 large onion, thinly sliced
  Flour
  Salt and freshly ground pepper
- 1 pound chicken livers, trimmed

Preheat oven to 200°F. Combine first 4 ingredients in small bowl. Melt 2 tablespoons butter in large skillet over medium-high heat. Add onion and sauté until browned and crisp, about 20 minutes. Transfer to platter and keep warm in oven.

Combine flour, salt and pepper in shallow dish. Dredge livers in flour, shaking off excess. Melt remaining butter in same skillet over medium-high heat. Add livers and brown about 1 minute. Turn livers over and add soy sauce mixture. Continue cooking, basting frequently, until livers are done, about 2 minutes. Arrange over onion and pour pan juices over.

OTHER FOWL

APRICOT GAME HENS

6 SERVINGS

- 1 cup Chunky Apricot Preserves (see page 42)
- ⅓ cup dry white wine
- ¼ cup (½ stick) butter, melted
- 2 8-ounce packages stuffing mix
- ¾ cup pecans
- 6 Cornish game hens, thawed, rinsed and patted dry
  Salt and freshly ground pepper
  Fresh parsley or watercress sprigs (garnish)

Preheat oven to 350°F. Combine first 3 ingredients in small bowl. Prepare stuffing mix according to package directions and stir in pecans. Sprinkle hens inside and out with salt and pepper. Fill loosely with stuffing, spooning remainder into small baking dish. Truss hens securely. Arrange in roasting pan. Brush each hen generously with some of apricot sauce. Bake hens and remaining stuffing, basting hens frequently until done, about 1 hour. Spoon remaining stuffing onto serving platter and arrange hens on top. Garnish with parsley or watercress.

POULET A LA DIABLE

4 SERVINGS

- 1 8-ounce jar Dijon mustard
- 3 ounces (¾ cup) breadcrumbs
- 2 Cornish game hens, washed and patted dry
  Parsley flakes
- 2 to 3 tablespoons (¼ to ⅜ stick) butter

Preheat oven to 350°F. Combine mustard and breadcrumbs in bowl and blend thoroughly. Spread some of mixture over entire surface of hens, patting firmly with hands. Spoon remainder into cavity. Sprinkle with parsley and dot lightly with butter. Place on rack and roast until tender, about 1¼ hours. If coating starts to overbrown, tent with foil.

DO AHEAD

CHICKEN

ROAST CHICKEN WITH CHINESE BASTING SAUCE

Stir-fried snow peas, water chestnuts and cucumber sticks dressed with soy sauce, vinegar and sesame oil round out the menu. Pour a Gewürztraminer or plum wine.

2 TO 4 SERVINGS

- 1 2½- to 3-pound fryer
- ¼ cup soy sauce
- 2 tablespoons honey
- 2 tablespoons cider vinegar
- ½ teaspoon grated fresh ginger root
- ½ teaspoon minced garlic

Place chicken in large deep bowl that holds it snugly. Combine remaining ingredients in blender or food processor fitted with steel knife and puree. Pour sauce over chicken, cover and refrigerate overnight. Drain chicken, reserving sauce, and roast, following directions for Basic Roast Chicken. After chicken has cooked 20 minutes, pour sauce over. Continue roasting, basting with sauce every 20 minutes.

GREAT CHICKEN

6 SERVINGS

- 1 8-ounce bottle Russian salad dressing
- 1 cup orange marmalade
- 1 envelope onion soup mix

1 3-pound chicken, quartered and skinned, or 3 whole chicken breasts, halved and skinned

Combine first 3 ingredients in large bowl and mix well. Add chicken, turning to coat. Cover and marinate in refrigerator overnight.

Preheat oven to 350°F. Arrange chicken in 9×13-inch baking dish and bake 15 minutes. Baste generously; turn chicken over and baste again. Continue cooking, basting occasionally, until chicken tests done, about 45 minutes.

CHICKEN FLORENTINE
See photograph page 136

6 SERVINGS

6 8-ounce chicken breast halves
1 cup seasoned breadcrumbs
2 tablespoons olive oil
2 tablespoons (¼ stick) butter
2 cups Sauce Marinara*
½ cup dry red wine
1½ cups boiling chicken stock
1 cup uncooked long grain rice
1 2½-ounce can sliced black olives, drained
2 10-ounce packages frozen chopped spinach, thawed and pressed dry
1 cup ricotta or cottage cheese
2 beaten eggs
½ teaspoon crushed marjoram
½ teaspoon salt
¼ teaspoon nutmeg
¼ cup grated Parmesan cheese

Preheat oven to 350°F. Coat chicken with breadcrumbs. Heat oil and butter in 12-inch skillet. Add chicken breasts and sauté until brown. Remove from pan and set aside.

Combine Sauce Marinara and wine. Place 1 cup sauce-wine mixture in skillet. Add chicken stock, rice and olives; stir thoroughly, scraping bottom of skillet. Place in a lightly oiled 3-quart casserole or paella pan.

Arrange chicken skin-side down atop rice. Cover tightly with foil and bake 20 minutes. Turn chicken, re-cover

with foil and bake another 25 minutes. Dish may be cooked ahead to this point.

While chicken is baking, combine spinach, ricotta, eggs, marjoram, salt and nutmeg. Spoon spinach mixture around edge of baking dish. Pour remaining sauce-wine mixture over chicken. Sprinkle with Parmesan. Bake uncovered, until spinach mixture is heated 10 to 15 minutes more.

This dish can also be prepared with cooked chicken or turkey, which would be added after rice is baked.

*Sauce Marinara

MAKES 3 CUPS

2 tablespoons olive oil
2 minced garlic cloves
1 28-ounce can tomato puree
1 tablespoon sugar
1 tablespoon fresh minced parsley
1 teaspoon oregano
1 teaspoon basil
1 teaspoon salt
¼ teaspoon pepper

In a 3-quart saucepan, heat olive oil and sauté garlic until golden brown. Add remaining ingredients and simmer for 15 minutes with the lid only partially covering pan to prevent spattering.

May be refrigerated for 2 weeks or frozen up to 6 months.

CHICKEN POLAR

6 SERVINGS

1 16-ounce can whole berry cranberry sauce
1 8-ounce bottle creamy French dressing
1 envelope onion soup mix
3 large whole chicken breasts, split

Combine cranberry sauce, dressing and onion soup in mixing bowl. Add chicken and coat well. Cover and marinate overnight, turning once or twice.

Preheat oven to 400°F. Arrange chicken in single layer in 9×13-inch baking dish. Bake 30 to 40 minutes, basting occasionally.

CHICKEN WITH PLUM SAUCE

Serve with steamed white rice and Chinese pea pods with water chestnuts. Chenin Blanc or Vouvray would be compatible wines.

4 SERVINGS

2 whole chicken breasts, skinned, boned and halved
3 tablespoons dry white wine
1 tablespoon catsup
3 tablespoons Chinese Plum Sauce*
½ teaspoon salt
½ teaspoon sugar
3 tablespoons oil
¼ cup chicken broth
1 teaspoon cornstarch mixed with 1 tablespoon water

Cut chicken into 1-inch cubes. In a bowl mix together wine, catsup, 2 tablespoons plum sauce, salt and sugar. Add chicken and marinate at least 30 minutes, preferably overnight.

Heat wok or skillet over high heat. Add oil. Stir-fry chicken until almost cooked, about 1 minute. Add chicken broth and remaining 1 tablespoon plum sauce. Simmer 2 to 3 minutes. Blend cornstarch and water mixture and add to pan. Simmer, stirring frequently, until sauce is thickened and translucent.

*Chinese Plum Sauce is available at oriental markets. If you can't find it, this is a good alternative:

Chinese Plum Sauce substitute

MAKES 1½ CUPS

1 cup plum jam
½ cup chutney
1 tablespoon vinegar
¼ teaspoon hot pepper sauce

Combine ingredients in saucepan. Cook over medium heat until thoroughly blended and bubbling. Pour into sterilized jar and cap tightly. Store in refrigerator.

LEMON CHICKEN

25 SERVINGS

- 6 pounds boned and skinned chicken breasts, cut into 1½×¾-inch pieces
- 1 cup peanut oil
- 2 tablespoons cornstarch
- 2 tablespoons salt
- ¼ cup finely grated lemon peel
- 2 cups chicken stock
- 1½ pounds snow peas (strings removed)
- 1½ cups sliced fresh mushrooms
- ¼ cup fresh lemon juice
- 3 tablespoons cornstarch mixed with 3 tablespoons cold water
- ½ teaspoon freshly ground white pepper
  Salt to taste

Combine chicken, ¼ cup oil and 2 tablespoons cornstarch in large bowl and blend well. Heat remaining ¾ cup oil with salt in large deep skillet or Dutch oven over medium-high heat until very hot. Add chicken and sauté until it just turns white (dish can be prepared ahead to this point and refrigerated).

Sprinkle with lemon peel. Add stock, peas and mushrooms and cook an additional 1 minute. Combine remaining ingredients and pour over chicken. Continue cooking, stirring constantly, until sauce thickens. Adjust seasoning. Transfer to large chafing dish and serve immediately.

OVEN-BARBECUED CHICKEN

4 SERVINGS

- 1 14-ounce jar hickory smoked barbecue sauce
- 2 tablespoons soy sauce
- 2 tablespoons bourbon
- 2 tablespoons Dijon mustard
- 1 3- to 4-pound chicken, cut into pieces

Pour barbecue sauce into bowl. Add soy sauce and bourbon to empty barbecue sauce bottle and shake well. Combine with barbecue sauce. Add mustard and stir to blend. Cover chicken with sauce and marinate overnight, turning once.

Preheat oven to 375°F. Bake uncovered 15 minutes. Reduce temperature to 350°F and continue baking until chicken is cooked, about 45 minutes. Serve.

OVERNIGHT BARBECUED CHICKEN

8 SERVINGS

- 2 broiler-fryer chickens, cut up
  Water

Marinade

- ½ cup wine vinegar
- 4 tablespoons Worcestershire sauce
- ½ cup water
- 1½ cups brown sugar
- 1½ cups catsup
- 2 teaspoons salt
- 1½ teaspoons pepper
- 2½ tablespoons dry mustard
- 2 teaspoons paprika
- 2 dashes hot pepper sauce

Poach chicken in 2 inches of water for 30 minutes in large covered pot, then drain thoroughly.

For marinade: Combine ingredients in blender and whirl until thoroughly mixed. Reserve 1 cup of this mixture and let chicken stand overnight in the remainder of marinade.

Grill chicken on barbecue until brown and crisp. While chicken is barbecuing, heat reserved marinade and simmer 5 minutes; pass separately with chicken.

SPICED CHICKEN STRIPS

8 BUFFET SERVINGS; 6 MAIN-COURSE SERVINGS

Marinade

- 1 medium onion, coarsely chopped
- 1 whole head garlic, peeled
- 5 tablespoons peanut oil
- ¼ cup red wine vinegar
- 3 tablespoons catsup
- 2 tablespoons fennel seeds
- 2 tablespoons ground cumin
- 1½ to 2 tablespoons paprika
- 20 whole peppercorns

- 1 1-inch piece fresh ginger, peeled and chopped
  Seeds from 8 cardamom pods
- 8 whole cloves
- 2 teaspoons ground coriander
- 2 teaspoons salt
- 1 teaspoon cinnamon
- ¼ teaspoon ground red pepper
- 3 pounds boned, skinned chicken breast, cut into strips about 1½ to 2 inches long and ½ inch wide

For marinade: Combine all ingredients in blender or processor and mix to smooth paste.

Place chicken in large bowl. Add marinade and stir to coat thoroughly. Cover and chill overnight.

Position rack so meat will be about 6 inches from heat source and preheat broiler. Spread chicken in shallow baking pan and broil until firm to the touch, about 4 minutes.

YOGURT CHICKEN

8 SERVINGS

- 4 to 5 pounds chicken pieces, skinned
- 2 to 3 garlic cloves, minced
- ½ teaspoon fines herbes
- ¼ teaspoon freshly ground pepper
- 3 cups plain yogurt
- 2 onions, finely chopped
- 3 tablespoons fresh lemon juice
- 1½ teaspoons soy sauce
- 1½ teaspoons turmeric
- ¾ teaspoon ground ginger
- ½ teaspoon cinnamon
- ½ teaspoon ground cloves

Rub chicken with garlic, fines herbes and pepper. Combine remaining ingredients in large bowl. Add chicken, turning to coat well. Cover and marinate in refrigerator overnight, turning occasionally.

Preheat oven to 350°F. Remove chicken from marinade and place in single layer in large roasting pan. Tent with foil and bake 30 minutes. Remove foil, turn pieces and bake until lightly browned, about 30 minutes, basting occasionally with marinade. Serve immediately.

BRAISED TURKEY WITH LEMON AND CINNAMON

See photograph page 159

4 TO 6 SERVINGS

- 4 to 6 tablespoons Greek olive oil
- ½ cup flour
- 1 to 2½ pounds boned and skinned turkey, cut into 1-inch chunks
- 3 tablespoons Greek olive oil
- 3 medium onions, chopped
- 1 garlic clove, minced
- ⅔ cup undrained canned tomatoes
- 3 tablespoons tomato paste
- 2 cinnamon sticks, broken in half
- 2 lemons (or more to taste)
- 1½ teaspoons crumbled Greek oregano
- ⅛ teaspoon ground allspice
- 2 to 3 cups rich turkey or chicken stock
  Salt and freshly ground pepper
- 1 pound ziti (Greek or Italian pasta in a hollow rod shape)
- 4 tablespoons (½ stick) butter
- ½ cup freshly grated imported Parmesan cheese

Heat 4 tablespoons oil in wok or large skillet over high heat. Place flour in bag, add turkey pieces and shake until well coated. Shake off excess flour. Stir-fry turkey in small batches until lightly browned, adding oil as needed. Remove from heat and set aside.

Heat 3 tablespoons oil in heavy 4- to 5-quart saucepan over high heat. Add onion and cook until golden brown. Stir in garlic and cook another 30 seconds. Reduce heat and stir in tomatoes, tomato paste, cinnamon, lemon juice, pulp and skin of squeezed lemons, oregano and allspice and simmer 5 minutes. Add stock and turkey. Bring to gentle simmer, cover partially and cook until turkey is tender, 1½ to 2 hours. Braised turkey can be prepared to this point up to 4 days ahead and refrigerated, or frozen up to 2 months ahead.

Taste and adjust lemon juice, cinnamon, oregano and/or salt and pepper. Remove lemon pieces and cinnamon sticks. Skim off excess fat and keep sauce warm over low heat while cooking pasta.

Bring 8 quarts of water to boil with 2 tablespoons salt. Break pasta into pieces about 3 inches long. Add to pot and boil, stirring frequently to prevent sticking, until pasta is tender but not mushy. (Pasta should be cooked a little beyond the al dente stage.) Turn into colander and toss to drain thoroughly. Turn pasta out onto heated large serving platter, dot with butter and toss to coat. Spoon turkey and sauce over pasta and sprinkle with Parmesan cheese. Serve immediately.

MICROWAVE

ROAST BUTTERY CHICKEN

4 SERVINGS

- 1 3½-pound whole roasting chicken
  Seasoned salt
- 1 large white onion, quartered
- ½ cup (1 stick) softened unsalted butter
- ½ teaspoon pepper
  Salt

Liberally sprinkle cavity of chicken with seasoned salt. Place onion in cavity and truss bird. Coat chicken generously with softened butter and season with pepper. (Do not be tempted to salt the outside of the bird. Salt will draw moisture to any large surface such as a whole chicken or roast of meat, forming a crust that will slow down microwave penetration.)

Cover tips of legs and wings as well as the breast tip with small strips of foil. This will prevent them from overcooking before the rest of the bird is done.

Place chicken on its side on an inverted saucer in a glass baking dish. Cover loosely with waxed paper.

Cook in center of oven 6 minutes on High. Baste. Siphon or spoon off any collected liquid.

After the first 6 minutes, turn chicken and cook 6 more minutes. Baste. Again siphon off liquid. Turn bird breast side up. Cook 6 more minutes. Baste well. Remove from oven, turn the bird breast down, wrap with foil. Let stand for 15 minutes.

Prick the thick part of the thigh with a fork. If juices run clear, the chicken is done; if juices are yellowish-pink, it will need another 3 minutes. Season to taste with salt. The chicken will be golden brown. If you like it browner or crisper, place it under the broiler of a conventional oven.

STUFFED ROAST CHICKEN

3 TO 4 SERVINGS

- 2 to 3 cups stuffing (see page 89)
- 1 3- to 4-pound chicken, cleaned, rinsed and patted dry
- 1 slice bread (preferably heel)
- 2 tablespoons (¼ stick) butter
- 1 tablespoon bottled browning sauce
  Garlic powder
  Freshly ground pepper

Spoon stuffing into chicken cavity. Cover opening with bread. Stuff neck if desired and secure with wooden picks. Put remaining stuffing in small dish.

Melt butter in measuring cup. Add browning sauce and mix thoroughly. Place chicken breast side up in baking dish. Brush liberally with butter mixture and sprinkle with garlic powder and pepper. Drape with paper towel to prevent spattering and cook on High 11 minutes. Turn dish and continue cooking on High an additional 12 to 14 minutes. Remove from oven. Cook remaining stuffing on High 3 to 4 minutes to heat through (the longer it cooks the crisper it will be). Carve chicken and serve with additional stuffing.

FRUITED CHICKEN ACAPULCO

6 SERVINGS

- 1 3- to 4-pound fryer, cut into pieces and skinned
- 2 tablespoons bottled browning sauce
- 1 tablespoon oil
- 1 teaspoon garlic salt
- ½ teaspoon powdered ginger
- 1 8-ounce can chunk pineapple, drained, juice reserved
- ½ cup plus 2 tablespoons coffee liqueur
- 1 tablespoon fresh lemon juice
- 1½ tablespoons cornstarch*
- 1 11-ounce can mandarin oranges, drained
- ¼ cup chopped green onion
  Freshly cooked rice

Rinse chicken and pat dry with paper towels. Combine browning sauce and oil and blend well. Brush chicken generously and sprinkle with garlic salt and ginger. Arrange skinned side down in shallow au gratin or other oval baking dish, with larger pieces of chicken toward outside of dish. Cover with waxed paper and cook on High 10 minutes.

Add pineapple juice to baking dish along with ½ cup liqueur and lemon juice. Turn chicken skinned side up, cover with waxed paper and cook on High until chicken is done, 10 to 14 minutes (allow 7 minutes per pound).

Remove chicken with slotted spoon and drain on paper towels. Skim fat from baking dish. Combine cornstarch with remaining liqueur and blend well. Stir into sauce. Cook on High until thickened and clear, about 2 to 3 minutes. Return chicken to dish. Add pineapple, mandarin oranges and onion. Spoon over chicken. Reheat 1 to 2 minutes. Serve immediately over rice.

*If you prefer a thicker sauce, increase cornstarch to 2½ tablespoons.

OLD WORLD CHICKEN IN THE POT

4 TO 6 SERVINGS

- Boiling water
- 1 4-pound chicken, cut up
  Giblets from chicken (do not use liver or kidney)
- 5 cups (about) water
- 4 large carrots, halved and cut into chunks
- 3 celery stalks, halved and cut into chunks (reserve tops)
- 1 onion
- 1 small parsnip, halved and cut into chunks
- 1 tablespoon concentrated chicken stock base
- ⅛ teaspoon freshly ground white pepper
  Minced fresh parsley (garnish)

Place chicken and giblets in 4-quart dish. Add remaining ingredients except celery tops and parsley, making sure water completely covers chicken. Add celery tops. Cover and cook on High 1 hour. Let rest 15 minutes. Remove celery tops. Strain broth if desired. Garnish with minced parsley.

PERUVIAN CHICKEN ESCABECHE

4 SERVINGS

- 3 garlic cloves, crushed
- 2 tablespoons fresh lemon juice
- ½ cup dry white wine
- ⅓ cup cider vinegar
- ⅓ cup water
- 1 bay leaf
- 8 peppercorns
- 1 tablespoon capers
- 1 teaspoon salt
- 1 3½-pound chicken, cut up

Combine all ingredients except chicken in a glass dish or bowl and bring to a boil. Arrange chicken pieces in a 9x13-inch casserole, placing meatier parts toward outside edge of dish. Pour hot marinade over chicken. Cover and cook 8 minutes on High. Turn chicken, cover and cook 8 minutes. Let set, covered, 5 minutes. Serve hot or cold.

POACHED CHICKEN BREAST

Keep a supply of chicken breasts on hand to poach instantly for use in sandwiches, tacos and quick salads.

2 SERVINGS

- 1 whole large chicken breast (about 1 pound), boned, skinned and halved
- ½ to 1 teaspoon chicken bouillon powder mixed with ½ cup boiling water or ½ cup chicken stock

Place chicken in small oval dish. Pour bouillon or stock over top. Cover and cook on High about 5 minutes. Baste with stock several times. Let cool completely in stock.

SUKIYAKI

Substitute any vegetables according to preference and what is available. Offer additional soy sauce at the table while serving.

4 SERVINGS

- ½ cup soy sauce
- ½ cup chicken broth
- ¼ cup dry sherry
- 2 tablespoons sugar
- 2 8-ounce chicken breasts, skinned and cut into ½-inch slices
- 6 small mushrooms, sliced
- 1 pound fresh spinach, stems removed
- ½ pound fresh bean sprouts
- ¼ pound fresh pea pods
- ½ cup sliced celery
- 1 medium onion, thinly sliced
- 1 bunch green onions, halved lengthwise and cut into 3-inch pieces

Combine soy sauce, chicken broth, sherry and sugar in large measuring cup. Cook on High 2 minutes. Combine remaining ingredients in 3-quart casserole and toss lightly. Pour sauce over top. Cover and cook on High 5 minutes, stirring once halfway through cooking time. Continue cooking until vegetables are tender, 2 to 3 minutes.

CORNISH HEN WITH WILD RICE STUFFING

4 TO 8 SERVINGS PER HEN

- ¼ cup sliced almonds
- 1 tablespoon butter
- 1 11-ounce can mandarin orange segments
- 1 6-ounce package long-grain and wild rice mix
- 4 Cornish hens, thawed
- 4 teaspoons bottled browning sauce
- 4 teaspoons oil
  Parsley sprigs or orange segments (garnish)

Combine almonds and butter in small measuring cup and cook on High until almonds are crisp, 2½ to 3 minutes. Set aside.

Drain mandarin oranges, reserving liquid. Add enough water to liquid to measure 1½ cups. Pour into 1½-quart casserole. Add rice mix with its seasoning packet and blend well. Cover and cook on High 10 minutes. Let stand covered 5 minutes. Add almonds and mandarin oranges and stir lightly until mixed.

Fill hen cavities, closing with toothpicks, or by placing ¼ slice of bread over opening. Reserve any remaining stuffing. Place hen breast side up in baking dish just large enough to accommodate.

Combine browning sauce and oil and brush over entire surface of hens. Cover with parchment or waxed paper and cook 10 minutes per pound on Medium (50 percent power), turning breast side down and basting with juices, if necessary, halfway through cooking. To serve, transfer hens to platter and surround with any remaining stuffing. Garnish with parsley or orange.

If using microwave with automatic meat probe, set temperature at 170°F. Internal temperature will rise about 10°F after being removed from microwave.

TURKEY BREAST WITH OLD FASHIONED DRESSING

Although it takes only a short time, this corn bread mixture tastes as if it had been cooking inside a turkey all day long.

MAKES 2–3 CUPS STUFFING

- ¼ cup diced onion
- ¼ cup diced celery
- 1 tablespoon butter or margarine
- 1 cup diced mushrooms
- ⅔ cup chicken stock, turkey stock or bouillon
- 1½ cups corn bread stuffing mix
- ½ turkey breast
  Paprika
  Minced fresh parsley

Combine onion, celery and butter in an au gratin-type dish just large enough to accommodate all ingredients. Cover with waxed paper and cook on High 3 minutes. Stir. Add mushrooms and cook 1 minute. Add stock or bouillon and blend well. Add stuffing mix and toss lightly, adding more liquid if necessary (mixture should be moist but not soggy). Set turkey on dressing. Sprinkle with paprika and parsley. Cover with waxed paper and cook on High 7 to 10 minutes per pound.

TURKEY BREAST

6 SERVINGS

- 1 5-pound turkey breast
- ½ teaspoon black pepper
- 3 to 4 cups stuffing (see recipe above)
  Salt and pepper

Place breast in center of small serving platter. Sprinkle with pepper.

Cook breast, skin side up, for 6 minutes on High. Baste well. Rotate platter ½ turn. Cook 6 minutes. Baste. Turn breast, skin side down. Baste. Cook 7 minutes. Baste. Remove breast, arrange bed of stuffing on the serving platter. Place breast, skin side up, in center. Baste. Cook 6 minutes. Baste well. Remove platter from oven. Wrap with foil and let stand for 5 minutes. Test for doneness. Season to taste.

ROASTED BONELESS TURKEY

Use of a meat probe is recommended to ensure complete cooking. If your microwave oven is not equipped with one, you might want to purchase an inexpensive microwave-safe thermometer.

6 TO 8 SERVINGS

- 1 5- to 5½-pound uncooked boneless young turkey, rolled and ready to cook (do not use precooked turkey roll)
  Oil
- ¼ teaspoon garlic powder or to taste
  Salt and freshly ground pepper
  Paprika

Set turkey on microwave-safe rack. Rub with oil. Sprinkle with garlic powder, salt, pepper and paprika. Cook on Roast setting (60 percent or 70 percent power) for 30 minutes. Turn roast over. Insert meat probe. Continue cooking on Roast until meat probe registers 160°F. Remove turkey from microwave and let rest until internal temperature reaches 175°F, about 10 to 15 minutes. Cut into slices and serve.

TURKEY LEGS BARBECUE

4 SERVINGS

- 2 turkey legs
  Oil
  Barbecue sauce

Prepare barbecue. Brush turkey with oil. Cover with lid, waxed paper or plastic wrap and cook on Roast setting (70 percent power) 10 minutes per pound. Transfer to grill and cook only until outside is crisp, turning and basting frequently with barbecue sauce.

ENTREES: Meats

Basic Ideas For Ground Beef

■ Combine 2 pounds lean ground beef with 1 egg, ½ cup soy sauce and ¼ cup each chopped red pepper, onion and pine nuts. Generously season mixture with herb seasoning blend and garlic powder. Form it into patties and broil, barbecue or pan-fry to desired doneness.

■ In addition to hamburgers, ground beef can be used for a myriad other simple suppers. And meat loaf is probably one of the easiest! Just mix together 1½ pounds lean ground beef, 1 8-ounce can tomato sauce with mushrooms, 1 lightly beaten egg and 1 3-ounce can fried onion rings, crumbled coarsely, in a large bowl. Pack the entire mixture in a 9 x 5-inch loaf pan and bake 45 to 50 minutes.

■ Add a fancy flair to 6 plain, uncooked meat patties (about ¼ to ¾ inch thick) seasoned with garlic powder, salt and pepper by topping each with about ½ cup wild rice, prepared according to package directions. Roll the patties up, with the rice inside, and secure them with toothpicks. Place them seam side down in an oiled baking dish and cover with a sauce made from a 10½-ounce can cream of mushroom soup and 2 tablespoons catsup. Bake for 1 hour in a 350° oven.

■ A special trick with hamburgers is to lightly shape each patty around a small ice cube to keep the meat moist.

■ Making chili is ridiculously easy by adding 2 15½-ounce cans kidney beans, drained, 2 10½-ounce cans tomato soup and 1½ soup cans water to 1 pound lean ground beef that has been browned in olive oil and drained. Bring entire mixture to a boil, then reduce heat to medium. Add 2 large onions, minced, and cover and cook. After 15 minutes, add about 2 tablespoons chili powder, 1 bay leaf and garlic powder and pepper to taste. Continue cooking another 45 minutes. Before serving, remove bay leaf and garnish with finely chopped celery, green pepper and/or grated cheddar.

■ Basic hamburgers can be spiced up by serving them with a selection of international condiments: Mexican hot sauce, Chinese soy sauce, Japanese teriyaki sauce, German mustard and, of course, American catsup.

BEEF

BASIC PAN BROILED STEAK

> 2 tablespoons (¼ stick) clarified butter or beef fat, or more
> 1 to 4 steaks (any tender cut), cut at least 1¼ inches thick
> Salt and freshly ground pepper

Heat butter over medium-high heat in heavy skillet large enough to hold steaks without touching. Add meat and sear well on both sides, turning with tongs; do not pierce with fork. Reduce heat to medium and continue cooking, turning often, until desired degree of doneness is reached (determine by timing or touch method). Sprinkle with salt and pepper to taste.

BASIC OVEN BROILED STEAK

> Tender steaks, cut at least 1½ to 2 inches thick
> Salt and freshly ground pepper

Set rack 4 inches from heat source and preheat broiler. Place steak on rack set over broiler pan and broil until browned, about 3 minutes per side. Turn oven to 375°F and continue cooking steaks, turning often, until desired degree of doneness is reached. Sprinkle steaks with salt and pepper to taste.

BASIC BARBECUED STEAK

> Tender steaks, cut 1½ to 2 inches thick
> Salt and freshly ground pepper

Preheat gas or electric barbecue, or prepare briquettes. (If grill has adjustable rack, coals should be white hot; if nonadjustable, allow coals to burn down a bit more.) Set rack about 2 inches from coals and sear steaks on both sides, about 3 minutes per side for rare meat. Raise rack to 4 inches above coals and continue to cook the steaks, turning frequently, until desired degree of doneness is reached.

BAKED STEAK

4 SERVINGS

> 1 large flank steak
> 2 large tomatoes, quartered

> 1 green pepper, sliced into thin rings
> 1 large Bermuda onion, sliced into thin rings
> 1 4-ounce can whole button mushrooms, drained
> 2 tablespoons (¼ stick) butter, cut into pieces
> 3 tablespoons chili sauce
> 3 tablespoons catsup
> 1 tablespoon Worcestershire sauce

Preheat oven to 350°F. Place steak in shallow baking pan. Cover with tomatoes, green pepper, onion and mushrooms and dot with butter. Combine remaining ingredients and pour over top. Bake uncovered until tender, about 45 minutes. Thinly slice across grain to serve.

FILLET OF BEEF

Serve with wild rice cooked in beef bouillon.

4 SERVINGS

> 1 tablespoon vegetable oil
> 1 garlic clove, crushed
> 4 fillets of beef tenderloin, about 1½ inches thick
> 1 pound fresh mushrooms, halved

Pan-broiling

■ This is a favorite way to prepare pork chops and, if done correctly, produces succulent results. Dry tough chops result from overcooking, cooking over too high a heat or lack of any marbling. Sear pork over rather high heat then quickly reduce heat to low. Cook, depending on thickness of cut, until chop is almost firm when pressed, about five to ten minutes to a side. If you have any doubts about doneness, use an instant-reading meat thermometer. A well-marbled chop or steak is at its peak at an internal temperature of 150°F.

■ Unaged top or bottom round, sirloin tip, and chuck without the rib eye are all excellent choices for pot roasts, stews and other braised dishes.

■ If you are among those who think ribs do not offer enough solid meat, follow these directions for cutting them into very generous portions:

With sharp pointed knife, cut alongside the first rib, as close to bone as possible. (This bone will now have no meat attached to it. Use for stock or discard.) Skip to third rib and cut against each side of bone to remove. This bone will now have no meat on it, but the second rib will have a generous portion on each side. Repeat with remaining ribs.

Plan on 1 or 2 beef ribs or 2 or 3 pork spareribs for each serving. Do not use this technique for lamb riblets.

1 bunch green onions, chopped
½ to ¾ cup dry vermouth
1 13-ounce can mushroom gravy
Salt and freshly ground pepper

In an electric skillet set at 400°F, heat garlic with oil, then brown fillets 3 to 4 minutes on each side. Remove fillets and keep warm. Discard garlic.

Turn skillet down to 350°F and sauté mushrooms and green onions in the same oil until soft but not brown.

Return beef to skillet. Mix vermouth with gravy and pour over meat and vegetables. Cover and cook at 350°F for 10 minutes (beef will be medium rare). Season with salt and pepper to taste just before serving.

MUSTARD AND HERB BROILED STEAK

2 SERVINGS

¼ cup Dijon mustard
1 garlic clove, minced
1 green onion, minced
½ teaspoon basil
2 uncooked steaks, cut at least 1½ inches thick

Combine mustard, garlic, green onion and basil in small bowl and mix well. Spread on both sides of steaks and broil.

SOPHOMORE STEAK

4 SERVINGS

¼ cup spicy brown mustard
¼ cup catsup
1 pound flank steak
Juice of ½ lemon
Freshly ground pepper

Mix mustard and catsup together and spread on steak. Place steak on broiling rack and broil until steaks are slightly charred, about 3 to 5 minutes. Remove from broiler and immediately sprinkle with lemon juice and pepper.

STEAK AU POIVRE

4 SERVINGS

Whole black peppercorns
4 1-inch-thick strip, club or filet mignon steaks, well trimmed
2 tablespoons (¼ stick) butter

1 tablespoon olive oil
½ pound mushrooms, sliced
½ cup red wine
¼ cup chopped fresh parsley
2 tablespoons brandy
1 tablespoon butter
¼ teaspoon fresh lemon juice
Dash of hot pepper sauce
Dash of Worcestershire sauce
Salt
1 teaspoon arrowroot

Place peppercorns on hard, flat surface and crush with pressing-rolling motion, using bottom of skillet or pan. Press steaks into crushed pepper using heel of your hand or flat side of cleaver.

Heat 2 tablespoons butter and olive oil in large heavy iron skillet over medium-high heat until mixture begins to brown. Sear steaks on both sides, then cook to desired doneness. Transfer to heated platter and keep warm. Reduce heat to medium.

Add remaining ingredients except arrowroot to same skillet. Stir small amount of sauce into arrowroot and blend well. Return to skillet and cook until slightly thickened. Pour over steaks and serve.

STEAK WITH GREEN PEPPERCORN AND MUSTARD SAUCE

2 SERVINGS

    2 steaks
    ½ cup brown sauce or beef stock
    ¼ cup whipping cream
    ½ teaspoon green peppercorns, or more to taste
    1 tablespoon Dijon mustard

Pan-broil steaks according to basic recipe and keep warm.

Pour off all but thin film of fat from skillet in which steaks were cooked. Place over medium-high heat and add brown sauce, cream and peppercorns. Bring to boil and boil 3 minutes, scraping up brown bits that cling to pan. Stir in mustard and cook 1 minute longer. Taste and adjust seasonings if desired. Pour over steaks and serve immediately.

STEAK WITH MILANESE WHITE WINE SAUCE

4 SERVINGS

    4 steaks
    5 tablespoons (⅝ stick) butter
    ½ cup minced shallot
    2 cups brown sauce
    ½ cup white wine
    2 teaspoons fresh lemon juice
       Salt and freshly ground pepper
       Minced parsley (garnish)

Broil steaks according to basic pan-broiled recipe and keep warm.

Pour off all fat from skillet in which steaks were cooked. Place over medium-high heat, add butter and shallot and cook 2 minutes. Add sauce, wine and lemon juice and bring to boil, scraping brown bits from pan, and cook 3 to 4 minutes. Season with salt and pepper to taste. Pour over steaks and sprinkle with parsley. Serve immediately.

STEAK WITH NEAPOLITAN TOMATO AND CAPER SAUCE

3 TO 4 SERVINGS

    3 to 4 flank, skirt, wedge bone sirloin, top round or chuck steaks
    ½ cup minced onion
    1 garlic clove, minced
    1 28-ounce can tomatoes, very well drained
    2 teaspoons basil
    ½ teaspoon oregano
    ¼ cup oil-cured black olives
    1 to 2 tablespoons capers (preferably large Italian variety), drained
       Salt and freshly ground pepper

Pan-broil steaks in olive oil according to basic recipe and keep warm.

Add onion to juices in skillet in which steaks were cooked and sauté over medium heat 3 minutes. Stir in garlic and cook 1 minute longer. Increase heat, add tomatoes, basil and oregano and boil 5 minutes, stirring frequently. Quickly mix in olives and capers. Season to taste with salt and pepper. Pour over steaks. Serve immediately.

STEAK WITH ONION, GREEN PEPPER AND TOMATOES

4 SERVINGS

    4 steaks, cut at least 1½ inches thick
    2 tablespoons oil
    1 medium onion, thinly sliced
    1 green pepper, seeded and thinly sliced
    1 large tomato, cut into chunks
       Salt and freshly ground pepper
       Steamed rice

Begin broiling steaks according to basic oven-broiled recipe.

While steaks are cooking, heat oil in wok or large skillet over high heat. Add onion and pepper and stir-fry 2 to 3 minutes. Add tomato and stir-fry 1 minute longer. Season with salt and pepper to taste. Divide mixture over steaks during last few minutes of cooking. Serve with steamed rice.

BEEF AND GREEN TOMATO

4 SERVINGS

    1 pound round steak, diagonally sliced into very thin strips
    1 tablespoon oil
       Salt and pepper
    2 medium green, very firm tomatoes, thinly sliced
    ¼ cup honey
    ½ teaspoon garlic powder or to taste
       Cooked rice or noodles

In a large skillet brown meat quickly in oil. Add salt and pepper to taste. Remove meat. Add tomato slices and heat until they begin to break apart. Add honey and garlic powder. Return meat to pan and cook until meat is hot. Serve meat mixture over cooked rice or noodles.

BEEF AND SCALLOP SAUTE

See photograph pages 106-107

Reprinted with permission of Barbara Kafka from the as yet untitled book to be published by Harper & Row in 1982.

In this delicate dish the beef picks up the mild flavor of the scallops rather than the other way around. Serve with a California Zinfandel.

4 SERVINGS

    2 tablespoons peanut oil
    1 teaspoon minced fresh garlic
    1 pound trimmed beef tenderloin (narrow end), cut into pieces ½ inch thick, then halved crosswise
    ¾ pound sea scallops
    1¼ cups diagonally sliced green onion
    1 tablespoon Flavored Brine*
       Freshly ground pepper
       Pinch of red pepper flakes

Heat oil in wok or large skillet until almost smoking. Add garlic and beef, then scallops, and stir-fry about 30 seconds. Add remaining ingredients and stir-fry beef and scallops another 20 to 30 seconds.

*Flavored Brine

Keeps almost indefinitely.

MAKES ABOUT 1½ CUPS

- 2 cups water
- 2 tablespoons sliced peeled ginger
- 1 tablespoon freshly ground white pepper
- 1 teaspoon red pepper flakes
- 1½ cups coarse salt

Combine water, ginger, pepper and pepper flakes in medium saucepan and bring to boil. Gradually stir in salt. Reduce heat and simmer 10 minutes. Strain through sieve lined with dampened towel. Store in tightly covered jar.

BEEF STROGANOFF

4 SERVINGS

- 1 1½- to 2-pound flank steak
- 1 envelope onion soup mix
- 1 10¾-ounce can cream of mushroom soup
- 1½ cups sour cream, room temperature
   Freshly cooked noodles or rice

Preheat oven to 325°F. Cut steak lengthwise into thirds and then crosswise into ¼-inch slices. Combine meat, onion soup mix and mushroom soup in 2-quart baking dish. Cover and bake 1 hour. Stir some of sauce into sour cream. Blend into meat mixture. Spoon over noodles or rice.

BROCCOLI BEEF

4 SERVINGS

- 1 pound fresh broccoli, trimmed and peeled
- 1 tablespoon oil
- 2 garlic cloves, minced
- ½ pound lean beef, thinly sliced
- ½ cup frozen whole pearl onions, thawed and drained
- ¼ cup diced pimiento
   Chow Sauce*

Chow mein noodles or freshly steamed rice

Cook broccoli in boiling water until crisp-tender, about 10 minutes. Drain. Cut off florets; slice broccoli stems diagonally.

Heat wok or skillet over high heat. Add oil and swirl to coat. Add half of garlic and stir-fry briefly; do not burn. Blend in beef and broccoli stems and stir-fry about 2 minutes. Add florets, onions, pimiento, Chow Sauce and garlic. Cover and cook until vegetables are crisp-tender, about 2 minutes. Serve over noodles or freshly steamed rice.

*Chow Sauce

- 2 tablespoons oyster sauce
- 2 tablespoons Chinese rice wine
- 1 tablespoon soy sauce
- 1 teaspoon cornstarch
- ½ teaspoon salt

Mix all ingredients in small bowl.

CHINESE PEPPER STEAK

4 SERVINGS

- 1 1½- to 2-pound flank steak, trimmed
- 3 tablespoons soy sauce
- 1 tablespoon dry sherry or Chinese rice wine
- 2 teaspoons cornstarch
- 1 teaspoon sugar
- 4 tablespoons peanut oil or vegetable oil
- 1 medium-size green pepper, cut into ½-inch dice
- 4 ⅛-inch slices peeled fresh ginger or ¼ teaspoon ground ginger
   Freshly cooked rice

Cut meat lengthwise into thirds and then crosswise into ¼-inch strips. Combine next 4 ingredients in medium bowl. Add meat, turning to coat. Cover and marinate in refrigerator 30 minutes.

Heat wok or skillet over medium-high heat. Pour in 1 tablespoon oil and swirl to coat. Add pepper and stir-fry until crisp-tender, about 3 minutes. Transfer to dish. Pour remaining oil into wok and heat over medium-high. Add ginger and stir-fry briefly. Add steak with marinade and stir-fry until meat is lightly browned and marinade is reduced, about 2 minutes. Discard fresh ginger. Return pepper to wok and stir-fry until heated through, about 1 minute. Serve over rice.

FLANK STEAK WITH GREEN BEANS

4 SERVINGS

- ¾ to 1 pound flank steak, cut into thin strips
- 1 tablespoon oyster sauce or soy sauce
- 1½ teaspoons cornstarch
- ¾ teaspoon sugar
   Few dashes of white wine
   Dash of ginger
- 1 pound green beans
- 2 tablespoons oil
- ¾ teaspoon garlic powder
- ½ teaspoon salt
   Freshly cooked rice

Combine first 6 ingredients in bowl and marinate 5 to 10 minutes.

Meanwhile, remove ends from beans; break beans in half. Place in 2- to 3-quart pan and cover with water. Bring to boil and boil 2 minutes. Remove from heat and immediately hold under cold running water until beans are cool. Drain beans thoroughly.

Heat oil in large skillet over high heat. When light haze forms, add beef and garlic powder and stir-fry until browned, 2 to 3 minutes. Remove with slotted spoon. Add beans and salt and stir-fry 2 to 3 minutes. Return beef to skillet and stir-fry another minute to heat through; add a few drops of water if necessary to prevent sticking. Adjust seasoning to taste and serve immediately over rice.

GREEN BEANS AND MEAT IN TOMATO SAUCE

4 SERVINGS

- ¼ cup (½ stick) butter
- 1 large onion, chopped
- 2 garlic cloves, minced
- 1½ pounds lamb, beef or pork, cut into ½-inch cubes
- 1 16-ounce can whole tomatoes, undrained
- 1 8-ounce can tomato sauce
- 1 teaspoon salt
- ½ teaspoon cinnamon
- 2 10-ounce packages cut green beans, partially thawed
  Noodle-Rice*

Melt butter in large skillet over medium-high heat. Add onion and garlic and sauté until golden, about 5 minutes. Add meat, stirring until it is no longer pink. Blend in tomatoes, tomato sauce, salt and cinnamon. Simmer until meat is tender, about 20 minutes. Add beans and simmer until crisp-tender, about 10 minutes. Serve over noodle-rice.

*Noodle-Rice

- 1 cup long-grain converted rice
- 2 tablespoons (¼ stick) butter
- ½ cup finely broken uncooked spaghetti
- 2 cups water
  Salt

Soak rice in enough water to cover. Meanwhile, melt butter in medium skillet over medium-high heat. Add spaghetti and sauté until browned. Drain rice and add to skillet. Blend in water and salt and bring to rolling boil, stirring occasionally. Reduce heat, cover and simmer until all water is absorbed and rice tests done, about 20 minutes. Fluff with fork before serving.

ONE-SKILLET GREEN PEPPER AND STEAK

4 TO 6 SERVINGS

- ½ cup water
- 1½ tablespoons cornstarch
- 3 tablespoons soy sauce
- 2 tablespoons brown sugar
- 2 tablespoons oil
- 1 pound round steak, sliced diagonally into ⅛-inch strips
- 1 to 2 green peppers, cut into thin strips 1 inch long
  Freshly steamed rice

Combine water and cornstarch in small bowl and blend well. Stir in soy sauce and brown sugar. Heat oil in large skillet over medium-high heat. Add meat and brown until no longer pink, about 10 minutes. Push meat to sides of skillet. Pour cornstarch mixture into center and stir until thickened. Blend in meat. Add green pepper and mix well. Cover and cook until pepper is crisp-tender, about 5 minutes. Spoon meat mixture over rice and serve.

HERB-SCENTED TENDERLOIN WITH MUSTARD-CAPER SAUCE

6 TO 8 SERVINGS

- 1 4-pound beef tenderloin butt, trimmed of all fat
- 3 tablespoons olive oil
- 8 branches fresh marjoram or oregano (or 4 tablespoons crumbled dried leaves)
  Mustard-Caper Sauce*

Let tenderloin stand at room temperature 30 minutes. Rub all sides of tenderloin with oil.

To barbecue, heat coals until gray ash forms. Spread into overlapping layer and let burn 15 minutes. Set grill 3 inches above coals.

Set beef on grill and cook about 8 minutes. Turn and continue cooking, frequently sprinkling coals with herbs, until meat thermometer inserted in thickest part of meat registers 125°F (very rare), 130°F (rare) or 135°F (medium-rare). Remove and let cool. May also use broiler.

When ready to serve, slice meat thinly and arrange on platter in overlapping pattern. Spoon ribbon of Mustard-Caper Sauce down center; pass remainder.

*Mustard-Caper Sauce

MAKES ABOUT 1½ CUPS

- 3 generous tablespoons moutarde de meaux (coarsely ground French mustard)
- 2 egg yolks, room temperature
- 1 small green onion, chopped
- ¼ teaspoon chopped fresh marjoram or pinch of dried, crumbled
  Juice of ½ large lemon (about 2 tablespoons)
- 1 cup light olive oil, room temperature
- ¼ to ½ cup whipping cream
- 1½ tablespoons capers, rinsed and drained

Combine first 5 ingredients in processor and mix until pale and creamy. With machine running, gradually add oil through feed tube in thin stream, stopping machine occasionally to be sure oil is absorbed. Add cream and capers and mix until blended.

Sauce can be prepared up to 3 days ahead and chilled. Serve at room temperature.

TOMATO BEEF

4 SERVINGS

- ¼ cup soy sauce
- 2 tablespoons grated fresh ginger
- 2 garlic cloves, minced
- 1 teaspoon cornstarch
- 1 teaspoon sugar
- 1 pound sirloin tip, thinly sliced
- 3 to 4 tablespoons oil
- 1 pound medium tomatoes, quartered
- 4 celery stalks, diagonally cut into 1-inch pieces
- 6 green onions, cut into ½-inch pieces
- 1 green pepper, cut into 1-inch squares
- 1 onion, cut into ½-inch strips
- 2 teaspoons cornstarch dissolved in ¾ cup water and 1 teaspoon soy sauce
  Freshly cooked rice

Combine first 5 ingredients in large bowl. Add meat and marinate at room temperature for 10 minutes. Discard marinade.

Heat 2 tablespoons oil in large skillet over high heat. When light haze forms, add meat and stir-fry about 2 minutes. Remove with slotted spoon and set aside.

Add 1 to 2 tablespoons more oil to skillet. When hot, add vegetables and stir-fry until crisp-tender. Reduce heat, add dissolved cornstarch mixture and simmer until thickened, 1 to 2 minutes. Stir in meat and simmer an additional 2 minutes to heat through. Serve over rice.

STANDING RIB ROAST

6 TO 8 SERVINGS

- ¾ cup flour
- 1 teaspoon salt
- ½ teaspoon freshly ground pepper
- 1 tablespoon paprika
- 3 garlic cloves, minced
- 1 3- or 4-rib roast, trimmed of excess fat; feather bone and ribs loosened and tied in place
  Horseradish Mousseline Sauce (see page 43)

Preheat oven to 325°F. Combine flour, salt, pepper, paprika and garlic. Rub roast completely with this mixture. Place roast fat-side up in shallow roasting pan. A rack is not necessary since bones form natural rack. Insert meat thermometer into thickest part of roast, making sure tip does not touch bone. To determine roasting time:

Very rare—15 to 17 minutes per pound or 130°F on thermometer.

Medium rare—18 to 20 minutes per pound or 150°F on thermometer.

Well done—22 to 28 minutes per pound or 165°F on thermometer.

When desired doneness is reached, turn heat off, leave oven door ajar and allow meat to rest 20 minutes, or remove roast and let stand in a warm place near the oven. (This makes carving easier, and less juices

will run out onto the platter so the meat will be more succulent.) Cut strings, and serve with Horseradish Mousseline Sauce.

TEXAS-STYLE HICKORY-SMOKED BARBECUED BEEF RIBS WITH PANHANDLE SAUCE

Cooking ribs with smoke is very much a Western tradition.

6 TO 8 SERVINGS

Panhandle Barbecue Sauce

- 1 cup bottled chili sauce
- 3 tablespoons minced onion
- 2 tablespoons minced green pepper
- 1 tablespoon brown sugar
- 1 fresh or canned jalapeño pepper, minced
- 1 teaspoon dry mustard
- 2 dashes Worcestershire sauce
- 3 cups hickory chips
- 5 pounds beef ribs, cut from rib of beef and trimmed (do not use short ribs)

For sauce: Combine all ingredients in small pan and bring to boil. Reduce heat and simmer 15 minutes.

Soak hickory chips 15 minutes in enough water to cover. Drain well.

Heat coals until gray ash forms. Spread into single layer and let burn about 30 minutes. Set grill 4 inches above coals.

Arrange ribs on grill. Add about half of hickory chips to fire. Cover barbecue if possible, leaving vents open. Cook ribs about 40 minutes, turning every 10 minutes and adding chips and more coals as needed. After 40 minutes, brush ribs generously with sauce and continue cooking, turning and brushing frequently, for about 20 minutes.

CHILI QUICK

6 TO 8 SERVINGS

- 1 pound lean ground pork
- 1 pound lean ground beef

- 1 medium onion, diced
- 1 tablespoon oil (optional)
- 2 15- to 15½-ounce cans chili without beans
- 2 medium tomatoes, diced
- 1 green pepper, diced
- 1 cup grated cheddar cheese (garnish)
- ½ cup chopped onion (garnish)

Sauté pork, beef and onion in large skillet over medium-high heat until meat is browned, adding oil if necessary. Drain off any excess fat. Reduce heat to medium, stir in chili and cook about 25 minutes, stirring occasionally. Add tomatoes and pepper and continue cooking until heated through, about 5 minutes. Serve in bowls or mugs. Garnish with cheese and onion.

CHILI WITH PEANUTS

6 TO 8 SERVINGS

- ¼ cup oil
- 2 cups minced onion
- 2 garlic cloves, minced
- 2½ pounds lean ground beef
- 1 16-ounce can tomatoes, undrained
- ⅔ cup chopped, skinned, unsalted peanuts
- 3 tablespoons tomato paste
- 3 tablespoons chili powder or to taste
- 1 tablespoon salt
- 1 teaspoon cumin seed
- 1 teaspoon chopped chilies or ¼ teaspoon hot pepper sauce
- ⅔ cup chopped, skinned, unsalted peanuts (garnish)
- ¼ cup minced parsley (garnish)

Heat oil in Dutch oven or soup pot over medium-high heat. Add onion and garlic and sauté until tender, about 5 minutes. Add beef and brown well. Stir in tomatoes, ⅔ cup peanuts, tomato paste, chili powder, salt, cumin and chilies. Reduce heat and simmer until thick, about 30 minutes, stirring occasionally. Spoon into individual bowls and pass remaining ⅔ cup peanuts and minced parsley for garnish.

LIVER WITH MUSHROOM WINE SAUCE

2 SERVINGS

 2 tablespoons flour
 2 tablespoons Parmesan cheese
 Salt and freshly ground pepper
 4 ¼-inch-thick slices calf's liver (about ⅔ pound)
 2 to 3 tablespoons oil
 1 large onion, chopped
 ¼ pound mushrooms, sliced
 6 tablespoons dry white wine
 6 tablespoons beef broth
 Chopped fresh parsley (garnish)

Preheat oven to 200°F. Combine flour, cheese, salt and pepper. Lightly coat both sides of liver, reserving remaining flour. Heat half of oil in large skillet over medium-high heat. Add onion and sauté until soft, about 10 minutes. Transfer to platter and keep warm in oven.

Heat remaining oil in same skillet. Add liver and sauté on both sides until brown and crusty, about 4 minutes per side. Arrange over onion on platter. Add mushrooms to skillet and sauté 2 to 3 minutes. Spoon over liver. Add remaining flour mixture to skillet. Gradually add wine, stirring constantly, and cook 2 to 3 minutes. Blend in broth and continue cooking until sauce is thickened. Pour over liver. Garnish with parsley. Serve immediately.

LAMB

BUTTERFLIED LAMB WITH LEMON-MUSTARD SAUCE
See photograph pages 110-111

The sauce can be prepared well in advance and reheated. The lamb should be as close to room temperature as possible before cooking. For easier carving, remember to let the meat rest 10 to 15 minutes after removing from the oven. The internal temperature will rise between five and ten degrees during this rest period so take this into account when you test for doneness. Very rare lamb is about 125°F, rare is between 130°F and 135°F, and medium-rare registers between 140°F and 145°F.

6 TO 8 SERVINGS

 1 7- to 8-pound leg of lamb, boned and butterflied
 Salt and freshly ground pepper
 Lemon-Mustard Sauce*

Adjust oven rack to about 6 inches below broiler and preheat broiler. Place lamb fat side up on rack in shallow pan. Broil meat 10 to 15 minutes. Turn and broil until instant-reading meat thermometer registers 130°F, about 8 to 10 minutes. Remove from oven and let rest in warm area 10 to 15 minutes. Season to taste with salt and pepper.

Slice lamb thinly and arrange on heated serving platter. Pour sauce over meat and serve.

*Lemon-Mustard Sauce

 6 tablespoons (¾ stick) unsalted butter
 2 large garlic cloves, minced
 3 tablespoons coarse-ground French mustard (moutarde de meaux)
 Shredded peel from 2 large lemons
 Juice of 1 lemon
 ¼ teaspoon dried oregano (preferably Greek) or to taste
 Salt and freshly ground pepper

Combine butter and garlic in small saucepan and cook over low heat 3 to 5 minutes. Just before serving, whisk in remaining ingredients; heat mixture briefly.

Trim leftover lamb of all fat. Cut meat julienne and toss with lemon-basil-chive flavored mayonnaise. Mound in lettuce cups and garnish with a few Greek olives and crisp cucumber sticks.

CHINESE ONE-DISH LAMB

2 TO 3 SERVINGS

 2 teaspoons cornstarch
 ⅔ pound boned lamb, sliced ⅛ inch thick
 2 tablespoons oil
 ½ cup shredded bok choy or thinly sliced celery
 ¼ cup shredded carrot
 ¼ cup bamboo shoots
 3 green onions, thinly sliced
 ½ teaspoon salt
 ½ teaspoon sugar
 Hoisin-Plum Sauce*
 Freshly steamed rice or deep-fried maifun (rice sticks)

Rub cornstarch into meat in bowl.

Heat wok or skillet over high heat. Add 1 tablespoon oil and swirl to coat. Add bok choy, carrot, bamboo shoots, onions, salt and sugar and stir-fry until vegetables are crisp-tender, about 3 minutes. Transfer to platter. Pour remaining oil into wok. Add lamb and stir-fry about 2 minutes. Blend in Hoisin-Plum Sauce and continue to cook about 1 minute. Reduce heat to medium, return vegetables to wok and stir-fry until heated through, about 2 minutes. Serve over rice or maifun.

*Hoisin-Plum Sauce

 2 teaspoons hoisin sauce
 1 teaspoon oyster sauce
 1 teaspoon plum sauce
 ½ teaspoon soy sauce
 ½ teaspoon tomato paste
 ½ teaspoon cornstarch
 ¼ teaspoon salt
 ¼ teaspoon sugar

Mix all ingredients in small bowl.

GREEN NOODLE AND LAMB CASSEROLE

6 TO 8 SERVINGS

 1½ pounds ground lamb
 ¼ cup chopped onion
 1 garlic clove, minced

1 10½-ounce can cream of mushroom soup
1 8-ounce can tomato sauce
½ cup water
½ teaspoon oregano
½ teaspoon salt
¼ teaspoon freshly ground pepper
8 ounces green egg noodles, cooked al dente and drained
¼ cup (½ stick) butter, melted
¼ cup freshly grated Parmesan cheese
1 cup ricotta cheese

Preheat oven to 350°F. Grease 3-quart baking dish. Brown lamb, onion and garlic in large skillet over medium-high heat; pour off excess fat. Blend in soup, tomato sauce, water and seasoning. Reduce heat and simmer 10 minutes. Meanwhile, toss cooked noodles, butter and Parmesan in large bowl. Add lamb mixture and ricotta and mix well. Turn into dish. Cover and bake until heated through, about 25 minutes. Uncover and continue baking until top is golden, about 5 minutes. Serve casserole hot.

GROUND LAMB AND EGGPLANT KEBABS
See photograph page 129

Seasoned ground lamb is known as köfte in Turkey or kafta in Lebanon and can be barbecued on an outdoor grill or cooked under the broiler. Either way, it's a fine aromatic filling for pita bread as well as an easy main dish to prepare after an extremely busy and active day.

6 SERVINGS

1½ pounds ground lamb
½ cup minced onion
½ cup minced fresh parsley
3 tablespoons flour
3 tablespoons red wine or water
1½ teaspoons salt
½ teaspoon freshly ground pepper

½ teaspoon allspice
¼ teaspoon cinnamon
¼ teaspoon cayenne pepper
1 medium eggplant (1 to 1½ pounds), cut into 6 lengthwise wedges
Olive oil
Garlic salt
Freshly ground pepper

Prepare charcoal and generously grease grill. (If broiling in oven, preheat briefly just before cooking.) Grease 6 skewers.

Combine first 10 ingredients and mix well. Shape into 18 meatballs. Cut eggplant wedges into 4 equal pieces. Alternate with meatballs on skewers, pressing firmly together. Brush cut surfaces of eggplant with olive oil and sprinkle with garlic salt and pepper. Place about 4 to 6 inches above glowing coals or broil about 4 inches from heat source turning often, until eggplant is tender and lamb is done, about 15 to 20 minutes.

LAMB CHOPS KORABIAK

4 SERVINGS

¼ cup (½ stick) butter or margarine
6 to 10 mushrooms, sliced
2 to 3 green onions, sliced
2 large or 4 small lamb chops
1 teaspoon minced fresh rosemary or ½ teaspoon dried, crumbled
Salt and freshly ground pepper
Garlic powder
1 cup dry red wine

Melt half of butter in large skillet over medium-high heat. Add mushrooms and onions and sauté until tender, about 5 to 10 minutes. Remove and keep warm. Melt remaining butter in same skillet over medium-high heat. Sprinkle chops with rosemary, salt, pepper and garlic powder. Add to skillet and sauté until browned on both sides, about 5 minutes. Reduce heat to medium and continue cooking until tender. Transfer lamb chops to heated platter. Pour wine into skillet and cook over medium-high heat, scraping up

any browned bits clinging to bottom of pan, until liquid is reduced by ⅓. Spoon vegetables over chops and top with sauce.

LAMB TART AVGOLEMONO

Serve with a salad of sliced beets and paper-thin slices of onion dressed with olive oil and cider vinegar lightly touched with ground cloves. A full dry red wine such as Barbera is a good choice.

6 TO 8 SERVINGS

1 unbaked 9-inch pastry shell
1 egg white, lightly beaten
1 pound ground lamb
2 slices homemade-style white bread (crusts trimmed), torn into pieces
¼ cup milk
¼ cup minced fresh parsley
1 large onion, minced
1 large garlic clove, minced
1 teaspoon minced fresh mint leaves or ½ teaspoon dried
1 teaspoon salt
½ teaspoon freshly ground pepper
¼ teaspoon allspice
3 eggs
½ cup chicken broth
¼ cup whipping cream
2 tablespoons fresh lemon juice
2 tablespoons grated lemon peel

Preheat oven to 400°F. Brush pastry with egg white and bake 5 minutes. Let cool while preparing filling.

Combine next 10 ingredients in large bowl and mix gently but thoroughly. Spoon into prepared shell. Beat eggs lightly. Add remaining ingredients and mix well. Pour into shell and bake 15 minutes. Reduce oven temperature to 350°F and continue baking until custard is firm, about 15 more minutes. Let stand 5 minutes before slicing.

PORK

PAN-BROILED PORK CHOPS

This basic recipe has almost limitless variations for pan sauces, two of which we also present here. One of the tricks for perfect pan-broiled chops is to start with a thick cut (about 1½ inches) trimmed of all fat. An instant-reading thermometer inserted in thickest part of chop should register 150°F.

4 SERVINGS

- 2 tablespoons oil or (¼ stick) clarified butter
- 4 1½-inch-thick center loin or sirloin pork chops, well trimmed (preferably close to room temperature)
  Salt and freshly ground pepper

Heat oil or butter in heavy 12-inch skillet over medium-high heat. Arrange chops in pan without sides touching and sauté on all sides until rich golden color, turning once (use wooden spoons or spatulas to turn so meat is not pierced). Reduce heat to low (if using electric range, remove pan from direct heat until burner cools down) and continue cooking chops, turning once, until they are semifirm when pressed with finger, about 10 minutes per side; do not overcook. Season with salt and freshly ground pepper.

VARIATIONS

Dijon Pork Chops with Green Peppercorns: Follow recipe for basic Pan-Broiled Pork Chops. Transfer chops to oven-proof platter, tent with foil and set in 350°F oven. Pour off all fat from skillet. Stir in 1 cup whipping cream, ¼ cup beef stock and 2 tablespoons green peppercorns, rinsed and drained. Boil over high heat, stirring constantly and scraping up any browned bits clinging to bottom of pan, until reduced by ⅓. Blend in 2 heaping tablespoons Dijon mustard. Taste and adjust seasoning. Pour sauce over top of pork chops.

Pork Chops with White Wine and Shallots: Follow recipe for basic Pan-Broiled Pork Chops. Transfer chops to oven-proof platter, tent with foil and set in 350°F oven. Pour off all but 2 tablespoons fat from skillet. Place skillet over high heat. Add ½ cup minced shallot and sauté until softened, about 1 minute. Stir in ½ cup dry white wine and ½ cup rich chicken stock. Boil over high heat, stirring constantly and scraping up any browned bits clinging to bottom of pan, until reduced by ½. Pour wine sauce over chops. Sprinkle with either minced fresh chives or green onion tops.

BARBECUED PORK CHOPS

4 TO 6 SERVINGS

- 8 to 12 thinly sliced pork chops
- 1 lemon, thinly sliced
- 1 large onion, thinly sliced
- 2 cups water
- 1 cup catsup
- 3 tablespoons Worcestershire sauce
- 1 teaspoon chili powder
- 1 teaspoon salt
- 2 dashes hot pepper sauce

Preheat oven to 450°F. Arrange chops in single layer in shallow baking dish. Cover each with lemon and onion slices. Bake 15 minutes. Combine remaining ingredients in large saucepan and bring to boil over medium-high heat. Pour over meat. Reduce oven temperature to 350°F. Continue baking, basting once or twice, until meat is done, about 30 minutes.

FRUITED PORK CHOPS

6 SERVINGS

- 6 loin or rib pork chops, 1 inch thick
  Salt

- 3 large tart green apples, unpeeled, cored and diced
- 3 tablespoons all purpose flour
- 1 11-ounce can mandarin oranges, drained (syrup reserved)
- 3 tablespoons molasses
- 2 tablespoons cider vinegar
- ⅓ cup raisins

Preheat oven to 350°F. In large skillet, brown chops on both sides over medium-high heat. Transfer to shallow baking dish. Sprinkle with salt and cover with apples.

Drain all but 3 tablespoons fat from skillet. Place skillet over medium heat, add flour and stir until mixture is browned and smooth. Add enough water to mandarin orange syrup to equal 1½ cups liquid. Blend into flour mixture. Stir in molasses and vinegar. Reduce heat to low and continue cooking, stirring constantly, until sauce is thickened. Add raisins and blend well. Pour over chops, cover and bake until chops are tender, about 1 hour. Arrange oranges over top of pork chops during last 10 minutes of cooking.

PORK CHOP MEAL

4 SERVINGS

- ¾ cup uncooked rice
- 4 pork chops cut 1 to 1¼ inches thick
- 1 tomato, sliced
- 1 green pepper, sliced in rings
- 1 onion, sliced
- 1 10½-ounce can beef broth
- ½ cup water (optional)
- 1 teaspoon Worcestershire sauce (optional)

Preheat oven to 375°F. Place rice in buttered 2-quart rectangular casserole. Brown meat in skillet over medium-high heat; arrange on top of rice. Place slice of tomato, green pepper and onion on each chop. Add broth. Cover tightly with foil and bake 60 minutes. Test chops with a fork for tenderness. If moisture has evaporated, add water and Worcestershire sauce.

PORK CHOPS AND SAUERKRAUT

4 SERVINGS

- 1 tablespoon oil or butter
- 4 pork chops (trimmed), ¾ inch thick
- 1 8-ounce jar sauerkraut, drained
- 1 teaspoon caraway seeds
- 1 pint (2 cups) sour cream, room temperature
  Paprika

Preheat oven to 350°F. Heat oil or butter in large skillet over medium-high heat. Add chops and brown well, turning once, about 3 to 4 minutes. Transfer to baking dish. Divide sauerkraut evenly over chops and sprinkle with caraway. Top each with ½ cup sour cream. Sprinkle generously with paprika. Bake until topping is golden, about 25 to 30 minutes. Serve hot.

PORK CHOPS IN WINE SAUCE

4 SERVINGS

- 1 teaspoon sage
- 1 teaspoon rosemary
- 2 medium garlic cloves, chopped
- 1 teaspoon salt
  Freshly ground pepper
- 4 center-cut pork chops, 1 inch thick
- 2 tablespoons (¼ stick) butter
- 1 tablespoon peanut oil
- ¾ cup dry white wine

Combine sage, rosemary, garlic, salt and pepper. Press a little of this mixture firmly into both sides of each of the pork chops.

Melt butter and oil in heavy 10- to 12-inch skillet. Brown chops on both sides, turning carefully with tongs. Remove and pour off all but a small amount of fat from pan. Add ½ cup wine and bring to boil. Return chops to pan. Cover, reduce heat and simmer until chops are tender when pressed with tip of knife, about 25 to 30 minutes.

When ready to serve, remove chops to heated plate. Add remaining wine to skillet and boil down to a syrupy glaze. Pour over chops.

STUFFED PORK CHOPS

4 SERVINGS

- 1 cup mixed dried fruit, cut up
- ¼ cup raisins
- 1 cup white wine
- 2 cups herb stuffing mix
- ¼ cup diced celery
- 2 tablespoons diced onion
- ¼ cup (½ stick) butter, melted
  Water
  Salt and freshly ground pepper
- 4 rib pork chops, 1½ inches thick (slit pocket in each)

Preheat oven to 350°F. Plump mixed fruit and raisins in wine; drain, reserving wine. Combine fruit, stuffing mix, celery and onion. Pour melted butter over and stir. Add water to moisten as desired and blend well. Taste and add salt and pepper as needed. Stuff each chop; lightly pack remaining stuffing in small casserole. Place meat in baking dish, pour reserved wine over, cover with foil and bake 30 minutes. Remove foil and continue baking 30 minutes along with remaining dressing.

SZECHWAN PORK PICNIC-STYLE IN LETTUCE LEAVES

4 SERVINGS

- 4 lean pork chops sliced 1 inch thick
  Boiling water
- 2 fresh red chili peppers or jalapeño peppers, seeded and finely minced, or ½ teaspoon dried red pepper flakes
- 2 cups cooked thin noodles
- 1 cup mixed fresh mint and basil leaves
- 12 large lettuce leaves

Szechwan Sauce

- 4½ tablespoons white vinegar
- 4½ tablespoons light soy sauce
- 4 to 5 small garlic cloves, minced

- 3½ tablespoons sesame oil
  Dash of sugar
  Salt
  Red chili oil* (optional)

Remove pork from bones. Cut meat into very thin slices. Cook in boiling water until done, about 6 minutes. Drain well. Set aside to cool.

For sauce: Combine all ingredients in small bowl and blend well.

Add pork to sauce and toss lightly. Cover and marinate about 30 minutes. Stir in chilies or pepper flakes.

To serve, place small amounts of noodles, pork, mint and basil leaves in each lettuce leaf and fold to enclose. Use additional sauce for dipping if desired.

*Available in oriental markets.

CHORIZO BURRITO

12 SERVINGS

- 12 large flour tortillas
- 2 tablespoons sesame oil
- 1 pound beef or pork chorizos (Mexican sausage), removed from casings
- 3 eggs, lightly beaten
- 1 1-pound 14-ounce can refried beans
- 1 cup grated cheddar or Monterey Jack cheese
- 1 7-ounce can green salsa
- 1 cup sour cream
- ½ bunch cilantro, snipped

Preheat oven to 350°F. Wrap tortillas in foil and place in oven until moist and pliable, about 5 minutes.

Heat oil in large skillet. Add chorizos and cook over medium heat until brown; drain well. Add eggs; cook and stir until set. Remove from heat.

To make burritos, assemble ingredients on each tortilla in following order: 3 to 4 tablespoons beans, 1 heaping tablespoon cheese, 2 to 3 teaspoons salsa (depending on spiciness desired), 1 heaping tablespoon chorizo-egg mixture. Roll or fold envelope-style and place seam side down on serving platter. Dollop with sour cream, garnish with cilantro and serve.

SAUSAGE NOODLE BAKE

This is a favorite after football games.

4 TO 6 SERVINGS

- 1 10½-ounce can cream of chicken soup
- ½ cup milk
- 1½ cups shredded cheddar cheese
- 1 pound pork sausage, cooked and crumbled
- ¼ pound noodles, cooked
- 2 tablespoons chopped green pepper
- 2 tablespoons chopped pimiento
  Buttered cracker crumbs

Preheat oven to 350°F. Generously butter a 2-quart casserole or baking dish. Combine soup and milk in large saucepan and blend well. Cook slowly, stirring occasionally, until sauce is heated through. Add 1 cup cheese and stir until melted. Add sausage, noodles, green pepper and pimiento and heat until well blended. Pour into prepared casserole. Top with cracker crumbs and remaining ½ cup cheese. Cover and bake 20 minutes. Remove lid then bake until top is golden brown and bubbly, about 15 minutes.

ONE-DISH SAUERKRAUT

4 TO 6 SERVINGS

- 2 32-ounce cans sauerkraut
- 1 pound pork spareribs, cut into serving-size pieces
- 1 medium onion, diced
- 1 pound hot Italian sausage
- 1 14½-ounce can chicken broth
- 2 8-ounce cans tomato sauce
- 1 6-ounce can tomato paste
- 3 4-ounce cans or jars mushrooms
- 1 garlic clove, mashed
  Soy sauce to taste
  Dash of hot pepper sauce

Rinse sauerkraut lightly and turn into large pan. Sauté ribs with onion in large skillet. Add to sauerkraut. Cook sausage until well browned. Cut into bite-size pieces and add to pan along with remaining ingredients. Cover and simmer until ribs are tender, about 45 minutes, stirring occasionally. Serve hot.

SWEET AND SOUR SPARERIBS

3 TO 4 SERVINGS

- 2½ to 3 pounds meaty pork spareribs
  Salt and pepper

Sauce

- ¼ cup firmly packed dark brown sugar
- 3 tablespoons lemon juice
- 1 small jar strained apricots, apricots-and-applesauce or pears
- 1½ teaspoons molasses
- 1½ teaspoons dark corn syrup
- ½ teaspoon ground ginger
  Dash of hot pepper sauce
- ¼ cup chili sauce
- 1 small garlic clove, pressed
- 1 tablespoon soy sauce
- ½ teaspoon dry mustard

Sprinkle ribs with salt and pepper. Broil 3 to 5 minutes per side. Place in 9×13-inch baking dish.

For sauce: Mix all ingredients in 1-quart pan. Heat briefly on medium-low, stirring until combined. Reduce oven to 350°F. Pour half the sauce over ribs and bake uncovered 30 minutes. Pour remaining sauce over spareribs and continue baking for another 30 minutes.

NORTHERN-STYLE ONE-POT CHINESE CASSEROLE

8 SERVINGS

- ¼ cup vegetable oil
- 1 pound ground pork
- 2 cups chopped cabbage
- 1 large onion, chopped
- 1 large carrot, shredded
- ½ pound green beans, french cut and sliced into 1-inch pieces
- 3 or 4 dried medium black mushrooms, soaked in hot water 30 minutes, well drained and minced
- 1 teaspoon minced fresh ginger
- ¼ cup soy sauce
- 1½ cups rice
- 2 cups chicken broth
- 2 small zucchini, shredded
  Salt and freshly ground pepper
  Soy sauce (optional)
  Minced green onion (garnish)

Heat oil in wok or large skillet over medium-high heat. Add pork and stir until meat loses pink color. Stir in cabbage, onion, carrot, beans, mushrooms and ginger and stir-fry 2 minutes. Mix in soy sauce. Add rice and stir gently. Pour in broth. Cover tightly and simmer until liquid is almost absorbed, about 20 to 25 minutes. Stir in zucchini and cook about 5 minutes longer. Season with salt and pepper to taste, and soy sauce if desired. Garnish with green onion and serve immediately.

SARDINIAN PORK STEAKS

Although Italian sweet peppers are preferable for this dish, green peppers can be substituted.

6 SERVINGS

- 2 ounces salt pork, diced
  Boiling water
- 2 tablespoons full-bodied olive oil
- 3 pounds pork steaks cut from shoulder, loin or leg
  Salt and freshly ground pepper
- 2 large sweet red peppers, cut into thin strips (about 2×¼ inches)
- 1 large sweet yellow pepper or ½ green pepper, cut into thin strips
- 1 large onion, cut into thin strips
- 1 small green pepper, cut into thin strips
- 1 large garlic clove, minced

1 to 2 small dried hot red peppers, rinsed, partially seeded and cut into thin strips, or 1 long mildly hot red pepper, cut into thin strips

½ cup (or more) veal or chicken stock

1 large tomato, peeled, seeded and chopped

½ cup oil-cured black olives, pitted and coarsely chopped

2 tablespoons capers, rinsed and drained

Blanch salt pork in boiling water 5 minutes; drain, rinse and pat dry. Combine olive oil with salt pork in heavy large skillet and cook over medium heat until pieces of pork begin to color.

Sprinkle steaks lightly on both sides with salt and pepper. Push salt pork to one side of skillet and increase heat to medium-high. Add steaks in batches so sides do not touch and brown on all sides. Remove steaks and set aside.

Increase heat to high. Add sweet red and yellow peppers, onion and green pepper and toss constantly until vegetables begin to color. Sprinkle lightly with salt and pepper. Add garlic and hot pepper and stir-fry briefly. Stir in stock and tomato. Return pork steaks to skillet and baste generously with sauce. Reduce heat, cover and simmer 45 minutes, adding more stock if necessary (mixture should be moist with small amount of liquid). (At this point dish can be refrigerated 1 to 2 days if desired.)

About 20 minutes before ready to serve, stir in olives and capers and reheat, stirring several times. Taste and adjust seasoning. Make bed of peppers and onion mixture on heated platter and arrange pork steaks over top. Moisten with sauce and sprinkle with any olives and capers left in skillet.

SAUTEED PORK WITH ARTICHOKES
See photograph page 108

4 TO 6 SERVINGS

4 large artichokes

1 lemon, halved

2 quarts water

3 tablespoons light olive oil

2 pounds pork sirloin, cut into 1-inch cubes

1 medium onion, minced

4 garlic cloves

1 to 1½ cups (or more) rich chicken stock

2 tablespoons minced fresh Italian parsley

1 tablespoon tomato paste

¼ teaspoon salt

⅛ teaspoon freshly ground pepper

1½ tablespoons minced fresh Italian parsley (garnish)

4 to 6 lemon wedges (garnish)

Snap off coarse outer layers from artichokes leaving meaty sections at base intact. Cut off top fourth of each artichoke and discard, rubbing cut portions with lemon halves as you work. Peel stems if desired. Quarter each artichoke starting from bottom. Cut away choke and purple-tinged inner leaves. Squeeze lemon halves into large bowl. Add water and artichokes and set aside.

Heat oil in large heavy skillet over medium-high heat. Add pork in 2 or 3 batches and sauté on all sides until deeply golden. Remove from skillet using slotted spoon and set aside.

Increase heat to high, add onion and brown quickly. Add drained artichokes and garlic and toss until artichokes begin to color. Stir in stock, 2 tablespoons parsley, tomato paste, salt and pepper and blend well. Return pork to skillet. Reduce heat, cover and simmer until pork is tender, adding more stock if mixture seems too dry, about 50 minutes. (If mixture seems too liquid, cook uncovered about 15 minutes to reduce sauce.) Taste and adjust seasoning. Turn out onto heated platter. Sprinkle with remaining parsley and garnish with lemon wedges.

TORTILLA DE PUERCO CON SALSA TOMATILLO

Refried beans mixed with sour cream is a perfect side dish. You can also serve this tortilla casserole with separate bowls of chopped lettuce, tomatoes, onions, olives and grated cheddar cheese.

8 TO 10 SERVINGS

6 cups (3 pints) sour cream

2 4-ounce cans chopped green chilies

1 2-ounce jar stuffed olives, drained and chopped

12 corn tortillas (thawed, if frozen) cut into 2-inch strips

3 cups cubed cooked pork

2 cups sliced zucchini
Salsa tomatillo (green tomato sauce)

Preheat oven to 325°F. Generously butter 3-quart rectangular casserole. Combine sour cream, chilies and olives and blend well. Alternate layers of tortillas, pork, zucchini and sour cream mixture in baking dish, ending with layer of tortillas topped with sour cream. Bake uncovered until bubbly and heated through, about 45 minutes to 1 hour. Pass salsa separately.

FENNEL SAUSAGES AND POTATOES

4 TO 6 SERVINGS

6 fennel-flavored sausages, thinly sliced

¼ cup (½ stick) butter

4 large potatoes, peeled and grated
Salt and freshly ground pepper

Sauté sausage in frying pan over medium-high heat until crisp. Drain on paper towels. In another frying pan melt butter over medium heat, add potatoes and cook until crisp. Stir in sausage and cook together several minutes. Season with salt and pepper to taste.

YUGOSLAV PORK WITH STRING BEANS

4 SERVINGS

    Oil
1 large onion, thinly sliced
1 large green pepper (or 2 small), seeded and thinly sliced
1 pound pork tenderloin, cut into bite-size chunks
¼ to ½ teaspoon paprika
    Salt and freshly ground pepper
½ pound green beans, trimmed
½ cup water
2 tablespoons flour
    Oil
    Paprika
    Sour cream (garnish)

Heat small amount of oil in large skillet over medium-high heat. Add onion and green pepper and sauté until browned. Stir in pork, paprika, salt and pepper to taste and continue cooking until meat is browned. Stir in beans and water, reduce heat, cover and simmer until pork is tender, about 45 minutes.

About 5 minutes before serving, brown flour in small amount of oil over low heat. Add paprika for color and stir constantly for 2 to 3 minutes. Add to meat and continue cooking until sauce thickens. Serve hot topped with sour cream.

VEAL

BRAISED VEAL CHOPS IN TARRAGON CREAM

Parslied pilaf is an excellent accompaniment to this dish.

4 TO 6 SERVINGS

1 cup whipping cream
2 tablespoons finely minced fresh tarragon
1 tablespoon Dijon mustard

4 to 6 rib veal chops cut ¾ inch thick
    Salt and freshly ground pepper
    Flour
2 to 3 tablespoons (¼ to ⅜ stick) butter
1 tablespoon oil
2 cups finely sliced onion
1 teaspoon finely minced garlic
¼ cup white wine vinegar
1 large sprig fresh tarragon
1 bay leaf
½ cup brown chicken stock or bouillon
    Finely minced fresh parsley (garnish)

Position rack in center of oven and preheat to 325°F. Combine first 3 ingredients and blend well; set aside.

Dry chops thoroughly with paper towels. Season with salt and pepper. Dredge lightly with flour, shaking off excess. Heat 2 tablespoons butter with a little oil in heavy 12-inch skillet over medium-high heat. Add chops 2 to 3 at a time and sauté until nicely browned, about 2 to 3 minutes per side. Remove.

If fat in skillet has burned, wipe out pan and add a little more butter and oil. Place over medium heat, add onion and garlic and sauté until onion is soft and nicely browned, about 5 to 6 minutes; do not burn. Season with salt and pepper. Add vinegar, tarragon and bay leaf. Bring to simmer and let cook until vinegar is reduced by half. Return chops to skillet and add a little of the stock. Cover and braise 25 minutes, adding a little stock about every 10 minutes and turning meat once.

Transfer chops to heated serving platter and keep warm. Discard tarragon and bay leaf. Bring pan juices to simmer over direct heat, add cream mixture and cook until sauce is reduced and heavily coats spoon. Taste and adjust seasoning. Spoon over chops, sprinkle with parsley and serve immediately.

Tarragon cream can also be used as a sauce to complement tournedos or hamburgers.

VEAL CHOPS WITH TOMATO SAUCE

5 SERVINGS

½ cup dry white wine
1 10½-ounce can onion soup
2 tablespoons tomato paste
½ teaspoon dried basil
¼ cup all purpose flour
    Salt and freshly ground pepper
5 thick veal chops, trimmed
3 tablespoons (⅜ stick) butter
2 tablespoons olive oil
    Freshly cooked buttered pasta

Preheat oven to 375°F. Blend first 4 ingredients in small bowl and set aside. Combine flour, salt and pepper in shallow dish. Dredge chops in flour, shaking off excess. Heat butter with oil in large skillet over medium-high heat. Add chops and brown evenly on both sides. Transfer to baking dish. Pour off any excess fat from skillet. Add wine mixture to skillet and stir over medium-high heat until sauce is thickened, scraping up any browned bits clinging to bottom. Pour over chops and bake tented with foil until meat tests done, about 25 minutes. Serve with freshly cooked and buttered pasta.

VEAL CORDON BLEU WITH MUSHROOM SAUCE

4 SERVINGS

8 thin slices ham or prosciutto
8 veal cutlets, pounded thin
2 tablespoons grated Romano cheese
2 tablespoons grated Parmesan cheese
    Flour
1 egg, beaten
¾ cup breadcrumbs seasoned with 1 tablespoon Parmesan cheese, ¼ teaspoon paprika and dash of salt
3 tablespoons (⅜ stick) butter

¼ cup chopped shallot
¼ cup chopped green pepper
1 garlic clove, minced
1 cup sliced fresh mushrooms
¼ teaspoon cracked black pepper
½ cup cream of mushroom soup
¼ cup milk
2 tablespoons dry Marsala wine
Chopped parsley (garnish)

Lay 2 slices ham on each of 4 veal cutlets. Sprinkle generously with Romano and Parmesan cheeses. Top with remaining veal and press edges together tightly to seal. Dredge lightly in flour. Dip in egg, then roll in seasoned breadcrumbs.

Melt butter in 10-inch skillet over medium-high heat. Add veal and sauté until golden, turning once. Remove from pan and keep warm. Add shallot, green pepper and garlic to skillet and sauté until almost tender. Stir in mushrooms and cracked pepper. Reduce heat, return veal to skillet and simmer about 2 minutes to heat through, turning once.

Meanwhile, combine mushroom soup and milk in small saucepan and bring just to boiling point, stirring frequently. Remove from heat and stir in Marsala. Add to skillet and continue simmering until sauce reaches desired consistency. Transfer veal to warmed serving platter, spoon sauce over top of meat and garnish with parsley.

VEAL NORMANDE

4 TO 6 SERVINGS

1½ tablespoons butter
1½ tablespoons oil
6 thinly sliced veal cutlets, pounded
5 tablespoons brandy
½ teaspoon freeze-dried shallots

1 10½-ounce can cream of mushroom soup
⅔ cup milk
1 tart medium apple, peeled, cored and thinly sliced
Freshly cooked wild rice

Melt butter with oil in large skillet over medium-high heat. Add veal and brown, turning once. Transfer to platter. Add brandy and shallots to skillet and stir, scraping up any browned bits clinging to bottom of pan. Blend in soup and milk. Return veal to pan with apple. Reduce heat and simmer, stirring once or twice, until heated through. Serve over rice.

Can substitute 6 chicken breast halves, skinned, boned and pounded.

VEAL IN SHERRY

4 SERVINGS

1 pound veal scallops, pounded thin
Salt and freshly ground pepper
Flour
⅓ cup (¾ stick) melted butter
½ cup dry sherry
½ cup chopped parsley (garnish)
Freshly cooked rice or buttered noodles

Sprinkle scallops with salt and pepper and dredge in flour. Heat butter in large skillet over medium heat. Add veal and sauté 4 to 5 minutes on each side. Add sherry and boil 1 minute, deglazing pan. Garnish with parsley and serve with freshly cooked rice or buttered noodles.

VEAL SCALOPPINE WITH MUSHROOM SAUCE

4 SERVINGS

Mushroom Sauce*
1 pound veal scaloppine
2 tablespoons flour
Salt and freshly ground pepper
1 egg
2 tablespoons water
1½ cups breadcrumbs

3 to 5 tablespoons oil
1 to 2 tablespoons butter

Prepare sauce and keep warm.

Pound meat between 2 sheets of waxed paper until very thin. Combine flour, salt and pepper in pie plate. Beat egg with water in shallow dish. Dredge meat in flour, dip into egg mixture and then roll in breadcrumbs. Lightly pound slices with flat of knife so crumbs adhere.

Heat 3 tablespoons oil with 1 tablespoon butter in large skillet over medium-high heat. Add meat in batches and sauté until browned, turning once, about 3 to 5 minutes, adding more oil and butter as necessary. Transfer to platter and spoon mushroom sauce over top of veal. Serve immediately.

Also works well with 1 pound chicken breasts, skinned and boned.

*Mushroom Sauce

¾ cup chicken broth
1 tablespoon flour
1 tablespoon butter
1 teaspoon finely chopped green onion, white part only
1½ cups thinly sliced mushrooms
½ cup whipping cream
Salt and freshly ground pepper
Nutmeg
Pinch of ground red pepper

Combine broth and flour in small bowl and stir until flour is dissolved. Melt butter in medium skillet over medium-high heat. Add onion and sauté until tender, about 1 minute. Reduce heat to medium. Add mushrooms and cook about 2 to 3 minutes. Stir in broth. Increase heat to medium-high and cook until slightly thickened, stirring occasionally, about 10 minutes. Blend in cream, salt and pepper. Season with nutmeg and red pepper.

DO AHEAD

BEEF

BEER STEAK

6 TO 8 SERVINGS

- ¼ cup (½ stick) butter, or ¼ cup bacon drippings
- 2 pounds round steak, about 1 inch thick
  Flour
- 1 large onion, chopped
- 1 cup beer
  Bouquet garni (1 bay leaf, sprig of parsley, ¼ teaspoon leaf thyme)
  Salt and freshly ground pepper

Preheat oven to 275°F. Heat butter or bacon drippings in large skillet over medium-high heat. Dredge meat in flour and brown quickly on both sides. Remove and set aside. Add onion and sauté until softened. Remove half and spread remaining onion evenly in skillet. Add meat and top with reserved onion. Pour in beer and add bouquet garni and salt and pepper to taste. Cover and bake until fork tender, about 2 hours.

CALIFORNIA MARINATED CHUCK STEAK

The secret of this excellent steak is to start with the tenderest cut of the chuck—the first cut right next to the rib portion of the steer. If the meat is aged prime or heavy choice, it will taste even better.

4 TO 6 SERVINGS

- 1 cup beer
- ¼ cup soy sauce
- ¼ cup pineapple juice
- ½ small onion, cut into chunks
- 2 garlic cloves
- 2 tablespoons brown sugar
- 2 tablespoons vinegar
- ¼ teaspoon grated fresh ginger
- 1 3- to 3¼-pound first cut (also known as blade) chuck steak, about 2½ to 3 inches thick, trimmed of all fat
  Watercress or parsley (garnish)

Puree all ingredients except meat and garnish. Pour marinade over steak. Cover tightly and marinate overnight in refrigerator, turning steaks over once.

Preheat broiler. Cover bottom of broiler pan with water and set rack in place. Drain marinade from steak. Broil meat about 2 to 4 inches from heat source until browned on each side. Reduce temperature to 375°F and continue cooking about 6 to 8 minutes per side for rare, 8 to 10 minutes for medium rare, and 10 to 12 minutes for medium. Place on heated platter and garnish. Separate meat from bones with sharp knife, then slice. Garnish steaks with watercress or parsley.

STEAK FLORENTINE

2 SERVINGS

- 2 T-bone or porterhouse steaks, cut at least 1¼ inches thick
- 2 to 3 tablespoons Italian olive oil
- ⅛ teaspoon freshly ground pepper
  Lemon wedges

Rub steaks with oil and pepper and let stand at room temperature 1 hour. Pan-broil according to basic recipe. Serve with lemon wedges, letting each guest flavor meat to his or her own taste.

CARAWAY BEEF STEW

6 SERVINGS

- ½ cup (1 stick) butter or margarine
- 3 pounds chuck, sirloin or top round, cut into 1-inch cubes
- 1 dozen medium onions, sliced
- 2 tablespoons sweet paprika
- 1 tablespoon caraway seeds
- 1 tablespoon marjoram
- 2 teaspoons salt
  Juice of half a lemon
- 1 large garlic clove, crushed (optional)
- ½ cup dry red wine
- 1 tablespoon flour
- 1 tablespoon tomato paste
  Chopped parsley (garnish)

In a large stewpot or Dutch oven, melt butter until it bubbles. Add meat all at once, turning until cooked on all sides. Mix in onions and half each of paprika, caraway, marjoram, salt and lemon juice. Add garlic clove, if desired, and wine. Stirring occasionally, simmer uncovered until cubes of meat are tender, about 1½ to 2 hours.

Blend in remaining paprika, caraway, marjoram, salt, lemon juice, and flour mixed with tomato paste and a bit of liquid from the stew. Simmer 15 minutes more. Garnish stew with parsley.

May be prepared the night before and then reheated.

Opposite
Czechoslovak Pepper Steak accompanied by buttery Caraway Noodles is a perfect do-ahead entrée.

Page 106–107
Both Beef and Scallop Sauté (above right) and Seafood Succotash (below left) combine traditional American tastes with a nouvelle cuisine light touch.

Page 108
Sautéed Pork with Artichokes combines perfectly browned loin with artichokes in a garlic-scented tomato sauce.

Page 109
Quick Potage Saint-Germain is a fresh-tasting start. Roast Chicken with Rosemary Butter rests on a bed of Stir-Fry of Sweet Peppers and Zucchini. Asiago with Pears are a light and different dessert.

Page 110–111
Sherried Scallops with Snow Peas is the perfect first course. Tangy Lemon-Mustard Sauce adds zip to Butterflied Lamb. Scallioned Rice in Lettuce Cups and Sautéed Carrots with Apricot are accompaniments. Coupe Marron is the rich finish.

Page 112
Smoked Salmon Tart is a glamorous entrée. The appropriate garnish for this superb creation? Red caviar, of course!

Czechoslovak Pepper Steak with
Caraway Noodles
Recipe page 113

106

Top right: Beef and Scallop Sauté
Recipe page 92
Bottom left: Seafood Succotash
Recipe page 74

Sautéed Pork with Artichokes
Recipe page 101

Potage Saint-Germain
Recipe page 38
Roast Chicken with Rosemary Butter
Recipe page 82
Stir-Fry of Sweet Peppers and Zucchini
Recipe page 144
Asiago and Pears
Recipe page 176

Sherried Scallops with Snow Peas
Recipe page 77
Butterflied Lamb with Lemon-Mustard
Sauce
Recipe page 96
Scallioned Rice in Lettuce Cups
Recipe page 163
Sautéed Carrots with Apricot
Recipe page 141
Coupe Marron
Recipe page 185

Smoked Salmon Tart
Recipe page 62

CZECHOSLOVAK PEPPER STEAK WITH CARAWAY NOODLES

See photograph page 105

Serve with a lightly chilled Gamay or Beaujolais.

4 SERVINGS

- 1½ pounds top sirloin or tender chuck, well trimmed and cut on the diagonal into slices ½ inch thick
  All purpose flour
  Salt
- 2 tablespoons lard, bacon fat or vegetable oil
- 1 medium onion, minced
- 1 small garlic clove, minced
- 2 teaspoons imported sweet Hungarian paprika (do not substitute Spanish paprika)
- 1 cup (about) beef stock
- ¼ cup tomato puree
- 2 red bell peppers cut into ¼-inch strips*
- 2 green bell peppers cut into ¼-inch strips*
  Salt and freshly ground pepper
- 1 cup sour cream (garnish)
  Caraway Noodles**

Place beef slices between 2 sheets of waxed paper and pound to thickness of ¼ inch. Sprinkle lightly with flour and salt.

Heat lard in heavy, large, non-aluminum skillet over medium-high heat. Add meat in 2 batches and brown well on all sides. Remove from pan and set aside.

Pour off all but 2 tablespoons fat from skillet. Add onion and sauté over medium heat until soft, about 10 minutes. Stir in garlic and cook about 20 seconds. Add paprika and cook a few seconds. Stir in stock and puree, scraping up any browned bits clinging to bottom of pan. Return beef to skillet and bring to simmer. Cover partially and cook until beef is almost tender, about 40 minutes. Pepper steak can be prepared to this point and refrigerated.

Add peppers, cover partially and simmer until slightly softened and beef is tender, about 20 minutes. Season to taste with salt and pepper. Transfer to heated shallow bowl and pass sour cream and noodles separately when serving.

*If available, substitute sweet Italian "frying" peppers for bell peppers.

**Caraway Noodles

- 4 quarts water
- 1 tablespoon salt
- ½ pound wide egg noodles
- 3 tablespoons (⅜ stick) butter
- 3 tablespoons minced onion
- 1 teaspoon caraway seeds
  Salt and freshly ground pepper

Bring water and salt to boil in large saucepan or Dutch oven. Add noodles and cook until tender but firm. Drain; rinse with warm water and drain again.

Melt butter in same pan over medium heat. Add onion and sauté until soft. Stir in caraway and cook about 1 minute. Add noodles, tossing to heat through. Season to taste with salt and pepper. Turn into heated serving bowl.

MARINATED FLANK STEAK

4 TO 6 SERVINGS

- 1 cup chili sauce
- ¼ cup soy sauce
- 2 tablespoons Worcestershire sauce
- 2 tablespoons molasses
- ½ teaspoon chili powder
- ½ teaspoon dried minced onion
- ½ teaspoon liquid smoke
- ¼ teaspoon garlic powder
  Salt and freshly ground pepper
- 1 2- to 2½-pound flank steak

Combine first 8 ingredients with salt and pepper to taste. Place meat in baking dish and pour marinade over. Refrigerate at least 2 hours or overnight, turning meat once or twice. Pan-fry or broil to desired degree of doneness. Carve flank steak by slicing diagonally.

STEAK TIPS WITH HORSERADISH SAUCE

Perfect party fare—an easy-to-prepare buffet dish with its own tangy sauce. Prepare the meat a day ahead, but don't slice it until the day of the party to ensure juiciness. Sauce can be prepared the night before the party and chilled.

25 SERVINGS

- 9 large garlic cloves or to taste, minced
- 6 to 7 tablespoons oil
- 3 2- to 2½-pound triangle tip roasts
  Salt and freshly ground pepper
  Horseradish Sauce*

Combine garlic and oil. Rub thoroughly into meat and sprinkle generously with salt and pepper. Let roasts stand at room temperature for 2 to 3 hours.

Prepare charcoal grill and preheat oven to 400°F. Grill meat very briefly just to seal in juices. Transfer to rack set in roasting pan and roast to desired doneness, about 45 to 60 minutes for medium-rare. Remove from oven and let cool. Wrap in foil and refrigerate overnight. Thinly slice and arrange on platter. Serve with Horseradish Sauce.

*Horseradish Sauce

MAKES 7 CUPS

- 4 cups (2 pints) sour cream
- 1 cup white horseradish, drained
- 5 slices fresh white bread (crusts trimmed), torn into fine pieces
- 2 cups whipping cream

Combine first 3 ingredients in large bowl and mash with fork to blend well. Whip cream until stiff. Stir ¼ into horseradish mixture to loosen, then gently fold in remainder. Cover and refrigerate until ready to serve.

SOUR CREAM SUPREME

8 SERVINGS

- 1 tablespoon oil
- 1½ pounds lean ground beef or veal
- 1 garlic clove, minced
- 2 8-ounce cans tomato sauce
- 1 teaspoon sugar
- 1 teaspoon salt
  Freshly ground pepper
- 1 8-ounce package (2½ cups) elbow macaroni
- 1 cup sour cream
- 1 3-ounce package cream cheese, room temperature
- 5 green onions including tops, minced
- ½ pound cheddar cheese, grated

Heat oil in medium skillet over medium heat. Add meat and garlic and brown well; drain off excess fat. Add tomato sauce, sugar, salt and pepper. Reduce heat and simmer 20 minutes, stirring occasionally.

Meanwhile, cook macaroni according to package directions. Drain thoroughly and set aside. Combine sour cream, cream cheese and green onions in small bowl and blend thoroughly.

Grease 9×13-inch baking dish or 2 8-inch square baking pans. Place macaroni on bottom, top with sour cream mixture, then meat sauce. Sprinkle with grated cheese. Cover and refrigerate overnight or wrap well and freeze.

When ready to use: If casserole has been refrigerated, preheat oven to 350°F and bake uncovered about 45 minutes. If dish has been frozen, preheat oven to 375°F and bake uncovered 55 to 60 minutes.

TAMALE PIE

6 SERVINGS

- 1 large onion, chopped
- 2 garlic cloves, crushed
- 4 tablespoons (½ stick) butter
- 2 pounds lean ground beef
- 1 8-ounce can tomato sauce
- 1 12-ounce can corn, drained (reserve liquid)
- 1 tablespoon chili powder
  Salt and pepper
- 1 4-ounce can diced green chilies, drained
- 1 15-ounce can chili and beans
- 1 16-ounce package corn muffin mix
- 2 eggs
- ⅔ cup milk
- 1 tablespoon dill
- 1 tablespoon cumin

Brown onion and garlic in butter. Add beef, ½ pound at a time. Break up with fork and sauté in skillet until beef is browned.

Add tomato sauce, corn, chili powder, salt and pepper to taste. Simmer mixture 15 minutes.

Add green chilies and chili and beans. If mixture is too dry, moisten with reserved corn liquid. Spoon mixture into a 2-quart baking dish. (Can refrigerate at this point, which will allow flavors to mingle.)

Preheat oven to 400°F. Stir dry corn muffin mix with eggs, milk and herbs. Pour over chili mixture and bake for 10 minutes. Reduce heat to 350°F and bake until top is nicely browned, about 30 minutes.

GREEK MEATBALLS

4 TO 6 SERVINGS

- 2 pounds lean ground beef
- ½ cup lightly packed chopped fresh mint
- ½ cup lightly packed chopped fresh parsley
- ¼ cup coarsely chopped pine nuts
- ¼ cup finely chopped onion
- 1 garlic clove, minced
- 1½ teaspoons salt
  Flour

Thoroughly combine all ingredients except flour. Form into 12 oval-shaped balls. Roll in flour; freeze. Grill or sauté over high heat until very brown outside and still rare inside. Set aside.

About 30 minutes before serving, preheat oven to 300°F. Place meatballs in baking dish and cook until as well done as desired, about 25 to 30 minutes.

ROSY MEATBALLS

6 TO 8 SERVINGS

- 1 pound ground beef
- ½ cup cracker crumbs or breadcrumbs
- 1 egg, beaten
- 1 teaspoon instant minced onion, rehydrated
- ¼ teaspoon dry mustard
  Salt and freshly ground pepper
- 1 16-ounce can whole berry cranberry sauce
- 1 8-ounce can tomato sauce

Combine ground beef, crumbs, egg, onion, mustard, salt and pepper and mix well. Shape into bite-size meatballs and brown carefully on all sides in large skillet over medium-high heat.

Mix cranberry and tomato sauces in small bowl and pour over meatballs. Simmer covered 30 minutes.

Recipe may be made ahead and reheated if desired.

MEAT LOAF WELLINGTON

4 SERVINGS

- 1 medium onion, chopped
  Butter
- 1 egg
- 1 pound lean ground beef
- ½ cup seasoned bread stuffing mix
- 3 tablespoons grated Parmesan cheese
- 2 tablespoons chopped parsley
  Salt and freshly ground pepper
- 1 egg
- 1 tablespoon water
- 1 package (8) refrigerated crescent rolls
  Easy Gravy*

Preheat oven to 350°F. Sauté onion in butter until softened. Lightly beat egg in medium mixing bowl. Add beef, stuffing mix, cheese, parsley, onion, salt and pepper to taste and combine gently but thoroughly. Form into loaf shape (about 8×4 inches) and place on baking sheet.

Beat remaining egg with water. Separate rolls and lay over top and sides of loaf patchwork fashion, sealing edges of rolls with egg-water glaze. Brush with remaining glaze and bake about 1 hour. Slice and serve with Easy Gravy.

If desired, additional rolls may be cut into shapes with cookie cutter and used to decorate top.

*Easy Gravy

   1 package instant brown gravy mix
   ½ cup port or red wine
   ½ cup water

Combine ingredients in saucepan and cook according to directions on packaged gravy.

LAMB

CHAMPAGNE LAMB CHOPS

2 TO 4 SERVINGS

   4 2-inch-thick loin lamb chops
   ½ bottle champagne
   1 teaspoon garlic powder
      Salt

Place all ingredients in baking dish. Marinate 45 minutes or overnight. Preheat oven to 350°F. Drain meat. Bake until cooked as desired, about 35 to 45 minutes.

MARINATED LAMB CHOPS

4 SERVINGS

   4 sirloin lamb chops, about 1 inch thick
      Stone-ground mustard
      Salt and freshly ground pepper
      Red wine

Rub both sides of chops with mustard. Sprinkle with salt and pepper to taste. Cover with wine and marinate

overnight in refrigerator. Rub again with mustard just before broiling or pan-frying to desired doneness.

MINTY LAMB CHOPS

4 SERVINGS

   ⅓ cup chopped fresh mint
   1 garlic clove, minced
      Juice of 1 lemon
   ½ cup olive oil
      Salt and pepper
   8 loin lamb chops
      Herb Butter*

Combine first 5 ingredients in food processor or blender. Pour over lamb chops. Marinate overnight at room temperature, turning once.

When ready to broil, remove chops from marinade. Blot on paper towels and broil until desired doneness is reached. Serve each chop with a dollop of Herb Butter.

*Herb Butter

   ½ cup (1 stick) butter, room temperature
   2 tablespoons minced fresh mint
   1 tablespoon minced parsley
   2 garlic cloves, minced

Blend all ingredients. Chill.

LAMB BANDIT

6 SERVINGS

   6 round or blade bone shoulder chops, boned and cut ¾ to 1 inch thick

Marinade

   2 large garlic cloves, minced
   1 teaspoon oregano
   ½ cup olive oil
   ½ cup dry sherry
   ¼ cup lemon juice
   1 medium onion, sliced
   2 tablespoons parsley
   2 tablespoons fresh mint
      Parchment paper or heavy-duty foil squares
   6 tomato slices, ½ inch thick
   6 tablespoons Feta cheese, rinsed and crumbled

   6 tablespoons coarsely shredded Kasseri cheese
   2 medium potatoes, thinly sliced
   2 medium carrots, julienned
   2 celery stalks, sliced
  12 boiling onions, halved
   1½ teaspoons oregano
   3 tablespoons fresh lemon juice
      Skordalia Sauce*

Remove all fat from chops. Place in single layer at bottom of a 9×13-inch baking dish.

For marinade: Puree first 8 ingredients in blender. Pour over chops, pricking meat with fork to allow marinade to penetrate. Chill overnight, turning several times.

Drain meat, reserving marinade, and brown quickly under broiler or in skillet. Brush one side of parchment paper or foil with a tablespoon of marinade. Place a chop on each. Top with remaining vegetables, cheeses and seasoning, in order listed, dividing evenly.

Preheat oven to 375°F. Drizzle 1 tablespoon marinade over ingredients. Fold parchment or foil over meat and vegetables. Crimp edges tightly. Bake on a cookie sheet 1 hour.

Serve from parchment, allowing guests to open their own packets and savor the aroma. Accompany with Skordalia Sauce if you wish.

Two-inch cubes of lean, boned lamb may be substituted for chops, allowing 2 pounds for 6 servings.

*Skordalia Sauce

   1 cup plain mashed potatoes (no milk or butter)
   ½ cup mayonnaise
   3 garlic cloves
   1 tablespoon olive oil
   1 tablespoon lemon juice or to taste
   ½ teaspoon salt
      Pepper to taste

Combine all ingredients in blender and puree at high speed. Taste for salt and pepper. Thin with additional mayonnaise, oil or lemon juice.

BARBECUED BUTTERFLIED LEG OF LAMB

A crisp green salad, steaming corn on the cob, crusty French bread, and a slightly chilled bottle of a fruity Gamay or Beaujolais will make this a memorable menu.

6 TO 8 SERVINGS

Sauce

- 1 cup catsup
- 1 cup water
- ¼ cup Worcestershire sauce
- ¼ cup vinegar
  Few drops of hot pepper sauce
- ¼ cup firmly packed brown sugar
- 1 teaspoon celery salt
- 1 teaspoon chili powder
- 1 teaspoon salt
- 1 6-pound leg of lamb, boned, trimmed and butterflied

For sauce: Combine ingredients in 2-quart pan. Bring to a simmer, but do not boil. Remove from heat and pour over lamb. Marinate overnight in refrigerator.

Barbecue lamb 8 to 10 inches from hot coals for about 50 minutes, turning often and basting every 10 to 15 minutes. Do not overcook. It should be crisp on the outside and pink inside. (May also broil.)

BUTTERFLIED LAMB IN THE STYLE OF THE SOUTH

"The South," in this case, is the southwestern area of France, where this seasoning and broiling combination supposedly originated.

6 TO 8 SERVINGS

- 16 branches fresh rosemary, lightly bruised, or 2 tablespoons crumbled dried leaves
- 12 branches fresh thyme, lightly bruised, or 2 teaspoons crumbled dried leaves
- 3 garlic cloves, lightly crushed
- 1 25.6-ounce bottle (1 fifth) Beaujolais
- ¼ cup olive oil

- 1 branch fresh sage, lightly bruised, or ¼ teaspoon crumbled dried leaves
- 1 teaspoon coarsely ground pepper
  Salt
- 1 6- to 7-pound leg of lamb, boned and butterflied

Combine all ingredients except lamb in large bowl and blend well. Set lamb in large shallow dish and pour marinade over. Cover and refrigerate overnight, turning at least once. Drain off marinade into bowl and pat the meat dry.

Heat coals until gray ash forms. Spread into overlapping layer and let burn 30 minutes. Set grill 4 inches above coals; let coals burn until moderately hot. (May also broil.)

Place lamb flat on grill and cook, brushing occasionally with marinade and adding coals to fire if necessary, until meat thermometer inserted in thickest part registers 135°F (medium-rare), about 20 minutes per side. Let stand about 10 minutes, then slice thinly.

RACK OF LAMB WITH FRESH MINT SAUCE

4 TO 6 SERVINGS

- 2 racks of lamb (1¾ to 2 pounds each), well trimmed
- ¼ cup brandy
- ½ teaspoon dried thyme
- ½ teaspoon salt
- ¼ teaspoon freshly ground pepper
  Flour
- 1 egg lightly beaten with 1 tablespoon half and half
- 1 cup Italian seasoned breadcrumbs

Sauce

- ½ cup olive oil
- ½ cup red wine vinegar
- 6 to 8 fresh mint leaves

- 1 teaspoon salt
  Freshly ground pepper

Place lamb in large shallow baking dish. Combine brandy, thyme, salt and pepper in small bowl and mix well. Pour over lamb, cover and marinate overnight.

Bring lamb to room temperature. Preheat oven to 450°F. Dip lamb in flour, shaking off excess. Dip in egg mixture and then roll in breadcrumbs to coat evenly. Bake fat side up until top is crusty and golden brown, about 30 to 35 minutes (meat will be between medium and medium-rare).

For sauce: While meat is cooking, combine ingredients in blender or food processor and blend thoroughly. Pass separately.

MUSTARD SHISH KEBABS

4 SERVINGS

- 1 2-pound lean, boned leg of lamb, cut into 1-inch cubes (not thicker)

Marinade

- 3 tablespoons Dijon mustard
- 2 tablespoons white wine vinegar
- 2 tablespoons olive oil
- ¼ teaspoon rosemary
- ¼ teaspoon sage
- 1 to 3 garlic cloves, minced
  Salt and pepper
- 1 large green pepper, cut into ¾-inch squares
- 1 large sweet red pepper, cut into ¾-inch squares
  Butter, room temperature (optional)

Combine first 6 marinade ingredients in medium bowl. Add lamb and sprinkle with salt and pepper. Mix to coat lamb thoroughly. Marinate in refrigerator overnight.

Remove meat from refrigerator ½ hour before cooking. Preheat broiler or barbecue. Alternate meat and peppers on skewers. Broil until meat is browned, brushing the cubes with butter if desired.

PORK

ROAST PORK

6 SERVINGS

- 1 3-pound boned pork loin
- 1 large onion, chopped
- 6 garlic cloves, crushed
- ½ cup soy sauce
- ¼ cup cider vinegar
- 2 tablespoons oil
- 1 tablespoon brown sugar
- 1 teaspoon curry powder
- 1 teaspoon oregano
- ½ teaspoon pepper
  Pungent Fruit Sauce (see recipe page 43)

Split meat lengthwise. Combine remaining ingredients except sauce in large bowl and add meat. Cover and marinate overnight, turning meat over occasionally.

Preheat oven to 375°F. Drain meat, place in shallow pan on rack and roast until meat thermometer registers between 170°F to 185°F, about 1½ hours. Serve roasted pork loin with Pungent Fruit Sauce.

"THE REAL THING" HAM

6 TO 8 SERVINGS

- 1 3-pound canned ham
- ¼ cup Dijon mustard
  Cloves
- ⅓ cup orange marmalade
- ¼ cup maple syrup
- 2 tablespoons cider vinegar
- 1 cup red wine
- ⅓ cup cola

Preheat oven to 350°F. Place ham, fat side up, in baking pan. Coat with mustard and stud with cloves. Add layer of orange marmalade; top with maple syrup. Combine vinegar, wine and cola and pour over ham, letting mixture drip down sides.

Bake 1 hour, basting every 15 minutes. Remove from oven and let ham stand another 15 minutes before you slice and serve.

CHARCUTERIE SALAD

4 TO 6 SERVINGS

- 1 pound cooked well-marbled pork, trimmed of all fat and cut into thin sticks
- ¼ cup light olive oil
- ¼ cup Spanish Sherry wine vinegar
- 6 cornichons, cut julienne
- 2 green onions, minced
- 1 large shallot, minced
- 1 pound new potatoes
- ¼ cup wine vinegar
- 3 tablespoons light olive oil
- 3 tablespoons minced sweet red onion
- 1 heaping teaspoon Dijon mustard
  Salt and freshly ground pepper
- 1 large head romaine
- 1 cup julienned roasted sweet red peppers
- 2 green onions, cut into very thin 2-inch strips
- 1 tablespoon capers, rinsed and drained

Combine pork, oil, Sherry vinegar, cornichons, minced green onion and shallot in medium bowl and toss ingredients gently. Cover mixture and refrigerate 1 to 2 days.

Boil potatoes in large saucepan in water to cover until tender. Drain well. Return to hot pan and place over heat to dry, shaking pan constantly. Let stand until cool enough to handle, then peel and cut into medium dice. Combine potatoes, wine vinegar, oil, red onion, mustard, salt and pepper in another bowl and toss lightly. Cover and refrigerate overnight.

To serve, arrange lettuce leaves on large platter, leaving center almost empty. Add peppers to pork mixture and toss well. Taste and season with salt and pepper. Arrange potato salad over lettuce in shallow ring

and sprinkle with green onion. Mound pork in center; top with capers. Serve lightly chilled.

OCCIDENTAL-ORIENTAL SPARERIBS

8 SERVINGS

- 1 1-pound can hoisin sauce
- ⅔ cup barbecue sauce (not hickory flavored)
- 2 tablespoons fresh lemon juice
- 1 rack (about 5 pounds) spareribs, cut into bite-size pieces

Combine sauces and lemon juice. Place ribs in 9×13-inch baking dish or shallow roasting pan and pour marinade over. Cover and refrigerate overnight, stirring once or twice. Bake, uncovered, at 350°F until meat is done, about 1 hour (time will depend on size of ribs).

MINNESOTA WILD RICE AND SAUSAGE CASSEROLE

6 TO 8 SERVINGS

- ¾ pound bulk pork sausage
- ½ cup chopped celery
- 1 tablespoon dehydrated bell pepper flakes
- 1 10½-ounce can cream of mushroom soup
- 1 cup hot water
- 1 4-ounce package (¾ cup) wild rice, soaked overnight
- ¾ cup grated American cheese
- 1 4-ounce can pimientos, drained and chopped
- 1 2-ounce can mushrooms, drained
- 1 tablespoon minced onion
- 1 teaspoon seasoned chicken stock base
- ½ teaspoon marjoram
- ½ teaspoon thyme

Preheat oven to 375°F. Grease 3-quart casserole. Crumble sausage into large skillet and brown over medium-high heat. Add celery and pepper flakes and cook until soft. Drain off fat. Add remaining ingredients and mix thoroughly. Turn into casserole and bake covered until all liquid is absorbed, about 1 hour.

SPARERIBS WITH ALABAMA BARBECUE SAUCE

If you refrigerate this sauce, it will keep quite well up to 2 weeks.

4 TO 6 SERVINGS

Alabama Barbecue Sauce

2 tablespoons oil
1 onion, minced
1 large garlic clove, minced
½ cup catsup
½ cup cider vinegar
⅓ cup honey
¼ cup Worcestershire sauce
2 teaspoons dry mustard
1 teaspoon ground ginger
1 teaspoon salt
   Juice of 1 lemon
4 pounds pork spareribs, well trimmed

For sauce: Heat oil in saucepan over low heat. Add onion and garlic and sauté until soft. Add all remaining ingredients (except ribs) and simmer 15 minutes. Remove sauce from heat and set it aside.

Heat coals until gray ash forms. Spread into overlapping layer and let burn 20 minutes. Set grill about 3 inches above coals. (Fire should be gentle so ribs do not burn. If it seems too hot, spread coals farther apart; if too slow, add more coals and push close together.)

Arrange ribs on grill and cook slowly 30 minutes, turning once. Brush ribs generously with sauce and cook another 20 minutes. Turn ribs, brush again with sauce and cook 20 minutes longer. (May also broil.)

COMPANY PORK

4 SERVINGS

8 pork tenderloin steaks, 1 inch thick
2 cups pineapple juice
½ cup soy sauce
2 garlic cloves, crushed

Place pork in shallow baking dish. Combine remaining ingredients and pour over pork. Cover and refrigerate overnight, turning once. Broil or barbecue, basting frequently with the marinade.

PICKLED PORK

4 TO 6 SERVINGS

2 pounds pork loin
   Pinch of brown peppercorn
1½ teaspoons salt
1 teaspoon saltpeter

Season pork with peppercorn, salt and saltpeter. Let stand in refrigerator overnight. Steam in wok 1½ hours. Cool to room temperature. Trim fat and slice thinly.

PIQUANT PORK KEBABS

6 SERVINGS

1 12-ounce jar apricot preserves
1 8-ounce bottle Russian salad dressing
1 envelope onion soup mix
1½ pounds boneless pork, cut into 1-inch cubes
4 large carrots, cut into 1-inch pieces
2 large zucchini, cut into 1-inch pieces
   Steamed rice

Combine first 3 ingredients in bowl. Add meat and stir to coat thoroughly. Cover and marinate overnight in refrigerator.

Prepare barbecue (or use broiler). Alternate meat, carrots and zucchini on skewers. Cook, turning and basting frequently with marinade, until meat is cooked through and carrots are tender. Serve pork kebabs on bed of freshly steamed rice.

MICROWAVE

PRIME RIB

8 SERVINGS

1 5-pound prime rib of beef
1 1½-ounce package onion soup mix
1 dozen large fresh mushrooms, sliced

Place roast on cooking platter and rub with soup mix. Arrange roast fat side down, with mushrooms over

top and around sides. Cook uncovered on High for 10 minutes. Remove roast from microwave, turn on one side and let stand 5 minutes (standing time permits microwaves to penetrate to center of roast). Return to microwave and cook 5 minutes. Remove from microwave, turn on other side, and let stand 5 minutes. Return to microwave for 5 more minutes. Turn roast again, let stand 5 minutes, and return to microwave. For medium rare, cook until microwave meat thermometer registers 125° to 130°, about 10 minutes more (roast will continue cooking after it is removed from microwave).* Allow the roast to rest before carving. This is important, since it allows the juices to be redistributed throughout the roast.

*If your microwave has a Medium or Roast setting, eliminate standing time between turnings, and, instead of cooking on High for the last 10 minutes, cook on Roast or Medium for about 20 minutes (check internal temperature after 10 minutes). The slower cooking in the final stage will permit microwaves to penetrate to center of roast, eliminating need for standing time in the earlier stage.

TENDERLOIN OF BEEF

4 SERVINGS

1 2- to 2½-pound beef tenderloin,* room temperature
½ envelope (about 2 to 3 tablespoons) dehydrated onion soup mix
½ pound medium fresh mushrooms, sliced

Place roast in small shallow dish and pat meat evenly with soup mix. Arrange mushroom slices over and around roast. Place paper towel loosely over top to prevent spattering. Cook on High 5 minutes. Turn roast over and spoon mushrooms and any drippings over top. If available, insert microwave meat probe into thickest part of roast. Cook on High an additional 5 minutes. Reduce to Roast (about 70 percent power) and cook until probe registers 130°F, about 5 minutes for medium-rare. Let stand 5 to 10 minutes. (Internal temperature will increase about 10 degrees during standing time.)

*Additional cooking time will be needed if using thicker butt end of fillet. Allow an additional 5 minutes on High power, or until desired degree of doneness is reached.

MIXED KEBABS

4 SERVINGS

- 8 slices bacon, folded in quarters
- 1 6-ounce filet mignon, cut into 8 chunks
- 8 scallops
- 2 canned pineapple rings, quartered
- 1 small Polish sausage, quartered
- ⅓ cup barbecue sauce

Line paper plate with paper towels. Arrange bacon in circle on top and cook on High 3 to 4 minutes to cook partially. Remove from oven and drain on paper towels.

Preheat broiler or prepare charcoal grill. Prepare kebabs using 4 long skewers and arrange food in following order for each: beef, scallop, bacon, pineapple, sausage, pineapple, bacon, scallop and beef. Brush with barbecue sauce and broil until cooked evenly on all sides, about 4 to 5 minutes. Serve immediately.

MEATBALLS

MAKES 20 TO 24

- ¾ pound lean ground beef
- ¼ pound lean ground pork
- ¼ cup tomato juice
- ¼ cup chopped onion
- 1 egg, lightly beaten
- 1 slice bread, soaked in water and squeezed dry
- 2 garlic cloves, finely chopped
- 1 tablespoon chopped fresh parsley
- 1 teaspoon Worcestershire sauce
- 1 teaspoon salt

⅛ teaspoon freshly ground pepper

Combine all ingredients in mixing bowl and blend thoroughly. Shape into 20 to 24 meatballs. Arrange in circle on microwave-safe rack set over plate or dish. Cover with waxed paper and cook on High 7 to 9 minutes, rotating rack if meatballs are cooking unevenly.

OLD-FASHIONED MEAT LOAF

6 SERVINGS

- 1½ pounds lean ground beef
- ½ cup catsup
- 2 eggs
- 1 medium onion, chopped
- 1 garlic clove, minced
- 2 slices bread, rinsed with cold water and squeezed dry
- 1 teaspoon Worcestershire sauce
- ½ teaspoon salt
- ¼ teaspoon freshly ground pepper
- 2 hard-cooked eggs
- ¼ cup catsup, room temperature

Combine first 9 ingredients in large mixing bowl and blend well. Pack evenly into 6-cup ring mold (or deep casserole dish with glass standing upright in center). Tuck hard-cooked eggs into beef so they are completely covered. Cook on High, turning dish once, until meat loaf has pulled away from edges of mold, about 10 minutes. Baste off accumulated juices. Invert loaf onto serving platter. Spoon remaining catsup evenly over top and serve.

PARMESAN-TOPPED MEAT LOAF

6 SERVINGS

- 1 pound ground chuck
- ½ pound ground pork
- 1 8-ounce can tomato sauce
- 2 large eggs, beaten
- ¾ cup breadcrumbs
- 2 tablespoons instant onion
- 2 tablespoons minced parsley
- 2 tablespoons Worcestershire sauce

- 2 teaspoons spicy mustard
- 1 teaspoon salt
- ½ teaspoon garlic salt
- ½ teaspoon pepper
- ½ cup grated Parmesan cheese

Combine all ingredients except Parmesan in large bowl and blend well. Lightly pack mixture into 1½-quart glass loaf pan. Sprinkle with half Parmesan. Cook uncovered 5 minutes on High. Rotate dish ½ turn. Cook another 5 minutes. Sprinkle with remaining Parmesan, rotate ½ turn and cook additional 5 minutes. Remove from oven, cover with foil and let meat loaf stand about 10 minutes before serving.

STUFFED GREEN PEPPERS

4 SERVINGS

- 4 large green peppers (tops removed), seeded
- ¼ cup water
- 1 pound lean ground beef
- ¼ cup chopped onion
- 1½ cups cooked rice
- 1 8-ounce can tomato sauce
- 1 large garlic clove, finely chopped
- 2 tablespoons chopped celery
- 1 tablespoon Worcestershire sauce
- 2 teaspoons minced fresh parsley
- ½ teaspoon salt
- ⅛ teaspoon freshly ground pepper
- 4 tablespoons catsup

Place peppers upright in deep casserole (they should fit snugly). Add water. Cover and cook on High 3 minutes. Let stand without draining while preparing filling.

Combine beef and onion in mixing bowl and cook on High 3 minutes. Stir to crumble beef. Add remaining ingredients except catsup and blend well. Divide among peppers. Cover and cook on High 10 minutes. Spread 1 tablespoon catsup over top of each. Cover peppers and let stand about 2 to 3 minutes to soften.

Vegetable

■ Here's a new twist for the pizza lover—Zucchini Pizza. This meatless meal will surprise and delight your friends. Cut zucchini lengthwise in quarter-inch slices, or in rounds if you have a large, overgrown zucchini. Top each slice with pizza sauce, finely chopped black olives, minced green onion and grated mozzarella or Monterey Jack cheese. Place the slices on a baking sheet about 5 inches below the heat source of a preheated broiler and broil until cheese is melted and bubbly and zucchini is crisp, about 4 minutes.

Eggs

■ With the help of your blender, this fluffy brunch dish is a snap to make. Whirl together 8 eggs and 1 cup cottage cheese with chives along with salt and pepper to taste at high speed for 1 minute and set aside. Saute 1 4-ounce can sliced mushrooms and ½ cup green peppers in butter in a 10- or 12-inch skillet. Pour egg mixture over tender vegetables and continue cooking, lifting mixture on sides and bottom until done. Garnish with parsley.

■ You won't have to make hash browns on the side for this breakfast: the potatoes are in the omelet! Heat olive oil in a large skillet and sauté 1 large, peeled and thinly sliced potato. Sprinkle the sautéed potatoes with salt and pour in 8 well-beaten eggs. Cook over medium heat until golden brown. Turn once, cut in wedges and serve.

Microwave Eggs

■ To hard-cook egg, break egg into small glass measuring cup. Pierce yolk with fork. Cover cup with paper towel and cook on High until egg just begins to firm, about 40 to 50 seconds (egg will continue to cook as it stands). Immediately begin mashing with fork, blending until egg is completely hard-cooked and grated.

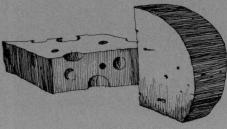

VEGETABLE

CRUSTLESS SPINACH QUICHE

6 SERVINGS

- 1 10-ounce package frozen chopped spinach
- 8 ounces Gruyère cheese, grated
- 2 slices day-old bread, crusts removed
- 6 eggs, lightly beaten
- 4 teaspoons grated onion
- ¼ teaspoon nutmeg
  Salt and pepper
  Sour cream (optional)

Preheat oven to 350°F.

Place spinach in colander to thaw; press out all moisture. Mix spinach with cheese, bread torn into small pieces, eggs, onion, nutmeg, salt and pepper to taste. Transfer to 8-inch buttered pie plate and bake until knife inserted in center comes out clean, about 30 minutes. Serve hot or cold, with or without sour cream garnish.

SPINACH BALLS

MAKES ABOUT 6 DOZEN

- 6 eggs
- 2 10-ounce packages frozen chopped spinach, thawed, drained and squeezed dry
- 2 cups herb stuffing mix
- 1 large onion, grated
- 1 cup freshly grated Parmesan cheese
- ¾ cup (1½ sticks) butter, room temperature
- 1 teaspoon poultry seasoning
  Salt and freshly ground pepper

Preheat oven to 350°F. Beat eggs lightly in large bowl. Add remaining ingredients and blend well. Roll into walnut-size balls. Transfer to baking sheet. Bake until golden, about 20 minutes. Serve hot.

Spinach balls can be partially baked for 10 minutes, cooled and frozen. Reheat thawed balls in 350°F oven for about 10 to 15 minutes before serving hot.

SPINACH NOODLE BAKE

8 SERVINGS

- 2 pounds fresh spinach, cooked just until wilted, drained and chopped, or 2 10½-ounce packages frozen chopped spinach, thawed and squeezed dry
- 1 pound penne or ziti noodles, freshly cooked and drained
- 1 pound ricotta cheese
- 2 15½-ounce jars marinara sauce
- 3 eggs, lightly beaten
- ⅔ cup freshly grated Parmesan cheese
- ⅓ cup chopped fresh parsley
- 2 teaspoons salt
- ½ teaspoon freshly ground pepper

Preheat oven to 350°F. Generously butter 3-quart casserole or baking dish. Combine all ingredients in large mixing bowl and blend thoroughly. Turn into prepared dish and bake until top is golden brown and sauce is bubbly, 25 to 30 minutes.

Cheese

Cheese

■ Welsh Rarebit for two is a warming entrée for brunch, lunch or a light supper on a cold winter day. Make your cheese sauce by combining 1 10½-ounce can cheese soup, ½ cup beer, 1 tablespoon Worcestershire sauce and ½ teaspoon dry mustard in a small saucepan over low heat. Top each of 6 slices toasted French bread with a thin slice of Spanish onion and a few strips crisp-fried bacon. Pour the heated sauce over the toast, sprinkle with paprika and garnish with halved cherry tomatoes and freshly chopped parsley.

■ Dress up a package of frozen cheese blintzes for an impressive weekend brunch. Place the blintzes, still frozen, in a 2-quart casserole and cover with ½ cup melted butter. In a separate bowl, mix together 2 cups sour cream, 6 eggs, ¼ cup each orange juice and sugar and 2 teaspoons each vanilla and salt. Pour mixture over blintzes and bake in a 350° oven until puffed and brown, about 1 hour. Serve with additional sour cream and/or fresh fruit.

■ Avoid stringiness in cooking by shredding, grating or breaking cheese into small cubes. This allows it to melt faster and disperse more evenly. This same effect can be achieved by blending cheese with other ingredients, such as a cream sauce, to reduce its density, or by using a double boiler or thick-bottomed pan to reduce the amount of direct heat applied to the cheese for melting.

■ Do not remove the rind from soft, ripened cheeses before serving. Do remove at least one side of the rind from a hard or waxed rind cheese.

■ Slice a wedge from a whole cheese before serving, to present a more inviting display.

■ Provide each cheese with its own spreading utensil, especially soft cheeses. This is a must particularly for all bleu cheeses.

■ Don't overpower delicate cheeses with strong-flavored bread, beverages or other foods.

■ Serve cheese at room temperature in order to bring out full flavor.

SPINACH AND POTATO CASSEROLE

4 TO 6 SERVINGS

    2 10-ounce packages frozen chopped spinach, cooked and drained
    1 10¾-ounce can cream of potato soup
    ½ pound cheddar cheese, shredded

Preheat oven to 350°F. Combine spinach and soup in 1-quart baking dish and mix well. Sprinkle cheese over top. Bake until heated through, about 20 minutes.

TOMATO-CHEESE CASSEROLE

6 TO 8 SERVINGS

    1 8-ounce package small elbow macaroni, cooked al dente, rinsed in cold water and drained
    1 10-ounce package extra-sharp cheddar cheese, grated
    ½ cup grated Parmesan cheese
    ½ cup (1 stick) butter
    1 28-ounce can whole tomatoes, drained (reserve liquid) and halved

    ¾ cup corn flakes, crumbled
    ¾ cup milk

Preheat oven to 325°F. Butter a 2-quart rectangular baking dish. Spread half of macaroni evenly over bottom of dish. Sprinkle with half of cheddar and Parmesan cheeses. Dot with half of butter. Arrange half of tomatoes over top. Add enough reserved tomato liquid to moisten. Repeat layering. Sprinkle with corn flakes. Slowly pour in milk around edges of dish. Bake until top is crisp, about 1½ hours.

TOMATO-OLIVE QUICHES

Freeze one of these cooked quiches to thaw and reheat later.

MAKES 2 9-INCH QUICHES

    2 unbaked 9-inch pie shells
    ¼ cup all purpose flour
    ½ teaspoon salt
       Freshly ground pepper
    2 large tomatoes cut into slices ½ inch thick
    2 tablespoons oil

    2 eggs
    1 cup shredded cheddar cheese
    1 cup whipping cream
    2 2-ounce cans sliced black olives, drained
    1 cup minced green onion
    2 ounces provolone cheese, thinly sliced

Preheat oven to 425°F. Bake pie shells for 8 minutes. Remove from oven and set aside. Reduce oven temperature to 375°F.

Combine flour, salt and pepper in small dish. Dip tomato slices into mixture, shaking off excess. Heat oil in large skillet over medium-high heat. Add tomatoes to skillet in batches and sauté until golden, turning once, about 3 to 5 minutes. Drain thoroughly.

Beat eggs lightly in medium bowl. Stir in cheddar and cream. Arrange half of olives, onion, provolone and tomatoes in one pie shell. Pour half of egg mixture over top. Repeat with remaining ingredients and pie shell. Bake until centers are set and tops are golden, about 40 to 45 minutes. Let cool 5 minutes before cutting.

TOMATO AND SAUSAGE TART

4 TO 6 SERVINGS

- 2 teaspoons Dijon mustard
- 1 unbaked 9-inch pastry shell
- ½ pound Italian sausage
- 2 to 3 medium tomatoes, peeled, cored and thickly sliced
- ½ teaspoon salt
- ¼ teaspoon freshly ground pepper
- ½ teaspoon dried basil
- ¼ cup minced fresh parsley
- 1½ cups shredded cheddar cheese
- ½ cup mayonnaise

Position rack in lower third of oven and preheat to 400°F. Spread mustard over pastry and bake 5 minutes. Cool thoroughly.

Remove sausage from casings. Sauté in small skillet, crumbling with fork, until cooked through. Drain and cool.

Sprinkle sausage over pastry. Cover with tomato slices and sprinkle with salt, pepper, basil and parsley.

Combine cheese and mayonnaise in small bowl and blend well. Spread over tomato slices, sealing completely to edges. Bake until hot and bubbly, about 35 minutes.

ZUCCHINI-CORN CASSEROLE

6 SERVINGS

- 2 tablespoons (¼ stick) butter
- 1 large onion, chopped
- 4 cups sliced zucchini (about 4 to 5 medium)
- 1 garlic clove, minced
- 2 tablespoons canned diced green chilies or to taste
- 2 tablespoons hot water
- 1 16-ounce can cream-style corn
- 1 cup grated sharp cheddar cheese
- 4 eggs, beaten
- 1 tablespoon chopped fresh parsley
  Salt and freshly ground pepper

Preheat oven to 350°F. Butter 1½-quart baking dish. Melt butter in large skillet over medium-high heat. Add onion and sauté until soft, about 5 minutes. Stir in zucchini and garlic, blending well. Mix in chilies and water. Reduce heat to medium, cover and cook until zucchini is tender, shaking pan frequently to prevent sticking, 5 to 10 minutes. Add corn, ½ cup cheese, eggs, parsley, salt and pepper to taste and mix well. Turn into dish and sprinkle with remaining cheese. Bake until set, about 45 to 50 minutes.

ZUCCHINI BAKE

6 TO 8 SERVINGS

- 1 cup shredded sharp cheddar cheese
- ½ cup cottage cheese
- 4 eggs, beaten
- 3 tablespoons minced fresh parsley
- 1½ teaspoons salt
- ¼ teaspoon freshly ground pepper
- 2 pounds zucchini, sliced into ¼-inch rounds
- ¾ cup breadcrumbs
- ¼ cup grated Parmesan cheese
- ¼ cup (½ stick) butter

Preheat oven to 375°F. Butter inside of shallow 2-quart baking dish. Combine first 6 ingredients in bowl and mix well. Place layer of zucchini in baking dish and layer with some of cheese mixture. Repeat, ending with cheese mixture. Combine breadcrumbs and Parmesan in small bowl. Sprinkle over casserole. Dot with butter. Tent with foil and bake 25 minutes. Remove foil and bake until top is browned, about 20 minutes. Serve immediately.

LEFTOVER VEGETABLE CHEESE PIE

6 TO 8 SERVINGS

- 1 9-inch deep-dish frozen pie crust
- 3 to 4 cups cooked vegetables (leftover or canned)*
  Frozen peas (optional)
- 1 to 2 medium tomatoes, quartered, or 6 to 8 cherry tomatoes, halved
- 1 medium onion, chopped
- 1 garlic clove, minced
- 1½ cups sliced or grated cheddar cheese
  Parmesan cheese
- 1 tablespoon butter, cut into bits

Preheat oven to 350°F. Prick bottom and sides of pie crust. Combine vegetables, onion and garlic and place in crust. Cover with cheddar cheese, sprinkle with Parmesan and dot with butter. Bake until vegetables are hot and crust is light golden brown, about 30 minutes.

*Consider color when preparing this pie. Almost any combination of vegetables will work well. A couple of suggestions: Carrots, corn, broccoli, green beans and tomatoes; or zucchini, summer squash, brussels sprouts, peas and tomatoes.

VEGETARIAN CHEESE TART

6 TO 8 SERVINGS

- ⅓ cup chopped cashews
- 1 9-inch frozen pie shell, thawed
- 3 tablespoons (⅜ stick) butter
- 3 medium zucchini, thinly sliced
- 2 garlic cloves, crushed
- ¼ teaspoon dried dill
- ¼ teaspoon salt
- ⅛ teaspoon freshly ground pepper
- 3 eggs, well beaten
- 1 cup cubed Monterey Jack cheese
- 2 tablespoons chopped fresh parsley

Preheat oven to 325°F. Sprinkle nuts evenly on crust. Melt butter in small skillet over medium heat. Add zucchini and garlic and sauté several minutes until softened. Sprinkle with dill, salt and pepper and toss lightly. Spoon into crust. Pour eggs over and sprinkle with cheese and parsley. Bake until set, about 45 minutes.

FESTIVE ITALIAN QUICHE

4 TO 6 SERVINGS

- 1 unbaked 9-inch pie shell
- 2 tablespoons oil
- 2 cups chopped zucchini
- ½ cup chopped onion
- 1 garlic clove, minced
- 1¼ cups shredded mozzarella cheese
- 3 eggs, beaten
- 1 cup cottage or ricotta cheese
- ⅓ cup milk
- ½ teaspoon salt
  Freshly ground pepper
  Tomato Sauce*

Preheat oven to 350°F. Bake pie shell 10 minutes. Remove from oven and let cool. Increase oven temperature to 375°F. Heat oil in medium skillet over medium-high heat. Add zucchini, onion and garlic and sauté until tender, about 10 minutes. Spread evenly in pie shell.

Mix 1 cup mozzarella with remaining ingredients except sauce. Spoon over vegetables and sprinkle with remaining cheese. Bake until knife inserted near center comes out clean, about 40 minutes. Let stand 5 minutes, then cut into wedges and serve with Tomato Sauce.

*Tomato Sauce

- 1 15-ounce can tomato sauce
- 1 tablespoon dried parsley flakes
- 1 teaspoon dried oregano
- ½ teaspoon dried basil leaves, crumbled
- 1 garlic clove, minced
  Salt and freshly ground pepper

Simmer ingredients in medium saucepan about 15 minutes, stirring occasionally.

EGG

ASPARAGUS AND POACHED EGGS

4 SERVINGS

- 3 to 4 tablespoons (⅜ to ½ stick) unsalted butter
- 3 pounds thin asparagus, trimmed and cooked crisp-tender
- 3 shallots, minced
- 4 eggs, poached until whites are firm but yolks are still soft
  Salt and freshly ground pepper

Melt butter in large skillet over medium-high heat. Add asparagus and shallots and sauté only until heated through. Divide among heated plates and top each with a poached egg. Sprinkle lightly with salt and pepper and serve.

EGGS FANTASTIC

6 SERVINGS

- 1 pound bulk sausage, crumbled
- ¼ pound mushrooms, chopped
- 1 medium onion, diced
  Salt and freshly ground pepper
- 6 eggs
- 3 tablespoons sour cream
- 6 tablespoons Mexican tomato and yellow chili hot sauce
- 16 ounces cheddar cheese, grated
- 8 ounces mozzarella cheese, grated

Preheat oven to 400°F. Grease 9 x 13-inch baking dish. Combine sausage, mushrooms and onion in large skillet. Sauté over medium-high heat until sausage is completely cooked. Season to taste with salt and pepper. Drain well.

Combine eggs and sour cream in blender and whip 1 minute. Turn into baking dish and bake until eggs are softly set, 4 to 7 minutes. Spoon

hot sauce evenly over top. Add sausage mixture and top with combined grated cheeses.

To serve immediately, broil until cheeses are melted. To serve next day, refrigerate until serving time, bake at 325°F until cheeses are melted, about 30 minutes.

GRATINEED EGGS (KITCHEN BUFFET BRUNCH)

8 TO 10 SERVINGS

- 1 pound sweet or hot Italian sausage, casings removed
- 1 tablespoon butter
- 8 mushrooms, sliced
- 1 medium red onion, chopped
- 12 eggs, beaten
- 1 cup milk
- 8 ounces mozzarella cheese, shredded
- 2 medium tomatoes, peeled and chopped
- ½ teaspoon salt
- ½ teaspoon freshly ground pepper
- ½ teaspoon dried oregano leaves, crumbled

Preheat oven to 400°F. Generously grease large ovenproof skillet or large shallow baking dish; set aside. Crumble sausage into skillet and fry over medium-high heat, stirring constantly, until sausage is no longer pink. Drain well and transfer to bowl.

Wipe out skillet. Add butter and melt over medium heat. Add mushrooms and onion and sauté until onion is soft but not brown. Stir into sausage. Blend in remaining ingredients, mixing thoroughly. Turn into prepared dish. Bake until knife inserted in center comes out clean, about 30 to 35 minutes.

HOPPEL POPPEL BRUNCH

6 SERVINGS

- 2 tablespoons (¼ stick) butter
- 10 eggs, lightly beaten
- ½ cup sour cream
- 8 slices salami, chopped
- 6 green onions, chopped
- 5 slices American cheese, chopped
- 12 cherry tomatoes, halved
- 1 4-ounce can button mushrooms, drained
  Salt and freshly ground pepper

Preheat oven to 350°F. Melt butter in 2-quart rectangular baking dish. Combine all remaining ingredients in mixing bowl and blend well. Pour into prepared dish. Bake until puffed and golden, about 30 to 40 minutes. Serve immediately.

MEXICAN EGGS

4 SERVINGS

- 1 tablespoon butter
- 1 green pepper, seeded and diced
- 1 medium onion, diced
- ⅓ to ½ cup diced green chilies
- 4 to 6 medium tomatoes, diced (peeled, if desired)
  Salt and freshly ground pepper
  Pinch of sugar
- 8 slices Monterey Jack or cheddar cheese
- 8 eggs

Heat butter in 10- to 12-inch skillet. Add pepper, onion and green chilies and sauté until softened. Stir in tomatoes, salt, pepper to taste and sugar and cook until thickened, stirring frequently. Place cheese slices atop sauce and let soften. Break eggs onto cheese, cover and let cook until eggs are desired doneness, about 3 to 4 minutes. Serve.

OEUFS A L'OSEILLE (EGGS WITH SORREL)

An easy first course for formal dinners, or allow 2 eggs per person and use as the main course for luncheon.

6 SERVINGS

- Small bunch of sorrel (18 leaves)
- 6 large eggs
- ½ cup whipping cream
- 1 tablespoon butter
  Salt and freshly ground pepper

Preheat oven to 325°F. Lightly butter 6 small individual soufflé dishes. Place 2 or 3 sorrel leaves in dish, top with egg and cover with cream. Dot with butter and sprinkle with salt and pepper. Place dishes in pan of hot water and bake until eggs are set, 15 minutes.

SAUCY EGGS

4 SERVINGS

- 2 cups Italian meat sauce
- 8 eggs
- 8 slices garlic toast
  Parmesan cheese, grated

Bring meat sauce to simmer. While sauce is heating, fry eggs sunny side up. Place each egg on a slice of toast and top with meat sauce and Parmesan cheese.

SPINACH AND SAUSAGE FRITTATA

6 TO 8 SERVINGS

- 2 Italian sausages, crumbled
- ¼ cup olive oil
- 1 10-ounce package frozen spinach, thawed and drained
- ⅓ to ½ pound mushrooms, sliced
- 1 medium onion, chopped
- 6 eggs
- 1 cup grated Parmesan cheese
- 2 garlic cloves, minced
- ½ teaspoon dried basil
- ¼ teaspoon dried marjoram

Salt and freshly ground pepper
1 cup grated mozzarella cheese

Brown sausage in large skillet over medium-high heat; remove and drain well. Pour off grease from skillet. Add oil and heat until light haze forms. Add spinach, mushrooms and onion and sauté until onion is translucent. Remove from heat.

Preheat oven to 350°F. Butter 9-inch pie plate. Combine eggs, ¾ cup Parmesan, garlic and seasonings in medium bowl and mix well. Stir in sausage and vegetables. Turn into pie plate and sprinkle with mozzarella and remaining Parmesan. Bake until set, about 25 minutes.

SUPER QUICK EGG FOO YOUNG

2 TO 3 SERVINGS

- ½ cup cooked meat (chicken, shrimp, beef or pork)
- 1 1-pound can mixed Chinese vegetables, drained
- 5 beaten eggs
- 1 teaspoon salt
  Oil

Combine meat, vegetables, eggs and salt. Spoon ¼ cup at a time into hot oil. When bottom is cooked, turn gently and cook until set.

Gravy

- 2 cups water
- ⅓ cup soy sauce
- 2 tablespoons cornstarch dissolved in ¼ cup water
- 1 tablespoon sugar

Heat water and soy sauce. Add cornstarch and stir over medium heat until gravy is slightly thickened.

VERMICELLI OMELET

6 SERVINGS

- ½ pound vermicelli or spaghettini
- ¼ cup olive oil

2 2-ounce cans anchovy fillets
6 eggs
⅓ cup grated Parmesan cheese
  Freshly ground black pepper

Cook vermicelli following directions on package. Drain well. Heat oil in a large skillet. Add cooked vermicelli and fry over medium heat, until vermicelli is golden and crisp on the bottom, about 8 to 10 minutes.

Chop all but 6 anchovies. Beat eggs and combine with cheese, chopped anchovies and pepper to taste. Pour over vermicelli, tilting skillet from side to side until eggs are just set.

Place skillet under broiler until top of omelet puffs and browns. Invert and slide onto heated platter. Garnish with reserved anchovy fillets arranged spoke fashion. Cut into wedges to serve.

This is the Sicilian way to use leftover pasta. A 6-ounce can of Italian-style tuna may be substituted for the anchovies.

WOK SCRAMBLED EGGS

6 TO 8 SERVINGS

8 eggs
2 tablespoons water
  Dash of hot pepper sauce
2 teaspoons peanut oil
1 garlic clove, minced
1 small onion, chopped
1 bunch green onions, chopped
1 small green pepper, seeded and chopped
½ cup diced celery
  Fines herbes
1 to 2 cups fresh bean sprouts
  Sliced mushrooms (optional)
  Salt and freshly ground pepper
  Paprika

Combine eggs, water and hot pepper sauce in blender and mix thoroughly at high speed. Heat oil in wok or large skillet until hot, coating all surfaces. Add garlic and stir briefly. Add onions, pepper, celery and fines herbes and stir-fry until onion is translucent. Add egg mixture, bean sprouts, mushrooms, salt and pepper to taste and stir until about ⅔ done. Remove from heat and allow eggs to finish cooking. Sprinkle liberally with paprika and serve immediately.

CHEESE

ALL-IN-ONE QUICHE

6 SERVINGS

1½ cups milk
½ cup biscuit mix
6 tablespoons (¾ stick) butter, room temperature
3 eggs
  Pinch of salt
1 cup diced ham, turkey, chicken, shrimp or bacon
2 green onions, chopped
1 4-ounce can sliced mushrooms, drained
1 cup grated sharp cheddar cheese

Preheat oven to 350°F. Combine first 5 ingredients in blender and mix well. Turn into ungreased deep 9-inch or regular 10-inch pie plate. Add meat or shellfish, poking into batter. Top with onions, mushrooms and cheese. Bake until top is golden, about 45 minutes. Let stand 10 minutes before serving.

CHEESE BAKE

8 SERVINGS

¾ pound Monterey Jack cheese, grated
1 cup buttermilk baking mix
½ cup milk
4 eggs
6 tablespoons (¾ stick) butter or margarine, cut into pieces
3 tablespoons cottage cheese
1 teaspoon caraway seeds

Preheat oven to 350°F. Combine all ingredients in large bowl and mix well. Turn into 2-quart rectangular baking dish. Bake until puffed and golden, about 45 minutes.

CHEESE PIE

6 SERVINGS

1 cup milk
¾ cup flour
1 egg
  Salt and freshly ground pepper
1 cup combined grated Monterey Jack, Swiss and/or cheddar cheese

Preheat oven to 400°F. Butter 9-inch pie plate. Blend milk, flour, egg, salt and pepper to taste using electric mixer. Stir in half of cheese. Pour into pie plate and bake until puffed and golden, about 25 minutes. Sprinkle remaining cheese evenly over top. Continue baking until cheese has melted, about 3 to 4 minutes. Cut into wedges and serve immediately.

CHEESE PIE OLE

This pie forms its own golden brown crust while baking.

6 SERVINGS

3 eggs
1 cup milk
¾ cup all purpose flour
½ teaspoon salt
  Pinch of freshly ground pepper
4 ounces cheddar, Muenster or Swiss cheese, shredded
3 green chilies, seeded and finely chopped
1 large or 2 small green bell peppers, chopped
2 small red bell peppers, chopped, or 1 pimiento, diced
2 tablespoons sliced pimiento-stuffed green olives

Preheat oven to 425°F. Grease 8-inch pie plate. Combine first 5 ingredients and beat well. Blend in half of cheese. Add chilies, green and red peppers or pimiento and olives and mix thoroughly. Pour into pie plate. Bake until set, about 25 minutes. Sprinkle remaining cheese over top and continue baking until cheese is melted, about 3 to 5 minutes. Let cool slightly. Slice into wedges before serving.

CHEESE SOUFFLE IN A BLENDER

4 TO 6 SERVINGS

    2 tablespoons (¼ stick) butter
    2 tablespoons Parmesan
       cheese
 1½ cups diced cheese (half Swiss
       and half cheddar)
    5 eggs, separated
    ¼ cup flour
    ½ teaspoon dry mustard
    ½ teaspoon salt
    2 cups hot (not boiling) milk

Make waxed paper collar around 1½-quart soufflé dish and secure with tape. Butter dish and paper and sprinkle with Parmesan.

Preheat oven to 375°F. Place cheeses, egg yolks, flour, mustard and salt in blender. Blend on high speed 15 seconds. Add to milk in 2-quart saucepan and cook slowly, stirring constantly, until mixture reaches custard consistency. Beat egg whites until they form stiff peaks. Fold whites gently into custard mixture.

Pour into prepared soufflé dish and bake until lightly browned, about 35 minutes. Serve immediately.

COTTAGE CHEESE QUICHE

6 TO 8 SERVINGS

    1 unbaked 9-inch pie shell
    2 cups cottage cheese
    ½ cup grated Swiss cheese
    2 eggs
    1 to 2 tablespoons chopped
       chives or onion
       Salt and freshly ground
       pepper
    ½ 3-ounce can french-fried
       onion rings, crushed, or
       seasoned fresh breadcrumbs*
       to taste

Position rack in lower third of oven and preheat to 400°F. Partially bake pie shell until golden, about 20 minutes. Remove from oven. Reduce temperature to 350°F.

Combine cottage and Swiss cheeses, eggs, chives, salt and pepper and beat well. Turn into pie shell. Bake

30 minutes. Remove from oven and sprinkle with crushed onion rings. Bake an additional 10 to 15 minutes. Let stand 5 minutes before slicing into wedges and serving.

*If using breadcrumbs, sprinkle over quiche at beginning of baking time.

CREAM CHEESE QUICHE

8 SERVINGS

    8 ounces cream cheese, room
       temperature
    2 eggs
    ¼ teaspoon salt
    ¼ teaspoon freshly ground
       pepper
    ½ cup chopped ham or other
       cooked meat
    2 tablespoons freshly snipped
       dill or 2 teaspoons dried dill
    1 unbaked 9-inch pie shell
    1 8-ounce package Swiss or
       cheddar cheese slices

Preheat oven to 400°F. Whip cream cheese with eggs. Add salt and pepper and blend well. Gently stir in ham and dill. Spoon into pie shell. Top with cheese. Bake until golden, about 30 minutes. Let stand 5 minutes before serving.

QUICK CHILI CASSEROLE

4 TO 6 SERVINGS

    1 pound sharp cheddar or
       Monterey Jack cheese, grated
    8 eggs
    1 4-ounce can whole green
       chilies, undrained

Preheat oven to 325°F. Grease a shallow 1½-quart baking dish and set aside.

Place cheese in large mixing bowl. Combine eggs and undrained chilies in blender and whirl on high until well blended. Combine egg mixture with cheese and stir until well mixed. Pour into prepared dish and bake until puffed and golden brown and knife inserted in center comes out clean, about 50 to 60 minutes.

Serve with a tossed green salad and warm corn or flour tortillas.

QUICKIE MUENSTER QUICHE

The cheese forms its own "crust."

4 SERVINGS

    2 8-ounce packages
       (approximately) sliced
       Muenster cheese
    6 eggs, beaten
    ½ cup milk
    ½ cup diced green chili peppers
    ¼ teaspoon monosodium
       glutamate (optional)
    ¼ teaspoon hot pepper sauce
    ¼ teaspoon salt

Preheat oven to 375°F. Line bottom and sides of 4 individual ramekins with cheese slices. Combine remaining ingredients and divide evenly among ramekins. Bake 20 minutes. Remove from oven and allow to stand 5 minutes before serving.

BARLEY CASSEROLE

6 SERVINGS

    ½ cup (1 stick) butter
    2 medium onions, coarsely
       chopped
    ¾ pound mushrooms, sliced
 1½ cups barley
    3 pimientos, coarsely chopped
    2 cups chicken stock
       Salt and freshly ground
       pepper

Preheat oven to 350°F. Melt butter in large skillet over medium-high heat. Add onions, mushrooms and barley and sauté until tender, about 5 to 10 minutes. Turn into shallow 2-quart baking dish. Blend in remaining ingredients. Cover and bake 50 minutes. Uncover and bake until all liquid is absorbed, about 10 minutes.

RUSSIAN SAUERKRAUT

4 TO 6 SERVINGS

    ½ pound bacon
    1 large onion, chopped
    1 27-ounce can sauerkraut,
       drained (reserve liquid), rinsed
       and squeezed dry
    2 to 3 dill pickles, chopped

2 tablespoons chopped pimiento

Cook bacon in large skillet over medium-high heat until crisp. Drain well. Crumble and set aside. Drain all but 2 tablespoons fat from skillet. Return skillet to medium-high heat. Add onion and sauté until golden, about 5 to 10 minutes. Add bacon with remaining ingredients and mix well. Cover, reduce heat and simmer, stirring occasionally and adding reserved sauerkraut liquid if mixture seems too dry, until heated, about 30 minutes.

ZUCCHINI PANCAKES

4 SERVINGS

3 cups coarsely grated zucchini
1 egg, lightly beaten
  Pinch of nutmeg
  Salt and freshly ground pepper
½ cup all purpose flour
1 teaspoon baking powder
  Oil
  Parmesan cheese (garnish)

Combine zucchini and egg and mix well. Add nutmeg, salt and pepper to taste. Sift flour and baking powder over mixture and blend thoroughly. Place large skillet over medium-high heat or heat griddle; oil lightly. Use ¼ cup batter for each pancake and cook until lightly golden, turning once. Transfer to platter and sprinkle with Parmesan.

DO AHEAD

BRUNCH CASSEROLE

Assemble this casserole the night before baking and refrigerate.

12 SERVINGS

4 cups cubed day-old firm white or French bread
2 cups (8 ounces) shredded cheddar cheese

10 eggs, lightly beaten
4 cups (1 quart) milk
1 teaspoon dry mustard
1 teaspoon salt
¼ teaspoon onion powder
  Dash of freshly ground pepper
8 to 10 slices cooked bacon, crumbled
½ cup sliced mushrooms
½ cup chopped peeled tomato

Generously butter 9×13-inch baking dish. Arrange bread cubes in dish and sprinkle with cheese. Beat together next 5 ingredients with pepper to taste and pour evenly over cheese and bread. Sprinkle with bacon, mushrooms and tomato. Cover and chill overnight.

Preheat oven to 325°F. Bake casserole uncovered until set, about 1 hour (tent with foil if top begins to overbrown).

MINI BLINIS

12 TO 16 SERVINGS

2 8-ounce packages cream cheese, room temperature
½ cup sugar
2 egg yolks
2 1-pound loaves thin sliced white bread, crusts trimmed
1 cup (2 sticks) butter, melted
  Cinnamon and sugar
  Sour cream and jelly

Combine cream cheese, sugar and yolks in mixing bowl and beat until smooth. Flatten each slice of bread with rolling pin and spread with some of cream cheese mixture. Roll jelly roll fashion and dip in melted butter. Sprinkle with cinnamon and sugar to taste. (If preparing ahead, place in single layer on baking sheet and freeze. When solidly frozen, transfer to plastic bags and return to freezer until ready to use.)

When ready to serve, preheat oven to 400°F. Leave blinis whole or cut each in half and place on baking sheet. Bake until light golden brown; fresh blinis 8 to 10 minutes, or frozen blinis (thawing is unnecessary) 10 to 15 minutes. Serve hot accompanied by sour cream and jelly on the side.

MEXICAN CHEESE PUFF

10 TO 12 SERVINGS

5 cups grated sharp cheddar cheese
4 cups grated Monterey Jack cheese
2 medium tomatoes, seeded and chopped
1 7-ounce can diced green chilies
1 2¼-ounce can sliced black olives, drained
½ cup all purpose flour
6 eggs, separated
1 5.33-ounce can evaporated milk
½ teaspoon salt
½ teaspoon dried oregano leaves, crumbled
¼ teaspoon ground cumin
¼ teaspoon freshly ground pepper
¼ teaspoon cream of tartar

Preheat oven to 300°F. Butter 9×13-inch glass baking dish. Combine first 5 ingredients with 2 tablespoons flour and mix well. Spoon into dish. (Casserole can be prepared to this point and refrigerated until ready to serve.) Beat egg yolks in large mixing bowl. Gradually blend in remaining flour and milk and beat until smooth. Add salt, oregano, cumin and pepper and mix well. Beat egg whites in medium bowl until foamy. Add cream of tartar and continue beating until stiff peaks form. Fold egg whites into yolk mixture, blending thoroughly. Spoon over cheese. Bake until top is golden brown and firm, about 1 hour. Let stand 15 minutes before serving.

QUICK EGG-CHEESE SOUFFLE

An easy brunch dish.

10 TO 12 SERVINGS

Butter
25 to 30 thin slices egg bread, crusts removed
20 slices sharp cheddar cheese
12 eggs
4 cups milk
Seasoned salt

Generously butter 9×13-inch baking dish. Place layer of bread in bottom and top with half of cheese. Repeat layering. Beat eggs, milk and salt in mixing bowl until well blended. Pour mixture over bread. Cover tightly and refrigerate overnight.

Bring soufflé to room temperature. Preheat oven to 350°F. Bake casserole until top is brown and puffy, about 45 minutes.

For variation, cooked shrimp or diced ham may be sprinkled over top of each cheese layer before adding egg mixture.

24-HOUR WINE AND CHEESE OMELET

12 SERVINGS

1 large loaf day-old French or Italian bread, broken into small pieces
6 tablespoons (¾ stick) unsalted butter, melted
¾ pound domestic Swiss cheese, shredded
½ pound Monterey Jack cheese, shredded
9 thin slices Genoa salami, coarsely chopped
16 eggs
3¼ cups milk
½ cup dry white wine
4 large whole green onions, minced
1 tablespoon Düsseldorf German mustard
¼ teaspoon freshly ground pepper
⅛ teaspoon ground red pepper
1½ cups sour cream

⅔ to 1 cup freshly grated imported Parmesan cheese or shredded Asiago

Butter 2 shallow 3-quart (9×13-inch) baking dishes. Spread bread over bottom and drizzle with butter. Sprinkle with Swiss and Jack cheeses and salami.

Beat together eggs, milk, wine, green onions, mustard, pepper and red pepper until foamy. Pour over cheese. Cover dishes with foil, crimping edges. Refrigerate overnight.

Remove from refrigerator about 30 minutes before baking. Preheat oven to 325°F. Bake casseroles covered until set, about 1 hour. Uncover; spread with sour cream and sprinkle with remaining cheese. Bake uncovered until crusty and lightly browned, about 10 minutes.

MICROWAVE

CALIFORNIA QUICHE

6 SERVINGS

2 cups grated Monterey Jack cheese
9 strips bacon, crisply cooked and crumbled
1 4-ounce can diced green chilies
3 green onions, thinly sliced
1 baked 9-inch deep-dish pie shell
1 13-ounce can evaporated milk (regular or nonfat)
4 eggs

Combine first 4 ingredients in small bowl and toss lightly. Sprinkle about ¾ of mixture over pie shell.

Heat milk in measuring cup on High 2½ minutes. Beat eggs in separate bowl. Add hot milk and beat again. Pour evenly into pie shell. Sprinkle

with remaining bacon mixture. Cook on Bake (60 percent power) until center is barely set, about 12 to 15 minutes. Let stand 5 minutes.

BACON AND EGG IN A CUP

1 SERVING

2 slices bacon, cooked crisp and broken into pieces
1 egg
1 tablespoon grated cheddar or Monterey Jack cheese

Sprinkle bacon in bottom of custard cup. Add egg. Pierce yolk twice with toothpick. Sprinkle egg with cheese. Cover and cook on Medium-High (70 percent power) until egg is slightly firm, about 1 to 1½ minutes.

Opposite
Grilled Ground Lamb and Eggplant Kebabs are tucked into pita pockets and served with a tangy Yogurt Sauce. Tabbouleh can be made earlier in the day.

Page 130–131
Peas à la Venitienne, Cold Bass in Sorrel Sauce and Asparagus with Mustard Sauce make a delightful spring dinner.

Page 132
Salmon with Apples, Pears and Limes, Brown Rice Milanese and Green Beans-Open Sesame are calorie-wise and picture-perfect.

Page 133
Gnocchi in Basil Butter is a silken semolina mixture enhanced with garlic, topped with Parmesan cheese and garnished with slivers of anchovy.

Page 134–135
Sauté of Shrimp l'Antiboise is a vivid melange of shrimp, red peppers, plum tomatoes and zucchini, scented with fresh thyme and enlivened with pungent garlic and hot chili pepper.

Page 136
Chicken Florentine nestles crisply browned chicken in a bed of spinach and ricotta cheese, sauced with Marinara.

Ground Lamb and Eggplant Kebabs
Recipe page 97
Yogurt Sauce
Recipe page 43
Tabbouleh
Recipe page 58

Peas à la Venitienne
Recipe page 73
Cold Bass in Sorrel Sauce
Recipe page 75
Cold Asparagus in Mustard Sauce
Recipe page 139

Salmon with Apples, Pears and Limes
Recipe page 62
Brown Rice Milanese
Recipe page 161
Green Beans-Open Sesame
Recipe page 140

Gnocchi in Basil Butter
Recipe page 166

Sauté of Shrimp l'Antiboise
Recipe page 78

Chicken Florentine
Recipe page 85

FLUFFY EGGS AND BACON

1 SERVING

- 2 teaspoons butter
- ¼ cup thinly sliced onion
- 2 eggs
- 1 tablespoon sour cream
- 2 slices bacon, cooked crisp and cut into pieces

Combine butter and onion in small gratin dish (about 4 × 7 inches). Cook on High until onion is softened, about 3 minutes. Stir through several times. Beat eggs with sour cream in small bowl. Pour over onion. Cook on High, stirring several times, until eggs are soft, about 1½ minutes. Sprinkle bacon along rim. Cook on High 30 seconds.

CHILES RELLENOS

4 SERVINGS

- 5 eggs
- 2 cups shredded Monterey Jack cheese
- 1 cup cottage cheese, very well drained
- ¼ cup all purpose flour
- 2 tablespoons diced green chilies or jalapeño peppers or ½ cup shredded green or red pepper, sautéed until softened
- ½ teaspoon baking powder

Combine all ingredients in mixing bowl and whisk until well blended. Pour into 10-inch quiche dish. Cook uncovered on Roast (70 percent power) until set, turning dish if eggs appear to be cooking unevenly, about 12 to 15 minutes.

EGGS BOMBAY

6 SERVINGS

- 3 tablespoons (⅜ stick) butter
- 3 tablespoons flour
- 2 teaspoons curry powder or to taste
- 2 cups light cream
  Salt and pepper
- 2 teaspoons instant minced onion
- 12 hard-cooked eggs, peeled and quartered

- 6 toasted, buttered English muffins

Melt butter in a glass casserole; blend in flour and curry powder. Cook 40 seconds on High, stirring into a smooth paste. Stir in cream gradually, cooking until sauce is smooth and medium thick, about 15 seconds between additions. Stir in salt and pepper to taste and onion. Cover and cook 2½ minutes on High. Stir. Add eggs, cover and cook until heated through, about 1½ minutes. Stir again. Serve hot, spooned over English muffins.

LOX AND EGGS

4 SERVINGS

- 2 tablespoons (¼ stick) butter or margarine
- 1 small onion, finely diced
- 2 ounces smoked salmon, diced
- 6 eggs
- 6 tablespoons milk
  Minced fresh parsley (garnish)

Melt butter on High in 8-inch pie plate. Tilt dish to coat completely. Sprinkle with onion and cook uncovered on High until onion is soft and beginning to crisp slightly. Add salmon and cook uncovered for an additional minute.

Whisk together eggs and milk. Add to dish and cook uncovered on High until set, stirring from outside to center as necessary, about 3 minutes. Stir again. Sprinkle with parsley before serving.

MEXICAN EGGS

4 SERVINGS

- 2 tablespoons (¼ stick) butter
- 2 medium yellow onions, chopped
- 1 large tomato, peeled, seeded, chopped and drained
- 2 teaspoons chili powder

- 1 tablespoon chopped parsley
- 8 medium-size eggs, beaten with 4 tablespoons cream
  Salt and pepper

Melt butter in a large glass casserole; add onion and cook on High 2 minutes. Stir in tomato and chili powder. Cook on High 3 minutes, stirring several times.

Gently stir in parsley and egg-cream mixture. Cover with waxed paper and cook 1½ minutes on Medium, stirring every 20 seconds. Cook another 60 seconds, stirring after 30 seconds. Eggs should appear undercooked—just set but not dry. Remove from oven and stir again. Cover and let set 2 minutes. Season to taste.

MEXICAN SCRAMBLED EGGS

4 SERVINGS

- 2 tablespoons (¼ stick) butter or margarine
- 2 small tomatoes, chopped and drained
- 1 4-ounce can diced green chilies
  Onion flakes
- 6 eggs
- 6 tablespoons milk
  Garlic powder
  Salt and freshly ground pepper
- 1 cup grated sharp cheddar cheese
  Minced fresh parsley (garnish)

Melt butter on High in 10-inch porcelain quiche dish or medium-size au gratin dish. Tilt dish to coat completely. Sprinkle evenly with tomatoes, chilies and onion flakes and cook uncovered on High until softened, about 1½ minutes. Beat eggs and milk with garlic powder, salt and pepper. Add to dish and cook uncovered on High until almost set, stirring frequently from outside to center, about 3 minutes (eggs should still be slightly moist).

Sprinkle cheese over top and cook on High until melted, about 1 to 2 minutes. Sprinkle with parsley.

Quick Ways to Add a Surprise Lift

■ A pleasing textural contrast: Sauté peeled, sliced sunchokes (Jerusalem artichokes) in butter, turning slices frequently, for 6 to 8 minutes. They should still be sweetly crisp. Season with salt and freshly ground pepper and serve with a tomato-sauced, well-seasoned meat loaf.

■ Glazed carrots always look exquisite—but they don't have to be difficult! Cut 10 fresh carrots in half crosswise then in quarters lengthwise and boil them until crisp-tender, or begin with a can of whole baby carrots. Combine 6 tablespoons (¾ stick) butter in a medium-size skillet with ½ cup sugar and ½ teaspoon ginger, stirring until butter is melted. Reduce heat to low and add drained carrots. Toss until well glazed.

■ Celery fritters provide taste and texture contrasts to gently sautéed calf's liver: Run a vegetable peeler down the back of celery stalks to remove strings and cut stalks into 1-inch half-moons. Dip into basic fritter batter scented with a dash of grated nutmeg. Deep fry in hot oil (375°F) until crisp, puffed and golden. Drain thoroughly and serve immediately.

■ Of all the possible ways to fix corn, the hands-down favorite is good old corn on the cob. To get around the perennial corn-buttering bother, put several lumps of butter—plus a tablespoon or two of minced parsley or chives—on a platter. Just before serving, roll the ears in butter mixture until they're well coated.

■ Baked potato jackets may be scraped, buttered, seasoned with salt and pepper, and placed in a hot oven to crisp for an appetizer (cut into pieces) or chopped as a soup topping.

■ Add a sweet touch to a 16-ounce can of whole small carrots. Just combine 6 tablespoons orange juice, 4 tablespoons marmalade and ¼ cup maple syrup in a medium saucepan and stir constantly. When this mixture comes to a boil, reduce heat and add drained carrots, stirring gently until heated through. Serve immediately.

VEGETABLE

ARTFUL ARTICHOKES

4 SERVINGS

- ⅔ cup mayonnaise
- ¼ cup (½ stick) butter, melted
- 2 tablespoons fresh lemon juice
- ½ teaspoon celery salt
- 1 15-ounce can artichoke hearts (packed in water), drained
- ¼ cup slivered almonds
- ¼ cup grated Parmesan cheese

Preheat oven to 425°F. Combine first 4 ingredients in small saucepan and whip until smooth. Place over low heat, stirring constantly until heated through; do not boil. Arrange artichokes in shallow baking dish just large enough to accommodate in single layer. Pour sauce over top. Sprinkle with almonds and cheese. Bake until heated through, about 10 minutes. Serve.

GRATIN OF ASPARAGUS

4 TO 6 SERVINGS

- 16 to 24 asparagus spears, scraped
  Salt
- 2 large eggs
- 2 egg yolks
- 1½ cups whipping cream
  Freshly ground pepper
- 4 to 6 slices baked ham, cut about 4×6×⅛ inches
- 2 tablespoons grated Swiss cheese
- 2 tablespoons freshly grated Parmesan cheese

Preheat oven to 350°F. Butter 7×11-inch baking dish. Cut off woody ends from asparagus leaving spears about 6 inches long. Tie into 3 bundles allowing one spear to remain separate for testing. Place about 4 cups salted water in 4-quart pan; bring to boil. Add asparagus and cook uncovered over medium heat until just tender, about 8 minutes. Drain and run under cold water. Gently untie spears and spread on layer of paper towels.

Blend eggs, yolks and cream thoroughly. Season with salt and ground pepper.

Wrap 4 asparagus spears in each slice of ham. Place seam side down in single layer in baking dish. Pour cream mixture over and sprinkle with cheeses. Bake until top is nicely browned and tip of knife comes out clean, about 40 minutes. Serve immediately directly from baking dish.

ASPARAGUS WITH PECANS

4 SERVINGS

- 2 pounds asparagus, trimmed and cooked crisp-tender
- 2 to 3 tablespoons (¼ to ⅜ stick) unsalted butter
- ½ cup crushed pecans
  Salt and freshly ground pepper

Preheat oven to 350°F. Generously butter 8- or 9-inch square baking dish. Place asparagus in dish, dot with butter and sprinkle with pecans. Bake until heated through, about 15 minutes. Season with salt and pepper and serve immediately.

ASPARAGUS SAUTE

4 SERVINGS

- ¼ cup chicken stock, completely degreased
- 2 teaspoons butter
- 2 to 3 pounds asparagus, trimmed and cooked crisp-tender

Storage

■ A pound of peas in their pods will yield about one cup of shelled peas. Though ideally you should use peas immediately upon purchase, if you must store them, leave them in their pods, wrapped in plastic to retain their moisture. Shell right before cooking. Cook them in a small amount of water until just tender, about 5 to 7 minutes.

■ If you are not going to use your asparagus immediately, store in a plastic bag, tip end first, and place in the vegetable section of the refrigerator. If very fresh, asparagus will hold well for up to 2 days. If they are in a borderline state between freshness and wilting, trim about an inch off the bottom of the stalks and place in a vaselike container. Pour in about an inch of water and lightly cover with plastic wrap. Refrigerate up to 2 days.

■ For Fresh Spinach: wrap in paper toweling, place in a plastic bag and refrigerate. Clean dry spinach should keep in the refrigerator for 1 week without further attention.

■ For Frozen Spinach: squeeze spinach dry in the corner of a towel or cheesecloth. If excess moisture remains in the vegetable, it could ooze during baking, producing a watery consistency in the entire dish.

Uses of Lemon

■ Lemon does wonderful things for both raw and cooked vegetables. For example: dip stalks of raw celery, fennel and florets of cauliflower into lemon juice before adding to the tray of crudités. This gives added flavor and protection against discoloration.

■ Add lemon juice to the cooking water of cauliflower, sunchokes and turnips both to preserve their color and to heighten and intensify flavor.

■ A squeeze of lemon added to rice and potatoes enhances flavor by adding a little zing.

■ Toss potatoes with a little lemon juice—color will be preserved as in cut surfaces of avocados, apples and other fruits.

Herbs as desired to taste (rosemary, marjoram, savory, tarragon, chives, basil or chervil, alone or in combination, for example)
Salt and freshly ground pepper

Combine stock and butter in large skillet over medium-high heat and boil 1 minute. Add asparagus and herbs and cook until asparagus is heated through. Season with salt and pepper to taste and serve.

ASPARAGUS TEMPURA

8 SERVINGS

　2　cups ice water
1 ⅔ cups all purpose flour
　1　egg yolk
　⅛　teaspoon baking soda
　3　cups oil
　2　pounds thin raw asparagus, trimmed
　　　Salt

Combine first 4 ingredients in medium mixing bowl and beat until smooth. Cover and refrigerate until ready to use.

To prepare, heat oil in wok or shallow pan to 375°F. Dip asparagus in batter and fry in batches until golden brown. Drain on paper towels, salt lightly and serve.

COLD ASPARAGUS IN MUSTARD SAUCE
See photograph pages 130-131

4 TO 6 SERVINGS

1½ to 2 pounds fresh asparagus, cleaned and tied into bundles
　1　hard-cooked egg
　1　raw egg yolk
1½ teaspoons Dijon mustard
　½　cup olive oil
1½ tablespoons white wine vinegar
　1　to 2 teaspoons well-drained capers
　　　Salt and freshly ground white pepper
　6　to 8 cooked medium shrimp, peeled and deveined (optional garnish)
　　　Vinaigrette dressing (optional)

　1　tablespoon finely minced pimiento
　1　tablespoon minced parsley

Bring about 4 cups salted water to boil in 6-quart pan. Add asparagus and cook uncovered until tender, about 10 to 12 minutes. Run immediately under cold water to stop further cooking and to retain color. Set aside to cool but do not chill in refrigerator.

Separate hard-cooked egg, reserving yolk; finely mince white.

Blend hard-cooked yolk, raw yolk and mustard in blender or food processor until smooth. Slowly add oil, beating until thick and creamy. Blend in vinegar. Transfer to small bowl. Add capers. Season with salt and white pepper.

Place asparagus on serving dish. Spoon sauce over, leaving tips exposed. If using shrimp garnish, dress with vinaigrette and place over mustard sauce. Sprinkle with egg white, pimiento and parsley. Serve at room temperature.

WHITE ASPARAGUS ESPANA

MAKES ABOUT ¾ CUP

- ½ cup olive oil
- ¼ cup red wine vinegar
- ½ teaspoon Spanish paprika
- ½ teaspoon salt
- ¼ teaspoon dry mustard
  Hot pepper sauce
  Freshly ground pepper
  Cooked white asparagus

Combine all ingredients except asparagus in small bowl and stir until well blended. Spoon over asparagus. Serve.

BROCCOLI CASSEROLE

6 SERVINGS

- 2 10-ounce packages frozen chopped broccoli, thawed and drained
- 1 10¾-ounce can cream of mushroom soup
- ½ cup mayonnaise
- ½ to ¾ cup grated cheddar cheese
- 1 2-ounce jar diced pimientos, drained
- 1 tablespoon fresh lemon juice
- 1 cup crushed cheese crackers
- ¼ cup slivered almonds

Preheat oven to 350°F. Butter shallow 2-quart baking dish. Combine first 6 ingredients in large bowl. Turn into dish. Sprinkle crackers and almonds evenly over top. Bake until heated through, about 20 minutes. Serve immediately.

BROCCOLI-CORN BAKE

6 SERVINGS

- 1 16-ounce can cream-style corn
- 1 10-ounce package frozen chopped broccoli, cooked and well drained
- 1 egg, beaten
- ½ cup coarsely crumbled crackers (about 12 crackers)
- 2 tablespoons (¼ stick) butter or margarine, melted
- 2 teaspoons dehydrated onion

  Salt and freshly ground pepper
- ¼ cup coarsely crumbled crackers (about 5 crackers)
- 1 tablespoon butter or margarine, melted

Preheat oven to 350°F. Combine first 6 ingredients in large bowl and mix thoroughly. Season with salt and pepper to taste. Pour into 1-quart baking dish. Combine remaining ingredients in small bowl and sprinkle evenly over top. Bake until golden, about 35 to 40 minutes.

BROCCOLI FLORETS WITH BROWNED BUTTER

8 TO 10 SERVINGS

- 2 large bunches broccoli, florets only
  Salt
- ½ cup (1 stick) butter

Cook broccoli florets in boiling salted water until crisp-tender, about 5 to 7 minutes; do not overcook. Transfer to colander and let drain 2 or 3 minutes. While broccoli is cooking, melt butter in saucepan over high heat, stirring constantly until it turns rich nutty brown. Arrange broccoli in heated serving dish and pour butter evenly over top.

CHEESY ONION BROCCOLI

4 SERVINGS

- 1 bunch broccoli
- ¼ cup (½ stick) melted butter
- ½ envelope onion soup mix
  Juice of ½ lemon
- 1 cup grated cheddar cheese

Steam broccoli until desired doneness is reached, about 7 minutes. Drain. Place in 1-quart baking dish; pour butter, onion soup mix and lemon juice over. Top with cheese, cover with foil and put under broiler until cheese melts, about 2 to 3 minutes. Serve immediately.

SESAME BROCCOLI

6 SERVINGS

- 1 large bunch broccoli, broken into florets, stems peeled
  Salt
- ½ cup sesame seeds, toasted
- ¼ cup sake
- 1½ tablespoons soy sauce
- 2 teaspoons sesame oil
- 2 teaspoons honey

Cook broccoli in boiling salted water until crisp-tender. Drain thoroughly. Let cool to room temperature. Combine remaining ingredients in large bowl. Shortly before serving, add broccoli and toss to mix well.

GREEN BEANS AND SWEET PEPPERS

8 SERVINGS

- 3 small red sweet peppers, sliced into rings
- 2 pounds green beans, cut into 5-inch lengths
  Salt

Use red pepper rings to circle bundles of green beans. Fasten with toothpicks if necessary. Steam 15 minutes over salted water.

GREEN BEANS-OPEN SESAME

See photograph page 132

6 SERVINGS

- 1 pound green beans, cut julienne
- 3 tablespoons tamari sauce
- 1 tablespoon sesame oil
- ¼ teaspoon nutmeg
- 4 large mushrooms, sliced
- ½ cup sesame seeds, toasted

Steam beans until crisp-tender, about 10 minutes. Meanwhile, combine tamari, oil and nutmeg in large skillet over low to medium heat. Add mushrooms and sauté until just tender. Add beans and toss lightly. Add sesame seeds and toss again. Serve immediately.

GREEN BEAN SAUTE WITH SHALLOTS

8 SERVINGS

- 1½ to 2 pounds green beans
- 2 to 3 tablespoons (¼ to ⅜ stick) butter
- 1 to 2 tablespoons minced shallots
  Salt and freshly ground pepper

Steam or boil beans briefly until just crisp-tender. Drain well and set aside. Melt butter in large skillet over medium heat. Add shallots and sauté until golden. Add beans, salt and pepper to taste and toss lightly until heated through.

BEAN CURD AND GREEN ONIONS

4 TO 6 SERVINGS

- 1 pound (approximately) tofu or dow foo (fresh bean curd)
- ¼ cup peanut oil
- 2 green onions, cut into 1-inch pieces (including stems)
- 1 teaspoon oyster sauce
- 1 to 2 teaspoons sugar or more to taste
  Salt

Pat bean curd dry with paper towels. (Be meticulous, it will take 8 to 10 towels.) Cut into 1-inch pieces. Heat oil in wok until quite hot. Add bean curd and stir carefully until brown, about 4 to 5 minutes. Add onions and oyster sauce. Stir 1 minute to thicken sauce slightly. Add sugar and salt and stir quickly, letting sugar form glaze. Serve hot.

SWEET RED CABBAGE

6 SERVINGS

- 1 red cabbage, shredded and finely chopped
- ½ cup apple cider vinegar
- ¼ cup sugar
- ¼ cup currant jelly
- 2 tablespoons (¼ stick) butter

- 1 teaspoon salt
  Fresh lemon juice (optional)

Combine first 6 ingredients in 3-quart saucepan over medium-low heat and cook 1 hour. Taste and adjust seasoning. Stir in lemon juice for tartness if desired.

COLESLAW

4 TO 6 SERVINGS

- 1 medium onion, chopped
- 1 cup sugar
- 1 cup oil
- ½ cup cider vinegar
- ⅓ cup mayonnaise
- ½ teaspoon celery seeds
- 1 teaspoon salt
- 1 medium cabbage, shredded

Combine onion and sugar in medium bowl. Let stand for 30 minutes. Add all remaining ingredients except cabbage and blend well. Cover and refrigerate. Just before serving, add cabbage and toss.

HOT SLAW

An unusual accompaniment to your favorite cold cuts.

4 SERVINGS

- 2 cups shredded cabbage
- 3 tablespoons (⅜ stick) butter
  Salt and freshly ground pepper
- ⅓ to ½ cup red wine vinegar
- 1½ tablespoons caraway seeds
- 1 teaspoon sugar or more

Place cabbage in medium saucepan with enough water to cover. Cook over medium-high heat until crisp-tender, about 6 to 7 minutes. Drain thoroughly.

Melt butter in large skillet over low heat. Increase heat to medium, add cabbage and toss to coat. Season with salt and pepper to taste. Stir in vinegar, caraway seeds and sugar. Toss gently and continue cooking over low heat until heated through and well blended, about 4 to 5 minutes. Serve.

SAUTEED CARROTS WITH APRICOT

See photograph pages 110-111

The apricots give a sweet-sour flavor accent that complements and blends beautifully with the carrots.

4 TO 6 SERVINGS

- 5 tablespoons (⅝ stick) unsalted butter
- 1 medium onion, cut into thin strips
- 1 pound carrots, shredded
- 4 ounces dried apricots, cut julienne
- ½ cup stock or water
- 1 to 2 teaspoons sherry wine vinegar (imported Spanish preferred)
  Salt and freshly ground pepper

Melt butter in large skillet over medium-high heat. Add onion and cook until browned. Add carrots and apricots and stir-fry about 2 minutes. Stir in stock and cook covered until carrots are crisp-tender, about 5 minutes. Uncover and cook until all liquid evaporates. Season with vinegar and salt and pepper to taste.

CARROTS MARGUERITE

4 SERVINGS

- 3 shallots or green onions (white part only), finely minced
- ¼ cup (½ stick) butter
- 1 pound carrots, peeled and shredded
- 3 tablespoons honey
- ½ teaspoon thyme
- ¼ teaspoon salt
  Dash of freshly ground pepper

Sauté shallots in butter a few minutes over low heat, until soft and just turning golden. Add carrots, honey, thyme, salt and pepper. Stir over medium heat to coat carrots evenly. Cover and cook 3 minutes. Serve immediately.

EGGPLANT FRITTERS

6 TO 8 SERVINGS

- 2 cups cooked mashed eggplant
- 1½ cups cooked white rice
- 1 cup (4 ounces) grated sharp cheddar cheese
- ⅓ cup finely chopped onion
- ⅓ cup (heaping) flour
- 2 eggs, well beaten
  Salt and freshly ground pepper
  Dash of red pepper sauce
  Oil

Combine all ingredients except oil. Heat ½ inch oil in large skillet over medium-high heat. Drop mixture by tablespoons into oil and fry until golden brown, turning once. Drain on paper towels. Serve hot.

Fritters can be frozen after frying and reheated in a 350°F oven until hot, about 10 minutes.

SHERRIED MUSHROOMS

4 TO 6 SERVINGS

- 4 to 6 patty shells, thawed
- 1 pound mushrooms, sliced
  Butter
- 1½ cups sour cream
- ¾ cup grated Parmesan cheese
- 3 tablespoons sherry
  Dash of garlic powder
  Parsley or watercress (garnish)

Heat patty shells according to package directions. Sauté mushrooms briefly in butter. Add sour cream, Parmesan, sherry and garlic powder and cook over low heat until warmed through. Serve in patty shells, garnished with sprigs of parsley or watercress.

SPINACH SOUFFLE STUFFED MUSHROOMS

- 1 12-ounce package frozen spinach soufflé, thawed
  Lemon-pepper seasoning
  Garlic powder
  Salt
- 12 to 18 mushrooms
  Melted butter
- 1½ tablespoons minced onion
- 3 tablespoons (⅜ stick) butter
  Freshly grated Parmesan cheese

Preheat oven to 375°F. Combine soufflé with lemon-pepper, garlic powder and salt.

Remove stems from mushrooms and set aside. Dip mushroom caps in melted butter and place on baking sheet. Finely mince stems. Add minced onion and blend well. Melt remaining butter in small skillet over medium heat. Add onion mixture and sauté until softened. Combine with spinach and blend well.

Fill mushroom caps with spinach mixture, mounding slightly in center. Sprinkle with cheese. Bake until filling is set and cheese is golden, about 12 to 15 minutes.

STUFFED MUSHROOMS

4 SERVINGS

- ¼ cup (½ stick) butter
- 3 tablespoons minced shallots
- ½ cup diced walnuts
- 8 giant mushroom caps, stems reserved and chopped
- ½ cup breadcrumbs
- ¼ teaspoon thyme
  Salt and freshly ground pepper

Preheat oven to 350°F. Butter baking dish. Melt butter in medium skillet over medium-high heat. Add shallots and sauté until wilted. Add nuts and chopped mushroom stems and cook 2 minutes. Mix in breadcrumbs, thyme and salt and pepper to taste. Fill mushroom caps, place in baking dish and bake until thoroughly heated, about 10 to 12 minutes.

SNOW PEAS AND TOMATOES

4 SERVINGS

- 2 to 3 tablespoons (¼ to ⅜ stick) butter or margarine
- 1 garlic clove, minced
- ¼ cup finely chopped onion
- 2 7-ounce packages frozen snow peas, thawed
- 1 8-ounce can water chestnuts, drained and sliced
- 1 tablespoon soy sauce
- 1 teaspoon salt
- 1 teaspoon dried oregano leaves, crumbled
- 3 medium tomatoes, cut into ¼-inch dice

Melt butter or margarine with garlic in large skillet over medium heat. Add onion and sauté until crisp-tender, about 1 minute. Blend in remaining ingredients except tomatoes and cook, stirring constantly, about 2 to 3 minutes. Stir in tomatoes and continue cooking until heated through, about 2 to 3 minutes. Serve hot.

PEA PODS WITH PETITS POIS

6 SERVINGS

  Butter
- 1 pound fresh snow peas, strings removed
  Pinch of fresh or dried dill
  Pinch of garlic salt
- 1 10-ounce package frozen petits pois, thawed

Melt a small amount of butter in medium skillet over medium-high heat. Add snow peas and stir-fry until just al dente. Add dill and garlic salt and mix well. Stir in thawed peas and heat through. (Add more butter, if desired.) Taste and adjust seasonings, if necessary.

CHILLED DILLED PEAS

4 TO 6 SERVINGS

- 1 cup sour cream
- 1 bunch fresh chives, snipped
- ¼ cup fresh snipped dill
- 1 teaspoon curry powder or to taste
  Salt and freshly ground pepper
- 1 16-ounce can tiny French peas, drained
  Snipped dill (garnish)

Combine sour cream, chives, dill, curry powder, salt and pepper to taste in bowl. Add peas and mix gently. Place in serving dish and garnish with dill. Chill thoroughly.

PAN-FRIED BAKED POTATOES

A clever way to use leftover baked potatoes.

4 TO 6 SERVINGS

- ¼ cup (½ stick) butter
- ¼ cup oil
- 6 to 7 large potatoes, baked, peeled and sliced into rounds ½ inch thick
- 4 green onions, minced
- ¼ teaspoon caraway seeds
  Salt and freshly ground pepper
- 1 cup sour cream

Heat butter and oil in large skillet over medium-high heat. Add potatoes and cook until golden, turning gently.

Add onions and caraway seeds and cook another few minutes. Season to taste with salt and pepper. Turn out onto platter and dollop with sour cream. Serve.

BRUNEDE KARTOFLER (SUGAR-BROWNED POTATOES)

6 TO 8 SERVINGS

- 18 small new potatoes, unpeeled
  Salt
- ½ cup (1 stick) unsalted butter
- ½ cup sugar

Cook potatoes in lightly salted boiling water until tender. Drain well. Let stand until cool, then peel.

Melt butter in heavy 10-inch skillet over low heat. Add sugar and cook, stirring frequently, until dissolved and mixture is slightly caramelized. Add one layer of potatoes and gently shake pan until all potatoes are thoroughly coated. Transfer to heated serving bowl and keep warm while cooking remaining potatoes. Serve immediately.

CREAMED SPINACH PUREE

6 SERVINGS

- ¼ cup (½ stick) butter
- 2 10-ounce packages frozen spinach, cooked, squeezed dry and finely chopped or pureed
- ½ cup whipping cream
- 2 tablespoons grated Parmesan cheese
  Pinch of grated nutmeg
  Salt and freshly ground pepper

Brown butter in medium saucepan over medium heat, being careful not to burn. Mix in remaining ingredients except salt and pepper and heat through, stirring constantly. Season to taste.

SPINACH CASSEROLE

4 TO 6 SERVINGS

- 2 cups (1 pint) sour cream
- ½ package onion soup mix (shake well before dividing)
- 2 10-ounce packages frozen chopped spinach, thawed and drained

Preheat oven to 350°F. Grease 1-quart baking dish. Combine sour cream and soup mix in medium bowl. Add spinach and blend thoroughly. Turn into dish. Bake until heated through, about 30 minutes.

SQUASH AND APPLESAUCE

2 TO 4 SERVINGS

- 1 large acorn squash, halved and seeded
  Salt
  Butter or margarine
  Brown sugar
- 1 cup applesauce

Preheat oven to 350°F. Arrange squash cut side down in shallow pan and bake until almost tender, about 35 minutes. Remove from oven. Turn cut sides up and add salt to taste. Brush with butter or margarine and sprinkle generously with

brown sugar. Divide applesauce between halves, return to oven and bake additional 15 minutes.

BAKED TOMATOES WITH SPINACH

8 SERVINGS

- 8 large firm tomatoes
  Salt
- 2 10-ounce packages frozen chopped spinach, thawed and squeezed dry
  Butter Topping*
- 1 cup grated Parmesan cheese
- ½ cup breadcrumbs

Preheat oven to 350°F. Halve tomatoes and remove center core and some seeds, leaving all pulp. Sprinkle with salt. Fill with spinach. Spread thickly with Butter Topping. Top with Parmesan mixed with breadcrumbs. Bake until soft, about 15 minutes. Place briefly under broiler to brown topping.

*Butter Topping

- 1 cup (2 sticks) butter
- 2 tablespoons minced shallots
- 2 garlic cloves, crushed
- 2 tablespoons minced parsley
- ½ teaspoon salt
  Freshly ground pepper to taste

Mix all ingredients together.

BROILED TOMATOES

6 SERVINGS

- ¼ cup mayonnaise
- ¼ cup grated Parmesan or Gruyère cheese
- ¼ cup minced shallot or green onion, white part only
- 2 tablespoons minced parsley
- 2 large ripe tomatoes, sliced into thirds, or 3 smaller tomatoes, halved

Preheat broiler. Combine all ingredients except tomatoes in small bowl and blend well. Gently spread mixture about ¼ inch thick on tomatoes. Broil 4 inches from heat source until lightly browned, about 2 to 3 minutes. Serve immediately.

STUFFED ZUCCHINI

6 SERVINGS

- 6 medium zucchini
- 1 cup sour cream
- ¾ to 1 cup grated sharp cheddar cheese
- 10 soda crackers
- 1 egg
- 2 heaping tablespoons grated Parmesan cheese

Preheat oven to 325°F. Parboil squash 3 minutes. Halve lengthwise and scoop out center. Cook pulp until soft. Blend with remaining ingredients except Parmesan. Spoon into squash shells, sprinkle with Parmesan and bake until tops are bubbly, about 20 to 30 minutes.

STIR-FRY OF SWEET PEPPERS AND ZUCCHINI

See photograph page 109

2 SERVINGS

- 3 to 4 tablespoons olive oil
- 1 large onion, cut into thin strips
- 1 large sweet red pepper, cut into thin strips*
- 2 small zucchini, cut into matchsticks
- 1 garlic clove, minced
- 2½ tablespoons fresh basil or 1½ teaspoons dried, crumbled
- ¼ teaspoon fresh thyme or generous pinch of dried
  Salt and freshly ground pepper

Heat oil in wok or large skillet over high heat. Add onion and red pepper and stir-fry until onion softens slightly, about 2 minutes. Add zucchini, garlic and herbs and stir-fry another 2 minutes. If not serving immediately, reheat by stir-frying over high heat about 3 minutes. Season with salt and pepper to taste.

*If fresh red pepper is unavailable, substitute 1 small green pepper and ½ cup bottled sliced roasted red peppers. Cook green pepper with onion and add red pepper at last minute or during reheating.

STIR-FRY VEGETABLES

4 SERVINGS

- ¼ cup (½ stick) butter
- 1 to 2 cups sliced carrots
- 1 cup chopped celery, including leaves
- 1 onion, chopped
- ½ cup peanuts
- 2 tablespoons soy sauce

Melt butter in wok or skillet over medium heat. Add remaining ingredients and stir-fry until vegetables are cooked through but still crunchy. Serve immediately.

FRUIT

RAW APPLESAUCE

MAKES ABOUT 1½ CUPS

- 3 apples, peeled, cored, and diced
- ¼ cup apple cider or juice or orange juice or grapefruit juice
- ¼ cup light corn syrup

Place all ingredients in blender or food processor and puree.

DANISH APPLESAUCE

A zesty accompaniment particularly pleasing with game or poultry.

MAKES ABOUT 4 CUPS

- 4 cups cooked pureed apples (4 to 5 large)
- ¼ cup sugar, or to taste
  Grated rind and strained juice of ½ orange
  Grated rind and strained juice of ½ lemon
  Sherry

Combine all ingredients except sherry in medium bowl and mix to blend. Add enough sherry to give the sauce a soft consistency.

HOT FRUIT COMPOTE

8 TO 10 SERVINGS

- 1 1-pound can pitted dark cherries

- 1 1-pound can sliced peaches
- 1 1-pound can pear halves
- 1 1-pound can apricots
- 1 1-pound can pineapple chunks
- 1½ cups syrup from drained fruits (any blend)
- 2 bananas, thickly sliced
- 8 ounces coconut macaroons (about 2 cups), broken up
- 1 cup Madeira
- ¼ cup (½ stick) butter, melted

Preheat oven to 350°F. Combine all ingredients gently but thoroughly in a 3-quart casserole. Bake covered about 1 hour.

Serve as a side dish with roast beef.

SCALLOPED PINEAPPLE CASSEROLE

4 SERVINGS

- ½ cup (1 stick) unsalted butter, room temperature
- ¾ cup sugar
- 4 eggs
- 1 20-ounce can crushed pineapple, drained
- 1½ teaspoons fresh lemon juice
- ¼ teaspoon freshly grated nutmeg
- 3 cups firmly packed cubed white bread (about 5 slices)

Preheat oven to 350°F. Butter 1½-quart baking dish. Cream butter with sugar in large bowl until smooth. Add eggs one at a time, beating well after each addition. Gently stir in pineapple. Blend in lemon juice and nutmeg. Fold in bread. Spoon into dish. Bake until top is lightly golden, about 50 minutes.

DO AHEAD

BROCCOLI HELENE WITH LIME SAUCE

25 SERVINGS

- 6 bunches broccoli, cut into florets with 3-inch stems

Italian salad dressing
Lime Sauce*

Peel broccoli stems if necessary. Cook broccoli in boiling water until crisp-tender and still bright green. Cool in ice water. Drain well. Refrigerate overnight.

Sprinkle broccoli lightly with dressing. Arrange on platter and serve with bowls of Lime Sauce for individual dipping.

*Lime Sauce

Can be made up to 3 days ahead.

MAKES 4 CUPS

- 2 cups mayonnaise
- 2 cups sour cream
- ⅓ cup fresh lime juice
- 1 tablespoon finely grated lime peel
- 2 teaspoons white horseradish
- 2 teaspoons Dijon mustard
- 1 teaspoon salt

Combine all ingredients in large bowl. Cover and refrigerate. Adjust seasoning before serving.

MARINATED CARROTS

6 TO 8 SERVINGS

- 1 cup cider vinegar
- 1 cup sugar
- ⅓ cup oil
- 4 16-ounce cans small carrots
- 1 4-ounce jar diced pimientos
- 1 cup chopped green onions
- 1 green pepper, diced

Boil vinegar, sugar and oil together until sugar dissolves. Cool.

Place carrots, pimientos, onions and green pepper in large bowl. Add cooled marinade and toss gently. Refrigerate, covered, up to one week, stirring occasionally.

When ready to serve, drain vegetables. Reserve marinade for future use.

Try substituting carrots with 4 16-ounce cans green beans, drained, or 1 pound fresh mushrooms, sliced.

CHEESE PUFFED POTATO CASSEROLE

8 TO 10 SERVINGS

- 4 eggs, separated
- 4 cups cooked instant mashed potatoes, seasoned according to package directions
- 1¼ cups shredded sharp cheddar cheese
- 1 tablespoon finely chopped onion
- 1 tablespoon finely chopped green pepper
- ½ teaspoon celery salt
  Salt
  Paprika

Preheat oven to 375°F. Generously grease 3-quart or 9×13-inch baking dish. Using electric mixer, beat egg yolks into potatoes until well combined. Blend in cheese, onion, green pepper, celery salt and salt to taste. Can be made ahead to this point, covered and refrigerated.

Just prior to baking, beat egg whites until soft peaks form. Fold into potato mixture. Spoon lightly into baking dish and sprinkle with paprika. Bake uncovered until top is golden brown, about 25 minutes.

MICROWAVE

APPLESAUCE

FOR EACH SERVING

- 1 tart cooking apple (peeled if desired), cored and sliced
- ¼ teaspoon cinnamon
- 6 strawberries (optional)

Arrange apple slices in 2-cup baking dish and sprinkle with cinnamon. Cover and cook on High 3 minutes. Transfer to processor, add strawberries and blend to desired consistency.

BROCCOLI CUSTARD

4 TO 6 SERVINGS

- 2 10-ounce packages frozen chopped broccoli, thawed, well drained and squeezed dry
- 2 cups shredded sharp cheddar or Monterey Jack cheese
- ¼ cup biscuit mix
- ¼ cup chopped fresh parsley
- 2 garlic cloves, minced
- ¼ teaspoon salt
- ⅛ teaspoon freshly ground pepper
- 4 eggs, well beaten
  Cherry tomatoes and parsley sprigs (garnish)

Coat 6-cup ring mold with melted butter. Combine all ingredients except eggs and garnish in large bowl and blend well. Mix in eggs. Spoon into mold, spreading evenly. Cook uncovered on High until mixture appears to set around edges, about 8 to 10 minutes. Let stand 5 minutes before unmolding onto platter. Fill with cherry tomatoes and parsley. Serve warm or chilled.

CELERY-PEA MEDLEY

5 TO 6 SERVINGS

- 1½ cups thinly sliced celery cut on diagonal
- ½ cup minced onion
- 2 tablespoons (¼ stick) butter
- ½ teaspoon salt
- 1 10-ounce package frozen peas
  Finely minced rosemary (optional)

Combine celery, onion, butter and salt in 1½-quart glass casserole. Cover and cook on High 4 to 5 minutes, stirring halfway through cooking time. Add peas and stir to blend. Cover and cook on High 5 to 6 minutes, stirring halfway through cooking time. Rest, covered, 5 minutes before serving. Sprinkle with rosemary, if desired.

CORN ON THE COB

Fresh sweet corn is spectacular cooked by microwave. There are three methods, all equally good.

1. Carefully strip back husk (do not tear it off) and remove all of the silk. Brush corn liberally with melted butter and season with salt. Pull husks back into place. Tie with string around the tip to keep husks in position. Cook on High.

2. Place buttered, salted ears in a large glass casserole. Add 1 tablespoon of water. Cover with plastic wrap. Cook on High.

3. Wrap each buttered, salted ear securely in waxed paper and arrange spoke-fashion on paper towels in the oven. Cook on High.

Cooking Times:

2 ears of corn: 4 to 6 minutes; turn corn halfway through cooking time.

4 ears of corn: 8 to 10 minutes; turn corn halfway through cooking time.

6 ears of corn: 9 to 11 minutes; turn corn halfway through cooking time.

Very large ears will need extra cooking time. The corn should set, covered, 3 to 5 minutes after cooking.

BRUSSELS SPROUTS WITH GARLIC AND PARMESAN

6 TO 8 SERVINGS

   1 pound fresh brussels sprouts
   ¼ cup water
   2 tablespoons (¼ stick) butter
   1 garlic clove, minced
     Salt and freshly ground pepper
   ¼ cup freshly grated Parmesan cheese

Discard any dry outside leaves from sprouts. Trim stems. Using small sharp knife, cut a shallow "x" in bottom of each stem. Combine sprouts and water in shallow 1-quart baking dish. Cover and cook on High 7 minutes. Let stand covered 3 to 4 minutes.

Meanwhile, combine butter and garlic in small glass measuring cup and cook on High 1 to 2 minutes. Drain water from sprouts. Add butter mixture, salt and pepper to taste and toss lightly to coat. Add cheese and toss again. Serve hot.

SPINACH AND FETA CHEESE QUICHE

6 TO 8 SERVINGS

   4 ounces Greek feta cheese, well rinsed, patted dry and crumbled
   ½ cup Parmesan cheese
   ½ cup chopped green onion
   ½ cup minced fresh parsley
   ¼ cup fresh breadcrumbs
   1 10-ounce package frozen chopped spinach, thawed, squeezed dry
   1½ cups grated Monterey Jack cheese
   1 baked 9-inch deep-dish pie shell
   1 cup whipping cream
   4 eggs
     Parmesan cheese
     Minced green onion
     Minced fresh parsley

Combine first 6 ingredients in mixing bowl and blend well. Sprinkle Jack cheese on pie shell. Spoon spinach mixture over top. Heat cream in measuring cup on High 1½ minutes. Beat eggs in separate bowl. Add hot cream and beat again. Slowly pour over spinach mixture, allowing spinach to absorb cream before adding more. Sprinkle top with Parmesan, onion and parsley. Cook on Bake (60 percent power) until center is barely set, about 12 minutes, turning if necessary to promote even cooking. Let stand 5 minutes before serving.

BAKED POTATOES

Although baking a potato in a conventional oven may be the easiest "recipe" in the world short of boiling an egg, speedy microwave cooking eliminates some of the steps of traditional preparation. Simply ele-vate the potato on a rack and cook until the outside feels slightly soft. Let stand for a few minutes to finish cooking before cutting into it. There is no need to pierce the skin first—you don't even have to turn it over since elevating it will prevent heat from being trapped underneath, thus keeping the potato from steaming. A medium-size potato will usually take 6 minutes on High.

A simple way to calculate for more than one is to increase cooking time by 5 minutes for each additional potato. Place potatoes in a circle if cooking more than one. If they are not all the same size, the smaller ones will be finished first just as they are in conventional cooking.

QUICK AND EASY LYONNAISE POTATOES

Keeping oil at a minimum is the secret to the crisp texture of these potatoes.

2 SERVINGS

   2 medium potatoes, peeled, rinsed and patted dry
     Garlic salt
     Garlic powder
     Paprika
   ⅓ cup dehydrated onion flakes
   2 tablespoons oil
     Parsley flakes

Slice potatoes thinly and evenly. Pat dry with paper towels. Arrange half of slices in dish just large enough to accommodate all potatoes being used. Sprinkle lightly with garlic salt, garlic powder and paprika. Top with half of dehydrated onion. Repeat layering. Pour oil over top. Cover and cook on High until potatoes are fork tender, about 10 minutes. Sprinkle with parsley flakes.

HOT POTATO SALAD

4 SERVINGS

   4 slices bacon
   2 small white onions, chopped
   1 10½-ounce can condensed cream of celery soup
   2 tablespoons chicken broth

2 tablespoons white vinegar

½ teaspoon salt

¼ teaspoon pepper

½ teaspoon sugar

¼ teaspoon crushed celery seeds

4 medium potatoes, baked, peeled and diced

2 tablespoons chopped parsley

Place bacon slices in a glass casserole, cover with paper towel to prevent splatter. Cook on High 4 minutes. Remove bacon and drain on a paper towel. Cool and crumble bacon. Set bacon bits aside.

Pour off all but 2 tablespoons of bacon fat. Add onions and cook on High 2 minutes. Stir in soup, chicken broth, vinegar, salt, pepper, sugar and celery seeds. Cook on High uncovered 2 minutes; stir; cook 2 minutes more.

Add potato cubes and bacon bits; cook on High 30 seconds, stir; cook on High 30 seconds. Sprinkle with parsley. Serve.

SWEET AND SIMPLE SWEET POTATOES

Both sweet potatoes and yams are cooked on lower settings to ensure even cooking. Because of their irregular shape, the narrow end sometimes has a tendency to overcook. Timing is approximately 4 minutes for each potato.

6 SERVINGS

6 medium (about 3 pounds) sweet potatoes

Pierce potatoes. Arrange in circle on rack in microwave (if size of potatoes varies, place larger ones outside the ring and smaller ones inside). Cook on Roast (70 percent power) until potatoes are soft on outside but still firm in center, about 20 minutes. Cover and let stand in microwave 3 to 4 minutes to equalize moisture and finish cooking.

Potatoes can be cooked in advance and reheated on Roast (70 percent power). Allow 1 to 2 minutes per potato to reheat.

SPAGHETTI SQUASH

The pastalike strands produced when this squash is cooked are excellent with low-calorie/low-fat sauces. Try it tossed simply with margarine, Parmesan cheese and salt and pepper.

4 SERVINGS

1 2- to 3-pound spaghetti squash

Wash outside of squash and pat dry. Pierce in several places with fork. Place on rack and cook on High 6 to 7 minutes per pound, turning once (it should feel soft in several places). Let stand 10 minutes. Halve lengthwise and scoop out inside with large fork.

For a quick snack, remove seeds from squash and let dry for an hour on paper towel or plate. Cook on High until just toasted, about 2 minutes. Season with salt.

ORANGE-GLAZED YAMS

6 TO 8 SERVINGS

1 40-ounce can yams, drained, or 3 large fresh yams, cooked, peeled and cut into chunks

¼ cup firmly packed brown sugar

¼ cup sugar

1 tablespoon cornstarch

⅛ teaspoon salt

1 cup fresh orange juice

1 teaspoon grated orange peel

2 tablespoons (¼ stick) butter

Arrange yams in 1½-quart baking dish. Combine sugars, cornstarch and salt in 4-cup measure. Stir in orange juice and peel. Cook on High 2 minutes. Whisk through several times. Continue cooking on High for 2 more minutes. Add butter, stirring until melted. Pour sauce over yams. Cook on High until heated through, about 3 minutes.

ZUCCHINI ITALIANO

4 SERVINGS

3 tablespoons olive oil

2 small white onions, chopped

1 garlic clove, mashed

1 pound firm, 1½-inch diameter zucchini, cut into ¼-inch slices

1 teaspoon seasoned salt

¼ teaspoon oregano

Combine oil, onion and garlic in an 8-inch square glass baking dish and cook 3 minutes on High. Stir in zucchini and season with salt and oregano. Cover and cook 3 minutes on High. Stir. Cook additional 3 minutes. Stir. Let stand, covered, 5 minutes, before serving.

ZUCCHINI MEDLEY

4 SERVINGS

2 medium zucchini, sliced diagonally

1 medium onion, halved and thinly sliced into rings

1 teaspoon dried oregano leaves, crumbled (or other herb)
Salt and freshly ground pepper

2 tablespoons (¼ stick) butter

2 medium tomatoes, sliced

½ green pepper, cut into ½-inch slices

½ cup shredded Parmesan, Monterey Jack or cheddar cheese (optional)

Arrange zucchini slices in bottom of 2-quart round casserole. Top with onion. Sprinkle with some of oregano, salt and pepper. Dot with some of butter. Top with tomatoes, then green pepper. Dot with remaining butter and sprinkle with remaining oregano. Cover and cook on High 7 minutes. Sprinkle with cheese if desired. (If using Monterey Jack or cheddar, cook on High 1 minute to melt cheese.)

Tips For Pasta

■ Faced with only a few minutes to whip up a meal, an Italian cook will reach into the refrigerator for a dash of this and a bit of that, all the while thinking—pasta!

■ What shape pasta to use for which sauce? That's simple. Heavier-textured sauces are generally combined with thicker pastas (fusilli, fettuccini, tagliatelle, linguine, shells, ziti etc.). And light or thin sauces are served with the finer pastas (capelli d'angelo, vermicelli, spaghettini, quadrettini etc.).

■ When it comes to the all-important cooking of the noodle, remember this rule. For every pound of pasta have six quarts of boiling water (with two tablespoons salt added). If cooking very large or filled pastas (ravioli or lasagne for instance), add three tablespoons vegetable oil to the water. Drop the pasta in and boil rapidly, stirring occasionally to avoid sticking, until the noodles are tender but still al dente, a little firm to the bite. This is the only proper way to serve pasta. If it overcooks, throw it out! Drain immediately in a colander, making sure to shake out all liquid.

Ideally combine the pasta with sauce at this point, but there is a way of holding it for several hours before serving. Rinse with hot water to remove starch and drain again. Now toss the noodles with a generous amount of butter or olive oil (whichever will blend well with your chosen sauce) and set aside. Shortly before serving, either toss with the sauce until heated through or place covered in a 350°F oven for 15 minutes and then blend.

PASTA

CAPELLI D'ANGELO WITH BUTTER AND CHEESE

4 TO 6 SERVINGS

- 1 cup (2 sticks) unsalted butter
- 1 pound capelli d'angelo, cooked al dente
- 1½ cups freshly grated imported Parmesan cheese
  Salt and freshly ground pepper

Melt butter in large skillet over medium heat. Add pasta and cheese and toss constantly until butter and cheese cling to noodles. Season to taste with salt and pepper and serve immediately.

For a variation, combine ⅓ cup each freshly grated bel paese, Gruyère, fontina and Parmesan cheeses and toss with pasta according to above directions. Just before serving, stir in ½ cup whipping cream and heat through. Serve immediately with a sprinkling of minced chives.

ZUCCHINI WITH FARFALLE

See photograph page 157

4 TO 6 MAIN-COURSE SERVINGS OR 6 TO 8 FIRST-COURSE SERVINGS

- 5 tablespoons light olive oil
- 5 small zucchini, cut into sticks about 1½ inches long
- 2 large onions, minced
- 1 garlic clove, minced
- ⅔ cup whipping cream
- 1 pound farfalle, cooked al dente
- ½ cup freshly grated imported Parmesan cheese
  Salt and freshly ground pepper
  Freshly grated imported Parmesan cheese

Heat oil in large nonaluminum skillet over medium-high heat. Add zucchini and sauté quickly until golden. Remove with slotted spoon and set aside. Add onion and sauté until golden. Add garlic and cook an additional minute. Stir in cream, increase heat and boil until sauce is reduced by ⅓. Add noodles, zucchini, ½ cup Parmesan, salt and pepper to taste and toss thoroughly until heated through. Serve with additional grated Parmesan.

EASY FETTUCCINE

4 MAIN COURSE OR 6 SIDE-DISH SERVINGS

- ¼ cup (½ stick) butter or margarine, room temperature
- 2 tablespoons dried parsley
- 1 teaspoon dried basil, crumbled
- 1 8-ounce package cream cheese, room temperature
  Freshly ground pepper
- ⅔ cup boiling water
- ¼ cup (½ stick) butter or margarine
- 1 garlic clove, minced
- 1 8-ounce package fettuccine, cooked al dente and drained
- ¾ cup grated Romano cheese

Combine ¼ cup butter, parsley and basil in medium bowl. Blend in cream cheese. Season with pepper to taste. Mix in water, blending thoroughly. Set bowl in larger pan of hot water to keep warm.

and Bread

Foolproof Rice Ring

■ Wonder why your beautiful rice ring fell apart when you unmolded it? Simple explanation: you probably used the wrong kind of rice. Long-grain rice, the most popular because it produces fluffy, separate grains when cooked, will not stick together as well as the glutinous, softer-textured medium-grain rice. The shorter the grain, in other words, the stickier the rice. That's one reason the Chinese use short- or medium-grain rice; the tender little clumps can easily be handled with chopsticks. The plumper short and medium grains—aside from their "moldable" appeal—also are especially good as binders or extenders in meat and fish loaves, croquettes and puddings.

■ Try this for a perfect Friday night supper. Melt ½ stick butter in a medium sauce pan and saute 1 onion, diced, and 3 cloves garlic, minced. Blend in 1 teaspoon flour. Add 1 6½- or 7-ounce can minced clams and ½ cup milk. Simmer 10 minutes, then add parsley and other seasonings to taste, while stirring constantly. Serve over your favorite pasta and garnish with steamed clams.

Quick Breads

■ Add variety to your dinner roll basket with these crispy cheese triangles. All you need is pita bread, melted butter and grated Parmesan cheese. Split the pita in half horizontally with a sharp knife and brush both sides with melted butter. Sprinkle generously with Parmesan. Cut into quarters, transfer to baking sheet and toast in a 400° oven for about 8 minutes.

■ Herbed biscuits spice up any company gathering and are made in minutes. Start by melting ¾ stick butter in an 8 x 8-inch pan and sprinkle it with an herb combination of your choice—parsley, onion flakes, dill, celery seeds—or Parmesan cheese. Top with 1 8-ounce package refrigerated biscuits and bake 12 to 15 minutes. Invert and serve immediately.

■ With a package of refrigerated crescent rolls and a container of cheese seasoned with garlic and herbs, such as Boursin or Rondelé, you can create wonderful mouth-watering rolls. Simply place the sheet of dough on a flat surface, spread with cheese (1 5-ounce container will fill 2 packages of rolls), then roll and bake the crescents according to package directions. Cream cheese and chopped prosciutto may be combined and used as another variation.

Melt remaining butter in large skillet over low heat. Add garlic and cook about 1 to 2 minutes; do not burn. Add pasta and toss gently. Sprinkle with ½ cup of cheese and toss again. Transfer to serving platter. Spoon sauce over top and sprinkle with remaining cheese.

FETTUCCINE WITH PEAS AND HAM

See photograph page 156

6 TO 8 SERVINGS

- 5 tablespoons (⅝ stick) unsalted butter
- 6 shallots, minced
- ½ pound mushrooms, sliced
- 1¼ cups whipping cream
- 1 10-ounce package frozen tiny peas, thawed
- 4 ounces boiled ham, chopped
- 1 cup freshly grated imported Parmesan cheese
- 1 pound fettuccine, cooked al dente and drained
  Salt and freshly ground pepper

Additional freshly grated Parmesan (optional)

Heat butter in heavy large non-aluminum skillet. Add shallots and sauté until soft. Add mushrooms, increase heat to high and cook until mushrooms are very lightly browned. Add cream and let boil 2 minutes. Stir in peas and cook about 30 seconds. Reduce heat to low; blend in ham, cheese and fettuccine and toss until heated, well combined and sauce clings to pasta. Season to taste with salt and generous amount of pepper. Turn into heated platter and serve. Pass additional cheese, if desired.

Sauce can be prepared an hour or so ahead to point of adding peas.

LASAGNE WITH PESTO

See photograph page 157

6 SERVINGS

- 1 pound ricotta cheese
- 1½ cups freshly grated imported Parmesan cheese
- 1 cup minced mozzarella cheese
- ½ cup minced fresh parsley
- ¼ cup minced green onion

- 1 egg yolk
- ½ teaspoon marjoram
- ½ teaspoon minced garlic
- ½ teaspoon dried basil or 1½ teaspoons fresh
- ¼ teaspoon oregano
  Salt and freshly ground pepper
- ¾ pound lasagne noodles, cooked al dente and cooled
- 1 recipe Ligurian Pesto Sauce (see on page 150)

Preheat oven to 350°F. Generously grease a shallow, 2½-quart baking dish. Combine first 10 ingredients with salt and pepper to taste in large mixing bowl and blend well. Spread portion of cheese filling over each lasagne noodle. Roll up individually jelly roll fashion and stand vertically in single layer in baking dish. Pour sauce over, cover and bake until sauce is bubbly and heated through, about 30 to 40 minutes.

Lasagne can be assembled 1 day before serving.

ARTICHOKE LINGUINE

4 SERVINGS

- ¼ cup (½ stick) butter
- ¼ cup olive oil
- 1 tablespoon flour
- 1 cup chicken broth
- 1 garlic clove, crushed
- 1 tablespoon minced fresh parsley
- 2 to 3 teaspoons fresh lemon juice
  Salt and freshly ground white pepper
- 1 14-ounce can artichoke hearts packed in water, drained and sliced
- 2 tablespoons freshly grated Parmesan cheese
- 2 teaspoons capers, rinsed and drained
- 1 tablespoon butter
- 2 tablespoons olive oil
- 1 tablespoon freshly grated Parmesan cheese
- ¼ teaspoon salt
- 1 pound linguine, cooked al dente and drained
- 2 ounces minced prosciutto or other ham (garnish)

Melt butter with oil in small saucepan over medium heat. Add flour and stir until smooth, about 3 minutes. Blend in broth, stirring until thickened, about 1 minute. Reduce heat to low. Add garlic, parsley, lemon juice, salt and pepper to taste and cook about 5 minutes, stirring constantly. Blend in artichokes, cheese and capers. Cover mixture and simmer about 8 minutes.

Melt remaining butter in large skillet over medium heat. Stir in remaining oil, cheese and salt. Add linguine and toss lightly. Arrange pasta on platter and pour sauce over. Garnish with prosciutto.

EASY LINGUINE ROMANO

4 TO 6 SERVINGS

- 8 ounces linguine
- ¼ cup (½ stick) butter
- 4 ounces chicken livers
- ¾ cup or more whipping cream
- ½ cup or more grated Parmesan cheese
  Salt and freshly ground pepper

Cook linguine according to package directions until al dente. Drain well. Meanwhile heat half the butter in medium skillet over medium-high heat. Add chicken livers and sauté; do not overcook. Let sautéed livers cool, then chop coarsely.

Combine all ingredients in heavy saucepan. Place over low heat and mix gently, adding more cheese or cream to reach desired consistency. Serve immediately.

LIGURIAN PESTO WITH BUCATINI, POTATOES, AND GREEN BEANS
See photograph page 157

This classic pesto sauce can be prepared in about 5 minutes with the help of a food processor or blender and then stored (covered by about ½ inch olive oil) in the refrigerator 3 to 4 months. It is marvelous by itself as a pasta sauce or as a seasoning for vegetable soups. When combined with bucatini (long, hollow rods of pasta), potatoes and green beans, it becomes a classic.

4 TO 6 SERVINGS

Sauce
- 2 cups tightly packed fresh basil leaves*
- ¼ cup freshly grated imported Parmesan cheese
- 2 garlic cloves, halved
- 1 tablespoon toasted pine nuts
  Salt and freshly ground pepper
- ⅔ to 1 cup full-bodied olive oil
- 3 tablespoons (⅜ stick) butter

- 6 ounces green beans, steamed until crisp-tender (halved if extremely long)
- 1 large potato, boiled until tender, peeled and cubed
- 1 pound bucatini, cooked al dente
  Freshly grated imported Parmesan cheese

For sauce: Combine ingredients in food processor or blender, adding enough olive oil to make thick, smooth sauce. Set mixture aside.

Melt butter in large skillet over medium-high heat. Add beans and potato and sauté 3 minutes. Add bucatini and pesto sauce and toss thoroughly. Serve immediately with Parmesan cheese.

*When fresh basil is not available, substitute 1½ cups tightly packed Italian (broadleaf) parsley and 2 tablespoons dried basil.

LINGUINE WITH TOMATO-BASIL SAUCE
See photograph page 160

This is a robust sauce that tastes of summer. If in season, use fresh tomatoes and basil. The sauce will keep in the refrigerator 4 to 5 days, or may be frozen up to 4 months. Make it in quantity as it lends itself to delicious variations.

4 TO 6 MAIN-COURSE SERVINGS OR 6 TO 8 FIRST-COURSE SERVINGS

- ¼ cup full-bodied olive oil
- 2 medium onions, chopped
- 1 large garlic clove, minced
- 1 28-ounce can tomatoes, undrained, seeded and chopped, or 2 pounds fresh tomatoes, peeled, seeded and chopped
- 1½ to 2 tablespoons dried basil or ¼ cup fresh
- ½ teaspoon dried oregano or 1½ teaspoons fresh
- 1 to 1½ teaspoons sugar
  Salt and freshly ground pepper

1 pound linguine, cooked al dente
Freshly grated imported Parmesan cheese

Heat oil in large heavy skillet over medium-low heat. Add onion and cook until soft and transparent, about 10 minutes. Add garlic and cook an additional 2 minutes. Blend in tomatoes and herbs. Increase heat to high, bring to boil and cook until some of liquid has evaporated, about 5 minutes. Add sugar, salt and pepper to taste. Add pasta and toss until blended. Serve immediately with Parmesan cheese.

For Abruzzo Tomato Sauce: Add 3 ounces blanched and chopped salt pork to olive oil. Cook over medium heat until pork is golden. Remove with slotted spoon and reserve. Add onion and proceed as directed in basic recipe. In addition to basil and oregano, add ½ teaspoon dried hot red pepper flakes to sauce. When sauce is finished, stir in reserved pork just to heat through.

For Bolognese Tomato-Cream Sauce: Substitute light olive oil for full-bodied oil in basic recipe. Before adding sugar, salt and pepper, stir in 1 cup whipping cream and ¼ cup (½ stick) unsalted butter. Simmer several minutes and then season to taste. The butter and cream give a rich, almost sweet quality to this sauce that makes it quite elegant.

ITALIAN MACARONI

2 SERVINGS

1 cup uncooked macaroni
Boiling water
1 tablespoon butter or oil
Salt
¼ cup grated Gruyère cheese
¼ cup grated Parmesan cheese
¼ cup (½ stick) melted butter
Pepper
Nutmeg

Cook macaroni in boiling water with butter and salt until it reaches desired doneness, about 10 to 12 minutes. Drain but do not rinse.

Add cheeses, butter and seasonings to taste. Toss quickly and serve.

Garnish with chopped ham or tongue, or sliced mushrooms or truffles, if desired.

PASTA PRIMAVERA

See photograph page 158

4 TO 6 MAIN-COURSE SERVINGS OR 6 TO 8 FIRST-COURSE SERVINGS

½ cup (1 stick) unsalted butter
1 medium onion, minced
1 large garlic clove, minced
1 pound thin asparagus, tough ends trimmed, cut diagonally into ¼-inch slices, tips left intact
½ pound mushrooms, thinly sliced
6 ounces cauliflower, broken into small florets
1 medium zucchini, cut into ¼-inch rounds
1 small carrot, halved lengthwise, cut diagonally into ⅛-inch slices
1 cup whipping cream
½ cup chicken stock
2 tablespoons chopped fresh basil or 2 teaspoons dried
1 cup frozen tiny peas, thawed, or 1 cup fresh young peas*
2 ounces prosciutto or cooked ham, chopped
5 green onions, chopped
Salt and freshly ground pepper
1 pound fettuccine or linguine, cooked al dente, thoroughly drained
1 cup freshly grated imported Parmesan cheese

Heat wok or large, deep skillet over medium-high heat. Add butter, onion and garlic and sauté until onion is softened, about 2 minutes. Mix in asparagus, mushrooms, cauliflower, zucchini and carrot and stir-fry 2 minutes. Remove several pieces of

asparagus tips, mushrooms and zucchini and reserve for garnish.

Increase heat to high. Add cream, stock and basil and allow mixture to boil until liquid is slightly reduced, about 3 minutes. Stir in peas, ham and green onion and cook 1 minute more. Season to taste with salt and pepper if desired.

Add pasta and cheese, tossing until thoroughly combined and pasta is heated through. Turn onto large serving platter and garnish with reserved vegetables.

*Frozen tiny peas tend to be sweeter than fresh peas from the market. If using fresh peas, cook them with the asparagus and shell just before adding.

Vegetables may be chopped several hours in advance, wrapped and kept in refrigerator.

For a variation, add 1 pound cooked, shelled shrimp when you prepare pea-ham mixture.

PASTA WITH SALSA DI PUTTANA

See photograph page 153

SERVES 4 TO 6

2 tablespoons olive oil
2 garlic cloves, minced
1 celery rib, minced
1 sweet red pepper, minced (optional)
1 2-pound, 3-ounce can Italian plum tomatoes (or 4½ cups)
8 anchovies, chopped
8 stuffed green olives, sliced
8 pitted black olives, sliced
1 teaspoon capers
1 teaspoon basil
¼ teaspoon dried red pepper

Heat olive oil in a large skillet. Sauté garlic, celery and sweet red pepper until soft. Press tomatoes through a food mill and add to skillet along with anchovies. Simmer for 10 minutes. Stir in olives, capers, basil and dried red pepper. Simmer, uncovered, for 20 minutes. Serve with hot pasta tossed with butter.

VEGETABLE PASTA

3 TO 4 SERVINGS

- 3 tablespoons olive oil
- 3 garlic cloves, minced
- ¼ cup chopped onion
- 1 pint cherry tomatoes, halved
- 2 cups chopped broccoli, cooked until crisp-tender and drained
- 1 tablespoon chopped fresh basil or ½ teaspoon dried, crumbled
- ½ teaspoon crushed red pepper flakes or to taste
  Salt and freshly ground pepper
- ½ pound fettuccine, cooked al dente and drained
  Freshly grated Parmesan cheese

Heat oil in large skillet over medium-high heat. Add garlic and onion and sauté until tender, about 5 to 10 minutes. Add tomatoes and cook until softened, about 10 minutes. Blend in broccoli and seasonings. Add fettuccine and toss lightly. Sprinkle lightly with Parmesan and toss again. Pass additional cheese at table if desired.

SPINACH PASTA WITH GORGONZOLA SAUCE

See photograph page 160

The rich, buttery flavor of Gorgonzola cheese makes this sauce unique. It can be prepared about an hour before serving and gently reheated.

4 TO 6 MAIN-COURSE SERVINGS OR 6 TO 8 FIRST-COURSE SERVINGS

- ¼ pound imported Gorgonzola cheese, crumbled
- ½ cup milk
- 3 tablespoons (⅜ stick) butter
- ⅓ cup whipping cream
- 1 pound spinach pasta, fettuccine or spaghetti, cooked al dente
- ⅓ cup freshly grated imported Parmesan cheese

Combine Gorgonzola, milk and butter in large, nonaluminum skillet. Place over low heat and stir until smooth. Add cream and stir until

sauce is hot and well blended. Add pasta and Parmesan and toss until noodles are evenly coated.

SPINACH PESTO

4 SERVINGS

- 3 cups fresh spinach leaves, stems discarded
- 2 cups fresh parsley (preferably Italian type)
- ½ cup grated Parmesan cheese
- ½ cup grated Romano cheese
- ½ cup oil
- ¼ cup blanched almonds
- ¼ cup (½ stick) butter or margarine, melted
- 2 tablespoons pine nuts
- 3 large garlic cloves, crushed
- 1 teaspoon salt
- 1 teaspoon oil
  Salt
- 1 pound pasta
  Grated Parmesan cheese

Puree first 10 ingredients in blender or processor until smooth; set aside.

Bring water to boil in large pan. Add oil and salt. Add pasta and cook over medium-high heat until al dente. Strain through colander, reserving ⅓ cup liquid. Blend hot liquid into puree and toss with pasta. Serve with Parmesan cheese.

SPAGHETTI WITH MUSSELS, SCALLOPS AND SHRIMP

See photograph pages 154-155

4 TO 6 MAIN-COURSE SERVINGS OR 6 TO 8 FIRST-COURSE SERVINGS

- 3 tablespoons light olive oil
- 1 large onion, minced
- 2 garlic cloves, minced
- ¼ cup dry white wine
- 1½ teaspoons dried basil or 1½ tablespoons fresh
- 1 teaspoon dried marjoram or 1 tablespoon fresh
- 1½ cups canned tomatoes, well drained
- 1½ pounds mussels, scrubbed and debearded, or 2 pounds small clams, scrubbed

- 1 pound sea scallops, halved
- 1 pound large shrimp, peeled, deveined and butterflied
  Salt and freshly ground pepper
- 1 pound spaghetti, cooked al dente

Heat oil in 4- or 5-quart saucepan over medium-high heat. Add onion and sauté until lightly golden. Add garlic and sauté an additional 30 seconds. Stir in wine, basil and marjoram and cook 1 minute. Add tomatoes, increase heat and boil 5 minutes. Reduce heat to medium, add mussels or clams, cover and cook until shells open about ½ inch, approximately 5 minutes. Add scallops and shrimp. Cover and cook until scallops and shrimp are barely firm, about 2 to 3 minutes. Season to taste with salt and pepper, add spaghetti and toss gently to mix.

Opposite
Pasta with Salsa di Puttana is a delectable combination of pasta with a tomato sauce.

Page 154–155
Spaghetti with Mussels, Scallops and Shrimp is a memorable dinner, ready on short notice.

Page 156
Antipasto Centerpiece Salad, Fettuccine with Peas and Ham, Herbed Cheese Bread and Amaretto Oranges with Sorbet are perfect for casual dining, Italian style.

Page 157
Ligurian Pesto (top), Zucchini with Farfalle (left) and Lasagne with Pesto (right) exemplify pasta joining forces in delectable and varied combinations.

Page 158
Pasta Primavera is a fresh and delicate vegetable medley tossed with pasta and Parmesan cheese.

Page 159
Braised Turkey with Lemon and Cinnamon nested in a bed of ziti, Bibb and Walnut Salad, Frozen Chocolate Pecan Pie and Spiced Cider with Calvados provide a hearty menu for hungry guests.

Page 160
Tomato-Basil Sauce and creamy Gorgonzola Sauce are perfect partners for any pasta on hand.

Pasta with Salsa di Puttana
Recipe page 151

Spaghetti with Mussels, Scallops
and Shrimp
Recipe page 152

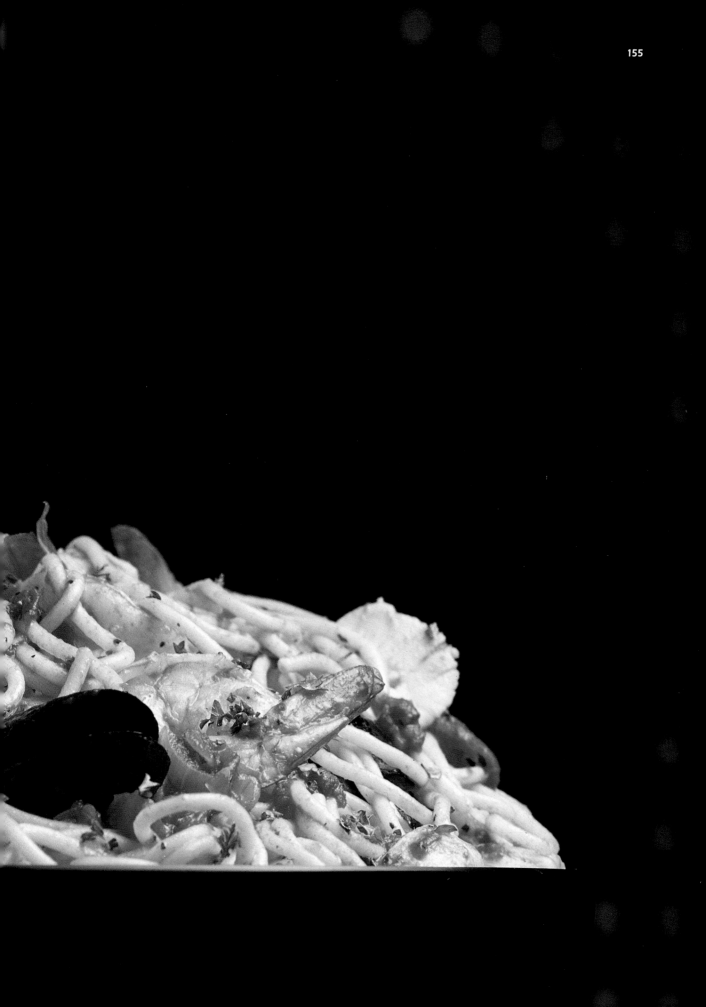

Antipasto Centerpiece Salad
Recipe page 48
Fettucine with Peas and Ham
Recipe page 149
Herbed Cheese Bread
Recipe page 165
Armaretto Oranges with Sorbet
Recipe page 175

Top: Ligurian Pesto
Recipe page 150
Left: Zucchini with Farfalle
Recipe page 148
Right: Lasagne with Pesto
Recipe page 149

Pasta Primavera
Recipe page 151

Braised Turkey with Lemon and Cinnamon
Recipe page 87
Bibb and Walnut Salad
Recipe page 49
Frozen Chocolate Pecan Pie
Recipe page 192
Spiced Cider with Calvados
Recipe page 24

160

Left: Linguine with Tomato-Basil Sauce,
Recipe page 150
Right: Spinach Pasta with Gorgonzola
Sauce,
Recipe page 152

BROCCOLI TAGLIERINI

6 SERVINGS

- 1 pound fresh broccoli, florets only, or 1 10-ounce package frozen broccoli spears
- ½ cup (1 stick) butter
- 1 garlic clove, halved
- 1 8-ounce package taglierini or fettuccine pasta, cooked al dente, rinsed and drained
- 1 cup grated Parmesan cheese

Cook florets in boiling salted water to cover until crisp-tender, or cook frozen broccoli according to package directions. Drain well. Cut spears into smaller pieces.

Melt butter with garlic in large skillet over medium heat; remove garlic. Add pasta and toss lightly until well coated. Add broccoli and toss again. Blend in cheese.

TAGLIATELLE WITH NUTS AND HAM

Tagliatelle are quarter-inch-wide ribbonlike strips of pasta. If not available, linguine may be substituted.

4 TO 6 MAIN-COURSE SERVINGS OR 6 TO 8 FIRST-COURSE SERVINGS

- ⅓ cup light olive oil
- ½ pound cooked ham, coarsely chopped
- ½ cup walnuts, coarsely chopped
- 2 to 3 tablespoons minced fresh Italian (broadleaf) parsley
- 1 garlic clove, minced
- 1 pound tagliatelle, cooked al dente
  Freshly grated imported Parmesan cheese

Heat oil in large skillet over medium-high heat. Add ham, nuts, parsley and garlic and sauté 3 to 4 minutes. Add pasta and toss until heated through. Serve immediately with Parmesan.

SPAETZLE

MAKES 6 TO 8 SERVINGS

- 8 eggs
- 1 teaspoon salt
- ¼ teaspoon nutmeg
  Freshly ground pepper
- 1¼ cups all purpose flour (about)
- 4 quarts chicken stock or broth, heated to boiling

Beat eggs thoroughly in medium bowl. Add seasonings. Beat in enough flour to make a doughy batter just thick enough to drop from teaspoon into boiling broth. (If batter is too thin, spaetzle will come apart and spread rather than remaining in individual balls.) Drop batter by scant teaspoonfuls (spaetzle will puff up). Simmer until done, about 12 minutes. Drain well and serve hot.

RICE

BAKED RICE

6 SERVINGS

- ¼ cup (½ stick) butter
- ¼ cup chopped green onion
- 2½ cups chicken broth
- 1 cup rice
  Few tablespoons of wild rice (optional)
- 1 cup golden raisins
- ¼ cup minced fresh parsley
- ½ cup sunflower seeds

Preheat oven to 350°F. Melt butter in medium skillet over medium heat. Add onion and sauté until slightly softened. Transfer to 2-quart baking dish. Stir in remaining ingredients except seeds. Cover tightly and bake until broth has been absorbed, about 45 minutes. Using fork, mix in sunflower seeds.

BROWN RICE MILANESE

See photograph page 132

6 SERVINGS

- 2 tablespoons (¼ stick) butter
- 2 shallots, chopped

- 1 garlic clove, minced
- 3 tablespoons dried chives
- ½ teaspoon dried dill
- 1 cup short-grain brown rice
- 2 cups cold water
- 1 cup freshly grated Romano cheese

Melt butter in large skillet or shallow heatproof casserole over medium heat. Add shallot and garlic and sauté until tender. Add chives and dill and sauté an additional 1 to 2 minutes. Stir in rice and sauté until it begins to crackle. Add water and bring to boil. Reduce heat to low, cover and simmer 45 minutes (do not remove cover during cooking time). Remove from heat and add cheese, tossing lightly until cheese is melted. Serve immediately.

Rice can be cooked ahead to point of adding cheese. Heat before adding Romano.

BROWN RICE AND VEGETABLES

4 SERVINGS

- 2 to 3 tablespoons water
- 2 to 3 tablespoons soy sauce or to taste
- 1 tablespoon oil
- 1 cup sliced zucchini (cut ¼ inch thick)
- 1 cup shredded cabbage
- ¼ cup quartered mushrooms
- ¼ cup chopped onion
- ½ cup cooked brown rice, room temperature
- ¼ cup chopped tomato
- ¼ cup grated carrot
  Toasted slivered almonds (garnish)

Heat water, soy sauce and oil in large skillet or wok over medium-high heat. Add zucchini, cabbage, mushrooms and onion and stir-fry 3 to 4 minutes. Blend in rice. Cover and heat through, about 5 minutes. Stir in tomato and carrot and continue cooking about 1 minute. Garnish with almonds.

COCONUT RICE

6 TO 8 SERVINGS

3 cups water
1½ cups long-grain converted rice
1 teaspoon curry powder or to taste
1 teaspoon salt
½ cup canned coconut milk
½ cup toasted coconut
¼ cup chopped green onion
2 tablespoons dark raisins
2 tablespoons light raisins
2 teaspoons butter

Bring water to boil in medium saucepan. Stir in rice, curry and salt. Reduce heat, cover and simmer until all water is absorbed and rice is tender, about 20 to 25 minutes. Add remaining ingredients, fluffing and mixing with fork, and heat through.

Coconut Rice may be prepared in advance and refrigerated. Bring to room temperature before reheating.

CHICKEN BROTH RICE

6 TO 8 SERVINGS

3 tablespoons (⅜ stick) butter
½ cup finely chopped onion
2 cups long-grain converted rice
Salt
Pinch of ground red pepper or dash of red pepper sauce
3 cups chicken broth
Bouquet garni (1 parsley sprig, 1 bay leaf and pinch of dried thyme)
Toasted sliced almonds, sliced pimientos or sliced mushrooms, sautéed

Melt 2 tablespoons butter in saucepan over medium-high heat. Add onion and sauté until soft, about 3 to 5 minutes. Add rice and stir until well coated. Blend in salt and red pepper or sauce. Add broth and bouquet garni and bring to boil. Reduce heat, cover and simmer until rice is tender and broth is absorbed, about 25 to 30 minutes. Discard bouquet garni. Add remaining butter and almonds, pimientos or mushrooms and toss lightly until butter is melted. Turn into dish and serve.

CHUTNEY RICE

4 TO 6 SERVINGS

1 cup mango chutney
4 cups cooked rice (freshly cooked or reheated)

Add chutney to hot rice and mix well. Place in heated bowl and serve immediately or refrigerate and serve when chilled.

FRIED RICE

4 SERVINGS

½ cup vegetable oil
1 Spanish onion, diced
2 large celery stalks, sliced
1 green pepper, cut into strips
2 cups diced cooked chicken or pork
½ pound (3 cups) brown rice, cooked
1 6-ounce can water chestnuts, halved
½ cup almonds, toasted
2 eggs, lightly beaten
Soy sauce

Heat oil in large skillet over medium-high heat. Add onion and sauté until translucent. Stir in celery and green pepper and cook until crisp-tender. Add meat, rice, water chestnuts and almonds and heat through, stirring constantly. Blend in eggs until mixture is thoroughly coated. Continue cooking, stirring frequently, until golden brown. Season with soy sauce to taste and serve immediately.

OVEN RICE

4 TO 6 SERVINGS

1 cup long-grain rice
2 10½-ounce cans beef consommé
1 small onion, chopped
1 4-ounce can mushrooms, undrained
½ cup (1 stick) butter or margarine, cut into pieces

Preheat oven to 350°F. Thoroughly combine all ingredients in heavy casserole. Cover and bake 45 minutes. Remove cover and continue baking 15 minutes. Fluff with fork just before serving.

MEXICALI ONE-DISH

4 TO 6 SERVINGS

3 cups sour cream
2 4-ounce cans diced green chilies
Worcestershire sauce
Salt
4 cups cooked long-grain rice
1 pound Monterey Jack cheese, diced
½ to ¾ cup grated cheddar cheese

Preheat oven to 350°F. Butter 3-quart baking dish. Combine sour cream, chilies, Worcestershire sauce and salt in large bowl. Spread ⅓ of rice in bottom of dish. Spread half of sour cream mixture evenly over top and sprinkle with half of Jack cheese. Repeat layering, ending with remaining rice. Sprinkle top with cheddar cheese. Bake until cheese is melted and casserole is heated through, about 45 minutes.

Add any leftover chicken, beef, pork, turkey, lamb or tuna for variation.

BACON-BAKED RICE

8 SERVINGS

>   2 cups white rice, cooked
>   according to package
>   directions
>   2 eggs
>   ¾ cup milk
>   6 strips bacon, fried crisp,
>   drained and crumbled
>   2 tablespoons chopped parsley
>   Salt and pepper

Preheat oven to 350°F. Mix all ingredients together and stir well. Spread in baking dish and bake until top is browned, about 10 minutes.

RICE PILAF WITH BULGUR

This dish, together with a spinach salad, will elevate a simple roast of lamb, veal or chicken into an interesting and elegant meal.

6 SERVINGS

>   ¼ cup (½ stick) butter or
>   margarine
>   1 medium onion, chopped
>   (optional)
>   ¾ cup long-grain converted rice
>   2 cups boiling chicken broth or
>   3 chicken bouillon cubes
>   dissolved in 2 cups boiling
>   water
>   ¼ cup bulgur
>   Salt and freshly ground
>   pepper
>   ½ cup raisins (optional)
>   ¼ cup pine nuts (optional)
>   ¼ cup fresh or frozen peas,
>   cooked briefly

Melt butter over medium-high heat in heavy 2-quart saucepan. Add onion and sauté until translucent. Reduce heat to medium, add rice and continue stirring until rice is golden but not browned, about 3 minutes. Add boiling broth, bulgur, salt and pepper to taste and stir well. Reduce heat, cover and simmer, without stirring, until all liquid is absorbed, about 20 minutes. Add raisins and/or nuts and peas and fluff with fork. Heat through and serve immediately.

SCALLIONED RICE IN LETTUCE CUPS
See photograph pages 110-111

4 TO 6 SERVINGS

>   2 tablespoons (¼ stick)
>   unsalted butter
>   3 large scallions, cut diagonally
>   into 1-inch pieces
>   2 cups water
>   ½ teaspoon salt
>   1 cup converted rice
>   3 tablespoons minced fresh
>   parsley
>   4 to 6 Bibb lettuce leaves

Melt butter in heavy 2- to 3-quart saucepan. Add scallions and toss about 30 seconds. Remove and set aside. Add water and salt to pan and bring to boil. Stir in rice. Reduce heat, cover and simmer 20 minutes. Remove from heat and let stand covered 5 minutes. Fluff with fork (if rice is too moist, cover with several paper towels). Reheat gently if needed and then toss with reserved scallions and parsley. Mound in lettuce cups and serve immediately.

SOUBISE

4 SERVINGS

>   ½ cup long-grain converted rice
>   6 tablespoons (¾ stick) butter
>   6 to 7 cups thinly sliced onion
>   Salt and freshly ground
>   pepper
>   ¼ cup grated Swiss cheese
>   1 tablespoon chopped fresh
>   parsley

Preheat oven to 300°F. Cook rice in boiling water 5 minutes. Drain well. Melt 5 tablespoons butter in ovenproof medium saucepan over medium-high heat. Add onion and stir to coat well. Stir in rice, salt and pepper. Cover and bake 1 hour, stirring occasionally. Blend in cheese and remaining butter. Top with chopped parsley.

SPICED FRIED RICE

6 TO 8 SERVINGS

>   ¼ cup soy sauce
>   1 tablespoon dry sherry
>   ¼ teaspoon sugar
>   5 to 7 tablespoons oil
>   2 garlic cloves, crushed
>   1 teaspoon crushed dried red
>   pepper flakes
>   1½ cups cooked cubed ham
>   1 medium onion, sliced
>   1 red bell pepper, halved,
>   seeded and cut julienne
>   1 green pepper, halved, seeded
>   and cut julienne
>   1 8-ounce can water chestnuts,
>   drained and sliced
>   1 8-ounce can bamboo shoots,
>   drained
>   ¼ pound bean sprouts
>   3 cups chilled cooked rice
>   2 eggs, lightly beaten
>   Salt and freshly ground
>   pepper

Combine soy sauce, sherry and sugar in small bowl and blend well. Set mixture aside.

Add 2 tablespoons oil to large skillet or wok over medium-high heat, tilting to coat. Add half of garlic and half of pepper flakes and stir-fry until garlic is browned. Discard garlic. Stir in ham and cook about 1 minute. Transfer to medium bowl. Add 2 to 3 more tablespoons oil to skillet with remaining garlic and pepper flakes and stir-fry until garlic is browned. Discard garlic. Add onion, red and green peppers, water chestnuts, bamboo shoots and bean sprouts and stir-fry 2 to 3 minutes. Add to ham. Add 1 to 2 tablespoons oil to skillet. Add rice, stirring until well coated with oil, about 2 minutes. Return ham and vegetables to skillet. Add soy sauce mixture and heat through. Make well in center. Pour in eggs and scramble until just beginning to set. Toss mixture thoroughly. Season with salt and pepper to taste and serve immediately.

VEGETABLE-RICE CASSEROLE

4 SERVINGS

- 2 cups cooked long-grain rice
- 1 10-ounce package frozen peas, cooked and drained
- 1 cup sour cream
- 1 cup diced celery
- ¼ cup minced onion
- 1 teaspoon curry powder or to taste
- ½ teaspoon salt
- ½ teaspoon dry mustard

Preheat oven to 350°F. Butter 1-quart baking dish. Combine all ingredients in large bowl and blend well. Turn into dish. Bake until heated through, about 25 minutes. Serve immediately.

WATER CHESTNUT AND RICE CASSEROLE

4 TO 6 SERVINGS

- ½ cup (1 stick) butter
- ¼ pound uncooked fine noodles
- 1 cup uncooked instant rice
- 1 10½-ounce can onion soup
- 1 10½-ounce can chicken broth
- ½ teaspoon soy sauce
- 1 8½-ounce can sliced water chestnuts, undrained

Preheat oven to 350°F. Melt butter in large skillet over low heat. Add noodles and cook until golden, stirring occasionally, about 10 minutes. Remove from heat.

Combine rice, onion soup, broth and soy sauce in large bowl. Add noodles and remaining butter. Drain water chestnuts (reserve liquid) and add to rice mixture. Measure liquid, adding enough water to equal ½ cup. Stir into rice. Turn into 2-quart rectangular baking dish. Cover and bake until rice is tender and liquid is absorbed, about 45 minutes.

WILD AND LONG GRAIN RICE STUFFING

FOR 15-POUND TURKEY

- 3 6-ounce packages wild and long-grain rice
- 6 cups chicken stock
- 3 tablespoons (⅜ stick) butter
- 3 tablespoons lemon juice
- 1½ teaspoons tarragon
- ¼ cup (½ stick) butter
- 1 pound mushrooms, sliced
- 1 large onion, minced
- 1 green pepper, chopped
- 1 teaspoon Sauce Diable
- ½ cup dry sherry
- ½ cup minced parsley
- 1 cup coarsely chopped toasted hazelnuts, pecans or walnuts
  Salt and pepper

Place rice, chicken stock and 3 tablespoons butter in 6-quart saucepan or Dutch oven. Cover tightly and bring to boil. Simmer gently 20 minutes. Remove cover and simmer until rice has absorbed chicken stock, about 10 minutes.

Add lemon juice and tarragon. Stir with a large fork. (This will keep rice grains separate.)

Melt ¼ cup butter in 10-inch skillet and sauté mushrooms, onion and green pepper until soft. Add Sauce Diable and sherry and cook 2 minutes. Remove from heat.

Combine vegetables with rice, using 2 forks; toss in parsley and nuts. Season with salt and pepper to taste.

May also be served in a casserole.

BREAD

ARTICHOKE BREAD

6 SERVINGS

- 3 cups loosely packed grated sharp cheddar cheese
- 2 6-ounce jars marinated artichoke hearts (drained), finely chopped
- 6 soda crackers, crushed
- 4 eggs
- 3 green onions, finely chopped

Dash of hot pepper sauce
Salt and freshly ground pepper

Preheat oven to 325°F. Grease 8-inch square baking dish. Combine all ingredients in large bowl and mix thoroughly. Turn into dish. Bake until tester inserted in center comes out clean, about 1 hour. Cool slightly before serving.

EASIEST, QUICKEST GARLIC BREAD

8 SERVINGS

- 1 loaf French or Italian bread
- ¾ cup (1½ sticks) softened butter
  Garlic salt
- ¾ cup Parmesan cheese, freshly grated
- ½ cup fresh parsley, chopped
  Paprika

Cut bread into 1½-inch slices. Spread each one generously with butter. Sprinkle with garlic salt, Parmesan cheese, parsley and paprika. Place bread under broiler until it starts to brown, about 3 minutes.

FRENCH MUSTARD BREAD

6 SERVINGS

- ½ cup (1 stick) butter, room temperature
- ¼ cup minced parsley
- 2 tablespoons chopped green onion
- 2 tablespoons prepared mustard
- 1 tablespoon sesame seeds, toasted
- 1 teaspoon lemon juice
- 1 1-pound loaf sliced French or sourdough bread

Preheat oven to 350°F. Thoroughly blend butter, parsley, onion, mustard, sesame seeds and lemon juice. Spread lightly on both sides of bread. Arrange in single layer on cookie sheets and bake until crisp, about 20 minutes.

GARLIC-CHEESE FRENCH BREAD

A favorite recipe from Finland— cheese fondue and bread all in one.

6 SERVINGS

1 large loaf French bread
½ pound Swiss cheese, grated
2 to 3 garlic cloves, crushed
¼ cup half and half
1 to 2 tablespoons minced parsley

Preheat oven to 400°F. Cut bread vertically, but not all the way through, into slices 1½ inches thick. Combine remaining ingredients and mix well. Pat between bread slices. Wrap loaf tightly in foil and bake until cheese is melted and bread is heated through, about 20 minutes.

HERBED CHEESE BREAD

See photograph page 156

6 TO 8 SERVINGS

½ cup (1 stick) unsalted butter
1 large garlic clove, minced
1½ tablespoons fresh basil or 1½ teaspoons dried leaves, crumbled
1 teaspoon fresh oregano or ¼ teaspoon dried (preferably Greek)
¼ teaspoon fresh marjoram or generous pinch of dried
Salt and freshly ground pepper
1 large loaf Italian or French bread, split in half lengthwise
3 ounces Swiss or Gruyère cheese, shredded
½ cup freshly grated imported Parmesan cheese

Combine butter, garlic, herbs, salt and pepper to taste in small saucepan and heat until butter is melted. Pour over cut sides of bread, then sprinkle with cheeses. Wrap in foil. About 20 minutes before ready to serve, place bread in oven and turn temperature to 375°F. Heat until bread is hot and crusty, about 20 minutes (if necessary, open foil to allow bread to crisp). Slice diagonally and pass in napkin-lined basket.

ONION-CHEDDAR CORN BREAD

10 TO 12 SERVINGS

6 tablespoons (¾ stick) unsalted butter
2 large onions, finely chopped
2 eggs
2 tablespoons buttermilk
2 17-ounce cans cream-style corn
1 1-pound package corn muffin mix
1 cup sour cream
2 cups shredded sharp cheddar cheese

Preheat oven to 425°F. Grease 9× 13-inch baking dish. Heat butter in skillet over medium-high heat and sauté onions until golden. Set aside. Combine eggs and buttermilk in large bowl and mix until smooth. Stir in corn and muffin mix, blending well. Turn into baking dish and spoon onion evenly over batter. Spread sour cream over onion and top with cheese. Bake until golden, about 30 minutes. Let stand 10 minutes before cutting.

PARMESAN POPOVERS

6 SERVINGS

¼ cup freshly grated Parmesan cheese
1 cup milk
1 cup all purpose flour
1 tablespoon butter, melted
¼ teaspoon salt
2 large eggs

Place oven rack on next to lowest shelf. Preheat oven to 450°F. Grease 6 deep muffin or custard cups and sprinkle with Parmesan; set aside.

Combine milk, flour, butter and salt in medium bowl. Beat in eggs just until blended (overbeating will reduce volume). Fill cups ¾ full. Bake 15 minutes. Reduce heat to 350°F

(do not open oven door) and bake 20 minutes more. Carefully remove popovers with spatula and serve.

CHEESE CRACKERS

MAKES ABOUT 2 DOZEN

1 cup all purpose flour
¼ teaspoon salt
6 tablespoons (¾ stick) butter or margarine
1 cup crisp rice cereal
1 cup grated sharp cheddar cheese
1 egg
½ teaspoon hot pepper sauce

Combine flour and salt in large bowl. Cut in butter until mixture resembles coarse meal. Add cereal and cheese, stirring with fork until thoroughly mixed. Beat egg with hot pepper sauce in small bowl. Drizzle evenly over cheese mixture and blend well. Transfer dough to large piece of foil. Divide dough in half and form into 2 cylinders, each about 1½ inches wide. Cover and chill at least 15 minutes.

Preheat oven to 350°F. Cut cylinders into ¼-inch slices. Arrange on baking sheet and press lightly with fingertips. Bake until golden and crisp, about 20 to 25 minutes. Let cool. Store in airtight container.

CHEESE PUFFS

MAKES ABOUT 3 TO 4 DOZEN PUFFS

4 ounces extra sharp cheddar cheese spread, room temperature
½ cup (1 stick) unsalted butter, room temperature
1 cup all purpose flour
Paprika

Combine cheese and butter in medium bowl and mix well. Blend in flour. Form into walnut-size balls and place on baking sheets. Dust with paprika. Refrigerate until thoroughly chilled.

Preheat oven to 350°F. Bake until bottoms of puffs are lightly browned, about 12 to 15 minutes. Serve puffs hot.

PITA POCKETS WITH ASSORTED FILLINGS

Fillings are designed to be mixed and matched for varied combinations.

6 SERVINGS

- 8 fresh pita rounds, top third removed

Fillings

- 2 cups alfalfa sprouts
- 3 tomatoes, sliced
- 3 avocados, peeled, sliced and coated with fresh lemon juice
- 1 red onion, thinly sliced
- 1 pound good quality country bacon, crisply cooked, drained and crumbled

DO AHEAD

GNOCCHI IN BASIL BUTTER

See photograph page 133

4 TO 6 SERVINGS

Basil Butter

- 3 to 4 tablespoons fresh basil leaves
- 2 to 3 tablespoons finely minced parsley
- 2 large garlic cloves, finely minced
- ½ cup (1 stick) unsalted butter, room temperature
- 3 to 4 anchovy fillets
  Salt and freshly ground pepper

Gnocchi

- 4 cups milk
- 2 teaspoons salt
- 1 cup semolina
- ¼ cup (½ stick) unsalted butter
- 5 to 6 tablespoons freshly grated Parmesan cheese

For butter: Combine first 3 ingredients in processor or blender and mix 30 seconds. Add butter and anchovies and blend until smooth, about 30 seconds. Taste and adjust seasoning, adding generous grinding of pepper. Set aside.

For gnocchi: Bring milk to boil in large saucepan. Reduce heat and add salt. Slowly add semolina, stirring constantly (preferably with electric mixer at medium speed) to prevent lumps. Continue cooking, stirring constantly (be careful not to scorch bottom of pan) until mixture is thick, about 15 minutes. Remove from heat and blend in butter and 3 tablespoons cheese.

Rinse 12×18-inch jelly roll pan or shallow baking pan under cold water, shaking off excess. Spread semolina mixture in pan, smoothing with dampened spatula (mixture should be about ½ inch thick). Let cool completely at room temperature, then cover and refrigerate until quite firm, 30 to 60 minutes.

Preheat oven to 350°F. Butter large shallow rectangular baking dish. Using small cookie cutter or glass about 1½ to 2 inches in diameter, cut rounds from semolina mixture. Arrange in slightly overlapping rows in prepared dish. Top each round with some of Basil Butter and sprinkle with some of remaining cheese. Cover tightly and bake for about 30 minutes. Sprinkle lightly with pepper and serve immediately.

Gnocchi can also be browned lightly under broiler after baking.

Gnocchi can be assembled 1 day ahead and refrigerated.

Basil Butter can be made ahead in larger quantities and refrigerated. It is also excellent as a topping for baked potatoes or mixed into a simple risotto or rice dish.

SPIEDINI

See photograph page 26

6 SERVINGS

- 1 cup (2 sticks) unsalted butter, room temperature
- 2 to 3 garlic cloves, minced
- 1¼ tablespoons dried basil
- 2 tablespoons capers, rinsed, drained and minced
  Salt
- 1 12-inch baguette French bread

- 12 to 16 ounces mozzarella cheese

Cream butter in small bowl. Blend in garlic, basil, capers and salt. Cover and chill if not using immediately.

Trim off top and side crusts of bread, leaving bottom crust intact. Slice bread almost through at about ¾-inch intervals. Cut cheese into as many slices as there are cuts in bread. Place cheese in each cut. Secure loaf with skewer if necessary. Wrap and refrigerate.

Just before serving, preheat broiler. Place loaf on piece of heavy foil, bringing up edges to form cradle but not covering top. Transfer to baking sheet. Spread top and sides with butter and run under broiler until brown and bubbly.

HUNGARIAN COFFEE CRESCENTS

See photograph page 180

MAKES 48 CRESCENTS

Pastry

- 3 cups all purpose flour
- 3 tablespoons sugar
- 1 cup (2 sticks) well-chilled unsalted butter
- 3 egg yolks, beaten
- 2 envelopes dry yeast or 2 cakes fresh yeast dissolved in ½ cup lukewarm milk
- 1½ teaspoons vanilla

Filling

- 3 egg whites, room temperature
- 1 cup + 8 teaspoons sugar
- ½ cup sugar
- 2 teaspoons cinnamon
- ½ cup ground walnuts or pecans
- 1 egg beaten with 2 teaspoons water
  Powdered sugar (optional garnish)

For pastry: Combine dry ingredients in processor or bowl. Cut in butter until mixture resembles coarse meal. Add yolks, yeast mixture and vanilla and blend until combined. Wrap tightly and refrigerate overnight.

Remove dough from refrigerator and divide into 6 equal pieces.

For filling: Beat egg whites until stiff peaks form. Gradually beat in ⅔ cup sugar. Combine remaining sugar with cinnamon and nuts.

Grease baking sheet(s) or use heavy-duty foil. Roll out 1 piece of dough into very thin round on lightly floured surface. Brush with egg white and then sprinkle with some of nut mixture. Using sharp knife, cut into 8 equal wedges. Starting at large end, roll wedges up, shaping gently into crescent. Transfer to prepared sheet(s) or foil, spacing about 2 inches apart. Repeat with remaining dough. Let stand at room temperature 30 minutes to rise.

Preheat oven to 350°F. Lightly brush each crescent with beaten egg. Bake until crisp and pale gold, about 20 minutes. Let cool on wire rack. Dust with powdered sugar.

If baking crescents ahead, let cool, wrap tightly and freeze. Defrost in refrigerator the day before serving. Crisp in 350°F oven on day of party. When cool, arrange on serving platter and cover lightly; do not return crescents to refrigerator.

FRESH APPLE-NUT BREAD

MAKES 1 9×5-INCH LOAF

- ¼ cup (½ stick) butter, room temperature
- 1 cup firmly packed light brown sugar
- 2 eggs
- 3 cups unsifted flour
- 2 cups peeled grated apple (about 2 large)
- ¾ cup chopped nuts
- 1½ teaspoons baking soda
- 1 teaspoon baking powder
- 1 teaspoon grated lemon peel
- 1 teaspoon salt
- 1 teaspoon cinnamon
- ¼ teaspoon nutmeg
- ¾ cup buttermilk

Preheat oven to 350°F. Grease and flour 9×5-inch loaf pan. Cream butter and sugar in medium bowl. Beat in eggs. Combine next 9 ingredients in separate bowl and blend into creamed mixture alternately with buttermilk. Turn into pan and bake until toothpick inserted in center comes out clean, about 1 hour. Cool 10 minutes. Remove from pan and cool completely on wire rack.

BANANA NUT BREAD

MAKES 1 9×5-INCH LOAF OR 2
5⅝×3⅛-INCH LOAVES

- ½ cup (1 stick) butter, room temperature
- 1 cup sugar
- 2 eggs, beaten
- 2 tablespoons sour milk
- 1 teaspoon fresh lemon juice
- ½ teaspoon baking soda
- 1½ teaspoons baking powder
- ¼ teaspoon salt
- 4 large very ripe bananas, mashed
- 2 cups flour
- 1½ cups walnuts or pecans

Preheat oven to 350°F. Grease and flour 1 9×5-inch loaf pan or 2 smaller pans. Cream butter, sugar and eggs in large bowl using electric mixer. Add remaining ingredients and mix on low until blended. Turn into pan(s) and bake until toothpick inserted in center comes out clean, about 1 hour. Cool 10 minutes. Remove from pan and cool completely on wire rack.

BLUEBERRY QUICK BREAD

MAKES 1 BUNDT CAKE; 2 9×5-INCH LOAVES
OR 4 5⅝×3⅛-INCH LOAVES

- 5 cups all purpose flour
- 1½ cups sugar
- 2 tablespoons baking powder
- 1 teaspoon cinnamon
- 1 teaspoon salt
- ¾ cup (1½ sticks) butter or margarine
- 1½ cups chopped walnuts
- 1 teaspoon grated lemon peel
- 4 eggs
- 2 cups milk

- 2 teaspoons vanilla
  Juice of 1 lemon
- 3 cups fresh or frozen blueberries, unthawed

Preheat oven to 350°F. Grease and flour 10-inch bundt or smaller pans. Combine flour, sugar, baking powder, cinnamon and salt in large bowl. Cut in butter until mixture resembles fine crumbs. Stir in walnuts and lemon peel.

Beat eggs lightly with fork in small bowl. Stir in milk, vanilla and lemon juice and mix well. Blend into flour mixture just until moistened. Gently stir in blueberries. Spoon evenly into pan(s) and bake until toothpick inserted in center comes out clean, about 80 to 90 minutes. Cool on wire rack 10 minutes. Remove from pan. Serve warm or cold. Wrap and store in refrigerator.

CRANBERRY NUT BREAD

MAKES 1 9×5-INCH LOAF

- 2 cups sifted all purpose flour
- 1 cup sugar
- 1½ teaspoons baking powder
- 1 teaspoon salt
- ½ teaspoon baking soda
- ¼ cup shortening
- 1 egg, well beaten
- ¾ cup orange juice
- 1 teaspoon grated orange peel
- 1 cup fresh cranberries, coarsely chopped, or 1 cup well-drained canned whole cranberries, coarsely chopped
- ½ cup chopped walnuts or pecans

Preheat oven to 350°F. Grease and flour 9×5-inch loaf pan. Sift dry ingredients into large bowl. Cut in shortening. Combine egg, orange juice and peel and add to dry ingredients, mixing just to moisten. Fold in berries and nuts. Turn into pan and bake until toothpick inserted in center comes out clean, about 1 hour. Cool on wire rack before removing from pan. Wrap and store overnight to develop flavors.

PINEAPPLE-ZUCCHINI LOAF

MAKES 2 9×5-INCH LOAVES

- 3 eggs
- 2 cups sugar
- 1 cup oil
- 3 tablespoons vanilla
- 2 cups peeled, grated and well drained zucchini
- 3 cups all purpose flour
- 1 teaspoon baking powder
- 1 teaspoon baking soda
- 1 teaspoon salt
- 1 8-ounce can crushed pineapple, undrained
- 1 cup chopped pecans or walnuts
- ½ cup raisins (optional)

Preheat oven to 350°F. Grease and flour 2 9×5-inch loaf pans. Beat eggs until fluffy. Add sugar, oil and vanilla and blend well. Add zucchini. Sift together flour, baking powder, soda and salt and add to batter. Stir in pineapple, nuts and raisins, if desired, and mix well. Turn into pans and bake until toothpick inserted in center comes out clean, about 1 hour. Cool on wire rack before removing from pans. Wrap and store overnight to develop flavors before slicing.

AMERICAN-STYLE LIPTAUER

SERVES 4–6

- 1 small baguette, about 8 inches, halved horizontally
- ¾ cup small curd cottage cheese
- ½ cup (1 stick) butter, room temperature
- 1 teaspoon onion juice or grated onion
- 1 teaspoon paprika
- 1 teaspoon prepared mustard
- 1 teaspoon caraway seeds

Carefully remove center from bread halves (leaving ½-inch shell) and place in food processor or blender. Process to fine crumbs. Combine remaining ingredients in small mixing bowl and beat with electric mixer until smooth. Add breadcrumbs a little at a time, beating well after each addition. Spoon into baguette halves. Wrap tightly and refrigerate overnight.

Just before serving, preheat broiler. Slice bread almost through into pieces ½ inch thick. Broil briefly until heated through and top is bubbly. Serve immediately.

FRENCH BREAD FARCI

12 SERVINGS

- 1 14-ounce package French rolls (12 per package)
- ⅔ cup water
- ½ cup minced parsley
- ¼ cup Dijon mustard
- 2 eggs, lightly beaten
- ½ teaspoon oregano
- ½ teaspoon freshly ground pepper
- 1 pound bulk sausage
- 1 pound ground beef
- 1 medium onion, chopped
- 6 tablespoons (¾ stick) butter
- 1 garlic clove, minced

Halve rolls lengthwise. Using fork or fingers carefully remove soft centers, leaving shells about ¼ inch thick. Let centers dry a bit.

Place dried bread in batches in blender or food processor (or simply use hands) and reduce to finer consistency. Transfer to medium bowl and add water, parsley, mustard, eggs, oregano and pepper.

Preheat oven to 400°F. Brown sausage, beef and onion in large skillet over medium-high heat until sausage is cooked through. Drain well. Combine meat and crumb mixtures, blending thoroughly. Divide equally among rolls, packing lightly, and place on ungreased baking sheet.

Melt butter in small saucepan; stir in garlic. Brush over filling and edges of bread. Bake until hot and browned, about 10 to 15 minutes. Serve immediately, whole or halved.

Shells may be filled with meat mixture and refrigerated overnight, or they may be frozen before baking. Brush with butter just before reheating, allowing about 5 to 10 minutes longer for frozen rolls

MICROWAVE

LASAGNE

6 TO 8 SERVINGS

- 1 pound lean ground beef
- 2 8-ounce cans tomato sauce
- ¼ pound mushrooms, chopped
- 1 small onion, minced
- ¼ teaspoon garlic powder or 1 garlic clove, minced and sautéed
- 1 teaspoon basil leaves
- ½ teaspoon oregano
- ½ teaspoon thyme
  Salt and freshly ground pepper
- 8 ounces lasagne noodles, cooked according to package directions and drained
- 1½ cups cottage cheese
- ½ pound mozzarella cheese, thinly sliced
  Freshly grated Parmesan cheese

Crumble ground beef into plastic colander set in 12×8-inch glass baking dish. Cook on High 4 minutes, stirring halfway through cooking time. Pour out drippings. Combine beef in 2-quart glass mixing bowl with tomato sauce, mushrooms, onion, garlic, basil, oregano, thyme, salt and pepper. Cook on High 6 to 8 minutes, stirring halfway through cooking time.

Layer ⅓ of cooked noodles in 12×8-inch baking dish. Top with ⅓ of meat mixture and ½ of cottage cheese and mozzarella. Repeat, ending with noodles and meat. Sprinkle generously with Parmesan. Cover with waxed paper and microwave on High 10 to 12 minutes, rotating dish ¼ turn halfway through cooking time. Rest, covered, 5 to 10 minutes before serving.

Lasagne can be assembled 1 or 2 days ahead and refrigerated. Allow 5 minutes additional cooking time if heating directly from refrigerator.

FETTUCCINI AL FORNO

6 TO 8 SERVINGS

- 1 pound fettuccine noodles, cooked according to package directions, drained
- ½ cup milk
- ½ cup (1 stick) butter, room temperature
- 4 eggs
- ¾ cup freshly grated Parmesan cheese
- 1 tablespoon minced fresh parsley
- ½ teaspoon garlic salt
- ¼ teaspoon freshly ground white pepper
- ¼ cup seasoned breadcrumbs

Combine all ingredients except breadcrumbs in pan in which noodles were cooked and stir constantly until butter is melted. Spread evenly in 12 × 8-inch glass baking dish and sprinkle with breadcrumbs. Cook on High 5 to 7 minutes, rotating dish ¼ turn halfway through cooking time. Let rest 5 to 10 minutes. Cut into squares and serve.

Fettuccine al Forno can be prepared ahead of time and refrigerated. To reheat, bring to room temperature, cover with plastic wrap (poke a few holes to allow steam to escape) and cook on High until heated through, about 4 to 5 minutes.

SEASONED RICE

Cooking rice in the microwave will give you perfect results every time.

4 SERVINGS

- 2 cups water
- 1 cup long-grain converted rice
- ¼ cup dehydrated onion
- 2 teaspoons chicken or beef bouillon mix

Combine all ingredients in 2-quart glass casserole. Cover and cook on High 12 to 14 minutes. Let stand covered until all water is absorbed, about 10 minutes.

To reheat, add about 2 tablespoons water for each cup of cooked rice and cook on High.

GARLIC BREAD

4 TO 6 SERVINGS

- 1 1-pound loaf French, Italian or sourdough bread
- ½ cup (1 stick) butter or margarine, melted
- 2 garlic cloves, minced
- ½ cup grated Parmesan cheese or to taste
  Paprika

Cut loaf into slices 1 inch thick without cutting all the way through to bottom. Set loaf on microwave-safe rack or in paper napkin-lined basket.

Combine butter and garlic and blend well. Using pastry brush, coat slices of bread with garlic butter. Sprinkle with cheese and paprika. Cook on High until heated through, 1 to 2 minutes.

PUMPKIN NUT MUFFINS

MAKES 1 DOZEN MUFFINS

- 1 cup mashed cooked pumpkin
- 1 cup sugar
- 1 cup oil
- ½ cup buttermilk
- 2 eggs
- 1⅔ cups all purpose flour
- 1 cup chopped walnuts
- 2 teaspoons pumpkin pie spice
- 1 teaspoon baking soda
- ½ teaspoon salt

Combine first 5 ingredients in large bowl and beat 1 minute. Add remaining ingredients and mix thoroughly. Pour batter into 12 ¾-cup glass custard cups, filling ⅔ full. Arrange 6 cups in circle on microwave-safe round platter. Cook on High 4½ minutes, turning platter if muffins appear to be cooking unevenly. Repeat with remaining batter. Loosen muffins from cups with thin knife and turn out onto racks. Serve muffins warm.

THE RICH BOY SANDWICH

8 SERVINGS

- 1 1- to 1½-pound loaf Italian or French bread
- 2 tablespoons mayonnaise
- 2 tablespoons prepared mustard
- 1 6-ounce jar marinated artichoke hearts
- 1 to 2 tablespoons capers, rinsed and drained
- ½ small onion, thinly sliced into rings
- ½ to 1 small tomato (optional), thinly sliced
- 1½ pounds assorted sliced Italian meats (mortadella, salami, prosciutto, roast beef, etc.)
- ½ pound sliced provolone cheese
- ¼ pound sliced Monterey Jack cheese

Halve bread horizontally through center and place halves cut side up on work surface. Spread mayonnaise on top half and mustard on bottom half. Drain artichokes and cut into small pieces. Arrange over mayonnaise. Sprinkle with capers. Top with onion and tomato slices. Layer overlapping slices of meat with cheese on other half of bread, draping meat over edge slightly. Close sandwich. Wrap tightly and refrigerate or freeze.

To serve, cut sandwich into 8 portions. Transfer to napkin-lined platter. Open sandwich filling sides up. Cook on High until cheese is melted and bread is heated through, about 40 seconds. Close sandwich and serve immediately.

DESSERTS

Fresh Fruit Finishers

■ A tray piled with plump grapes, pears and apples provides a delightful and easy-to-prepare dessert when accompanied by one or two good cheeses. No matter what the season, there are always fresh fruits to be fashionably dressed for dessert. Serve tart plums and cracked walnuts with Camembert; pears with provolone; apricots with Brie; kumquats with a touch of Roquefort.

■ Marinate 6 peeled, halved and pitted peaches in 2 tablespoons orange liqueur and ¼ cup honey. Refrigerate. When ready to serve, place 2 peach halves in each of 6 champagne or wine glasses and add champagne to cover. Garnish each portion with one perfect long-stemmed strawberry.

■ Cut a cantaloupe in half, remove the seeds and scoop out the melon. Dice the melon and marinate in port wine for several hours. Just before serving, return the melon to the cantaloupe shell and garnish with mint.

■ Put out a large crystal bowl of fresh grapefruit and orange segments and slices of pineapple dusted with finely grated coconut. Offer a small pitcher of orange liqueur.

■ Mix figs in yogurt with just a skimpy sprinkling of raw or brown sugar.

■ Bake bananas in their skins in a preheated 350°F oven for 20 minutes. Peel them and serve hot with a squeeze of lemon.

■ Mix together ¼ cup honey and 2 tablespoons of lime juice, and spoon over thin slices of pineapple.

■ Fresh fruits go well with many liqueurs. Some of our favorites are: Curaçao with oranges, pineapple or mandarin oranges; Grand Marnier with grapefruit, oranges, tangerines or strawberries; Kirsch with bananas, peaches, pineapple or melon balls and sherry with grapefruit or watermelon. And of course, Champagne with strawberries or figs in Ruby Port. But if no fresh fruit is in season try: canned pears, drained and served with Curaçao and orange juice; peaches with heavy cream and a few drops of almond extract.

■ Bathe papaya and pineapple chunks in plum wine.

■ With the exception of the fragile raspberry, too delicate to withstand rinsing, berries should be washed just before use.

CAKES

ANGEL FOOD BRITTLE CAKE

12 TO 14 SERVINGS

  2 cups whipping cream
  2 tablespoons powdered sugar
  1 cup crushed peanut brittle
  1 large angel food cake

Combine whipping cream and powdered sugar in medium bowl and beat until stiff. Gently fold in peanut brittle. Frost top and sides of cake. Chill before serving.

BEST CHOCOLATE CAKE

24 TO 30 SERVINGS

  2 cups sugar
  2 cups all purpose flour
  ¼ cup cocoa
  ½ cup (1 stick) margarine or butter
  1 cup water
  ½ cup oil
  2 eggs
  ½ cup buttermilk
  1½ teaspoons baking soda
  1 teaspoon vanilla

  1 16-ounce box powdered sugar
  1 cup chopped nuts, toasted
  ¼ cup cocoa
  ½ cup (1 stick) margarine or butter
  ⅓ cup buttermilk
  1 teaspoon vanilla

Preheat oven to 350°F. Combine first 3 ingredients in large bowl. Melt margarine or butter with water and oil in small saucepan over medium-high heat and bring to boil. Pour over dry ingredients and mix well. Add eggs, ½ cup buttermilk, baking soda and 1 teaspoon vanilla and blend thoroughly. Pour into 18×11-inch rectangular roasting pan. Bake until tester inserted in center of cake comes out clean, approximately 20 to 25 minutes.

Meanwhile, combine powdered sugar, nuts and remaining cocoa in mixing bowl.

Remove cake from oven. Melt remaining margarine or butter in small saucepan over medium heat. Add to sugar mixture with remaining buttermilk and vanilla and blend thoroughly. Immediately pour over cake, spreading evenly to edges. Let cake cool completely in pan.

BISCUIT CAKE

8 TO 10 SERVINGS

  1¼ cups sugar
  1¼ teaspoons cinnamon
  ½ cup raisins
  ½ cup strawberry or raspberry preserves or marmalade
  2 tablespoons chopped nuts
  2 packages (16) butterflake biscuits
  ½ cup (1 stick) butter, melted

Preheat oven to 375°F. Butter bottom of 6- to 6½-cup ring mold.

Combine sugar, cinnamon and raisins. Place teaspoons of preserves at ½-inch intervals around mold. Sprinkle with nuts. Dip biscuits in butter and then in cinnamon mixture. As each is coated, stand upright in mold, spacing evenly. Sprinkle with remaining sugar mixture. Drizzle rest of butter over top.

Place on cookie sheet on rack in middle of oven. Bake until deep golden and crusty, about 30 minutes. Let stand 5 minutes before inverting on serving platter but do not remove mold. Lift off carefully after 5 more minutes and serve.

Sweet Endings

■ Sweet liqueurs like crème de menthe, crème de cacao and others like almond or coffee liqueurs make sweet endings to a spur-of-the moment meal. Along the same line, sherry or sweet port are classic endings. Candies, macaroons or mints also add a final sweet touch.

Special Hints

■ To avoid excessive browning, use solid vegetable shortening as opposed to butter or oil to grease baking sheets or foil.

■ Freeze extra egg whites in a jar or in sections of an ice cube tray for use later in meringues or angel cakes.

■ Look to your faithful blender to help when you're in a jam. Out of powdered sugar, for instance? Just toss some granulated sugar in and whirl at high speed for a minute or two to powder it. If it's too grainy, whirl a bit longer.

■ Recrisp cookies by baking in 400°F oven for about 3 minutes.

■ Vary crusts by adding finely ground walnuts, pecans, filberts or almonds to the crumbs, or add a teaspoon or two of brandy, fruit liqueur or rum.

BUNDT CAKE

10 TO 12 SERVINGS

    1 cup solid white vegetable
       shortening
    2 cups sugar
    2 eggs
    2 teaspoons vanilla
    3 cups sifted cake flour
    ¼ cup cocoa
    2 teaspoons baking soda
    2 cups milk
       Powdered sugar

Preheat oven to 350°F. Cream shortening with sugar in large bowl. Beat in eggs and vanilla until smooth. Resift flour with cocoa and baking soda into another large bowl. Repeat twice. Add flour mixture to creamed mixture alternately with milk, beating well after each addition. Pour into 12-cup bundt cake pan. Bake until tester inserted in center comes out clean, about 35 to 40 minutes. Let cool about 5 minutes. Invert onto rack and let cool completely. Dust cake lightly with powdered sugar.

CAKE OF THE ANGELS

6 SERVINGS

    1¼ cups sugar

    ½ cup water
    6 egg yolks
    6 to 12 thin slices angel food
       cake
    2 cups bite-size pieces ripe
       fresh pineapple

Combine sugar and water in saucepan. Boil just until sugar dissolves. Cover pan and allow syrup to cool slightly. Beat yolks well. Beating constantly, pour syrup in a thin stream into yolks. Pour mixture back into saucepan and cook over low heat, stirring constantly, until mixture is thickened and loses translucency; do not let it boil (this may take 15 minutes). Strain and allow the sauce to cool to room temperature, stirring occasionally. Do not refrigerate.

Pass cake slices for each person to place on dessert plate. Pineapple is spooned lightly over cake and sauce ladled generously over both.

DUTCH BUTTER CAKE

6 TO 8 SERVINGS

    2 cups flour
    1½ cups sugar
    1 cup (2 sticks) unsalted butter,
       melted

    1 egg, separated

Preheat oven to 450°F. Sift flour and sugar together in medium bowl. Pour in butter and blend well. Add yolk and knead thoroughly. Press into 9-inch metal pie pan. Brush lightly with beaten egg white. Bake 15 minutes. Reduce oven temperature to 225°F and continue baking until top is golden and edges are browned, about 15 to 20 minutes. Cool before cutting. Use sharp thin knife to slice.

FROSTED RUM CAKES

MAKES 16 SERVINGS

    2 to 2½ cups powdered sugar
    ½ cup (1 stick) butter, softened
    ½ teaspoon rum extract
    ¼ cup (about) light rum
    1 large loaf angel food cake
    1 8¼-ounce jar dry roasted
       skinless cashews or peanuts,
       finely chopped

Cream sugar and butter in mixing bowl. Beat in extract. Slowly add enough rum to achieve spreading consistency. Cut cake into 2-inch cubes and frost on all sides. Sprinkle with chopped nuts. Refrigerate until ready to serve.

MOCHA BUNDT CAKE

12 TO 15 SERVINGS

- 1 package white cake mix
- 1 3¾-ounce package instant chocolate pudding mix
- 4 eggs
- 1 cup oil
- ⅔ cup vodka
- ⅓ cup coffee liqueur
- ¼ cup water
- ¼ cup coffee liqueur
- ¼ cup powdered sugar

Preheat oven to 350°F. Grease and flour bundt cake pan, shaking out excess. Combine first 7 ingredients in large bowl and beat thoroughly. Pour into pan. Bake until tester inserted in center comes out clean, about 50 to 60 minutes. Let cool 5 minutes in pan, then invert onto rack. Blend ¼ cup coffee liqueur with powdered sugar in small bowl until smooth. Drizzle evenly over warm cake.

RICOTTA CAKE

4 SERVINGS

- 1 pound whole milk ricotta cheese
- ¾ cup sugar
- 2 eggs
- ½ teaspoon freshly grated lemon peel
- ½ teaspoon vanilla
  Lemon and/or orange slices (garnish)
  Fresh fruit or fruit sauce (optional)

Preheat oven to 350°F. Generously butter a 6-cup bundt pan. Combine all ingredients except garnishes in food processor or blender and mix until smooth. Pour into prepared pan and cover with foil. Place in pan of water and bake until firmly set, about 1 hour. Allow to cool. Dip bottom of pan in hot water and unmold onto serving platter. Refrigerate until ready to serve. Garnish with lemon and/or orange slices, and fresh fruit or sauce, if desired.

POPPY SEED CAKE

10 TO 12 SERVINGS

- 1 18½-ounce package yellow cake mix
- 1 3¾-ounce package instant vanilla pudding mix
- 4 eggs
- 1 cup sour cream
- ½ cup (1 stick) melted butter
- ½ cup cream sherry
- ⅓ cup poppy seeds

Preheat oven to 350°F. Butter bundt cake pan and flour lightly, shaking out excess. Combine all ingredients in large bowl and beat 5 minutes. Pour batter into pan. Bake until tester inserted in center comes out clean, about 1 hour. Let cool completely in baking pan. Invert onto platter and serve.

STRAWBERRY POKE CAKE

20 SERVINGS

- 1 18½-ounce package yellow cake mix
- 1 3-ounce package strawberry gelatin
- 1 cup boiling water
- 1 cup strawberry soda
- 2 cups milk
- 1 3¾-ounce package instant vanilla pudding mix
- 1 4-ounce carton nondairy whipped topping

Prepare cake mix according to package directions and bake in 9×13-inch pan. Meanwhile, combine gelatin and water in small saucepan over medium-high heat and stir until gelatin is dissolved. Blend in strawberry soda and set aside.

When cake is done, remove from oven and poke entire surface with toothpick. Pour gelatin evenly over top. Cool completely, about 1 hour.

Combine milk and pudding mix in medium bowl and blend according to package directions. Chill until set, about 5 minutes. Fold in topping. Spread over cake. Cover and chill cake at least 1 hour or overnight before serving.

COOKIES AND CONFECTIONS

BASIC BUTTER COOKIES

MAKES ABOUT 30 COOKIES

- 1 cup all purpose flour
- ½ cup cornstarch
- ½ cup powdered sugar
- ¾ cup (1½ sticks) butter, room temperature
- ½ cup coarsely chopped or sliced walnuts

Preheat oven to 300°F. Sift first 3 ingredients into large bowl. Add butter and mix well. Stir in walnuts. Drop by teaspoons onto baking sheet. Bake until cookies are lightly golden, about 20 to 25 minutes.

JAMMIES

MAKES 4½ TO 5 DOZEN COOKIES

- ¾ cup (1½ sticks) butter, room temperature
- ⅔ cup sugar
- 1 egg
- 1 teaspoon vanilla
- 2 cups all purpose flour
- ½ teaspoon baking powder
- ½ teaspoon cinnamon
  Jam

Preheat oven to 350°F. Cream butter with sugar in large bowl. Add egg and vanilla and beat well. Combine flour, baking powder and cinnamon and add gradually to creamed mixture, blending well after each addition. Divide into four equal portions, rolling each into cylinder about 12 inches long. Transfer to baking sheet(s). Make an indentation about ¼ inch deep down center of each cylinder and fill with jam. Bake until golden, about 15 minutes. Let cool slightly, then slice cylinders diagonally into cookies ¾ inch wide.

BUTTERSCOTCH BROWNIES

MAKES ABOUT 24

- ½ cup (1 stick) butter
- 2 cups firmly packed dark brown sugar
- 2 teaspoons vanilla
- 2 eggs, lightly beaten
- 1 cup flour
- 2 teaspoons baking powder
- 1 teaspoon salt

Preheat oven to 350°F. Cream butter and brown sugar with electric mixer or in food processor. Beat in vanilla and eggs. Sift together flour, baking powder and salt. Stir into creamed butter and brown sugar.

Butter a 9 x 13-inch baking pan. Add batter and spread evenly. Bake 35 to 40 minutes. Do not overbake. Cool brownies completely before cutting into squares.

CHOCOLATE FUDGY BROWNIES

MAKES 16 BROWNIES

- ½ cup (1 stick) butter
- 2 ounces (2 squares) unsweetened chocolate
- 1 cup sugar
- ½ cup all purpose flour
- ½ teaspoon baking powder
- 2 eggs
- 1 teaspoon vanilla
- ½ cup chopped walnuts

Preheat oven to 450°F. Grease an 8-inch square baking pan. Melt butter with chocolate in medium saucepan. Remove from heat. Combine sugar, flour and baking powder in large bowl. Add eggs and vanilla and beat well. Pour in chocolate mixture and blend thoroughly. Stir in walnuts. Pour into pan. Bake until tester inserted in center comes out clean, about 15 to 20 minutes. Cool completely in pan before cutting into squares.

DANISH ELEPHANT EARS

MAKES 6 DOZEN

- 1 cup (2 sticks) unsalted butter
- 2 cups flour (lightly packed)

- 7 tablespoons ice water
- 1 cup sugar

In medium bowl cut butter into flour until dough resembles coarse meal. Gradually add water, stirring just until dough forms ball. Divide into 2 balls. Refrigerate 1 hour.

Grease baking sheets. Roll dough out to ¼-inch thickness and cut into 1½-inch rounds. Transfer to baking sheets and chill at least 30 minutes.

Preheat oven to 450°F. Dip rounds into sugar in shallow dish. Prick dough with fork. Bake until lightly browned, about 8 minutes, then turn and sprinkle again with sugar. Continue baking until sugar caramelizes, about 1 minute.

GRAMMYS

10 TO 12 SERVINGS

- 2 packages graham crackers (approximately 22 whole crackers)
- 1 cup (2 sticks) butter, melted
- 1 tablespoon cinnamon
- ¾ cup sugar
- 1 cup sliced almonds (3¾-ounce package)

Preheat oven to 275°F. Break crackers into various sizes. Place on ungreased cookie sheet with sides, allowing crackers to touch but not overlap. (This will be similar to putting a jigsaw puzzle together.) Drizzle half the melted butter over crackers. Mix cinnamon and sugar and sprinkle half over crackers. Top with half the almonds. Drizzle with remaining butter and finish with sugar and almonds.

Bake just until crackers look soft, 10 to 15 minutes. Watch carefully or sugar will burn. (Crackers crisp up while cooling.) Cool 10 minutes before removing from cookie sheet.

Great with ice cream, custard and fruit, or just as a solo snack.

RAISIN-GRANOLA COOKIES

See photograph page 26

MAKES 4 TO 5 DOZEN COOKIES

- 1 cup (2 sticks) butter, room temperature

- ¾ cup firmly packed dark brown sugar
- ¾ cup sugar
- 1 egg
- 1 teaspoon vanilla
- 1½ cups all purpose flour
- 1 teaspoon baking soda
- 1 teaspoon salt
- 1¾ cups granola
- 1 cup seedless raisins
- ½ cup unsalted peanuts

Preheat oven to 375°F. Generously grease baking sheets. Cream together butter and sugars. Add egg and vanilla and continue beating until well blended. Sift together flour, baking soda and salt. Add in small amounts alternately with granola, beating well after each addition. Continue beating 2 to 3 minutes, until batter is very well blended. Stir in raisins and peanuts.

Drop batter by heaping teaspoons about 2 inches apart on prepared sheets. Bake until the cookies are lightly browned around edges but still soft, about 12 to 15 minutes. Loosen with spatula and allow to cool completely on racks. Store in container.

Raisin-Granola Cookies freeze well.

SCOTCH SHORTBREAD

8 SERVINGS

- 1¼ cups all purpose flour
- ¼ cup sugar
- ½ cup (1 stick) butter, sliced, room temperature
- 3 tablespoons cornstarch
- 1 tablespoon sugar

Preheat oven to 375°F. Combine first 4 ingredients in medium bowl and blend until finely crumbled. Pat dough into 8- to 9-inch baking pan with removable bottom, spreading evenly. Press edges with tines of fork; gently prick bottom. Bake until lightly golden, about 25 minutes. Cool in pan 5 minutes. Cut into wedges using sharp knife. Sprinkle top with remaining sugar. Let cool completely in pan before serving, about 30 minutes.

CARAMELS

MAKES ABOUT ¾ POUND

- 6 tablespoons sugar
- ½ cup pure maple or golden syrup
- ¼ cup (½ stick) unsalted butter
- 5½ ounces (¾ cup minus 1 tablespoon) half and half
- 1 teaspoon vanilla

Generously butter 8-inch square pan and heavy 3-quart saucepan. Combine all ingredients except vanilla in saucepan. Place over medium heat and stir gently with wooden spoon until mixture is an even golden caramel color, very thick and breaks with big bubbles, about 20 to 25 minutes. (Test by dropping a little in cold water; it should form firm ball.) Remove from heat and stir in vanilla. Pour into greased pan. Cool about 30 minutes, then chill. When ready to serve, cut into squares. Store in refrigerator.

FUDGE

MAKES 1¼ POUNDS

- 2 1-ounce squares unsweetened chocolate
- ¾ cup milk
  Dash of salt
- 2 cups sugar
- ¼ cup (½ stick) butter
- ½ teaspoon vanilla
- ½ cup chopped walnuts

Melt chocolate in top of double boiler or over very low heat. Add milk and salt and stir well. Stir in sugar and bring to a full boil over medium heat. Cook without stirring to 235° until a small amount of mixture on teaspoon forms a soft ball in ½ cup cold water, remove chocolate from heat.

Add butter and vanilla and blend well. Stir in walnuts. Beat well with a large spoon until mixture begins to thicken. Pour quickly into a buttered 8- or 9-inch pie plate. Refrigerate.

FRUIT

ONE-BOWL APPLE CAKE WITH CREAM CHEESE FROSTING

24 SERVINGS

Cake

- 1 16-ounce can apple pie filling
- 2 cups all purpose flour
- 2 cups sugar
- ½ cup vegetable oil
- 2 eggs
- 2 teaspoons cinnamon
- 2 teaspoons baking soda
- 1 teaspoon salt

Frosting

- 1 cup powdered sugar
- 1 3-ounce package cream cheese, room temperature
- ¼ cup (½ stick) butter, room temperature
- 1 teaspoon vanilla

For cake: Preheat oven to 350°F. Butter 9×13-inch baking dish. Combine all ingredients in large bowl and blend well. Turn into prepared dish and bake until cake tests done, about 1 hour. Cool.

For frosting: Combine remaining ingredients and mix to spreading consistency. Frost cake.

APPLE-WALNUT SQUARES

MAKES ABOUT 24 SQUARES

- 2 cups all purpose flour
- 2 cups firmly packed brown sugar
- ½ cup (1 stick) butter, room temperature
- 1 cup chopped walnuts
- 1 teaspoon cinnamon
- 1 teaspoon baking soda
- ¼ teaspoon salt
- 1 egg
- 1 cup sour cream
- 1 teaspoon vanilla
- 2 cups finely chopped peeled tart apples (about 2 large)
  Vanilla ice cream

Preheat oven to 350°F. Lightly grease 9×13-inch baking dish.

Combine first 3 ingredients in medium bowl and mix until finely crumbled. Stir in nuts. Press 2 cups of mixture evenly into bottom of prepared dish. Add cinnamon, baking soda and salt to remaining mixture and blend well. Beat in egg, sour cream and vanilla. Gently stir in apples. Spoon evenly into dish. Bake until cake begins to pull away from sides of dish and tester inserted in center comes out clean, about 35 to 40 minutes. Let cool completely in pan. Cut into squares. Top with vanilla ice cream.

BAKED APPLES

8 SERVINGS

- 8 medium apples, peeled, halved and cored
- ⅓ cup sugar

Preheat oven to 400°F. Place apples cut side up on baking sheet. Sprinkle each half with 1 teaspoon sugar. Bake 10 minutes.

BAKED APPLE DESSERT

10 TO 12 SERVINGS

- 6 tart apples, peeled, cored and sliced
- 2 tablespoons fresh lemon juice
- 2 tablespoons cinnamon
- 1 18½-ounce package yellow cake mix
- ½ cup (1 stick) melted butter
- 1 cup chopped walnuts
  Vanilla ice cream

Preheat oven to 350°F. Grease 9×13-inch baking dish. Combine apples, lemon juice and 1 tablespoon cinnamon in large bowl and toss well. Spoon evenly into dish. Sprinkle cake mix over apples, patting gently. Dust with remaining cinnamon and drizzle butter evenly over top. Sprinkle with nuts. Cover with foil and bake until apples begin to bubble, about 15 to 20 minutes. Uncover and continue baking until top is browned and apples are tender, about 30 minutes. Serve warm or chilled, topped with ice cream.

BANANES L'ARCHESTRATE

Although this simple but elegant dessert may be cooked on the kitchen stove, a much more dramatic presentation is to prepare it at the table over a portable burner.

FOR EACH SERVING

> 1 tablespoon butter
> 1 banana, ripe but firm, sliced ⅜ inch thick
> 1 tablespoon sugar
> 1 tablespoon Cognac or brandy
> 1 scoop vanilla ice cream

Melt butter in sautoir or small skillet over medium-high heat. Add banana, sprinkle with sugar and stir gently but thoroughly until sugar has caramelized slightly and slices are golden.

Add Cognac and let warm for a moment or two. Carefully ignite and stir until flame subsides. Spoon over ice cream and serve immediately.

For best results prepare no more than two servings at a time.

BANANAS WITH ORANGE SAUCE

6 SERVINGS

> 3 to 4 firm bananas
> 1 6-ounce can frozen orange juice concentrate, partially defrosted
> Fresh mint (garnish)

Peel bananas and slice into serving bowl. Pour orange concentrate over bananas and toss to coat each slice. Remove with slotted spoon to individual serving dishes and garnish each with sprig of mint. Pour remaining concentrate into chilled sauceboat to pass separately. Serve.

MELON BALLS WITH LIME

6 SERVINGS

> 1 large ripe honeydew melon
> 1 ripe cantaloupe
> 6 wedges fresh lime

Cut honeydew into 6 equal pieces and discard seeds. Halve cantaloupe and discard seeds. Using melon baller, carefully scoop out fruit. Arrange in honeydew shells. Cover and chill, if preferred. To serve, slit each lime wedge and secure to one end of melon shell.

If there are extra melon balls, they may be passed separately.

AMARETTO ORANGES WITH SORBET
See photograph page 156

6 TO 8 SERVINGS

> 4 to 5 large navel oranges, peeled and thinly sliced into rounds
> ¼ cup Amaretto liqueur
> 1 to 1½ pints lemon, grapefruit or melon sorbet (if unavailable, substitute sherbet)
> Fresh mint leaves or scented geranium leaves (optional garnish)

Place orange slices in bowl and sprinkle with liqueur. Refrigerate until serving time. Drain slices and arrange in overlapping fan pattern on dessert plates. Using 2 tablespoons, scoop sorbet into 6 to 8 egg-shaped mounds and set each on plate at base of fan pattern. Garnish with leaves and serve immediately.

BAKED ORANGE PINEAPPLE

6 SERVINGS

> ¾ cup sugar
> ½ cup (1 stick) margarine, room temperature
> 4 eggs
> 2 11-ounce cans mandarin oranges, drained
> 1 8¼-ounce can crushed unsweetened pineapple, drained
> 6 slices white bread, crusts removed, cubed

Preheat oven to 350°F. Grease 1¾-quart baking dish. Cream sugar and margarine in large bowl until fluffy. Add eggs one at a time, beating well after each addition. Stir in oranges, pineapple and bread and blend well. Turn into dish and bake until golden, about 1 hour.

HOT ORANGE FRITTERS

4 TO 6 SERVINGS

> 1 large egg
> 2 tablespoons sugar
> Juice of 1 lemon
> 1 cup less 2 tablespoons flour
> 1 teaspoon baking powder
> Pinch of salt
> ⅔ cup milk
> Oil for deep frying
> 4 medium oranges, pith and seeds removed
> Sour cream
> Nutmeg

Combine egg and sugar in medium bowl and beat until thick and light. Add lemon juice and stir well. Sift together flour, baking powder and salt. Add to egg batter alternately with milk, beating well after each addition (batter consistency should be thick but smooth).

Preheat 1 inch oil in skillet until hot. Cut oranges into ⅓-inch slices, dip into batter and fry until puffed and golden, turning once. Remove with slotted spoon and drain on paper towels. Serve hot with cold sour cream and a dusting of nutmeg.

INSTANT ORANGE MOUSSE

6 TO 8 SERVINGS

> ⅔ cup hot water
> 2 envelopes unflavored gelatin
> ½ cup sugar
> 1 6-ounce can orange juice concentrate, partially defrosted
> 2 tablespoons whipping cream
> ½ teaspoon vanilla
> 2 cups ice cubes

Pour hot water and gelatin into blender. Whirl on high 30 seconds. Add sugar and blend on high 5 seconds. Add orange juice concentrate, whipping cream, vanilla and ice cubes. Blend on high until ice is evenly distributed into mixture, about 25 seconds. Pour immediately into parfait glasses and chill. Dessert will set almost immediately.

ASIAGO WITH PEARS
See photograph page 109

2 SERVINGS

- 2 ripe Anjou pears
- 4 to 5 ounces Asiago cheese (domestic or imported)
  Unsalted butter (optional), room temperature
- 5 to 6 slices French bread

Divide pears and cheese between 2 dessert plates. Present with dessert knives and forks. Serve butter in small crock or ramekin to spread on bread.

SPARKLING RASPBERRIES

FOR EACH SERVING

- 1 bowl fresh raspberries
- ¼ bottle sparkling Muscat

Place bowl of raspberries before guest. Pour into bowl about 2 ounces of sparkling wine and accompany with a glass of wine.

DELECTABLE STRAWBERRY DESSERT

8 SERVINGS

- 3 pints strawberries, cleaned and hulled
- 1 10-ounce package frozen raspberries, thawed and undrained
- 2 tablespoons sugar
- ¼ cup orange liqueur
- 1 8-ounce carton raspberry yogurt
- 1 cup frozen whipped topping, thawed, or ½ cup whipping cream, whipped
- 1 bakery pound cake

Reserve approximately 2 pints of largest berries; chill. Combine remaining strawberries with raspberries in blender. Add sugar and liqueur and blend 15 seconds; chill. Combine yogurt and topping or whipped cream and mix gently but thoroughly; chill.

Cut cake into 8 slices. Top each slice with whole strawberries, some of puree and a dollop of chilled yogurt mixture.

STRAWBERRIES IN FONDANT CHEMISES

6 SERVINGS

- 2 pints large strawberries, preferably with stems
- 2 3-ounce packages cream cheese, room temperature
- 3 cups powdered sugar
- 2 egg yolks
- 2 tablespoons kirsch
  Whipping cream (optional)

Wash strawberries and dry on paper towels. Beat cream cheese until light and fluffy. Add sugar, yolks and kirsch and continue beating until fondant has reached dipping consistency. Add cream if mixture seems too thick, blending well. Dip each berry halfway in fondant and place on baking sheet or waxed paper in cool area until firm.

FRUIT KUCHEN

The dough for this kuchen is simply pressed into the baking dishes; rolling is unnecessary.

12 TO 16 SERVINGS

German Sweet Dough

- 2 cups all purpose flour
- 2 to 4 tablespoons sugar
- 1 teaspoon baking powder
  Pinch of salt
- ¾ cup (1½ sticks) butter or margarine, sliced
- 1 egg, beaten
- 1 to 2 tablespoons liquid (milk, cream, rum or water)
  Grated lemon peel

Filling

- 3 cups peeled, cored and thinly sliced apples, or fresh or thawed frozen peaches (or combination)
- ½ cup sugar

- 1 teaspoon cornstarch
- 1 cup sour cream
- 2 eggs, beaten
- 2 teaspoons rum, or rum extract and water

For dough: Combine flour, sugar, baking powder and salt in medium bowl. Cut in butter until mixture resembles coarse meal. Add egg, liquid and peel, working into dough with fingers. Chill. Press into bottom and sides of 2 9-inch square or round baking pans.

For filling: Preheat oven to 400°F. Arrange apple or peach slices over dough. Combine sugar and cornstarch and sprinkle evenly over fruit. Bake 20 to 25 minutes. Remove pans from oven and reduce heat to 350°F. Combine sour cream, eggs and rum and pour over top of fruit. Return to oven and continue baking until custard is firm, about 15 minutes. Allow to cool before serving.

Opposite
Crème Fraîche with strawberries and blueberries is a colorful celebration of natural flavor.

Page 178–179
Cassata is a delicious do-ahead extravagance.

Page 180
Explorateur Cheese with Grape Clusters, light and golden water biscuits and the not-too-sweet Hungarian Coffee Crescents are an elegant dessert trio.

Page 181
Three steps to the perfect Petites Buches au Chocolate: Cake layer is spread with sweetened whipped cream, rolled, then coated with Chocolate Icing and chopped walnuts—a festive dessert presentation.

Page 182–183
Ice Cream Bombe is a tempting dessert with molded layers of ice cream.

Page 184
Vanilla ice cream with Chocolate Sauce is the ultimate easy delight.

Instant Crème Fraiche
Recipe page 188

Cassata
Recipe page 189

180

Explorateur Cheese with Grape Clusters
Recipe page 186
Hungarian Coffee Crescents
Recipe page 166

Petites Bûches au Chocolate
Recipe page 190

Ice Cream Bombe
Recipe page 190

Chocolate Sauce
Recipe page 194

MINTED FRUIT DIP

MAKES 1 CUP

- 1 8-ounce carton lime yogurt
- 1 tablespoon green crème de menthe
  Grapefruit sections, sliced bananas, pineapple, fresh strawberries, sliced peaches, honeydew, cantaloupe and/or ladyfingers

Combine yogurt and crème de menthe in small bowl and mix until thoroughly blended. Serve as dip for assorted types of fresh fruit and/or ladyfingers.

FRUIT SOUP

MAKES ABOUT 5 CUPS

- 1 21-ounce can cherry pie filling
- 1 10-ounce package frozen strawberries, thawed and drained
- 1 10-ounce package frozen raspberries, thawed and drained
- 1 teaspoon almond extract
  Ice cream or pound cake
  Sliced toasted almonds (garnish)

Combine first 4 ingredients in large bowl and blend well. Cover and chill. Spoon over ice cream or pound cake. Garnish with almonds.

Fruit Soup is also excellent served with plain yogurt.

ICE CREAM

BERRY SHERBET

MAKES ABOUT 2 CUPS

- 1½ cups unsweetened frozen blueberries, strawberries or raspberries, slightly thawed
- ½ cup sugar
- 1 egg white

Puree all ingredients in processor or blender until smooth. Pour into shallow pan. Cover and freeze until firm.

BLENDER FRUIT DESSERT

4 SERVINGS

- 1 pint vanilla ice cream
- 1 split chilled champagne (2 cups)
- ½ cup fresh or drained canned peaches, or other favorite or seasonal fruit

Place all ingredients in blender and whirl until smooth and creamy. Pour into stemmed glasses and serve immediately. (May also be frozen until ready to serve.)

CHERRY ICE CREAM

MAKES ABOUT 1½ QUARTS

- 4 ounces dark sweet chocolate, coarsely chopped
- ½ cup drained canned pitted black cherries, chopped
- 1½ quarts good quality French vanilla ice cream, softened
  Cherry liqueur

Fold chocolate and cherries into ice cream, blending evenly. Refreeze. To serve, scoop ice cream into individual serving dishes and top each serving with ½ to 1 tablespoon of the cherry liqueur.

CHOCOLATE "CRUMB" SUNDAE

4 TO 6 SERVINGS

- 1 6-ounce hazelnut or other crunchy chocolate bar
- 1 pint vanilla or other favorite ice cream or sherbet

Freeze chocolate bar. Place in double plastic bags and cover with brown paper sack. Pound with potato masher, mallet, rolling pin or hammer until chocolate is broken into small pieces. Return to freezer.

Spoon ice cream into goblets or wine glasses and top each serving with chocolate crumbs.

COUPE MARRON

See photograph pages 110-111

A devastating dessert that's very simple to prepare. Ice cream can be scooped into glasses and returned to the freezer several hours before serving and garnishing.

6 SERVINGS

- 1½ pints vanilla ice cream, softened
- 1 cup (about) imported marron (chestnut) pieces in vanilla-flavored syrup*
- ½ cup whipping cream, whipped
- 3 tablespoons shaved bittersweet chocolate (optional)

Scoop ice cream into 6 wine glasses. Spoon chestnuts and their syrup over top. Garnish with whipped cream and sprinkle each serving with shaved chocolate.

*Marrons are available in jars or cans in gourmet or specialty food stores.

FROZEN FRUIT SPECIAL

4 SERVINGS

- 1 20-ounce package frozen mixed fruits, thawed
- ¼ cup kirsch or Grand Marnier
- 1 pint rainbow, lemon or other sherbet
  Fresh mint leaves (optional)

Mix fruits with liqueur. When ready to serve, place fruits in glass serving dish and top with scoops of sherbet. Garnish with mint, if desired.

ICE CREAM GRASSHOPPERS

2 SERVINGS

- 3 large scoops vanilla ice cream
- ½ ounce green crème de menthe
- ½ ounce crème de cacao

Combine all ingredients in blender or processor until thick. Serve in frappé glasses.

ICED LIME DESSERT

4 TO 6 SERVINGS

- 1 12-ounce package frozen raspberries, thawed
- 3 tablespoons cherry-flavored liqueur
  Lime sherbet or vanilla ice cream

Place raspberries in blender or food processor and puree. Stir in liqueur and pour puree over scoops of lime sherbet or vanilla ice cream.

QUICK MANDARIN SHERBET

4 SERVINGS

- 1 pint tangerine sherbet
- 1 11-ounce can mandarin oranges, drained
  Curaçao to taste
  Mint leaves (garnish)

Scoop sherbet into dessert dishes. Arrange orange slices over top. Sprinkle with liqueur and garnish with mint.

SWEET AVOCADO CREAM

4 SERVINGS

- 2 large ripe avocados, peeled and seeded
- ½ cup milk
- ½ cup sugar or to taste
- ½ teaspoon cinnamon

Combine all ingredients in medium bowl and beat until smooth. Spoon into individual freezerproof goblets or dessert dishes. Cover and freeze until thoroughly chilled and firm, about 1 hour.

PIES

MAGIC PIE CRUST

MAKES 1 UNBAKED 9- OR 10-INCH CRUST

- 1½ cups all purpose flour
- ¼ teaspoon salt
- ¾ cup solid white vegetable shortening

- 1 egg
- 2 tablespoons cold water
  Flour

Combine 1½ cups flour and salt in large bowl. Cut in shortening until mixture resembles coarse meal; do not overmix. Beat egg with water in small bowl. Add to flour mixture, tossing briefly with fork until just moistened. Gently form into ball. Generously flour work surface and rolling pin. Pat dough into circle and roll out. Turn dough over and flour again. Roll into 12-inch circle. Fold dough in half and then in half again. Transfer to pie plate. Unfold dough and fit into plate, trimming excess dough 1 inch beyond rim of pan. Turn excess under to make narrow rolled rim. Flute decoratively or press edge with fork.

THE AMAZING INTERCHANGEABLE DO-IT-YOURSELF TIPSY PIE

With this basic filling, an unlimited supply of liqueurs and potables at your disposal and a freewheeling spirit of adventure, you can create an almost infinite number of pies—each different, all delectable. Choose the most appropriate crust and proceed.

Graham Cracker Crust

- 1½ cups graham cracker crumbs (about 20 crackers)
- 3 tablespoons sugar
- ⅓ cup (¾ stick) butter, melted

Preheat oven to 350°F. Mix all ingredients together and press into 9-inch pie plate. Bake 10 minutes. Cool.

Cookie Crust

- 1½ cups crushed cookies (vanilla or chocolate wafers or gingersnaps)
- ¼ cup (½ stick) butter, melted

Preheat oven to 350°F. Mix all ingredients together and press into a 9-inch pie plate. Bake 10 minutes. Allow to cool.

Filling

- 1 cup sugar
- 1 envelope unflavored gelatin

- 4 eggs, separated
- ½ cup water
  Flavorings (suggestions follow)

In small saucepan stir together ½ cup sugar and gelatin. Blend egg yolks with water and flavorings of your choice. Stir into sugar mixture. Cook over medium heat, stirring constantly, until mixture comes to boil. Remove from heat, cool and refrigerate, stirring occasionally, until mixture is cool and thickened.

Beat egg whites until foamy. Add remaining ½ cup sugar, 1 tablespoon at a time, beating until egg whites form stiff, glossy peaks. Fold gelatin mixture into meringue and spoon into prebaked 9-inch pie shell.

Flavoring suggestions:

Butterscotch Collins Pie

- 5 tablespoons Scotch
- 2 tablespoons Scotch liqueur
- 1 tablespoon lemon juice
  Orange slices (garnish)
  Cherries (garnish)

Gimlet Pie

- 6 tablespoons gin
- 2 tablespoons lime juice
  Grated peel of 1 lime
  Juice of ½ lime

Brandy Alexander-The-Great Pie

- 5 tablespoons brandy
- 3 tablespoons crème de cacao

Daiquiri Pie

- 5 tablespoons golden rum
- 2 tablespoons fresh lime juice
- 1 tablespoon fresh lemon juice

Black Russian Pie

- 7 tablespoons vodka
- 3 tablespoons coffee liqueur

Comin' Through The Rye Pie

- ¼ cup rye or bourbon whiskey
- ¼ cup fresh orange juice
- 2 tablespoons grated orange peel

DIVINE SOUR CREAM RAISIN PIE

8 SERVINGS

- 2 cups seedless raisins
  Boiling water
- ¾ cup sugar
- ¼ teaspoon salt
- 1 teaspoon cinnamon
- ½ teaspoon nutmeg
- ¼ teaspoon ground cloves
- 2 lightly beaten eggs
- 1 cup sour cream* (not commercial)
- 1 unbaked 9-inch pie crust

Preheat oven to 450°F. Pour boiling water over raisins to cover and allow raisins to soak for 15 minutes.

Add dry ingredients to eggs and mix together well.

Add sour cream and mix thoroughly. Drain raisins and add to mixture.

Pour mixture into pie shell and bake 10 minutes. Reduce oven temperature to 350°F and bake 30 to 35 minutes longer.

*Sour Cream

- 1 tablespoon light vinegar or lemon juice
- 1 cup whipping cream

Mix together and allow to stand for 30 minutes.

PECAN PIE

This southern specialty has a surprisingly light texture similar to custard.

6 TO 8 SERVINGS

- 1 partially baked 9-inch pie crust
- 1 egg white, lightly beaten
- ¼ cup (½ stick) butter, room temperature
- 1 cup firmly packed light brown sugar
- 4 eggs
- ¾ cup light corn syrup

- 1 teaspoon vanilla
- 2½ ounces pecan halves

Preheat oven to 375°F. Brush pie crust with egg white. Cream butter and sugar in medium bowl until smooth. Add eggs one at a time, beating well after each addition. Blend in syrup and vanilla. Pour into crust. Arrange pecans over top in circular pattern. Bake until tester inserted in center comes out clean, about 40 minutes. Let cool slightly. Serve warm or chilled.

QUICK LIME RUM PIE

4 SERVINGS

- 2 14-ounce cans sweetened condensed milk
- 4 egg yolks
  Juice and grated rind of 2 fresh limes
- ⅓ cup light rum
- 1 baked 9-inch pie shell or graham cracker crust
  Lightly sweetened whipped cream

Pour condensed milk into deep bowl. Add egg yolks and stir well with a fork, hand-beater or blender. Add lime juice, rind and rum; stir well. Pour into pie shell and refrigerate until ready to serve.

Just before serving, spread pie with a thin layer of whipped cream.

TOP CRUST COCONUT CUSTARD PIE

8 TO 10 SERVINGS

- 2 cups milk
- 1 cup coconut, flaked or shredded
- 4 eggs
- ⅔ cup sugar
- ½ cup sifted all purpose flour
- ½ cup (1 stick) butter or margarine, room temperature
- 1 teaspoon vanilla
- 1 teaspoon baking powder
  Pinch of salt

- ¼ cup jam (optional)
- 3 tablespoons orange liqueur (optional)
  Frozen, canned or fresh fruit, drained, sliced or chopped (optional)
  Whipped cream (optional)

Preheat oven to 350°F. Grease 10-inch baking dish or pie pan.

Combine first 9 ingredients in blender and whirl on high until thoroughly mixed. Pour into prepared baking dish and bake until golden, about 30 to 40 minutes.

While still warm, spread top with jam and sprinkle with liqueur, if desired. Chill. Top with fruit and/or whipped cream. Serve chilled or at room temperature.

UNBELIEVABLE PIE

6 SERVINGS

- ½ cup coarsely chopped toasted nuts
- 1 unbaked 8-inch graham cracker crust
- 1 square semisweet chocolate
- ½ cup (1 stick) unsalted butter
- 1 cup sugar
- 2 eggs, well beaten
  Whipped cream or ice cream

Preheat oven to 350°F. Sprinkle nuts on bottom of pie shell and set aside.

Combine chocolate and butter in top of double boiler over gently simmering water. Whisk until melted and well blended. Remove from heat and whisk in sugar. Beat small amount of warmed chocolate into eggs. Add to chocolate mixture and blend well. Pour into pie shell (uncooked mixture will not fill shell) and bake until filling is puffed, about 25 minutes. Serve warm or at room temperature with whipped cream or ice cream.

OTHER DESSERTS

ALMOND CREME

MAKES ABOUT 1 CUP OR 4 TO 6 SERVINGS

   1 cup sour cream
   3 tablespoons powdered sugar
1½ tablespoons almond liqueur
   1 teaspoon almond extract
      Strawberries, pineapple or bananas
  ½ cup blueberries (thawed if frozen)

Combine first 4 ingredients in small mixing bowl and stir well to blend. Cover and chill until ready to use. Serve over fresh fruit and sprinkle blueberries over the top.

EXPLORATEUR CHEESE WITH GRAPE CLUSTERS
See photograph page 180

This triple crème cheese is rich and silky. Taste before you buy since it is quite perishable. One and a half pounds will serve 12 to 16 generously, but buy a slightly larger piece for a more dramatic presentation.

Place the room temperature cheese on a board and arrange three large bunches of perfect grapes around one side of it. Accompaniment would be plain crisp crackers such as water biscuits. For easy serving, have grape scissors and cheese knife available to guests.

If Explorateur isn't available, substitute another double or triple crème such as Excelsior, Boursault, Brillat-Savarin or Caprice des Dieux.

CHOCOLATE FONDUE

12 SERVINGS

   6 1-ounce squares unsweetened chocolate
1½ cups sugar
   1 cup whipping cream
  ½ cup (1 stick) butter

1½ ounces (3 tablespoons) crème de cacao
      Cake or fruit, cut into bite-size pieces

Combine first 4 ingredients in double boiler over warm water and stir frequently until melted, about 10 minutes. Add crème de cacao and blend mixture well. Serve with cake or assorted fruit.

QUICK AND EASY CHOCOLATE MOUSSE

4 TO 6 SERVINGS

   2 cups (12 ounces) semisweet chocolate chips
1½ teaspoons vanilla
      Pinch of salt
1½ cups whipping cream, heated to boiling point
   6 egg yolks
   2 egg whites
      Whipped cream (optional)

Combine chocolate, vanilla and salt in blender, or food processor fitted with steel knife, and mix 30 seconds. Add boiling cream and continue mixing until chocolate is completely melted, about 30 seconds. Add yolks and mix about 5 seconds. Transfer to bowl and allow to cool.

Beat egg whites until stiff peaks form. Gently fold into chocolate mixture. Place in serving bowl or wine glasses, cover with plastic wrap and chill. Serve the mousse with whipped cream if desired.

INSTANT CREME FRAICHE
See photograph page 177

Use this only as an accompaniment; it is not appropriate for use as an ingredient in cooking.

MAKES 1½ CUPS

   1 cup whipping cream, whipped with 2 tablespoons powdered sugar or to taste
   3 to 4 tablespoons sour cream

Fold whipped cream into sour cream. Cover mixture and keep chilled until ready to serve.

Instant Crème Fraîche will keep covered in refrigerator for 1 or 2 days.

COFFEE MARSHMALLOW MOUSSE

4 TO 6 SERVINGS

1½ cups double-strength coffee, or espresso
 48 large marshmallows
   1 cup whipping cream, whipped
      Grated chocolate (garnish)

Heat coffee or espresso in 3-quart saucepan over medium-high heat. Add marshmallows and stir with wooden spoon until melted. Turn into medium bowl and chill until thickened, about 20 to 30 minutes. Fold in whipped cream and chill until ready to serve. Spoon into dessert dishes or goblets and garnish with chocolate.

DUSTY RICOTTA

4 SERVINGS

   1 pound ricotta cheese
  ½ cup powdered sugar
   2 tablespoons rum or brandy
   1 to 2 tablespoons instant espresso plus 1 teaspoon for garnish

Combine ricotta, sugar, rum or brandy and espresso in medium bowl and whisk until thoroughly blended. Turn into individual ramekins and chill well. Just before serving, dust with remaining espresso

EASY ZABAGLIONE

Just about any sweet wine goes well with zabaglione.

FOR EACH SERVING

   1 egg yolk
   1 tablespoon sugar
   2 tablespoons Marsala or dry white wine
      Dash of vanilla or any liqueur (optional)
      Grated orange or lemon rind (garnish)

Place egg yolk, sugar and wine in top of double boiler and beat until thoroughly blended. Continue beating over boiling water until zabaglione is thick and fluffy. Be careful not to let water in bottom of double boiler touch pan in which zabaglione is being beaten. Serve either hot or cold. Flavor, if you like, with vanilla or liqueur. Garnish with grated orange or lemon rind.

DO AHEAD

CAKES

BLENDER CHERRY CAKE

6 SERVINGS

    1½ cups milk
    4 eggs
    ½ cup all purpose flour
    ¼ cup sugar
    2 teaspoons vanilla
    2 16- or 17-ounce cans pitted sour cherries, drained and patted dry
       Powdered sugar (garnish)

Position rack in middle of oven and preheat to 350°F. Generously butter 2-quart rectangular baking dish or 10-inch pie plate. Combine milk, eggs, flour, sugar and vanilla in blender and mix on high speed 15 seconds. Scrape down sides of container with spatula. Blend on high 30 seconds. Spread cherries in baking dish. Pour batter evenly over top. Bake until top is golden brown, about 1½ hours. Dust with powdered sugar. Before serving, warm cake in low oven.

CASSATA

See photograph pages 178-179

12 SERVINGS

    1 9×5-inch pound cake
    2 cups ricotta cheese
    4 1-ounce squares semisweet chocolate
    1 ounce orange liqueur
    1½ cups raspberry jam
    2 cups chocolate frosting or whipped cream

    Toasted whole almonds (optional garnish)

Bake or buy a pound cake. Chill for 1 hour. Trim edges and uneven places so that cake is level on all sides and top. Slice cake horizontally into ½-inch slices and place base layer of cake on serving platter.

Force cheese through a sieve into a bowl. Beat until smooth.

Chop chocolate into fine bits in blender or food processor. Mix chocolate bits with liqueur and jam. Spread base layer with a portion of the ricotta cheese and spread cheese with part of raspberry-chocolate-liqueur mixture. Repeat using all cake, cheese and raspberry mixture, ending with a top layer of plain pound cake.

Press the filled cake gently. Use a spatula to even up sides. Cover with plastic wrap and leave cake in refrigerator overnight.

Before serving, frost cake with a favorite chocolate frosting or whipped cream. Garnish cake with whole almonds if desired.

MOCHA BROWNIE TORTE

This dish should be made 1 or 2 days in advance.

16 SERVINGS

Cake
    ⅔ cup (¾ stick) softened butter
    ⅓ cup sugar
    4 egg yolks
    3 1-ounce squares grated semisweet chocolate
    4 egg whites
    1½ cups finely ground almonds
    ½ cup sifted flour
    ⅛ teaspoon baking powder
       Coffee Cream Filling*
    ⅓ cup seedless raspberry jam
       Chocolate Icing*
    8 halved almonds (garnish)
       Whipped cream (optional)

Preheat oven to 350°F. Cream butter and sugar; add egg yolks and beat until light and fluffy. Thoroughly blend in grated chocolate.

Beat egg whites to soft peaks. Gently fold into chocolate mixture along with ground almonds.

Sift flour and baking powder together. Fold in gently but thoroughly. Pour batter into buttered and floured 8×8×2-inch pan. Bake until cake shrinks from sides of pan, about 30 to 40 minutes. Cool and remove from pan. Cover and refrigerate overnight.

To assemble: Split cake in half horizontally; place on serving plate. Spread Coffee Cream Filling on bottom layer. Cover with top layer. Wrap and return to refrigerator for several hours or overnight.

Coat top layer with raspberry jam. Score cake into 16 even squares, without slicing completely through. Pour Chocolate Icing over top and sides of cake, using knife to cover sides completely. Refrigerate.

After icing is set, cut squares through. Place a split almond in center of each square. Refrigerate cake for at least 1 hour before serving. Decorate with a frill of whipped cream, if desired.

*Coffee Cream Filling
    1 teaspoon instant coffee powder
    1 tablespoon hot water
    ¼ cup (½ stick) unsalted butter, room temperature
    ¼ cup sugar
    1 egg yolk

Dissolve coffee in hot water. Cream butter and sugar together; add egg yolk, beat thoroughly. Add coffee liquid. Beat again until fluffy.

*Chocolate Icing
    4 1-ounce squares semisweet chocolate
    ½ cup (1 stick) unsalted butter

Melt chocolate and butter over low heat, stirring until smooth and well blended. Cool slightly.

PETITES BUCHES AU CHOCOLAT
See photograph page 181

These small chocolate rolls (or logs) are filled with walnut marzipan and crème chantilly, thinly frosted with chocolate icing and rolled in either walnuts or chocolate sprinkles.

24 TO 26 SERVINGS

Chocolate Roll

> 6 ounces semisweet chocolate
> 3 tablespoons water
> 5 eggs, separated
> ¼ teaspoon cream of tartar
> ¾ cup sugar
> 1 teaspoon vanilla

Walnut Marzipan

> 12 ounces walnuts, grated (3 cups)
> 8 ounces vanilla wafers, finely grated (2 cups)
> ⅔ cup powdered sugar (optional)
> ⅓ cup light corn syrup
> ⅓ cup dark rum or coffee liqueur
> 2½ tablespoons unsweetened cocoa

Crème Chantilly

> 1 cup whipping cream, well chilled
> ¼ cup powdered sugar
> 1 teaspoon vanilla
> ½ cup powdered sugar
> ¼ cup unsweetened cocoa
>   Chocolate Icing*
> ½ cup toasted chopped walnuts or chocolate sprinkles (decoration)

For roll: Preheat oven to 350°F. Butter 15½×10½×1-inch jelly roll pan. Line with waxed paper, extending paper a few inches over each end; oil paper lightly.

Melt chocolate with water in top of double boiler over simmering water. Stir until smooth. Let cool.

Beat egg whites until foamy. Add cream of tartar and beat until soft peaks form. Gradually add half the sugar and beat until stiff but not dry. In large bowl combine egg yolks, remaining sugar and vanilla and beat until thick and pale yellow. Blend in chocolate; mix well.

Stir 2 large spoonfuls of whites into yolks and mix thoroughly. Gently fold in remaining whites; do not overfold. Turn into prepared pan, spreading evenly. Bake until edges of cake shrink slightly from pan, about 15 to 20 minutes. Cover cake with slightly dampened towel and let cool in pan.

For marzipan: Combine ingredients in processor, or electric mixer fitted with paddle attachment, and mix thoroughly. Roll between 2 sheets of waxed paper into same size as top of chocolate cake.

For crème: Combine ingredients in chilled mixing bowl and beat until thick. Cover and refrigerate.

To assemble: Remove towel from cake. Combine powdered sugar and cocoa and sift over surface. Cover with 2 overlapping layers of waxed paper, place a board or bottom of another jelly roll pan on top and invert cake onto work surface. Gently peel off waxed paper.

Remove top layer of waxed paper from marzipan and invert over cake. Remove the other sheet of waxed paper. Spread crème over marzipan. Cut cake lengthwise into 2 halves. Roll long edge toward center to form long thin cylinder. Wrap with plastic and place in freezer. Repeat with second half.

When solidly frozen, unwrap rolls and pour thin coating of Chocolate Icing slowly over tops, rotating to cover sides. Roll in chopped walnuts or sprinkles and chill to set the icing. Cut into 1-inch pieces and place each in decorative paper cup with a scalloped edge.

*Chocolate Icing

> 2 cups powdered sugar
> ⅔ cup unsweetened cocoa
> 1 tablespoon vegetable oil
> 4 tablespoons (about) strong hot coffee

Combine sugar and cocoa and sift into bowl. Add oil and 2 tablespoons coffee and beat vigorously. Blend in additional coffee 1 teaspoon at a time until icing is thin enough to pour.

ICE CREAM

HOW TO MAKE A BOMBE
See photograph pages 182-183

For gala parties and special celebrations one of the most spectacular grand finales is the ice cream bombe—a rainbow of ice cream flavors and colors in a dome shape. Bombes involve successive layers of various flavors of ice cream arranged so that when sliced, each serving presents different bands of color. They can be made in ordinary mixing bowls. Here are some guidelines to be followed in creating the layers:

The bombe mold must be thoroughly chilled in the freezer before you line it with ice cream. If the mold is warmer than the ice cream, ice cream will slide down the sides.

To facilitate unmolding, brush inside of mold with unflavored oil and line with two strips of waxed paper about an inch wide crisscrossed at the bottom and extending over top.

Before constructing the bombe, allow the first ice cream to set in the freezer for at least two hours after it is churned to assure that it will be hard enough to pack.

The ice cream used in the outside layer, which is the support of the mold, must be one that hardens with age. Ice creams with sugar or liquor additions are unsuitable for the outside layer, although they are fine for the middle of the bombe.

The center of your bombe may be any ice cream, or for a more dramatic presentation, fill it with chopped nut brittle or chopped sweet chocolate, which will spill out attractively when the bombe is cut open for serving.

To launch you in the art of bombe making we suggest any of the following combinations:

Outer layer of vanilla, middle layer of mocha and a finely grated sweet chocolate center.

Outer layer of coffee, middle layer of vanilla, and a center of combined prune and Armagnac.

Outer layer of vanilla, middle layer of coffee-almond brittle, and a center of toasted almond bits.

Set aside a fourth of the outside ice cream to produce a "floor" when the bombe is inverted.

To ensure an absolutely even first layer, pack the ice cream firmly about 1½ inches thick onto the sides and bottom of the bowl. Then take another kitchen bowl the size of the cavity and place it in the empty space—pushing down gently to eliminate any air pockets. Fill second bowl with ice cubes. This holds the walls while the ice cream hardens.

Keep the bombe frozen hard between periods of assembly.

When the first layer has frozen hard (probably the next day), pour a little hot water into the small support mixing bowl and twist it. It will slide out. Now pack in your second layer. Freeze again until hard.

To unmold, invert the frozen bombe onto a pre-chilled serving platter.

Dampen a kitchen towel with hot water and cover the outside of the mold. To encourage the mold to loosen, tug gently on the ends of the waxed paper ribbons. Immediately return the unmolded bombe to the freezer and, just before serving, garnish it with shaved chocolate, toasted slivered almonds, coconut, whipped cream rosettes, or whatever your imagination dictates.

GRANITA DI CAFFE (FROZEN ESPRESSO)

6 SERVINGS

    4 cups espresso coffee
      Sugar
      Whipped cream

Place coffee in a medium bowl. Sweeten to taste. Freeze, stirring frequently, until set, about 2 to 3 hours. (The more you stir the finer the texture will be. It is helpful to set a timer for 15-minute intervals.) Serve topped with a dollop of whipped cream.

HONEY ICE

6 SERVINGS

    1½ cups cold water
    ½ cup honey
    1 cup orange juice
    2 tablespoons lemon juice
    1 teaspoon grated orange peel
    ½ teaspoon cinnamon
      Pinch of salt
    1 cup whipping cream
    6 tablespoons Grand Marnier
    3 tablespoons chopped pistachio nuts (garnish)

Beat water and honey in saucepan until thoroughly blended. Place over medium heat and bring to boil. Let boil for 2 minutes without stirring. Remove from heat and add next 5 ingredients. Strain into ice tray or shallow dish. Freeze.

When ready to serve, whip cream. Scoop ice into bowls and pour a tablespoon of Grand Marnier over each. Top with whipped cream and pistachio nuts.

PAPAYA SHERBET

Delicious with fresh fruits or cookies.

4 TO 6 SERVINGS

    4 cups ripe papaya pulp (about 3 to 4 papayas)
    1 to 2 cups sugar*
      Juice of 2 lemons or ½ cup bottled lemon juice
    2 egg whites, room temperature

Combine papaya with sugar and lemon juice in bowl and mix well. Beat egg whites until stiff peaks form. Fold into papaya mixture. Pour into bowl or loaf pan and freeze, without stirring, until consistency of sherbet, approximately 1 hour.

*With 1 cup sugar, this dessert will have the consistency of ices; 2 cups will result in a sweeter taste and creamier texture.

PIES

CHERRY CREAM CHEESE PIE

8 SERVINGS

    1 8-ounce package cream cheese, room temperature
    ½ cup sifted powdered sugar
    ½ teaspoon vanilla
    1 cup whipping cream, whipped
    1 baked 9-inch deep-dish pie crust
    1 21-ounce can cherry pie filling, well chilled

Whip cream cheese with sugar until fluffy. Blend in vanilla. Fold in whipped cream, blending thoroughly. Spoon into pie shell. Spread cherries evenly over top. Refrigerate pie overnight.

FROZEN CHOCOLATE PECAN PIE
See photograph page 159

6 TO 8 SERVINGS

Crust

- 2 cups finely chopped pecans, toasted
- 5 tablespoons plus 1 teaspoon firmly packed brown sugar
- 5 tablespoons (⅝ stick) butter, chilled, cut into small pieces
- 2 teaspoons dark rum

Chocolate Filling

- 6 ounces semisweet chocolate
- ½ teaspoon instant coffee powder
- 4 eggs, room temperature
- 1 tablespoon dark rum
- 1 teaspoon vanilla
- 1½ cups whipping cream
- 3 tablespoons shaved semisweet chocolate

For crust: Blend all ingredients until mixture holds together. Press into bottom and sides of 9-inch pie plate. Freeze for at least 1 hour.

For filling: Melt chocolate with coffee in top of double boiler over hot water. Remove from heat and whisk in eggs, rum and vanilla until mixture is smooth. Let filling cool for about 5 minutes.

Whip 1 cup cream until stiff. Gently fold into chocolate mixture, blending completely. Pour blended mixture into crust and freeze.

About 1 hour before serving, transfer pie to refrigerator. Whip remaining ½ cup cream and dollop or pipe over pie. Sprinkle finished pie with chocolate shavings.

Pie can be frozen up to 3 months.

FROZEN GINGER CREAM

8 TO 10 SERVINGS

Crust

- 2½ cups almond cookie crumbs (about 20 cookies)
- 2 tablespoons (¼ stick) butter, melted

Filling

- 6 egg yolks
- ¾ cup sugar
- 4 egg whites
- ¼ cup sugar
- 1 cup whipping cream
- ¼ cup Grand Marnier
- ½ cup chopped crystallized ginger

For crust: Combine cookie crumbs and butter. Reserve small amount and pat remainder on bottom and slightly up sides of 8- or 9-inch springform pan. Chill crust mixture while making filling.

For filling: Beat egg yolks with ¾ cup sugar in top of double boiler over warm water until thick, about 6 to 10 minutes. Turn into large bowl and let cool 5 minutes, then beat 1 more minute.

Beat egg whites until foamy. Gradually add ¼ cup sugar and beat until stiff. Fold into yolks. Whip cream in another bowl until thickened. Add liqueur and beat until stiff. Fold into egg mixture. Spoon into pan alternately with ginger. Sprinkle with reserved almond cookie crumbs and freeze until ready to serve.

Frozen Ginger Cream can be made up to 1 week before serving.

KEY LIME PIE

8 SERVINGS

- 4 eggs, separated
- 1 14-ounce can sweetened condensed milk
- ½ cup fresh lime juice
- 1 9-inch graham cracker crust
- ½ cup sugar

Combine egg yolks and milk in medium bowl. Using spoon or rubber spatula, fold in lime juice. Pour into graham cracker crust and refrigerate for about 1 hour.

Preheat oven to 400°F. Beat egg whites in large mixing bowl until foamy. Gradually add sugar, beating constantly until stiff and glossy. Spread completely over filling, sealing to edges. Bake until meringue is golden, about 5 minutes. Remove

from oven and let cool slightly. Refrigerate overnight before serving. Serve directly from refrigerator.

PUMPKIN ICE CREAM PIE

8 SERVINGS

- 1 quart vanilla ice cream, softened
- ¾ cup canned pumpkin
- ¼ cup honey
- ½ teaspoon cinnamon
- ¼ teaspoon ground ginger
- ¼ teaspoon salt
- ⅛ teaspoon nutmeg
- ⅛ teaspoon ground cloves
- 1 baked 9-inch pie shell, cooled
- ⅓ cup chopped pecans
  Whipped cream and pecan halves (garnish)

Combine first 8 ingredients in mixing bowl and blend well. Pour into pie shell. Sprinkle with chopped nuts. Freeze until serving time. Garnish with whipped cream and pecan halves just before serving.

60-SECOND LEMON CHIFFON PIE

6 TO 8 SERVINGS

- 2 8-ounce cartons lemon chiffon yogurt
- 1 8-ounce carton frozen whipped topping, thawed
- 1 graham cracker pie crust
  Lemon zest (optional)

Fold yogurt and topping together and spoon into crust. Sprinkle with zest, if desired. Freeze until set. Remove from freezer about 15 minutes before serving.

SLY LEMON PIE

6 TO 8 SERVINGS

- 1 quart vanilla ice cream, softened
- 1 6-ounce can frozen lemonade concentrate, thawed
- 1 baked 9-inch pie shell
  Sliced lemon twists (garnish)

Combine ice cream and lemonade in blender or processor until smooth. Pour into pie shell. Freeze until firm, about 1½ hours. Let stand 10 minutes before serving. Garnish with lemon twists.

STRAWBERRY GLAZED PIE

8 SERVINGS

- 1 cup fresh strawberries
  Water
- ½ to ¾ cup sugar
  Pinch of salt
- 1 teaspoon cornstarch dissolved in 1 tablespoon water
- 1 baked 9-inch pie shell
- 2 cups (or more) strawberries, hulled
  Softly whipped cream (garnish)

Crush 1 cup strawberries; add enough water to equal 1 cup. Strain. Combine with sugar and salt in small saucepan and simmer, stirring constantly, until sugar is dissolved. Slowly stir in dissolved cornstarch and cook until clear and slightly thickened. Let cool slightly. Brush bottom of pie shell with some of glaze. Arrange remaining berries tip sides up in shell. Pour remaining glaze over top. Chill 2 to 3 hours or overnight. Top with softly whipped cream or pass separately.

OTHER DESSERTS

FROZEN LEMON MOUSSE

May be prepared up to 2 weeks in advance of serving.

12 SERVINGS

- 30 lemon or vanilla wafers (about)
- 4 egg yolks
- ½ cup fresh lemon juice
- ¼ cup sugar
- 1½ tablespoons grated lemon zest
- 4 egg whites
- ⅛ teaspoon cream of tartar

- ⅛ teaspoon salt
- ¾ cup sugar
- 1½ cups whipping cream

Line bottom and sides of 8- or 9-inch springform pan with wafers. Combine next 4 ingredients in large bowl and blend well. Let mixture stand at room temperature.

Beat egg whites until foamy. Add cream of tartar and salt and continue beating until soft peaks form. Gradually add remaining sugar, beating constantly until stiff and glossy. Whip cream until stiff. Gently fold whites and cream into yolk mixture. Carefully spoon into pan. Cover with foil and freeze overnight. Let mousse soften in refrigerator about 1 hour before serving.

MARVELOUS FROZEN MANGO MOUSSE

It's a good idea to freeze mango and milk all day or overnight before preparing mousse.

6 SERVINGS

- 1 very ripe large mango, peeled and cut into 1-inch pieces
- 1½ cups skim milk
- 2 tablespoons sugar
  Juice of 1 lime

Arrange mango pieces on baking sheet without sides touching. Pour 1¼ cups milk into shallow pan. Freeze until solid.

Just before serving, break frozen milk into chunks. Spoon into processor. Add remaining ¼ cup milk with sugar, lime juice and mango and mix well, stopping machine as necessary to scrape down sides of bowl, until mixture resembles smooth sherbet. Spoon into goblets or bowls.

MELON MOUSSE

4 SERVINGS

- 8 ounces peeled, seeded cantaloupe or other ripe sweet melon
  Juice of ½ lemon

- 2 teaspoons chopped fresh mint
  Pinch of salt
- ¼ teaspoon unflavored gelatin
- ¾ cup whipping cream
- 2 cantaloupe or other ripe sweet melons, halved
  Fresh mint sprigs (garnish)

Puree melon in processor or blender until smooth, stopping to scrape down sides of container. (You should have 1 cup of puree.) Transfer to small bowl and add lemon juice, mint and salt. Let stand at room temperature several hours or overnight. Press through fine sieve.

Transfer puree to small saucepan. Sprinkle with gelatin and let stand several minutes to soften. Stir over low heat until gelatin is dissolved. Refrigerate until cooled and just slightly thickened, about 15 minutes.

Beat cream in chilled bowl until stiff. Stir ¼ into melon puree to loosen. Gently fold in remainder. Cover mousse and refrigerate overnight, folding occasionally.

To serve, mound mousse in melon halves and garnish with mint.

PEARS POACHED IN RED WINE

Marinate the pears two days before serving, so they can absorb flavor.

6 SERVINGS

- 2 cups dry red wine
- ½ cup sugar
- 2 tablespoons lemon juice
- 1 2-inch cinnamon stick
- 6 small pears, peeled, halved and cored

Combine first 4 ingredients in large saucepan. Bring to boil over medium-high heat, stirring until sugar dissolves. Add pears and partially cover pan. Simmer over low heat until pears are soft but not mushy, about 20 minutes. Let cool, then pour into bowl. Cover and refrigerate 2 days before serving turning pears in liquid occasionally so they absorb color evenly.

PINEAPPLE PUDDING

6 SERVINGS

- 2 tablespoons flour
- 2 tablespoons cornstarch
  Juice of 1 large lemon (about ¼ cup)
- 1 20-ounce can crushed pineapple in its own juice
- 1 8-ounce can crushed pineapple in its own juice
- 3 eggs, separated
- ½ cup sugar
- 1½ teaspoons lemon peel
- ½ teaspoon baking powder
  Whipped cream (garnish)

Blend flour, cornstarch and lemon juice in 2-quart saucepan until smooth. Add pineapple, egg yolks, sugar and lemon peel and mix well. Bring to boil over medium-high heat, stirring constantly until thickened, about 5 minutes. Remove from heat and let cool slightly. Beat egg whites with baking powder until stiff peaks form. Fold into pineapple. Cover and refrigerate until set, about 2 hours. Spoon into bowls and top pudding with dollops of whipped cream.

RASPBERRY-STRAWBERRY BAVARIAN

8 TO 10 SERVINGS

- 1 6-ounce package strawberry gelatin
- 2 cups boiling water
- 1 cup sour cream
- 1 pint strawberry ice cream, cut into chunks
- 2 10-ounce packages quick-thaw whole frozen raspberries in syrup (left at room temperature 10 minutes)
- 1 tablespoon fresh lemon juice
- 2 cups whipping cream
- ½ cup powdered sugar, sifted
- 1½ teaspoons vanilla
  Chocolate curls (optional garnish)

Combine gelatin and boiling water in large bowl and stir until gelatin is dissolved. Beat in sour cream until mixture is smooth. Transfer to blender or food processor fitted with steel knife, add ice cream and mix until smooth.

Return to mixing bowl, add fruit and lemon juice and stir until fruit is broken up and mixture begins to set, about 2 minutes. Pour into serving bowl or individual dessert dishes. Cover and refrigerate overnight.

To serve, whip cream with powdered sugar and vanilla. Spoon generously over bavarian and garnish with chocolate curls, if desired.

RODGROD

MAKES ABOUT 2½ CUPS

- 2 10-ounce packages frozen unsweetened raspberries, thawed, or 1½ pounds fresh raspberries
  Sugar
- 2 tablespoons arrowroot mixed with ¼ cup cold water
  Whipped cream (garnish)
  Toasted slivered almonds (garnish)

Puree raspberries in processor or blender until smooth. Transfer to medium saucepan. Add sugar to taste, place over medium heat and bring to boil, stirring constantly. Add arrowroot mixture, reduce heat and simmer until thickened; do not boil. Pour into bowl and let cool. Cover and refrigerate at least 2 hours before serving. Spoon into goblets. Top with whipped cream and sprinkle with slivered almonds.

ENGLISH TRIFLE

6 TO 8 SERVINGS

- 3 or 4 firm bananas, peeled and sliced
- 1 basket raspberries, washed and drained*
- 1 basket strawberries, washed and hulled*
- 1 basket blueberries, washed*
- 1 3¾-ounce package pecans, shelled and chopped
- ½ 15-ounce package raisins
- 1 3¾-ounce package vanilla pudding
- 1 sponge cake, sliced
- 1½ ounces brandy
  Whipped cream mixed with 1 teaspoon brandy

Mix together all fruits and nuts.

Prepare vanilla pudding as directed on pudding package.

Arrange a layer of sponge cake slices in a large glass bowl. Top with a layer of mixed fruits and nuts, and sprinkle with brandy. Continue in layers until about 2 inches from top of bowl. Spread vanilla pudding evenly over top of trifle.

Mound whipped cream over trifle. At this point, trifle may rest in refrigerator for 1 hour or more for flavors to mingle. To serve, spoon down through trifle so that each serving consists of whipped cream, pudding, fruit and cake.

*If fresh berries are not available, use frozen drained berries, 1 10-ounce package of each kind.

CHOCOLATE SAUCE

See photograph page 184

MAKES ABOUT 1 CUP

- 8 ounces chocolate (milk or semisweet)
  Whipping cream

Soften chocolate in top of double boiler. Add sufficient cream to achieve desired consistency. Serve hot or at room temperature.

For Mint Chocolate Sauce, add a few drops of mint extract.

MICROWAVE

CHOCOLATE TAFFY

MAKES ¾ POUND

- 1 cup sugar
- ¾ cup light corn syrup
- ½ cup water

¼ teaspoon cream of tartar

1 ounce (1 square) unsweetened baking chocolate, coarsely chopped

Generously grease 9-inch square baking pan. Combine sugar, corn syrup, water and cream of tartar in 2-quart measuring cup or bowl and mix well. Cook on High until mixture boils, stirring once, about 5 to 10 minutes. Continue cooking on High without stirring until candy thermometer registers 266°F (or until small amount of mixture forms ball hard enough to hold its shape but still pliable when dropped into very cold water), about 12 minutes. Stir in chocolate, blending well. Pour into prepared pan. Set pan on rack. Let stand until cool, at least 30 minutes.

Grease hands well and pull taffy until satiny and elastic. Cut into pieces. Wrap in waxed paper, twisting ends closed. Store pieces of taffy in airtight container.

CHOCOLATE MOUSSE

12 SERVINGS

1 envelope unflavored gelatin

1¼ cups water

1 3.2-ounce envelope instant chocolate flavored nonfat dry milk or four .675-ounce envelopes hot cocoa mix

2 tablespoons unsweetened cocoa

1 9-ounce container nondairy whipped topping

Sprinkle gelatin over water in 4-cup measure and stir to soften. Blend in powdered milk and cocoa and mix well. Cook on High 2½ minutes. Whisk through, making sure milk and cocoa are thoroughly dissolved. Cool completely.

Fold in whipped topping, reserving small amount for garnish. Spoon into individual dessert dishes and refrigerate or freeze until ready to serve. Dollop with remaining whipped topping.

CHOCOLATE NUT BROWNIES

MAKES ABOUT 20 BROWNIES

2 ounces unsweetened baking chocolate

½ cup (1 stick) unsalted butter

2 eggs

¾ cup sugar

½ cup all purpose flour

1 tablespoon vanilla

1 teaspoon baking powder

¼ teaspoon salt

1 cup coarsely chopped walnuts

1 cup chocolate chips Powdered sugar (optional)

Combine chocolate and butter in 2-quart measuring cup and cook on High until butter is melted, about 1½ minutes. Stir to blend (chocolate will not appear to be melted until you have stirred it).

Beat eggs in large bowl until well mixed. Add chocolate mixture, sugar, flour, vanilla, baking powder and salt and blend thoroughly. Stir in nuts and chocolate chips. Turn into 9-inch pie plate or quiche dish. Cook on High 6 minutes (mixture will still be moist, but will firm as it cools). Let cool completely before cutting into squares.

QUICK PARTY MINTS

MAKES ABOUT 6 DOZEN

3 tablespoons (⅜ stick) unsalted butter

3 tablespoons milk

1 15-ounce box white creamy frosting mix

1 teaspoon peppermint extract Green food coloring

Combine butter and milk in 2-quart measuring cup or bowl and cook on High until butter is melted, about 45 to 60 seconds. Blend in frosting mix. Continue cooking on High, whisking through several times, until mixture is creamy, about 2 to 3 minutes. Whisk in extract and enough food coloring to give mixture light green hue. Drop by teaspoons onto waxed paper. Let cool; then refrigerate until firm.

PEANUT BRITTLE

MAKES ABOUT 1 POUND

1 cup sugar

½ cup dark or light corn syrup

1¾ to 2 cups dry roasted unsalted peanuts

1 teaspoon unsalted butter

1 teaspoon vanilla

1 teaspoon baking soda

Generously grease baking sheet. Combine sugar and corn syrup in 2-quart measuring cup or bowl and cook on High 4 minutes. Stir in peanuts using wooden spoon. Continue cooking on High 3 minutes. Stir in butter and vanilla and cook until candy thermometer registers 300°F (or until small amount of mixture separates into hard and brittle threads when dropped into very cold water), about 2 to 2½ minutes. Blend in baking soda and stir until mixture is light and foamy. Pour onto prepared sheet, spreading quickly to edges using back of wooden spoon. As candy cools, stretch into thin sheets using palms of hands. Let cool completely. Break into pieces. Store pieces of peanut brittle in airtight container in cool place.

PECAN PIE

8 SERVINGS

¼ cup (½ stick) unsalted butter

1½ cups whole pecans

1 cup sugar

½ cup light or dark corn syrup

3 eggs, lightly beaten

1 teaspoon vanilla

1 baked 9-inch pie shell (in glass or ceramic pie plate)

Melt butter in 2-quart measure on High. Add nuts, sugar, corn syrup, eggs and vanilla and blend well. Pour into pie shell. Cook on High until center is set, about 8 to 9 minutes. Serve either at room temperature or chilled.

MENUS

Meals in 30 Minutes

SPECIAL OCCASION FOR 2

Butter Sauce (halve recipe page 44) with
Cooked Artichokes

Mustard and Herb Broiled Steak (recipe page 91)
Stir-Fry of Sweet Peppers and Zucchini
(recipe page 144)
American-Style Liptauer (halve recipe page 168)

Bananes l'Archestrate (recipe page 175)

HEARTY LUNCHEON FOR 4

Indian Soup (recipe page 39)

Beef Salad with Asparagus and Broccoli
(recipe page 49)
Garlic-Cheese French Bread (recipe page 165)

Hot Orange Fritters (recipe page 175)

CLASSIC SUPPER FOR 4

Mushroom and Nut Pâté (recipe page 5)

Easy Scampi (recipe page 73)
Broiled Tomatoes (recipe page 143)
Creamy Vinaigrette (recipe page 55) with
Salad Greens

Chocolate Fondue (halve recipe page 188)

MICROWAVE MENU FOR 4

Galley Dip for Vegetables
(recipe page 2) with Crudités

Baked Salmon Steaks (recipe page 78)
Seasoned Rice (recipe page 169)
Spinach Salad (recipe page 59)

Pecan Pie (recipe page 195)

PRE-THEATER DINNER FOR 4

Spinach Dip (recipe page 2) with
Assorted Crackers

Steak au Poivre (recipe page 91)
Carrots Marguerite (recipe page 141)
Coleslaw (recipe page 141)

Strawberries in Fondant Chemises (recipe page 176)
Cafe Royale (recipe page 21)

MID-WEEK SUPPER FOR 6–8

Marinated Mushrooms (recipe page 7)

Baked Fish Mozzarella (recipe page 60)
Green Beans-Open Sesame (recipe page 140)
Vermont Fruit Salad (recipe page 55)

Angel Food Brittle Cake (recipe page 170)

ITALIAN DINNER FOR 6

Hot Clam Dip (recipe page 8)

Pasta Primavera (recipe page 151)
Easiest, Quickest Garlic Bread (recipe page 164)
Quick Mixed Salad (recipe page 51)

Amaretto Oranges with Sorbet (recipe page 175)
Cappuccino (halve recipe page 22)

CASUAL DINING FOR 8

Artichoke Soup Annette (recipe page 36)

Italian Stir-Fried Chicken (double recipe page 83)
Herbed Cheese Bread (recipe page 165)

Frozen Fruit Special (double recipe page 185)

Meals in 45 Minutes

SUNDAY BRUNCH FOR 6

Melon Balls with Lime (recipe page 175)

Smoked Salmon Tart (recipe page 62)
Spinach, Bacon and Apple Salad (recipe page 51)

Biscuit Cake (recipe page 170)
Cafe Orange (recipe page 21)

AFTER WORK DINNER FOR 4–6

Camembert Spread (recipe page 4)

Lamb Chops Korabiak (recipe page 97)
Chutney Rice (recipe page 162)
Asparagus with Pecans (recipe page 138)

Iced Lime Dessert (recipe page 186)

BIRTHDAY DINNER FOR 6

Easy Cheese Canapés (recipe page 8)

Wrapped Herb Chicken (recipe page 84)
Pea Pods with Petits Pois (recipe page 142)
Baked Tomatoes with Spinach (recipe page 143)
French Mustard Bread (recipe page 164)

Bundt Cake (recipe page 171)

MEXICAN DINNER FOR 10–12

Perfect Lemonade (recipe page 19)
Salsa Cruda Dip (recipe page 2)

Chorizo Burrito (recipe page 99)
Mexicali One-Dish (double recipe page 162)
Vinaigrette Dressing (recipe page 56) with
Mixed Salad Greens

Chocolate Fudgy Brownies (recipe page 173)

Meals in 60 Minutes

AFTERNOON LUNCH FOR 4–6

Lettuce Soup (recipe page 37)

Shrimp and Scallop Salad with Snow Peas
(recipe page 52)
Parmesan Popovers (recipe page 165)

Quick and Easy Chocolate Mousse (recipe page 188)

COMPANY'S COMING TO DINNER FOR 6

Lemon Froth (recipe page 19)
Kiwifruit with Prosciutto (recipe page 6)

Braised Veal Chops in Tarragon Cream (recipe page 102)
Broccoli Taglierini (recipe page 161)
Walnut Avocado Salad (recipe page 50)

Unbelievable Pie (recipe page 187)

ORIENTAL MENU FOR 4–6

Chinese Hot and Sour Soup (recipe page 39)

Beef and Scallop Sauté (recipe page 92)
Sesame Broccoli (recipe page 140)
Chicken Broth Rice (recipe page 162)
Oriental Salad Dressing (recipe page 56) with
Sliced Cucumbers

Basic Butter Cookies (recipe page 172) and
Ice Cream

FAMILY DINNER FOR 4–6

Stuffed Mushrooms (recipe page 142)

Barbecued Pork Chops (recipe page 98)
Brunede Kartofler (Sugar-Browned Potatoes)
(recipe page 143)
Raw Applesauce (recipe page 144)

Cherry Ice Cream (recipe page 185)

Do-Ahead Meals

FIRESIDE SUPPER FOR 4

Three Cheese Ball (recipe page 4)

Czechoslovak Pepper Steak
with Caraway Noodles (recipe page 113)
Broccoli Florets with Browned Butter
(halve recipe page 140)

Pumpkin Ice Cream Pie (recipe page 192)

PICNIC CELEBRATION FOR 4-6

Caviar Eggs (recipe page 5)

Potato, Ham and Swiss Cheese Salad with Shallot
Dressing (recipe page 50)
Chilled Dilled Peas (recipe page 142)
Cheese Shoestrings (recipe page 8)

Raisin-Granola Cookies (recipe page 173)
Strawberry Coolers (recipe page 24)

ELEGANT DINNER FOR 6

Almond Pâté (recipe page 12)

Tomato-Yogurt Soup (recipe page 36)
Braised Turkey with Lemon and Cinnamon
(recipe page 87)
Bibb and Walnut Salad (recipe page 49)

Frozen Chocolate Pecan Pie (recipe page 192)
Spiced Cider with Calvados (recipe page 24)

GREEK BARBECUE FOR 6

Raw Asparagus with Cream Cheese Dipping Sauce
(recipe page 6)

Ground Lamb and Eggplant Kebabs (recipe page 97)
Yogurt Sauce (recipe page 43) with
Pita Bread
Tabbouleh (recipe page 58)

Grammy Almond Cookies (recipe page 173)

BUSY DAY DINNER FOR 6-8

"Black Tie" Appetizer (recipe page 5)

Chicken Florentine (recipe page 85)
Cherry Tomato Salad (recipe page 57)

Mocha Brownie Torte (recipe page 189)

EASY ENTERTAINING FOR 4-6

Walnut and Cheese Stuffed Mushrooms (recipe page 11)

Salmon with Apples, Pears and Lime (recipe page 62)
Green Bean Sauté with Shallots (recipe page 141)
Brown Rice Milanese (recipe page 161)

Strawberry Glazed Pie (recipe page 193)

AUTUMN BUFFET FOR 12

Chicken Livers in Sage Cream (triple recipe page 9)
Spiced Apple Bowl (recipe page 33)

24-Hour Wine and Cheese Omelet (recipe page 128)
Cranberry Nut Bread (recipe page 167)
Day-Ahead Spinach Salad (double recipe page 58)

Cassata (recipe page 189)

FESTIVE APPETIZER BUFFET FOR 24

Fish House Punch (recipe page 24)

Dilled Mushrooms (recipe page 13)
Thistle Dip (recipe page 12)
Shrimp and Dip (recipe page 13)
Scallop Kebabs (recipe page 13)
Chicken Triangles (recipe page 8)
Oriental Chicken Appetizers (recipe page 12)
Sesame Beef Strips (recipe page 15)
Cocktail Party Meatballs (recipe page 10)

Kitchen Staples

You've completed the marketing, selecting from the freshest produce, meat and fish, and you're all set for a week of good, family meals. But what do you do about spur-of-the-moment entertaining for company? With this list of staples, you are all prepared: a bit of this, some of that and a *Bon Appétit* TOO BUSY TO COOK? recipe make it easy.

Breads and Grains

All purpose baking mix
Bread—whole wheat, pita bread, sourdough, French, Italian
Breadcrumbs
Crackers
Flour—all purpose, self-rising, whole wheat
Pasta and noodles—spaghetti, fettuccini, spinach pasta, egg noodles
Rice
Tortillas

Prepared Sauces and Condiments

Catsup
Chili sauce
Gravy—Beef gravy, mushroom gravy
Hot pepper sauce
Mayonnaise
Mustard—dry, prepared
Olive oil
Salad dressing
Soy sauce
Spaghetti sauce
Steak sauce
Tomato paste
Tomato sauce
Vinegar—white, red wine, white wine, wine tarragon, cider
Worcestershire sauce

Prepared Soups

Beef broth
Cheese soup
Chicken broth
Cream of celery
Cream of chicken
Mushroom
Tomato

Chicken and beef bouillon cubes or granulated powder
Onion soup mix

Frozen and Canned Foods

Sausages

Crabmeat
Salmon
Shrimp
Tuna fish

Butter
Margarine

Biscuits
Phyllo dough (strudel dough)
Pie shells
Puff pastry shells
Rolls

Lemon juice concentrate
Orange juice concentrate

Artichoke hearts
Bamboo shoots
Chinese pea pods
Green chilies
Hearts of palm
Kidney beans
Olives
Water chestnuts

Baking Essentials

Corn syrup
Instant coffee powder
Jam, jelly, preserves
Maple syrup
Nuts—almonds, pecans, peanuts, walnuts
Oil—vegetable, peanut
Raisins
Semisweet chocolate morsels

Solid vegetable shortening
Sugar—granulated, brown, powdered
Unsweetened cocoa powder

Wines and Spirits

Brandy
Chocolate liqueur
Coffee liqueur
Dry red wine
Dry white wine
Orange liqueur
Rum
Sherry
Vermouth
Vodka

Cheeses

Cheddar
Cream cheese
Monterey Jack
Parmesan
Swiss

Herbs and Spices

Keep a selection of dried herbs and spices at hand in airtight containers away from the light. Replace them as soon as they lose their scent, for they will have lost their flavor too.

When fresh herbs are available, buy some to freeze. Blanch clean herbs in boiling water, then immediately plunge into iced water and drain. Seal in foil and freeze. Bring to room temperature before using. When cooking with fresh herbs, try to reserve a little to add toward the end of the cooking time.

Herbs

Basil One of the most aromatic herbs, basil has a sweet, mildly pungent flavor. A favorite of Italians, it is a natural with tomatoes, both cooked and in salads, and forms the base for the classic pesto sauce. Use it sprinkled on pork or lamb chops just before cooking and to flavor salads, soups, stews, sauces and egg dishes.

Bay leaves One leaf is usually sufficient for most dishes: the greener the leaf, the more flavor. Float a leaf in water while cooking onions, carrots, tomatoes or rice. Alone, or as a part of a bouquet garni, use to flavor soups, especially tomato, sauces and fish dishes. Don't forget to remove it before serving. Place a bay leaf in the mold before baking a pâté or terrine.

Chervil A member of the parsley family, this delicate, feathery herb has a slightly anise flavor. It is excellent in butter and cream sauces and soups and as a garnish for salads and vegetables. Finely chopped fresh chervil is delicious sprinkled on grilled fish.

Chives Finely chopped chives add a delicious hint of onion to dishes with a short cooking time. They combine well with other herbs and are excellent in omelets and scrambled eggs, sauces and poached fish and sprinkled on salads, baked potatoes and cream soups, especially vichyssoise.

Cilantro Also known as coriander and Chinese parsley, cilantro is used extensively in Mexican, Chinese, Indian and Thai cooking. It is an essential ingredient in ceviche, combines well with celery, and is an excellent garnish for pork and rice dishes and guacamole. The ground seeds are an important flavoring in Indian and Moroccan dishes and are good used in stuffings.

Dill This aromatic herb has a lemony caraway flavor. It is delicious in soups, particularly lentil and pea, eggs, tomato dishes, poached fish and pickles. Try it in a white sauce to accompany fish or cauliflower or sprinkled over new potatoes tossed in butter. Add fresh dill sprigs to cider or white wine vinegar and use in salad dressings.

Fennel A feathery herb which looks something like dill and can be used in the same way though it will impart a mild licorice flavor. It is excellent in fish sauces and salad dressings and combines well with lemon. The bulbs of fennel add a tasty crunch to salads and are delicious braised and added to stir-frys.

Garlic An ancient bulb made up of individual sections called cloves which, when peeled, can be pushed through a special press or crushed with the flat side of a heavy knife. It is difficult to imagine French, Italian or Oriental cooking without garlic. It can be used sliced and inserted into meat before roasting, rubbed into a salad bowl before adding greens, in salad dressings, casseroles, pasta, mixed with butter and tossed with crunchy green beans or spread on bread and baked in the oven.

Horseradish Horseradish is a thick root with a strong, peppery flavor used mainly as a condiment. It must be peeled and grated, which is easier said than done, but worth while since it is delicious added to cream sauce or whipped cream and served with roast or boiled beef or mixed with melted butter and served with fish.

Marjoram A sweet and spicy member of the mint family, this is one of the most versatile herbs. Use marjoram to flavor stews, soups, meat—especially pork and sausage—stuffings, tomato sauces and tossed in with buttered root vegetables or string beans.

Mint The many varieties of mint are used to flavor sauces, vegetables, jelly, fruits, alcoholic beverages, tea and candy. When chopped and mixed with a little boiling water, vinegar and sugar, it makes a delicious sauce to accompany roast lamb. Add a few sprigs when cooking fresh peas or new potatoes or stir chopped mint into green pea soup, potato salad, applesauce, shredded cabbage or fruit salad.

Oregano A relative of marjoram, oregano is a natural with tomatoes and tomato sauces and so is a favorite in Italian and Mexican dishes. It is also delicious sprinkled on chicken and meat before roasting and in stuffings for both meats and vegetables.

Parsley This is the most available fresh herb and valuable for its vitamin and mineral content. Finely chopped, it adds flavor, aroma and color to sauces, soups and stews, salads, stuffings and egg and cheese dishes. Italian parsley, with flatter leaves, has more flavor but choose the curly variety for a more decorative garnish.

Rosemary This unique herb has a sweet, spicy, pungent flavor. For delicious roast lamb, insert rosemary into slits in the meat before cooking. It is also an interesting flavoring for veal and chicken, and good sprinkled on potatoes and greens and in sauces and stews.

Saffron Probably the most expensive herb, saffron adds color as well as zest. It is used in risotto, fish soups, and is a main ingredient of paella. Try using it also to make unusual breads and cakes.

Sage Sage should be used with care since it has a strong fragrant flavor. It is familiar mixed with onion as a stuffing for pork, chicken, duck and goose. A pinch added to soups and stews or to cheese spreads is also good.

Savory Savory has an aromatic, peppery flavor. Both the summer and the more pungent winter varieties can be used to flavor green beans, bean salad, breadcrumb coatings for veal or fish, salads and split-pea soup.

Tarragon A sweet, aromatic herb with the flavor of anise, tarragon is much used in French cooking. It is delicious added to melted butter and is a main ingredient in béarnaise sauce. It is good with fish, poultry and in salads. A large sprig added to good white wine vinegar provides a base for salad dressings and tartar sauce.

Thyme Thyme's strong flavor and odor are excellent in soups and stews, particularly those containing wine. Use it combined with parsley to flavor stuffing. Add it to melted butter and dribble over grilled shellfish or use to toss carrots, mushrooms or onions.

Spices

Allspice This dried berry has a fragrant flavor that tastes like a blend of cinnamon, nutmeg, mace and cloves. Use it ground to season pumpkin pie, sausage, sauces for fish, carrots and eggplant or whole in pot roast and beef stews, fresh pea soup, pickles and marinades.

Caraway seeds These dark brown seeds have a warm, aromatic flavor. They are often used in dark breads and are delicious with many vegetables especially sauerkraut, red cabbage and beets. Try tossing new potatoes in butter and caraway seeds. Use also with pork, sausage, goose and cheese.

Chili powder Chili powder is a blend of hot peppers, cumin, garlic, paprika and oregano and varies in intensity. It is used in stews, soups and sauces when a richness of color and flavor are desired and is, of course, an important ingredient in chili.

Cinnamon Cinnamon comes from the dried inner bark of the cinnamon tree. Its familiar sweet spicy flavor and fragrant odor add interest to cakes, apple desserts, hot mulled wine, baked ham, and sliced fresh fruits. Sprinkle on coffee and chocolate drinks and for an unusual marinade for pork chops, mix a little cinnamon with garlic, rosemary, orange juice and Marsala.

Cloves Cloves are the unopened flower buds of an evergreen tree and have a hot spicy flavor. Use whole in pickles, fruit dishes, especially apple pie, and for studding ham before baking. Ground cloves are delicious in cakes and gingerbread.

Cumin With its strong scent and flavor, cumin is an important ingredient in Mexican food and curries, and is delicious in meat loaf and dried bean dishes. Try adding a pinch to chicken pot pie, stews and stir-fried vegetables.

Ginger Finely chopped ginger root is an essential ingredient in oriental food where it often combines with freshly chopped garlic. In fact, adding this combination with a little soy sauce will give an oriental feel to any stir-fry. Use ground ginger in applesauce, rhubarb desserts, chutneys and try rubbing it on steaks and chops before broiling.

Mace Mace is the dried outer sheath of the fruit kernel of the nutmeg tree and stronger in flavor than nutmeg. It combines well with chocolate and can be used in pickling, marinades and in oyster stew.

Nutmeg The dried seed of the fruit of the nutmeg tree retains its flavor longer if kept whole and grated as needed. Use nutmeg in baking, sauces, puddings and fish dishes. Add a dash to pureed potatoes and parsnips and sprinkle on baked custard and quiches, chocolate drinks and eggnog. Try a pinch in pastry for fruit and meat pies.

Paprika Rich in color though mild in flavor, paprika is used a great deal in Spanish, Moroccan and especially Hungarian dishes such as goulash. It is also good with eggs, seafood, vegetables and lamb and to dust potato salad, cottage cheese and anything that needs enlivening visually.

Pepper White, black and green peppercorns are from different stages of the same plant. White pepper has a stronger aroma but not as much bite as black pepper. Keep black peppercorns in a pepper mill and grind them fresh as needed. Green peppercorns are prized by the French and used in sauces for veal and duck and pressed into steaks for pan frying.

Turmeric Turmeric is the dried and ground root of a member of the ginger family but is much more subtle in flavor than ginger. It imparts a rich yellow color to foods but use carefully for it will also make anything else it comes into contact with a rich yellow, too! It is the main ingredient of curry powder and is also used in mustards, relishes, dressings and seafoods.

Vanilla The long seed pods of a tropical orchid family are also known as vanilla beans. Keep one in a jar of sugar and use the sugar to flavor custards and puddings. Use the beans in ice cream or steamed milk. The extract form is good for baking, preserves and desserts.

Spice Pointers

Ground spices impart their flavors to food immediately, so they should be added only ten or fifteen minutes before the end of cooking time. Whole spices are best in slow cooking dishes because they require longer simmering periods to release their full flavors and aromas.

Use whole, not powdered, spices in beverages and for pickling to avoid clouding liquids.

When planning a menu, consider balance. When one dish is heavily spiced, don't use the same seasoning or one of equal intensity in the rest of the meal.

If trying a new-to-you spice, use less than the recipe calls for and *taste*. As a guide, start with no more than one-fourth teaspoon to a pint of sauce, soup or vegetable or to a pound of meat. You can always add more.

For cooking, tie whole spices in a square of cheesecloth or put them in a hinged metal tea steeping spoon or ball for easy retrieval after cooking.

Try using cinnamon sticks as stirrers for after-dinner coffee, hot tea and après-ski drinks.

Keep containers tightly closed and avoid overexposure of spices to air.

When grating nutmeg, figure that one whole nutmeg should yield about one tablespoon of spice.

Buying in bulk to save money is a good idea, but only for ground spices used frequently and for whole spices, which have a longer shelf life than ground, crushed or powdered spices.

Unless your pepper grinder is thoroughly washable, do not use it to grind other spices. It is better to have one grinder for pepper and one for other whole spices.

Wine and Cheese Guide

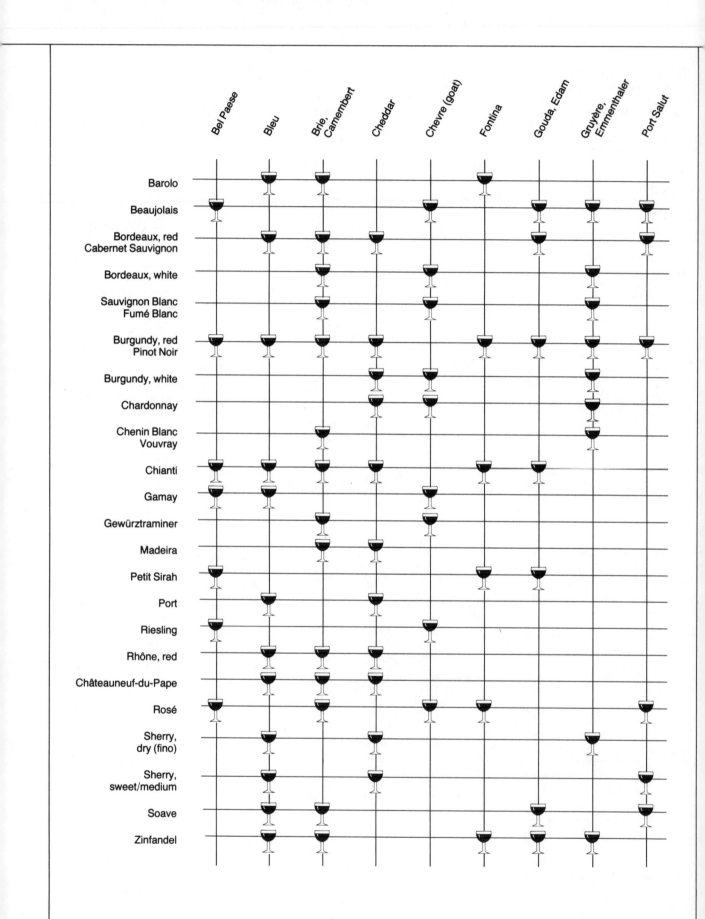

Conversion Charts

VOLUME

Cups and Spoons	Quarts and Ounces	Metric Equivalents
4⅓ cups	1 quart 2 ounces (1.056 quarts)	1 liter or 1,000 milliliters
2 cups plus 2½ Tablespoons	17 ounces (16.907 ounces)	½ liter
1 cup plus 1¼ Tablespoons	8 ounces (8.454 ounces)	¼ liter
⅓ cup plus 1 Tablespoon	3½ ounces (3.381 ounces)	1 deciliter or ¹⁄₁₀ liter or 100 milliliters
3⅓ Tablespoons	1¾ ounces (1.690 ounces)	½ deciliter or 50 milliliters
1 Tablespoon	½ ounce	15 milliliters
2 Teaspoons	⅓ ounce	10 milliliters
1 Teaspoon	¹⁄₁₆ ounce	5 milliliters

EQUIVALENTS

⅓ cup = 5 Tablespoons + 1 Teaspoon	½ cup = 8 Tablespoons	1 cup = 16 Tablespoons
⅜ cup = ¼ cup + 2 Tablespoons	⅔ cup = 10 Tablespoons + 2 Teaspoons	2 cups = 1 pint
⅝ cup = ½ cup + 2 Tablespoons	¾ cup = 12 Tablespoons	4 cups = 1 quart
⅞ cup = ¾ cup + 2 Tablespoons	¼ cup = 4 Tablespoons	3 Teaspoons = 1 Tablespoon

RECIPE TIMING ADJUSTMENT CHART FOR MICROWAVE OVENS

600 to 700 Watt Ovens Use cooking times as given in the recipes	500 to 600 Watt Ovens Add 15% to the recipes' cooking times	400 to 500 Watt Ovens Add 35% to the recipes' cooking times
15 secs.	17 secs.	20 secs.
30 secs.	35 secs.	41 secs.
1 min.	1 min. 9 secs.	1 min. 21 secs.
2 mins.	2 mins. 22 secs.	2 mins. 42 secs.
3 mins.	3 mins. 27 secs.	4 mins. 3 secs.
4 mins.	4 mins. 36 secs.	5 mins. 24 secs.
5 mins.	5 mins. 45 secs.	6 mins. 45 secs.
10 mins.	11 mins. 30 secs.	13 mins. 30 secs.
15 mins.	17 mins. 15 secs.	20 mins. 15 secs.
20 mins.	23 mins. ———	27 mins. ———
25 mins.	28 mins. 45 secs.	33 mins. 45 secs.
30 mins.	34 mins. 30 secs.	40 mins. 30 secs.

Freezing Guide

Avocado. Peel and puree. For each ¾ cup puree, add 2 teaspoons lemon juice. Freeze in small containers. Use for guacamole and salad dressings.

Béarnaise or hollandaise sauce. Freeze leftover sauce and reheat on top of double boiler, stirring until thickened. Texture will be altered. Use for basting chicken, fish or veal, but not as a pouring sauce.

Béchamel sauce. Freeze in polystyrene cups or plastic containers. Defrost at room temperature. Can be used as basis for mornay, and other sauces.

Beef ribs. Preroasted and cut into serving portions before freezing, deviled ribs get dinner off to a fast start. Reheat, without thawing, at 425°F, allowing 45 to 60 minutes.

Breadcrumbs. Crusts and stale bread make great crumbs. If necessary, dry bread in the oven. Crumble as fine as desired in food processor or blender. No need to thaw before using in breading, for au gratin or stuffing.

Butter. Keeps for months in the freezer. Unsalted butter and unsalted margarine should always be stored frozen. (Keep a little out in the refrigerator for daily use.) An elegant touch: Dip a melon ball cutter in hot water, scoop balls out of butter brick and drop into ice water. After flash freezing, pack in a bag or other container. Serve butter balls in a decorative pyramid or on individual plates. Thawing time is 10 to 15 minutes.

Butter, flavored. Butters such as maître d'hôtel, garlic, onion, parsley, anchovy, seafood, horseradish, herb, caper and curry can be packaged in small cups. Cream the butter, beat in the flavoring agent, then freeze. Thawed, the butters can be used on cooked dishes or applied to meat, fish and poultry during cooking.

Cheese. Swiss, Gruyère and Parmesan should be purchased in whole pieces, grated and frozen. They'll be ready to add to any dish. Mozzarella, Monterey Jack and provolone used as toppings should be added only after a dish is reheated, then placed under the broiler or in the oven just before serving. Bleu cheese or Roquefort should be wrapped in plastic wrap, then foil. Thaw at room temperature. Cheese will be crumbly but good on salads or in dressings and dips. Grate dried up odds and ends of cheese and freeze.

Chicken breasts. Bone, pound, layer with waxed paper and wrap carefully before freezing. Great for Chinese dishes. When defrosted, they are delicious wrapped around fingers of herb butter, dusted with flour, dipped in lightly beaten egg, rolled in flavored breadcrumbs, chilled a minimum of ½ hour, then fried or brushed generously with butter and baked in 350°F oven until golden, about 45 minutes. Baste frequently with butter or stock.

Chicken, cooked. Store in stock, ready for curries, crepes, casseroles.

Chicken giblets. Store in a large bag or other container for up to 3 months. They make delicious soup alone or can enhance other chicken soups. You can also make a fricassee by adding meatballs, lots of onions and paprika. Serve with rice.

Chicken livers. Freeze raw livers for use in pâté, chopped chicken liver, mushroom and liver in omelets or on toast points, or small liver strudels (which also freeze well).

Cream. Leftover cream can be frozen in its container, but it will not be suitable for whipping or for coffee. After thawing in the refrigerator, use for cooking. Make whipped cream rosettes, flash freeze, then pack in layers separated by waxed paper. Frozen, they can be used to decorate pies, cakes, ice cream and soup.

Crème pâtissière. Freeze this French custard in pint containers. Defrost overnight and rewhip with a whisk. Use for tarts or for fruit-topped pies.

Crepes. Stack each crepe separated with plastic wrap; freeze covered with foil. Crepes thaw quickly in a colander over boiling water. Use for breakfast or brunch or fill with meat, cheese, vegetables for a quick dinner. For dessert, fill with chocolate mousse or sliced ripe fruit tossed with a bit of apricot glaze.

Croutons. Cube stale bread. Toast in oven with or without melted butter. Freeze in bag or container. Thaw at room temperature 5 minutes and use to garnish soup or to stir into cooked vegetable dishes.

Duxelles. Freeze this concentrate of chopped mushrooms, shallot and wine in small containers. Use in canapés or in place of chopped mushrooms in any recipe. Add to sauces and soups, serve on beef, lamb or veal. Also marvelous in omelets. For a delightful hot mushroom pastry, spread on fresh, crustless, generously buttered, white sandwich bread that has been rolled thin with a rolling pin. Shape into small jelly rolls. Brush again with butter, place seam down on cookie sheet, bake at 375°F until golden, about 10 minutes.

Egg whites. Don't mix them. Pack in individual polystyrene cups or ice cube trays. Thaw at room temperature before beating. Thawed, they will keep in the refrigerator for 1 or 2 days. Eight large egg whites equal 1 cup. Great for soufflés, meringues and more.

Egg yolks, hard-cooked. Grate and freeze in small plastic bags. Defrost and use to sprinkle over canapés, vegetables and salads.

Egg yolks, raw. Beat lightly with a fork. For use in non-sweet dishes, stir in a teaspoon of salt. For sweet dishes, mix in a tablespoon of sugar or corn syrup for each cup of yolks (12 large yolks equal 1 cup). Good for omelets and baking. Freeze in small container or ice cube tray, thaw in or out of refrigerator; use immediately.

Fruit purees. Freeze in amounts called for in your favorite hot or cold soufflé or dessert. Defrost in refrigerator or at room temperature. Excellent folded into whipped cream for a sauce over poached or fresh fruit.

Game birds, trout and other fresh fish. Freeze in liquid or stock. Pop a bird or fish into a milk carton, fill with liquid, staple. It will stay fresh-tasting and juicy.

Gravy. Place in small containers or ice cube trays. Heat directly from the freezer to enrich sauces or sliced meat.

Green onions. Many recipes call for the white part of the green onion, but don't toss out the tops. Chop and freeze in plastic bags. Add to the skillet before sautéing fish for a lovely flavor variation or add to other onions being sautéed.

Green peppers. Wash, halve, remove stem and seeds and pack double-wrapped in heavy-duty plastic bags so the aroma doesn't permeate. They're perfect for dressing up hot dishes. In salads there's a slight loss of crispness.

Lasagne and cannelloni. They freeze well. Plain pastas, however, are better cooked just before serving.

Lemon juice and peel. Freeze fresh lemon juice in 8-ounce polystyrene cups or in ice cube tray. Each cube equals 2 tablespoons of lemon juice. Freeze the grated lemon peel, with juice, in a polystyrene cup. Strained, it makes a wonderfully fresh-tasting rind. Use in pastries, sherbets, cold or hot soufflés, or add frozen to sauces.

Meatballs. Take the time to cook miniature meatballs. Convenient for spaghetti, hors d'oeuvres and in barbecue sauce. Flash freeze, then scoop into plastic bags or cartons.

Milk. For emergencies, pasteurized and homogenized milk can be frozen at 0°F for about 3 weeks.

Mushroom caps, broiled. Brush with melted butter and broil 2 minutes, cup side up. Freeze. Thaw 10 minutes. Stuff or finish broiling.

Mushrooms, raw. May be frozen up to 3 weeks. Don't wash them. Flash freeze, then scoop into plastic bag or container. Use without thawing. Rinse and sauté or use in soups or stews.

Mushrooms, sautéed. These are excellent frozen. Slice 1 pound of mushrooms and sauté in ¼ cup (½ stick) butter for 5 minutes, stirring occasionally. Package in ½-pint containers. Heat through to use over broiled steak or in sauces. Or thaw ½ hour, then stir into cooked vegetables, rice or pasta.

Nuts. Freeze whole or chopped. They last indefinitely. Toast before using in baking or cooking.

Onions and shallots. Chop coarsely in blender or food processor, drain well, spread out in a single layer and flash freeze. Break up with fork and pack in small containers. These can be used without thawing. When onions start to sprout, trim and put into the freezer.

Parsley. Just before parsley gets tired, chop it in the blender or food processor and freeze in small plastic bags. It's excellent in soups, sauces or stews.

Pesto. Freeze pesto sauce to use with fresh-cooked pasta or as a topping for broiled tomatoes.

Piecrust. Freeze crust and filling separately. Roll out crust and line aluminum foil pie plates with dough. Don't prick. Flash freeze, then stack crusts together with plastic wrap between, ready for pies and quiches. After thawing for 15 minutes, they can be used as the recipe specifies.

Pie fillings. One quart of fruit will fill a 9-inch pie. Line a pie plate with foil, fill with fruit flavored as desired, cover with foil and freeze. When hard, remove from pie plate and store in freezer. For baking, place in pie shell and add French crumb topping: ½ cup sugar, ⅓ cup butter, ¼ cup flour (chopped nuts optional). Crumble ingredients with fingertips. Spread over fruit. Bake in lower third of 375°F oven.

Potatoes, mashed white or sweet. Freeze in patties or rosettes. Reheat by browning in butter.

Praline. Store in tightly covered plastic container. Delicious and useful for decorating iced cakes, mousses, soufflés, or as a coating for ice cream balls. Boil 1⅓ cups sugar and ½ cup water, swirling pan gently as liquid begins to boil to be sure sugar is completely dissolved. When syrup gradually turns a light caramel color, add 1½ cups walnuts or almonds; stir with wooden spoon to mix thoroughly. Turn out onto lightly greased baking sheet. In about 30 minutes, when mixture has cooled, use mallet or rolling pin to break mass into 1-inch pieces. Then coarsely chop in food processor. Some pieces should be about ⅛ inch to give texture to praline.

Puff paste. Wrap carefully for freezing; defrost in refrigerator overnight. Use for pastries and hors d'oeuvres.

Relishes and chutneys. Freeze in pint-size containers. A welcome addition to a curry dinner or as garnish for cold meats or poultry.

Soups. Bases for cream soups like vichyssoise can be frozen but freeze without cream. Add cream and other liquids before heating to serve.

Spaghetti and marinara sauces. Can be frozen in quart-size milk containers or in smaller amounts. An 8-ounce cup of sauce when defrosted can top a frozen pizza or 1 or 2 portions of pasta. Marinara sauce is also handy frozen in an ice cube tray; each cube equals 2 tablespoons, enough to enrich any dish that needs a touch of tomato.

Stock. Chicken, veal, beef or fish stock freezes well. Store in milk containers. When frozen, staple carton top. When ready to use, tear off carton and heat the frozen block. Great for poaching and in sauces, soups and other cooked dishes.

Tomato paste. Freeze in 1-tablespoon amounts in small plastic bags. Use frozen in sauces.

Vegetable purees. Cauliflower, pea and carrot are just a few possibilities. Defrost and use as a vegetable or to fill large mushroom caps or artichoke bottoms. Combined with stock and milk (or cream or yogurt), they make quick and delicious soups.

High Risk—Not Recommended

Hard-cooked egg white. It gets hard and rubbery unless chopped very fine and used in small proportions in a recipe such as chopped liver.

Aspics and gelatin salads or desserts. They get rubbery and weepy.

Raw salad ingredients. Crispness will be lost.

Cooked potatoes or rice frozen in soups or stews. Potatoes become mealy and rice soggy.

Mayonnaise. It curdles unless used in small ratio to other ingredients.

Stuffing in cooked or raw poultry. Can be a health hazard.

Broiled or quickly cooked meat and fish. These would be overcooked when reheated. The exception is rare tenderloin, carefully wrapped in plastic and foil. Defrosted in the refrigerator, this steak can be sliced thin and served with a hot brown stock-based sauce such as mushroom or red wine.

Cooked shrimp. Freezing toughens them. Uncooked shrimp freeze well.

Index

Credits

Acknowledgements

The following readers of *Bon Appétit*® contributed material included in the book:

Gene Adcock
Charles Allenson
Bob Arganbright
Susan Baerwald
Susan S. Bailis
Dr. Alvin Balaban
Liz Barclay
Lisa Bauman
Nancy Behrman
James Bellah
Linda Berman
Dorothy Berry
Mary Bijur
Ann Binder
Betsy Blankett
Joan Borinstein
Scott Brake
Daphne Bransten
Shanna Breen
Robert Broder
Martha Buller
James Burrows
Joan Cable
Phil Capka
Jane Jennifer Carey
Judith Carrington
Sandra Carter
Carol Chabot
Ashby Chadburn
Genny Chapman
Rose Cohimia
Claudette Cole
Michael Collyer
Bill & Shelby Conti
Jennifer Kane Coplon
Kathleen Ballard Cowell
Anne Darby
Barbara Darnell
Janet DeLand
Lucille DeLucena
Daphne Doerr
Diane Dodd-MacKenzie
Diane S. Dym
Myron (Mike) Emery
Debra Fergusan
& Owen Taylor
Claudia Feurey
Terry Flettrich
Karalee Fox
Phyllis Fox-Krupp
Tricia Gadsby
Edith Gaines
Robert L. Gaines
Rebekah Gibson
Val Gitlin
Connie Glenn
Sue Goldstein
Steven Green
Susan Grode
Nicki Grossman
Robert &
Hannah Grossman
Judy Haden
Betsy Halpern
Patsy Hanson
Fai Harris
Nancy Hinckley
Gail-Nancy Hirschel
Mary Onie Holland
Kirk Huffard
Ann Hunt
Jacquolene Young Hursey
Beverly Jackson
Dr. Jerome H. Jacobi
Jim and Linda Jenkins
Donna Jessee
Ellen Jones
Diane Jubelier

Vivian Kaplan
Sandy Katz
Ann Kohn
Isobel Robins Konecky
Kristina Korabiak
Dr. Jeffery Kottler
Maggie Kozelek
Saralee Kucera
Dona Kuryanowicz
Elise Lalor
Susan Lane-Tschopp
Cindy Lazof
Amy Levin
Cara Lieb
Scott & Darlene Lieblich
Amy Lovett
Ivy Rosequist Mann
Marie Masters
Susan Maxman
Joan McCormick
Tom & Sheri McCoy
Amanda Nyce McIntyre
Berenice McLaughlin
Carmela Meely
Maureen Mignosa
Charles B. Mincks
Glenn O. Mittelstadt
Jan Ellen Murray
Lori Nadler
Delores Nash
Michelle Naumburg
Douglas Nelms
Pam Nelson
Della Nevens
Gloria Lorch Nimetz
Mae Norris
Diane Ocon
Judith N. Olert
Lori Openden
Babette Pollard
Mary K. Pollard
Margaret Prochaska
Elizabeth Ebers Press
Sharon Puttmann
Elizabeth J. Quigley
Irene Raven
Theodora Raven
Robert Renn
Jack & Ginger Riley
Arthur Rissman
Fredric Roberts
Helyne Robin
Lois Robinson
Ellen Rose-Kuperman
George Rosenfeld
Bonnie Rothenburg
Nell Rugee
Phyllis Kasha Rukeyser
Norma Schechner
Eleanor G. Schultz
Patricia Scully
Marcia Seltzer
Kathy Sengenberger
Andrea Shapiro
Sharron Sheehy
Pat Shue
Renée Simmons
Patricia Skinner
Susan Slak
Dave Smith
Jean Bowen Smith
Mary Vanek Smith
Lois Solle
Lucille Stakee
Robert V. Strauss
Gerry Tausch
Barbara Tenenbaum

Barbara Tomorowitz
Alice Uchiyama
Susan Unterberg
Jim Van Arsdel
Elaine Wally
Sheri Wayne
Robert Weiss
Alice Welsh
Audrey White
Val White
Ronald S. Wirth
Faye Woocher
Linda Wysocki
Ensign Mark Zecca

The following food experts contributed material included in the book:

Ed Asner
Anna Teresa Callen
Cecilia Chiang
Elizabeth Schneider Colchie
Susan Countner
Terry D'Ancona
Gordon Davidson
Judi Davidson
Michel de Santis
Phyllis Diller
Mrs. John R. Drexell III
Kate Firestone
Naomi French
Paul Gillette
Sally Goldman
Bess Greenstone
Zack Hanle
Barbara Harris *
Ray Henderson
& Robert Ehrman
Rita Holmberg
Barbara Kafka
Barbara Karoff
Lynn Kasper
Terry Allen Kramer
Gilda Latzky
Rita Leinwand
Rodney Madden
John Loring
Perla Meyers
Jinx & Jefferson Morgan
Anna Muffoletto
Thelma Pressman
Norman S. Roby
Shirley Sarvis
Telly Savalas
Lari Siler
Richard Simmons
Jack Denton Smith
Doris Tobias
May Wong Trent
Jan Wiemer
Ann Willan
La Varenne Cooking School, Paris
Stella Wilson
Janet & Roger Yaseen

* Recipes for Baked Salmon Steaks, page 78; Celery Pea Medley, page 145; Crab Puffs, page 15; Fettuccine al Forno, page 169; Green Salad with Dill Dressing, page 59; Lasagne, page 168; Nachos, page 16; Seafood Combo, page 79; Spiced Cider, page 33 reprinted with permission from *Let's Cook Microwave!* by Barbara Harris, © 1979.

TOO BUSY TO COOK? was conceived, edited and published by The Knapp Press under the direction of:

Alice Bandy
Vice President, General Manager

Lynn Blocker
Traffic Coordinator

Richard E. Bye
Chairman of the Board

David Dexter
Proofreader

Anthony P. Iacono
Production Director

Philip Kaplan
Executive Graphics Director

Anita Keys
Copy Editor

Paige Rense
Editor-in-Chief

Jan Stuebing
Editorial Assistant

Don Umnus
Production Manager

Ellen Winters
Production Editor

Veronica Zagarino
Production Coordinator

Special thanks to:

Janet Barrows
Assistant Editor, Bon Appétit

Rita Leinwand
Food Editor, Bon Appétit

Bernard Rotondo
Art Director, Bon Appétit

Marilou Vaughan
Managing Editor, Bon Appétit

Design and Production:

Design Office
Bruce Kortebein
Andrew H. Ogus

Running head illustrations
by Heather Taylor

Photographers:

Tom Bartone, pages 178–179
Arthur Beck, page 68
Irwin Horowitz, pages 32, 66–67, 69, 70, 71, 72, 106–107, 112, 154–155, 157, 159, 160, 180, 181, 182–183
Brian Leatart, pages 28–29, 132, 158
Rudy Legname, pages 25, 65, 105, 133, 134–135
Ron Schwerin, pages 30–31
Victor Scocozza, pages 108, 109, 110–111, 156
Michel Tcherevkoff, page 177
Dan Wolfe, pages 26, 27, 129, 130–131, 136, 153, 184